LOST LANDSCAPES

of Palaeolithic Britain

The contribution of projects funded by the Aggregates Levy Sustainability Fund 2002–2011

Edited by Mark White, with Martin Bates, Matthew Pope, Danielle Schreve, Beccy Scott, Andrew Shaw and Elizabeth Stafford

Illustrated by
Julia Collins and Magdalena Wachnik

Oxford Archaeology Monograph 26
2016

This publication has been generously funded by Historic England (formerly English Heritage)

Published by Oxford Archaeology
Oxford Archaeology, Janus House, Osney Mead, Oxford OX2 0ES

Registered Charity No. 285627

Brought to publication by Elizabeth Stafford and Rebecca Nicholson,
Oxford Archaeology South

www.oxfordarch.co.uk

ISBN 978-0-904220-77-3

Cover illustration: Late Pleistocene hunters encamped on the high ground of the Isle of Wight observe a migrating reindeer herd following the now submerged Solent River. In the distance the chalk ridge of Portsdown behind modern day Portsmouth can be seen. Original artwork by Peter Lorimer

Typeset by Production Line, Oxford
Printed and bound in Great Britain by Latimer Trend & Company Ltd, Plymouth, UK

This book is dedicated to the memory of

Jon Humble (1958-2015)

Inspector of Ancient Monuments, Senior National Minerals and Environmental Adviser for Historic England, and Palaeolithic enthusiast

Contents

CHAPTER 4: TERRESTRIAL FLUVIAL LANDSCAPES *by Danielle Schreve*

CHAPTER 5: SITE AND ARTEFACT STUDIES *by Andrew Shaw and Beccy Scott*

List of authors

Dr Martin Bates

Department of Archaeology, University of Wales, Trinity Saint David, Lampeter, Ceredigion SA48 7ED

Dr Matthew Pope

UCL Institute of Archaeology, 31–34 Gordon Square, London WC1H 0PY

Dr Beccy Scott

Department of Prehistory and Europe, The British Museum, Franks House, 28–55 Orsman Road, London N1 5QJ

Dr Andrew Shaw

Centre for the Archaeology of Human Origins, Department of Archaeology, University of Southampton, Highfield, Southampton SO17 1BF

Professor Danielle Schreve

Department of Geography, Royal Holloway, University of London, Egham Hill, Egham TW20 0EX

Professor Mark White

Department of Archaeology, Durham University, South Road, Durham, DH1 3LE

List of Figures

CHAPTER 3

CHAPTER 4

CHAPTER 5

List of Tables

Text boxes and figures within boxes

Summary

This volume is concerned with disseminating the results and implications of various Palaeolithic and Pleistocene projects funded through the British Government's *Aggregates Levy Sustainability Fund* (ALSF), which ran from 2002 to 2011. This fund underwrote Palaeolithic and Pleistocene research in England and showcased it on an international stage. A wide variety of archaeologists and scientists participated and benefited from this scheme and this is demonstrated by the range of reports that resulted from the fund. Some of these works have found their way into formal publication in monographs and papers while others remain in the archive as grey literature. For these reasons this volume has been written and the research described is targeted not only at the informed audience but also at the archaeologists less familiar with Palaeolithic archaeology. The book has a major role to play in terms of practical outcomes for conservation and management, by facilitating the expansion of data on the Palaeolithic resource and nurturing greater collaboration between various stakeholders, particularly in updating Historic Environment Records (HERs) and developing mineral plans.

The five chapters in this volume present an overview of the results from the different projects. In Chapter 1 Mark White examines the background to the ALSF and how projects undertaken are contextualised within previous Palaeolithic research in the UK. There follows a series of chapters examining certain key themes in the work. Martin Bates and Matthew Pope (Chapter 2) consider the methodological approaches to field investigations in Palaeolithic archaeology including techniques appropriate to field investigation at a variety of scales. This is followed by an examination of the nature of the marine and marine-terrestrial transition zone by Matthew Pope and Martin Bates (Chapter 3), an area of increasing importance today with extensive gravel extraction in the offshore region as well as the development of the renewables sector. Danielle Schreve (Chapter 4) then considers the nature of the terrestrial landscape-based projects at the site and valley scale. She also discusses a major flagship project of the ALSF, the National Ice Age Network (NIAN). Next, Andrew Shaw and Beccy Scott (Chapter 5) discuss the technology, behaviour and settlement history of Palaeolithic humans.

This book is written for the non-specialist and focuses on providing a commentary on the Palaeolithic material record. The book uses case studies to open up to a wide audience the nature, potential and pitfalls of the Pleistocene record. A commonly recurring theme throughout the volume is scale. We have attempted to highlight how the scale of landscape investigations range from the pan-European down to the individual site, and timescales include deposits of varying ages. The concept of scale is important in the Palaeolithic, as often the results of site investigation provide information about the archaeological record at a variety of scales that are hard for the non-specialist to grasp.

The final chapter has been written by Mark White as an attempt to use the insights gathered through the ALSF projects to define future priorities and milestones and to offer pointers for all stakeholders regarding reasonable responses and mitigation to development at different locations. He identifies three basic strategic aims, each of which subsumes outreach and education:

- Extending the Pleistocene record (the discovery of new sites). This will require better predictive modelling.
- Enhancing the Pleistocene record (creation of an up-to-date online national database of collections and archives).
- Engaging with the Pleistocene record (engaging with stakeholders across a variety of forums).

Sommaire

Cette publication est axée sur la dissémination des résultats et implications des différents projets de recherche du Paléolithique et du Pléistocène, exécutés entre 2002 et 2011 et financés par le Fonds ALSF (*Aggregates Levy Sustainability Fund*) du gouvernement britannique. Ce financement a sécurisé la recherche sur le Paléolithique et le Pléistocène britannique et l'a exposée sur la scène internationale. Divers archéologues et scientifiques ont participé à et bénéficié de ce programme, illustré par un ensemble de rapports permis par ce financement. Certains de ces travaux ont donné lieu à des publications officielles sous forme de monographies et d'articles, tandis que d'autres demeurent encore au stade d'archive comme rapport de diagnostic. C'est pour ces raisons que ce volume a été créé : la recherche décrite cible non seulement un public averti, mais aussi les archéologues moins familiers avec l'archéologie du Paléolithique. Cet ouvrage a un rôle majeur à jouer en matière de résultats pratiques pour la conservation et la gestion, tout d'abord en facilitant l'expansion des données sur le Paléolithique, mais aussi en encourageant une plus grande collaboration entre les diverses parties prenantes, plus particulièrement en actualisant les registres HER (*Historical Environment Records)* et en développant des plans miniers.

Les cinq chapitres de ce volume présentent une vue d'ensemble des résultats de ces projets distincts. Dans le chapitre 1, Mark White examine les antécédents du ALSF et la manière dont les projets mis en œuvre s'insèrent dans de précédentes recherches du Paléolithique en Grande-Bretagne. Puis s'ensuit une série de chapitres sur certains thèmes clés du projet. Martin Bates et Matthew Pope (chapitre 2) étudient l'approche méthodologique de la recherche Paléolithique de terrain, dont des techniques appropriées à cette recherche à différentes échelles. Ceci est suivi par l'examen par Matthew Pope et Martin Bates (chapitre 3) de la nature de la zone de transition marine et marine-terrestre, zone aujourd'hui d'une importance grandissante avec l'extraction intensive de gravier dans les régions offshore et le développement du secteur des énergies renouvelables. Danielle Schreve (chapitre 4) considère ensuite la nature des projets basés sur l'aménagement du paysage terrestre à l'échelle du site et de la vallée. Elle évoque aussi le projet emblématique du ALSF: *National Ice Age Network* (NIAN). Andrew Shaw et Beccy Scott, quant à eux (chapitre 5), analysent la technologie, le comportement et l'histoire de l'établissement de l'humanité au Paléolithique.

Rédigée pour le non spécialiste, cette publication s'attache à commenter les témoignages matériels du Paléolithique. Il y est fait usage d'études de cas permettant d'exposer à un public large la nature, le potentiel et les écueils des archives du Pléistocène. La notion d'échelle constitue un thème récurrent dans cet ouvrage. Nous avons tenté d'attirer l'attention sur la façon dont l'envergure des investigations varie du paneuropéen à l'échelle du site-même, ainsi qu'à travers une série de périodes. Le concept d'échelle est important pour le paléolithique; les résultats de recherche sur le terrain renseignent fréquemment le relevé à des échelles variables, difficiles à appréhender par le novice.

Le chapitre final, rédigé par Mark White, tente d'utiliser les connaissances amassées au fil des projets du Fonds ALSF à la fois pour définir les priorités et étapes futures, mais aussi pour conseiller toutes les parties intervenantes sur des réponses satisfaisantes et une atténuation du développement en divers emplacements. Ce dernier chapitre identifie trois objectifs stratégiques de base, chacun englobant une dimension de sensibilisation et d'éducation :

- Augmenter les archives du Pléistocène (découverte de nouveaux sites), ce qui nécessitera une meilleure modélisation prédictive.
- Mettre en valeur les archives du Pléistocène (création d'une base de donnée nationale des collections et des archives mise à jour et accessible via internet).
- S'efforcer de comprendre les archives du Pléistocène (en collaborant avec les différents acteurs sur une variété de forums).

Zusammenfassung

Dieser Band befasst sich mit den Ergebnissen mehrerer paläolithischer und pleistozäner Projekte, die vom *Aggregates Levy Sustainability Fund* (ALSF) in der Zeit von 2002 bis 2011 durchgeführt und von der Britischen Regierung finanziert wurden. Die Finanzierung hatte das Ziel paläolithische und pleistozäne Forschung in England zu unterstützen und der internationalen Öffentlichkeit zu präsentieren. Eine Vielzahl Archäologen und Wissenschaftler nahmen an dem Vorhaben teil und profitierten davon, dies wird durch die zahlreichen Dokumentationen und Ergebnisse untermauert. Einige Arbeiten wurden in Monographien und Artikeln publiziert, während andere in der grauen Literatur archiviert wurden. Aus diesem Grunde wurde der vorliegende Band geschrieben und die darin vorgestellten Forschungsergebnisse sollen nicht nur den Fachleuten, sondern auch Archäologen, die mit der paläolithischen Forschung weniger vertraut sind, erreichen. Das Buch wird bei der Verbreitung paläolithischer Informationsquellen eine Hauptrolle im Bereich des Denkmalschutzes und der Verwaltung einnehmen und die Zusammenarbeit verchiedener daran interessierter Personen fördern, besonders beim Aktualisieren der "Historic Environment Records" (HERs) und beim Erarbeiten von Mineralplänen.

Die fünf Kapitel in diesem Band geben einen Überblick der Resultate der geförderten Projekte. Im ersten Kapitel untersucht Mark White den Hintergrund der ALSF und wie die durchgeführten Projekte im Kontext der paläolithischen Forschung in Großbritannien eingeordnet werden können. Dem folgen einige Kapitel, welche die Hauptthematiken der Arbeiten untersuchen. Martin Bates und Matthew Popes (Kapitel 2) prüfen die methodologische Vorgehensweise der Feldarbeit in der paläolithischen Archäologie, inklusive Grabungstechniken, die bei einer Vielzahl von Projekten angewandt werden kann. Darauf folgt eine Betrachtung der Eigenschaften der marinen und marine-terrestrischen Transitzonen von Matthew Pope und Martin Bates (Kapitel 3), ein Bereich der zunehmend wichtiger wird im Angesicht von umfangreichem Kiesabbau auf offener See und der Entwicklung erneuerbarer Energien. Danielle Schreve (Kapitel 4) untersucht im Weiteren den Charakter terrestrischer landschaftsraum basierter Projekte sowohl im Kleinen, auf Grabungsgröße, als auch bezogen auf ganze Täler. Sie erörtert außerdem ein bedeutendes Projekt des ALSF, das "National Ice Age Network" (NIAN). Danach befassen sich Andrew Shaw und Beccy Scott mit der Technologie, der Lebensweise und der Siedlungsgeschichte paläolithischer Menschen.

Dieses auch für den Laien verfasstes Buch zielt darauf ab die paläolithischen Hinterlassenschaften vorzustellen und zu bewerten. Das Buch nutzt Fallstudien um einem breiten Publikum Wesen, Potential und Schwierigkeiten der Forschung über das Pleistozän nahezubringen. Ein wiederkehrendes Thema in diesem Band ist der Umfang der behandelt wird. Wir haben versucht deutlich zu machen, dass einige Untersuchungen gesamteuropäisch einzuordnen sind, sich andere auf individuelle Grabungen beziehen und auch die Zeitspannen der Ablagerungen variieren. Maßstäbe richtig zu erfassen ist bei der Betrachtung des Palälithikums von großer Bedeutung, da Resultate von Grabungen oft Informationen auf einer Vielzahl von Skalen wiedergeben, die für den Laien schwer zu erfassen sind.

Das letzte Kapitel wurde von Mark White geschrieben als ein Versuch die Einblicke die durch ALSF gesammelt wurden zu nutzen und zukünftige Prioritäten und Meilensteine zu definieren, es soll interessierten Personen helfen passende Strategien zu entwerfen um die Auswirkungen von Entwicklungsprojekten an diversen Standorten zu vermindern. Er identifiziert drei wesentliche strategische Ziele, welche alle Öffentlichkeitsarbeit und Bildung umfassen.

- Das pleistozäne Schriftgut erweitern (neue Fundstätten entdecken). Dies erfordert eine besser vorausschauende Modellierung.
- Das pleistozäne Schriftgut verbessern (Herstellung einer aktuellen online- Datenbank aller Kollektionen und Archive)
- Sich mit dem pleistozänen Schriftgut beschäftigen (Austausch mit Interessierten durch eine Vielzahl von Foren).

Acknowledgements

The Lost Landscapes of Palaeolithic Britain project was funded by English Heritage (now Historic England) and formed a key component of the National Heritage Protection Plan, specifically Activity 3A3, 'Deeply Buried/Subterranean Pleistocene and Early Holocene Archaeology'. The project was monitored for English Heritage by Helen Keeley and Jonathan Last.

Project design and management was undertaken by Elizabeth Stafford for Oxford Archaeology, with support and advice from Klara Spandl and Anne Dodd. Julia Meen carried out the majority of the work collating the artefact database together with Gary Jones. Dr Peter Marshall of Historic England is thanked for his input into Box 2.5. Danielle Schreve gratefully acknowledges English Heritage (historic England) and Natural England (through the Aggregates Levy Sustainability Fund) for supporting the National Ice Age Network project, which highlighted many of the issues raised in Chapter 4. The late David Keen, Simon Buteux, Andy Howard, Alex Lang and Barbara Silva are thanked for much fruitful scientific discussion and fieldwork companionship during the NIAN project. Beccy Scott would like to thank Dr Nick Ashton and Dr Rob Hosfield for their input and the Calleva Trust (Pathways to Ancient Britain Project) for ongoing support.

This monograph has been copy-edited by Rebecca Nicholson and indexed by Chris Hayden. The principal illustrator was Julia Collins, with additional support from Hannah Kennedy, Magdalena Wachnik and Elizabeth Stafford. French and German summaries have been translated from English by Charles Rousseaux, Nathalie Haudecoeur-Wilks and Markus Dylewski. Peter Lorimer designed and produced the illustration for the front cover. Typesetting was undertaken by Charlie Webster of Production Line, Oxford.

We would like to warmly thank the very many colleagues and institutions who have provided advice and data, supplied images and allowed us the use of copyright material detailed below. As a work of synthesis, this volume draws information from many published reports, monographs and grey literature sources. Every effort has been made to present the information as accurately as possible and any remaining errors are the responsibility of the authors.

Illustration credits

Where illustrations that have been sourced from works cited in the main text of the volume, the relevant publication is identified in the following list by a short reference and full details can be found in the bibliography. Full references are only given in this list for works which are not otherwise cited in the main text.

Text Figures

Fig. 1.1 Oxford Archaeology, background map contains OS data © Crown Copyright 2015, AL 100005569; Fig. 2.1 adapted from data in Lisiecki, L E and Raymo, M E, 2005 A Pliocene-Pleistocene stack of 57 globally distributed benthic d18O records, *Paleoceanography* 20, PA1003 (upper curve) and Bassinot *et al.* (1994) (lower curve); Fig. 2.2 adapted from data in Martinson *et al.* 1987; Fig. 2.3 courtesy of Francis Wenban-Smith; Figs 2.4-2.10 courtesy of Martin Bates; Fig. 2.11 photo Oxford Archaeology; Fig. 2.12 and 2.13 photo courtesy of Martin Bates; Fig. 2.14 and 2.15 after Bates *et al.* 2004, 2007a; Fig. 2.16 adapted from Bates *et al.* 2010, fig 5a; Fig. 2.17 after Bates *et al.* 2004, 2007a; Figs 2.18-2.21 from Wenban-Smith *et al.* 2007a, courtesy of Francis Wenban-Smith; Fig. 2.22 from Bates *et al.* 2007c, fig 9 with permission from Elsevier; Fig. 2.23 from Gupta *et al.* 2004 fig 3-89 courtesy of Historic England, data © Dr Sangeev Gupta; Fig. 2.26 from Bates *et al.* 2007c, fig 4 and fig 8 with permission from Elsevier .Fig. 2.27 photo courtesy of Martin Bates; Fig. 2.28 from Boismier *et al.* 2012, courtesy of Historic England; Fig. 2.29 after Bates *et al.* 2004; 2007a; Fig. 3.1 from P. Gibbard 2007, *Nature Precedings* (doi:10.1038/npre. 2007.1205.1), adapted from Bourillet J-F, Reynaud J-Y, Baltzer A, Zaragosi S, 2003 The "Fleuve Manche": the sub-marine sedimentary features from the outer shelf to the deep-sea fans, *Journal of Quaternary Science* 18, 261-282 and reproduced courtesy of P. Gibbard and J-F Bourillet; Fig. 3.2 Photo courtesy of Martin Bates; Fig. 3.3 Reproduced with the permission of the Boxgrove Project; Fig. 3.4 The barbed point from Lemen and Ower banks (no 10), reproduced from Clark, J G D & Godwin, H, 1956 A Maglemosian site at Brandesburton, Holderness, Yorkshire, *Proceedings of the Prehistoric Society* 22, PL II reproduced with permission from Cambridge University Press; Fig. 3.5 reproduced courtesy of Wessex Archaeology; Fig. 3.6 reproduced with permission from the Dutch National Museum of Antiquities; Fig. 3.7 reproduced with permission of the artist © John Sibbick; Figs 3.8 and 3.9 reproduced courtesy of Wessex Archaeology; Fig. 3.10 – Fig. 3.12 reproduced courtesy of the Boxgrove Project; Fig. 3.13 courtesy of Martin Bates; Fig. 3.14 reproduced from Gupta *et al.* 2004 courtesy of Historic England, data © Dr Sanjeev Gupta; Fig. 3.15 reproduced courtesy of the Boxgrove Project; Fig. 3.16 photo by Nigel Larkin, with permission; Fig. 4.1 reproduced courtesy of Luton Museum Services; Fig. 4.2 and Fig. 4.3 reproduced from Bridgland, DR, 2014 Lower Thames terrace stratigraphy: latest views, in D R Bridgland, P Allen and T S White *The Quaternary of the Lower Thames & Eastern Essex, Field Guide*, fig. 4 and fig. 1A with permission from David Bridgland and the Quaternary Research Association; Fig. 4.3 from Morigi *et al.* 2011, fig. 2.6, based on Schreve 2004 and Bridgland 2006 fig. 1a; Fig. 4.4 adapted from Bridgland 2000; Fig. 4.5 background map contains OS data © Crown Copyright 2015, AL 100005569; Figs 4.5-4.10 from Corcoran *et al.* 2011 courtesy of the Museum of London Archaeology (MOLA) and Carlos Lemos; Fig. 4.11 from Warren 1912; Fig. 4.12 and 4.13 adapted from Essex Co. Council and Kent Co. Council 2004; Fig. 4.14 photo by Gary Coates/Birmingham Archaeology © Birmingham Archaeology; Fig. 4.15 photo © Phil Crabb of the Natural History Museum Photographic Unit, from Schreve *et al.* 2013 reproduced with permission from the Quaternary Research Association; Figs 4.16 is image (NWHCM: 2010.7, slide No 1144) reproduced courtesy of the Norfolk Museums Service, and 4.17 is modified from Boismier *et al.* 2012, reproduced with permission from Historic England; Fig. 4.18 photo courtesy of Dr Robert Hosfield; Fig. 5.1 © Beccy Scott; Fig. 5.3 Image reproduced courtesy of the AHOB Project; Fig. 5.4 Images reproduced courtesy of the British Museum; Fig. 5.6 Images 1 and 2 modified from Boëda 1993 and Images 3-6 reproduced courtesy of the Lithic Studies Society.

Figures within Boxes

Fig. 2.1.3 adapted from Lowe and Walker 1997 fig 6.5, after Shackleton and Opdyke, 1973 with permission from Pearson Education Inc; Fig. 2.2.1 from Bates *et al.* 2007 fig. 3 and Briant *et al.* 2012, fig. 2 courtesy of Martin Bates, Fig. 2.2.2 after Briant *et al.* 2012 with permission; Fig. 2.3.4 after Bates *et al.* 2010, fig 9; Fig. 2.3.5 after Bates *et al.* 2010, fig 2; Fig. 2.3.1 and 2.3.2 courtesy of Martin Bates; Fig. 2.3.3 Oxford Archaeology; Fig. 2.3.4 –2.3.6 from Brown 2012 courtesy of T Brown and L Basell; Fig. 2.4.1 and 2.4.2 courtesy of Martin Bates; Box 2.4.3 after Bates *et al.* 2004, 2007a; Fig. 2.4.4 from Bates *et al.* 2009 with permission from the Quaternary Research Association; Fig. 2.4.5 courtesy of Martin Bates; Fig. 2.4.6 from Bates *et al.* 2007b; Fig. 2.5.1 courtesy of Martin Bates; Fig. 2.5.2 from Basell *et al.* 2007 with permission from the Quaternary Research Association; Fig. 2.5.3 from Hosfield *et al.* 2011 with permission from the Quaternary Research Association; Fig. 2.6.1-2.6.2 and 2.6.3 B. from Penkman *et al.* 2008; Fig. 2.6.3 A. adapted from Bridgland 1994 fig. 4.3; Fig. 2.7.1 from Hijma *et al.* 2012 with permission from Elsevier; Fig. 2.8.1 from Bates *et al.* 2010 fig. 16; Fig. 2.8.2 from Bates *et al.* 2010 fig. 17; Fig. 2.8.3 reproduced courtesy of the Derby Museum and Art Gallery; Fig. 2.9.1 and 2.9.4 adapted from Bates and Heppell 2007, figs 5, 9, 12 and 21); Fig. 2.10.1-2.10.5 courtesy of Matt Pope; Fig. 4.2.1 from Boismier *et al.* 2012 reproduced with permission from Historic England; Figs 5.1.1-5.1.4 courtesy of Matt Pope and the Boxgrove project; Fig. 5.2.1 image courtesy of Laura Basell; Fig. 5.3.2 Photograph by Alan Straw; Fig. 5.3.3 Reproduced from Alabaster and Straw 1976, Proceedings of the Yorkshire Geological Society Vol 41 (1977) by permission of the Council of the Yorkshire Geological Society; Fig. 5.4.1 reproduced from Hosfield and Green 2013, fig 4.1 courtesy of Rob Hosfield; Fig. 5.4.2 reproduced from Hosfield and Chambers 2004, from the C.E. Bean collection, with permission from Dorset County Museum; Fig. 5.5.1 photo © Francis Wenban-Smith; Fig. 5.5.3 from Wenban-Smith 2004, courtesy of Francis Wenban-Smith; Fig. 5.6.1 drawings after Ashton and White 2003 courtesy of Mark White, photo © Mark White; Figs 5.6.2 and 5.6.3 reproduced courtesy of Wessex Archaeology; Fig. 5.7.1 © Simon Parfitt and Craig Williams, courtesy of Simon Parfitt; Fig. 5.8.1 photo courtesy of Mark White.

Chapter 1: Palaeolithic archaeology, commercial quarrying and the Aggregates Levy Sustainability Fund

by Mark White

INTRODUCTION, AIMS AND OBJECTIVES

If you have picked up this book and thought 'do we really need another tome on the British Palaeolithic', give me a moment to explain. The purpose of this volume is not to provide another synthesis of sites and interpretations, all of which can be found in other recent books (eg Morigi *et al.* 2011; Pettitt and White 2012). Rather, this volume is concerned solely with more widely disseminating the results and implications of the various Palaeolithic and Pleistocene projects funded through the British Government's *Aggregates Levy Sustainability Fund* (ALSF) which ran from 2002 to 2011.

The key drivers behind the ALSF are discussed below, but it is important to note from the start just how significant this fund has been in developing British Palaeolithic and Pleistocene research and showcasing it on an international stage. As noted in both the *Research and Conservation Framework for the British Palaeolithic* (Pettitt *et al.* 2008) and the benchmark reports on the impact of ALSF (Miller *et al.* 2008; Flatman *et al.* 2008; Richards 2008), it is hard to overstate the importance of the ALSF, which 'on the world stage... is held up as a model of innovative heritage management providing proactive, collaborative research benefit to all stakeholders' (Flatman *et al.* 2008). Indeed, through the provision of financial resources 'unimagined' at the turn of the millennium (Pettitt *et al.* 2008, 2), the ALSF facilitated unique opportunities to examine landscapes, deposits and materials that would otherwise not have been possible (Miller *et al.* 2008, 6). The research described in this volume also had significant practical outcomes for conservation and management, by facilitating the expansion of data on the Palaeolithic resource and nurturing greater collaboration between various stakeholders, particularly in updating Historical Environment Records (HERs) and developing mineral plans (Flatman *et al.* 2008).

However, the wider impact of these projects is somewhat more limited. As Flatman *et al.* (2008) found, awareness of the results of ALSF projects among curators and academics is extremely patchy (and this can almost certainly be extended to units, industry and contractors), largely because their outcomes and proposals are presented in sources not used by or available to all stakeholders. Most are either buried, among the publicly available as summaries on the Archaeological Data Service (ADS), as yet unpublished, or published in specialist literature (see http://-archaeologydataservice.ac.uk/archsearch. Useful search terms include ALSF, Aggregates Levy or individual project names, acronyms or numbers). There is thus an urgent need to ensure that all stakeholders are able to access and act upon ALSF project results. A comprehensive summary of each project considered in this volume is included in Appendix 1, along with reference to elements of the archive available on the ADS, published monographs and papers.

This volume therefore aims to bridge the gap between achievement and awareness through a synthetic conspectus of the most significant ALSF projects, and to provide pointers where further information might be sought. The primary target audience of this volume is thus the professional but not necessarily the specialist, and while students and scholars of the Quaternary period will hopefully find it a useful digest, it is primarily intended to raise awareness and widen understanding of the particular issues facing curators, developers, consultants, industry and archaeological units when dealing with the Palaeolithic resource.

More specifically, it is hoped that the book will:

- Improve access to data and interpretations currently provided in the grey literature or specialist journals
- Provide an overview and comparative investigation of Pleistocene landscapes across England (and in English offshore waters), an exercise last attempted in the 1990s by the *The English Rivers Palaeolithic Survey* (TERPS)
- Inform future research activities undertaken through national programmes of best practice and the development of research priorities

It is important to note that this book concentrates on Lower and Middle Palaeolithic sites (as did TERPS), as these dominate the British record and were the main focus of the ALSF projects. This bias is understandable when one recalls that for the Upper Palaeolithic, a period spanning only 30,000 of the 1,000,000 years humans have been visiting Britain, we have just eight Aurignacian sites, seven Gravettian ones, not a single shred of evidence for Solutrean occupation, and much of our Magdalenian comes from caves rather than fluvial contexts.

FORMAT OF THIS VOLUME

The remainder of this chapter provides the background for understanding the development and significance of the ALSF in the context of Palaeolithic research in Britain, sets out the aims and objectives of the programme, and lists the many Palaeolithic and Pleistocene projects that benefited from it (Table 1.1 and Fig. 1.1). Four themed chapters follow this, each exploring a different element of ALSF projects. Each chapter adopts a

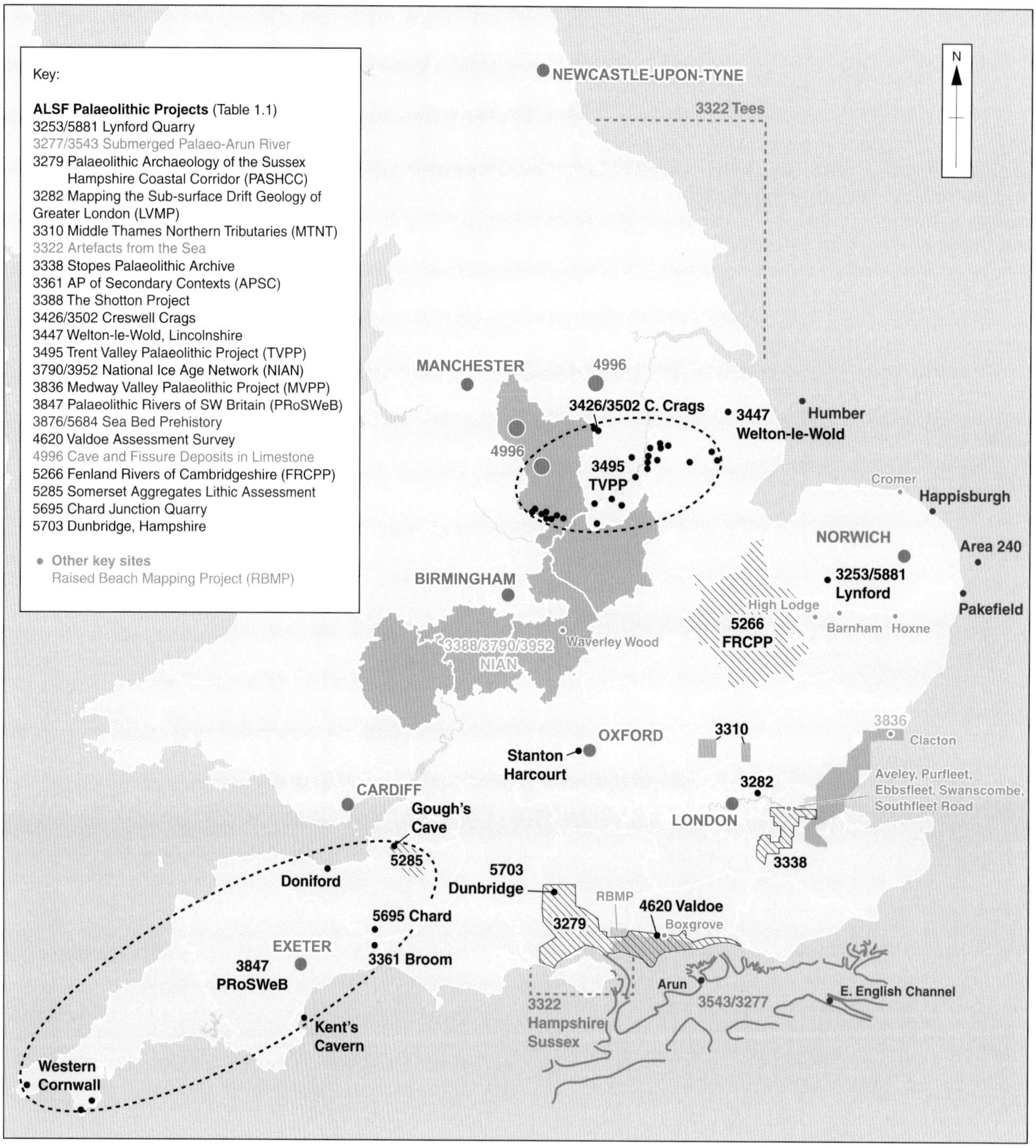

Fig. 1.1 Location of key Palaeolithic archaeological sites in Britain and ALSF projects referred to in this report. Contains Ordnance Survey data © Crown Copyright 2015

Table 1.1 List of projects related to Palaeolithic research funded by the ALSF 2002-2011. Data from Shape (shape.english-heritage.org.uk). The list excludes additional funding for dating, EH dissemination programmes and backlog clearance projects

PALAEOLITHIC PROJECTS (* Projects not located on Fig. 1.1)

EH project no.	*Project name*	*Acronym*	*Lead organisation*	*Total funding*
3253/5881	Lynford Quarry		Norfolk Archaeological Unit/ Northamptonshire Archaeology/ Royal Holloway, UoL	£404,286.90
3263/3913	The Thames Through Time Volume I	TTT	Oxford Archaeology	£162,198.90
3277/3543	Submerged Palaeo-Arun River: Reconstruction of Prehistoric Landscapes		Imperial College London	£379,247.00
3279	Palaeolithic Archaeology of the Sussex/ Hampshire Coastal Corridor	PASHCC	University of Wales, Lampeter	£308,097.50
3282	Mapping the sub-surface drift geology of Greater London (also known as The Lea Valley Mapping Project)	LVMP	Museum of London Archaeology	£232,839.70
3310	Middle Thames Northern Tributaries	MTNT	Essex County Council	£83,582.50
3322	Artefacts from the sea		Wessex Archaeology	£110,920.00
3333	Late Quaternary landscape history of the Swale-Ure		Durham University	£274,477.60
3338	Stopes Palaeolithic Archive		University of Southampton	£74,116.80
*3351	Archaeological Potential of Aggregate Deposits in the SW		University of Exeter	£1,500.00
3361	Archaeological Potential of Secondary Contexts	APSC	University of Southampton	£73,338.70
*3362	Re-assessment of the archaeological potential of Continental Shelves		University of Southampton	£84,606.00
*3363	Provenancing of flint nodules		University of Southampton	£2,620.00
3388	The Shotton Project: A Midlands Palaeolithic Network		University of Birmingham	£119,195.60
3426	Creswell Crags Limestone Heritage Area Management Action Plan		Creswell Heritage Trust	£166,570.20
3447	Welton-le-Wold, Lincolnshire: An understanding of the Ice Age		Heritage Lincolnshire	£38,671.10
3495	The Lower and Middle Palaeolithic occupation of the Middle and Lower Trent (also known as the Trent Valley Palaeolithic Project)	TVPP	Durham University	£217,141.30
3502	Creswell Crags: Management of Pleistocene Archives and Collections		Creswell Heritage Trust	£17,905.00
*3645	BMAPA Protocol for reporting Finds of archaeological interest		Wessex Archaeology	£138,135.10
3790/3952	National Ice Age Network	NIAN	University of Birmingham/ Royal Holloway, UoL	£312,037.40
3836	Medway Valley Palaeolithic Project	MVPP	University of Southampton	£254,554.40
3847	The Palaeolithic Rivers of SW Britain	PRoSWeB	University of Exeter	£208,141.10
*3854	Chronology of British Aggregates using AAR and degradation		University of York	£26,297.00
3876	Seabed Prehistory R2		Wessex Archaeology	£296,332.10
4600	Happisburgh/Pakefield exposures		Wessex Archaeology	£50,125.00
4620	Valdoe Assessment Survey		University College London	£148,782.80
4814	Late Quaternary Environmental & Human History of the Lower Tees Valley		Durham University	£60,446.60
4996	Archaeological Potential of Cave & Fissure Deposits in Limestone		Archaeological Research and Consultancy at the University of Sheffield	£30,193.80
*5088	J J Wymer Archive		Wessex Archaeology	£61,030.00
5266	Lower and Middle Palaeolithic of the Fenland Rivers (also known as Fenland Rivers of Cambridgeshire Palaeolithic Project)	FRCPP	Durham University	£82,450.00
5285	Somerset Aggregate Lithics Assessment	SALSA	Somerset County Council	£10,600.00
5684	Seabed Prehistory: Site Evaluation Techniques (Area 240)		Wessex Archaeology	£286,471.40

5695	Chard Junction Quarry, Dorset: Palaeolithic Archaeological Resource	Southampton University	£131,183.00
5703	Palaeolithic material from Dunbridge, Hampshire	Wessex Archaeology	£32,435.70
	Stanton Harcourt Pleistocene material	Katherine Cropper	£915.00
	Boxgrove Acquisition, West Sussex	Wragg & Co	£100,000.00

MINERAL PLANNING RELATED PROJECTS

Project no.	*Project name*	*Lead organisation*	*Total funding*
3041	Vale of York Alluvial landscapes	University of Newcastle/ York Archaeological Trust	£328,599.00
3374	Greater Thames Survey of Known mineral extraction sites	Essex/Kent County Councils	£185,038.00
3928	Aggregate Extraction in the Ribble Valley	University of Liverpool/ Oxford Archaeology North	£304,434.10
4653	Aggregate extraction in Warwickshire	Warwickshire County Council	£97,632.00
4778	Durham – assessment of archaeological resource in aggregate areas	Durham County Council	£271,219.30
4828	East Riding of Yorkshire – assessment of archaeological resource in aggregate areas	Humber Field Archaeology	£62,482.50
5229/5707	Aggregate Landscapes of Derbyshire and the Peak District	Derbyshire County Council	£205,120.00
5319	East Sussex – assessment of archaeological resource in aggregate areas	East Sussex County Council	£22,334.00
3346	Gloucestershire – assessment of archaeological resource	Gloucester County Council	£64,595.00
3365	Modelling exclusion zones for marine dredging	Southampton University	£258,486.00
3430	Hertfordshire Mineral Local Plan Review	Hertfordshire County Council	£15,442.00
3966	Worcestershire Resource assessment	Worcestershire County Council	£77,068.40
3987	Suffolk – assessment of archaeological resource in aggregate areas	Suffolk County Council	£102,720.90
3994	Somerset – assessment of archaeological resource in aggregate areas	Somerset County Council	£77,168.00
4633	Lincolnshire – assessment of archaeological resource in aggregate areas	Lincolnshire County Council	£66,324.20
4681	Warwickshire – assessment of archaeological resource in aggregate areas	Warwickshire County Council	£94,229.00
4766	Hampshire – assessment of archaeological resource in aggregate areas	Hampshire County Council	£155,327.90
4794	Isle of Portland Archaeology Survey	AC Archaeology	£27,612.70
4832	NMP: Leadon & Severn Valleys	Gloucestershire County Council	£44,232.00
5241	Norfolk – assessment of archaeological resource in aggregate areas	Norfolk Museums Service	£110,689.00
5292	Leicestershire and Rutland – assessment of archaeological resource in aggregate areas	Leicestershire County Council	£49,548.00
5339	North Yorkshire – assessment of archaeological resource in aggregate areas	North Yorkshire County Council	£4,053.80
5366	Whole-site first assessment toolkit for sands and gravels	Leicester University	£128,746.00
5381	Palaeolithic Research Framework	University of Sheffield/ Wessex Archaeology	£3,848.00
5713	Quarrying, caves and mines: a review of evaluation and mitigation techniques	York Archaeological Trust	£24,427.50
5725	Enhancing the geoarchaeological resource in the Lower Severn Valley	Worcestershire County Council	£81,940.70
5759	Bedfordshire aggregates archaeological resource assessment	Bedfordshire County Council	£52,343.00
5769	Assessment of archaeological resource in aggregate areas within the IOW	Museum of London Archaeology	£85,226.00
5784	Oxfordshire Aggregates Archaeological Resource Assessment	Oxford Archaeology	£53,723.80
5787	Notts Aggregate resource assessment	Trent and Peak Archaeology	£62,671.00
5794	South Gloucestershire Aggregate Resource Assessment	Cotswold Archaeology	£26,105.10
5807	Wiltshire and Swindon Aggregate Resource Assessment	Cotswold Archaeology	£36,949.30
5810	Essex Aggregates Resource Assessment	Essex County Council	£78,124.00
5849	Assessment of archaeological resource in aggregate areas within the London Borough of Havering	Museum of London Archaeology	£27,747.50

5850	Assessment of archaeological resource in aggregate areas within the Bath and NE Somerset	Museum of London Archaeology	£41,698.00
5898	West Berkshire Aggregates Resource Assessment	Museum of London Archaeology	£62,247.30

PROJECTS WITH DIRECT RELEVANCE TO THE PALAEOLITHIC RESOURCE

Project no.	*Project name*	*Lead organisation*	*Total funding*
3350	Aggregate Extraction related archaeology in England	University of Exeter	£86,494.00
3357	Predictive Modelling at a river confluence	University of Exeter	£296,978.00
3364	High resolution sonar and marine aggregates deposits	Southampton University	£96,460.00
3964	Aggregates industry in the Trent Valley: a history and archaeology	University of Sheffield	£57,178.80
4613	3D seismics for mitigation mapping of the southern North Sea	University of Birmingham/CBA	£241,807.70
4716	Marine Research Framework	Southampton University	£71,264.00
4772	Suffolk river valleys and aggregate extraction	Suffolk County Council	£78,005.50
4776	Unlocking the Past: archaeology from aggregates in Worcs - HER	Worcestershire County Council	£65,419.70
	AAR/Biogenic carbon OSL	University of Wales, Aberystwyth	£25,488.80
	Archaeology and the QPA		£5,238.00
	Archaeology of the Mendip Hills: conference	University of Worcester	£4,225.00

Annual Totals

2002	**2003**	**2004**	**2005**	**2006**	**2007**	**2008**	**2009**	**2010**
£1,522,101.40	£1,023,476.70	£1,340,887.90	£1,048,740.90	£1,223,588.40	£1,121,124.40	£418,371.20	£715,260.00	£369,016.0

scalar approach – that is, they examine the different potentials and problems that emerge from Palaeolithic investigations that operate at different levels of inquiry from the micro-scale of *in situ* find horizons and sites through the meso-scales of gravel quarries to the macro-scale of landscape surveys.

In Chapter 2, Martin Bates and Matthew Pope examine the range of methods used by various ALSF projects to explore the Pleistocene record. This reaches out to units and development controllers by exploring cost-effective methods as well as state-of-the-art techniques. It kick-starts the scalar approach advocated in this volume by looking at how different questions engender different approaches, and is particularly concerned with generating a greater appreciation among non-specialist stakeholders of the importance of sites with a range of environmental proxies but no hint of a human presence.

Chapter 3, by Matthew Pope and Martin Bates, deals with the record from marine and marine-land transitional zones. The marine resource has become something of a celebrity – perhaps even a cause célèbre – over the past decade, as awareness has grown that potentially high-quality archaeology can be found in intact sediments, particularly in the North Sea basin and immediate on-shore contexts. Pope and Bates examine the different ALSF projects that have tackled these issues, while also putting to rest some emerging misconceptions about this record. Vitally, they also question whether loss of marine habitat and lack of any contextual information is a price worth paying, or whether this is a resource best left to another generation.

In Chapter 4, Danielle Schreve examines the impact of the ALSF on terrestrial landscape based projects. This concentrates on the scale of the site, and of the valley, but also discusses the highs and lows of a major flagship project – the National Ice Age Network (NIAN). This chapter also offers the best insights into the Impact of ALSF in terms of social and cultural benefits to local and national communities, and in helping address policy at a national level.

In Chapter 5, Andy Shaw and Beccy Scott discuss the technology, behaviour and settlement history of Palaeolithic humans. The text of this chapter focuses on providing a commentary on the Palaeolithic material record for the non-specialist. Taking up the theme of scales, it begins with a useful outline of the nature of the material (including its taphonomic and collection history). A temporal run-down of the key types of artefact and technologies most commonly found at Palaeolithic sites is then provided and is intended to act as a brief guide to what one might expect to find in deposits of different ages. The value of waste flakes is also discussed, as well as changes in landscapes and the use of the landscape in structuring the archaeological record, aiming once again to provide useful insights into the value (or otherwise) of various sites for various stakeholders. Finally, the authors provide a guide to interpreting the record, in terms of taphonomy, site function and landscape use. Each of the themes discussed is exemplified using ALSF projects, which are in this chapter delivered through text boxes.

The final chapter is an attempt to use these insights to define future priorities and milestones, and offers pointers for all stakeholders regarding reasonable responses and mitigation to development at different locations.

FOR THE LOVE OF CLASTS

Palaeolithic archaeology has a singular love-hate relationship with the aggregates industry. Were it not for the commercial extraction of sands and gravels, most deeply buried Palaeolithic sites would remain just that: deeply buried. Instead, there are literally thousands of findspots (Roe 1968; Wymer 1968; 1985; 1999). The most profitable period for Palaeolithic archaeology was the era when quarries and brickpits were dug by hand (essentially from the landmark year of 1859 to the late 1920s), which is when most of our known and celebrated Palaeolithic sites were first discovered (Wymer 1968; 1985; 1999; Roe 1981; Pettitt and White 2012). It is fair to say that we are still reaping these dividends – almost all of the flagship excavations of the past 30 years have been re-investigations of the best finds of this vintage (see for example Roberts and Parfitt 1999; Ashton *et al.* 1992; Ashton *et al.* 1998; Ashton *et al.* 2005; Ashton *et al.* 2008; Gowlett *et al.* 2005). Equally, for their part, the early quarry workers could augment their salaries by 'keeping an eye out for palaeoliths', with many collectors willing to part with fairly large sums of money and occasional legs of mutton for the right pieces from the right sites – although this did occasionally lead to sharp practices including forgery and seeding sites from other localities (cf Smith 1894). Records of Worthington Smith's purchasing activities held in the British Museum and the Ashmolean Museum show that he was willing to pay over £1 for a prized piece, from his total annual income of £52. He was certainly not alone.

On the other hand, since the advent of large-scale mechanised extraction the very process of exposure has become the process of destruction, with the potential for lithic scatters, find horizons and indeed whole sites to be swept away in a few scoops of a giant bucket. Access to sites and collections has become increasingly difficult and now mostly involves chance finds on a sorting belt or spoil heap by quarry employees or local enthusiasts, some of the latter entering sites without permission and rarely registering their finds on the local HER. Rates of discovery have consequently slowed to about one or two major sites per generation and only a handful of truly significant new discoveries since the 1950s really spring to mind: Boxgrove, Purfleet, Aveley, Lynford, Waverley Wood, Glaston, Happisburgh and Pakefield being the most notable, the last two due to coastal erosion rather than extraction (see references in Pettitt and White 2012).

Equally, a number of historical, logistical and productivity-linked issues has made the Mineral Products Association as a body, and some (but not all) quarry managers as individuals, reluctant to allow Palaeolithic archaeologists access to their operations. This is easy to appreciate, especially when quarry companies have already conformed to legislation and often paid out large sums of money for archaeological investigations of the Holocene sediments above the Pleistocene aggregate. However, it does represent a misunderstanding as to the very different nature of Palaeolithic and Pleistocene remains and how these should be recorded and investigated. The latter occupy a rather enigmatic position among the various stakeholders. For archaeological units and scholars of later periods, Pleistocene sediment is the 'natural' (and of limited interest); for the quarry company, it is pay-dirt; and for the Palaeolithic specialist, it is the critical archaeological resource – the 'lost landscapes' of the Pleistocene. In other words, industry and Palaeolithic archaeology are interested in the same resource – Pleistocene deposits – just for very different reasons.

There is no easy solution to this, and balancing the protection of the Palaeolithic heritage with the needs of the aggregates industry is a fraught business, especially with new agendas driven towards a 'presumption in favour of sustainable development' (National Planning Policy Framework 2012, 14). I do not intend here to become embroiled in the rights or wrongs of the situation, nor to engage in period-specific special pleading, but a few operational issues should be outlined. As Wenban-Smith (1995b) points out, most archaeological legislation in the UK has focussed on the more visible, accessible and better documented sites and monuments of the Neolithic onwards. The non-structural nature of open-air Palaeolithic sites means that they are excluded from statutory protection on archaeological grounds – put simply, they are not monuments. However, some cave sites are Scheduled Monuments, which may appear incongruous since the caves are certainly not of human construction. In some cases caves are affected by aggregates quarrying of hard rock such as limestone, with Creswell Crags, Coygan Cave, Westbury, and Uphill Quarry being examples. The last three of these were actually destroyed by quarrying.

Environmentally significant sites that lack artefacts also fall outside the generally accepted definition of the archaeological resource and are rarely considered (Wenban Smith 1994, 1995a and 1995b), although both artefactual and non-artefactual sites may be afforded some protection if they are considered to be Sites of Special Scientific Interest (SSSI) by Natural England, usually on the basis of geology or fossil fauna (see sites in Bridgland 1994).

In counterpoint, it must be emphasised that for practical rather than legal reasons, Palaeolithic sites are incredibly hard to evaluate using normal planning procedures – either Planning Policy Guidance 16 (PPG16) or its successor the National Planning Policy Framework (NPPF) (see also Last *et al.* 2013). As it stands, local authorities are tasked with ensuring that, where proposed developments impinge upon heritage assets with archaeological interest (including Palaeolithic interests), developers should fund an appropriate desk-based assessment and, where necessary, a field evaluation. But for the Palaeolithic, how is this to be done with any degree of accuracy? New quarry sites are unlikely to have previously produced any Palaeolithic artefacts and will thus be largely absent from the Historic Environment Records (HERs). The uneven distribution of finds both vertically and horizontally (depending on what part of these lost landscapes are being exploited today and in the past) means that Palaeolithic occurrences pose several evaluative/predictive/mitigative problems. For example, one cannot simply assume that because a particular terrace gravel at Quarry A contained 1000 handaxes, the lateral extension of that gravel a kilometre away at Quarry B will contain anything at all. And all of this says nothing of the unique issues of monitoring marine aggregates – as recently brought home by the discovery of Palaeolithic artefacts dredged from Area 240 in the North Sea off East Anglia (Wessex Archaeology 2008; Tizzard *et al.* 2015) and the Neanderthal frontal bone found off the Netherlands (Hublin *et al.* 2009).

As described in Chapter 2, the distribution of artefacts across landscapes depends entirely on past palaeogeographies – in this case the precise part of the river channel that had once been exploited by Palaeolithic hominins and is now of interest to modern development. The quarry company or developer might also rightly ask whether another 1000 rolled handaxes from southeast England is actually telling us anything about the past we didn't already know (ie that Pleistocene hominins often made handaxes and these often ended up as clasts in rivers). If those 1000 rolled handaxes came from the relatively barren north of the country, however, their importance would be significantly greater, but they would still be derived and the details of their original context contextual depleted. In many respects other than in fine-grained well-preserved locations watching briefs are the best one can hope for. The Palaeolithic community and quarry industry must also be alive to a responsive as well as a predictive method of evaluation. That said, building such contingency into any development proposal may stumble over the imperative of presumption in favour of development. Obviously, new methods and measures are needed and predictive tools must be top of the agenda (see Chapter 2).

THE ENGLISH RIVERS PALAEOLITHIC SURVEY, 1991–1997

Following directly from concerns such as these was one of the greatest successes for English Heritage and British Palaeolithic research, *The English Rivers Palaeolithic Survey* (TERPS). This project was initiated in 1991 in response to growing awareness that the huge increase in the quantity of sand and gravel being extracted for road building and construction was potentially destroying evidence of the Palaeolithic period without record (Wymer 1999), although its proximate impetus appears to have been proposed mineral extraction at the rich site of Dunbridge, Hampshire (Gamble 1992; Wenban-Smith 1995a). This site had, incidentally, yielded about 1000 handaxes in earlier phases of extraction (Roe 1968). At the time, although Government policy was to encourage the increased use of recycled aggregate resources, there were no means to significantly reduce the threat posed to the Palaeolithic archaeological record. TERPS began life as the *Southern Rivers Palaeolithic Project* (SRPP), directed by John Wymer under the auspices of Wessex Archaeology, and aimed to provide a detailed survey of the known Palaeolithic material south of the Thames. In 1994 this work was extended to cover the whole country (thus becoming TERPS), which divided Britain into 12 regions, primarily based on major river drainage systems.

The specific aims of the survey were (quoted from Wymer 1999, 1):

- To identify, as accurately as possible, the findspots of Lower and Middle Palaeolithic artefacts and the deposits containing them in order to demonstrate fully the distribution of known Palaeolithic sites in England
- To confirm, where necessary, the validity of previous identifications of artefactual collections
- To verify, where necessary, the provenances of discoveries, and to note the current physical condition of such sites
- To chart the extent of relevant Quaternary deposits
- To review previous aggregate extraction so as to understand the circumstances of the earlier discovery of Palaeolithic material
- To consider current established and potential mineral extraction policies so as to recognise the threat to the Palaeolithic resource
- To assess the varying relative importance of discoveries and the potential for future finds throughout the study area in order to develop predictive models; to make recommendations to English Heritage in the light of potential threats
- To disseminate the results as quickly as possible in forms appropriate to different users
- To inform the academic fraternity of the progress and results of the survey

It is clear from this that curation lay at heart of TERPS. The results were initially disseminated to HERs, county planning offices and project members as a set of maps (containing information on past, present and future mineral extraction) and gazetteers (Wymer 1992-1997). While these had a very limited print run, the results were summarised in Wymer's final book: *The Lower Palaeolithic Occupation of Britain* (Wymer 1999). TERPS remains the most comprehensive survey of Lower and Middle Palaeolithic archaeology in the British Isles or anywhere else for that matter, and the resulting dataset has underpinned British Palaeolithic research since its publication.

THE AGGREGATES LEVY SUSTAINABILITY FUND, 2002-2011

In April 2002, the UK Government imposed a new levy on sales of primary marine and terrestrial aggregate, so that market prices better reflected the social and environmental costs of primary extraction. The Department for Environment, Food and Rural Affairs (Defra) used a proportion of the revenue generated to fund research designed to mitigate the impact of aggregate production in affected areas: this was known as the Aggregates Levy Sustainability Fund. The fund was distributed by a number of delivery partners, with the lion's share being funnelled through English Nature (now Natural England) and English Heritage (now Historic England), the latter primarily involved in mitigating the impact of aggregate extraction on the historic environment, both marine and terrestrial (ALSF Annual Report 2002-3). The scheme ran through four phases over 10 years: the Pilot Phase from 2002-4, Phase 2 from 2004-6, the Phase 2 Extension in 2007, and Phase 3 which ran from 2008 to 2011.

In total English Heritage distributed £28.8 million (Tim Cromack pers. comm.), with almost £8.8 million going to projects with relevance to Palaeolithic archaeology and wider Pleistocene research (Table 1.1). Such levels of funding were indeed unimagined when the first Palaeolithic framework document was published three years prior to the commencement of the scheme (English Heritage/Prehistoric Society 1999), and outshines funding from the Research Councils UK (RCUK) and charitable sources over the same period in reach and distribution, if not necessarily in actual cash. Also outlined in Table 1.1, but not discussed in detail in this volume, are the regional frameworks and mineral assessment plans funded by the ALSF. Such plans are critical to developing an understanding of what is left of Pleistocene landscapes, and when viewed against regional and national surveys of artefact distributions in space and time, they provide the pathways towards the holy grail of predictive modelling.

Both the Pilot and Phase 2 of the ALSF in England had the following objectives, as defined by Defra in 2002 (ALSF Annual Report 2004-5, 3):

Objective 1: minimising the demand for primary aggregates

Objective 2: promoting environmentally friendly extraction and transport

Objective 3: reducing the local effects of aggregates extraction

In March 2005, the third objective was reworded, and a fourth objective was added, thus:

Objective 3: to address the environmental impacts of past aggregates extraction

Objective 4: to compensate local communities for the impacts of aggregates extraction

The priorities and initiatives set out by English Heritage for the disbursal of ALSF funding also evolved over the lifetime of the scheme. For the Pilot, English Heritage focussed on three key areas (ALSF Annual Report 2002-3, 3):

- Projects that delivered reliable predictive information and techniques to enable planning authorities and the aggregates industry to minimise the future impact of extraction on the historic environment
- Projects aimed at increasing understanding in both the public and professional spheres of knowledge gained from past work on aggregate extraction landscapes
- Targeted buying-out of old mineral permissions for the benefit of long-term management and sustainability of the historic environment

English Heritage were also mindful of the possible need to use part of the funding for excavation, analysis and dissemination of unforeseen archaeological remains encountered during developer-funded excavation in advance of aggregate extraction, provided normal planning procedures had been followed (ibid).

During Phase 2, English Heritage continued to address the impact of aggregate extraction on the historic environment (initially Objectives 2 and 3, and eventually 4), specifically targeting projects that:

- Developed the capacity to manage aggregate extraction landscapes in the future Delivered to public and professional audiences the full benefits of knowledge gained through past work in advance of aggregates extraction
- Reduced the physical impacts of current extraction where these lie beyond current planning controls and the normal obligations placed on minerals operators
- Addressed the effects of old mineral planning permissions
- Promoted understanding of the conservation issues arising from the impacts of aggregates extraction on the historic environment

The final phase saw another variation, with projects now broken down into two themes, each with a different set of objectives (ALSF Annual Report 2007-8, 3):

Theme 1: quarries

- Identification and characterisation of the historic environment in key existing or potential areas of terrestrial aggregate extraction

- Research and development of practical new techniques to locate hidden historic environment assets in aggregate landscapes
- Conservation and repair of vulnerable historic assets directly impacted by aggregates extraction or directly associated with historical extraction
- Emergency funding for the recording, analysis and publication of nationally significant archaeological remains discovered during aggregates extraction

Theme 2: marine

- Identification and characterisation of the historic environment in key existing or potential areas of marine extraction
- Research and development of practical new techniques to locate seabed historic environment assets
- Marine historic environment training, dissemination and communication

Throughout its lifetime, knowledge transfer, communication and outreach lay at the core of ALSF objectives. As a recipient of several grants it was always very clear that projects needed to talk not to a purely academic audience, but to a variety of stakeholders, ranging from the general public and local interest groups, to government agencies, contractors, developers and the quarrying industry. Furthermore:

> "One of the most important roles of the ALSF [was] the ability to fund projects that raise awareness of conservation issues, not only across the historic environment sector but also amongst the wider community and the aggregate extraction industry. Many who work in the quarry industry will have some awareness of the archaeology that often comes to light during operations but it is important that these discoveries are better recognised and understood and that an accurate record is made of them."
> (ALSF Annual Report 2004-5, 20)

Given the recent winding up of the ALSF, as well as several other major funded projects such as the Leverhulme Trust's *Ancient Human Occupation of Britain* project (AHOB), it is timely to consider the many successes of the scheme, and use this to help build the future of the British Palaeolithic.

Chapter 2:
Methods for reconstructing Ice Age landscapes

by Martin Bates and Matthew Pope

INTRODUCTION

The practice of Palaeolithic archaeology in the field is firstly about geology: the sediments and landscapes features that form the preservational context of archaeological remains. In nearly all instances (certainly for the Lower Palaeolithic), these preservational contexts have been deposited naturally and understanding their formation and spatial distribution is fundamental to a correct interpretation of the archaeological signatures found in them. Such an approach is therefore in essence about reconstructing Pleistocene geographies and palaeolandscapes (Butzer 1982) and using this information to inform our understanding of the Palaeolithic archaeology. As a discipline these interests can be traced into the mid-19th century when workers in northern France and southern England demonstrated an early human presence in geological deposits of great antiquity using collaboration between the earth sciences, zoology and archaeology (Trigger 1989; O'Connor 2007).

Today, those involved in undertaking, curating or designing schemes aimed at recovering or preserving Palaeolithic remains require a scaled understanding of the associated ancient palaeolandscapes. In other words, Pleistocene specialists of all flavours must turn their hand to the field of palaeogeography: the study and reconstruction of past landscapes. The study of palaeogeography entails the reconstruction of patterns of the earth's surface both at specific times and through time using a wide range of material evidence including geological, biological and archaeological information. In particular, it focuses on the ancient sedimentary environments and the contemporary ecological conditions that may allow us to fix the location of shorelines, position of rivers and source areas of raw material (ie for human use). Understanding such an approach is of particular importance in a discipline that is totally familiar to only a limited audience (ie specialist Palaeolithic archaeologists and Quaternary scientists) but where the informed lay-person (ie development control officer) might well be required to construct and oversee the implementation of an investigation framework for a site that contains a Palaeolithic interest. As such, it is important not only in enabling us to understand any excavated finds, but also for developing strategies to locate those places in the modern landscape where we may expect to find evidence for our earliest ancestors (Bates and Wenban-Smith 2011).

The adoption of a palaeogeographical approach was fundamental to many of the ALSF funded projects. This not only facilitated novel investigations of known and new archaeological sites, but also allowed the reconstruction of landscape contexts in situations where archaeological remains were absent but where important biological, geological or dating material was available. To those less familiar with the Palaeolithic archive and a palaeogeographic approach to Pleistocene deposits, it might be tempting to suggest that in the absence of direct archaeological evidence (ie a lack of artefacts) from a given area, a verdict of no archaeological interest can be given. However, by accepting that a palaeogeographic stance to the investigation of past landscapes is in fact the only logical approach to the Palaeolithic past – perhaps epitomised by Foley's (1981) argument of spatially continuous use of the landscape – areas devoid of apparent archaeological remains become an integral part of the broader archaeological (landscape) picture. They provide evidence for vegetation patterns, vertebrate and invertebrate faunas, climate and such like, which may be absent from archaeological sites themselves. They thus require investigation and are certainly legitimate objects of study within the context of both research and developer funded projects. In other words, artefacts or not, they are all part of the hominin landscape.

The processes involved in palaeogeographical reconstruction and the location and successful recovery of Palaeolithic archaeological remains include all aspects of palaeoenvironmental reconstruction (see Lowe and Walker 1997). However, success within the context of an archaeological project depends on an appreciation of scale. The scale of investigation needs to be considered in both spatial and temporal frameworks. In particular, approaches need to be scaled towards the nature of the archaeological question posed, which in part are directed by the resolution of the information available. Indeed, attempts to reconstruct past Pleistocene landscapes are often hampered by fragmentary evidence, incomplete sequences, poor dating control and an absence of evidence for the faunal and floral aspects of the landscapes. We are also often let down by a reticence to examine the success (or otherwise) of a project, and an inability to examine so-called 'failure' adequately in print following completion of a project. Indeed, there is a common perception that 'failure' equates to no recovered archaeology. However, as argued above, this perception is a function of an inadequate understanding of the Palaeolithic resource and what constitutes knowledge gain in the discipline, by practitioners with perhaps limited experience of working with the Palaeolithic record. Allied to the problems of investigating the past is the probability that Pleistocene landscapes and environments in the UK and elsewhere are unique and have no modern analogues. Consequently, in order to investigate this past a modified 'principle of uniformitarianism' needs to be adopted.

This chapter seeks to set out how we can investigate and enhance our understanding of the Palaeolithic past by looking at approaches to investigating these palaeogeographies that have been used within ALSF projects. It is not designed to be an exhaustive attempt to summarise all approaches to reconstructing past environments and landscapes (for this again see, for example, Lowe and Walker 2015) but simply to demonstrate how some of these approaches have been used within the context of furthering our understanding of the Palaeolithic record in Britain through this pioneering scheme. In order to do this we seek to outline the nature of the Pleistocene past and highlight some of the techniques that are available to us to reconstruct the past landscapes within which Palaeolithic peoples lived and acted out their day-to-day lives. Consequently in the next section, we consider the nature of the Pleistocene period and the frameworks in use, and examine some of the key methods we can use to investigate the remote period of human prehistory. Finally, we examine a range of case studies of landscapes at a variety of archaeological scales.

THE PLEISTOCENE PERIOD: FRAMEWORKS FOR PALAEOLITHIC ARCHAEOLOGY

Currently, the earliest evidence for human activity in the UK is recorded in East Anglia (Fig. 1.1; Parfitt *et al.* 2005; 2010), with the most recent work suggesting that this occupation dates to before 780,000 BP, perhaps as early as 980,000 BP (Parfitt *et al.* 2010). These discoveries represent the culmination of 30 years of re-evaluation and research into Palaeolithic archaeology, which have seen major changes in our understanding of the nature of this record (McNabb 2007; Pettitt and White 2012) and a near doubling of the length of time humans have been present in the UK (Parfitt *et al.* 2005; 2010). These changes have gone hand in hand with signif-

Table 2.2 Summary of Marine Isotope Stages (MIS) in relation to other aspects of the Palaeolithic record

Epoch	*Age kBP*	*MI stage*	*Traditional stage (Britain)*	*Climate*
Holocene	Present–10,000	1	Flandrian	Warm – full interglacial
Late Pleistocene	25,000	2	Devensian	Mainly cold; coldest in MIS 2 when Britain depopulated and maximum advance of Devensian ice sheets; occasional short-lived periods of relative warmth ('interstadial'), and more prolonged warmth in MIS 3
	50,000	3		
	70,000	4		
	110,000	5a-d		
	125,000	5e	Ipswichian	Warm – full interglacial
Middle Pleistocene	190,000	6	Wolstonian complex	Alternating periods of cold and warmth; recently recognised that this period includes more than one glacial - interglacial cycle; changes in faunal evolution and assemblage associations through the period help distinguish its different stages
	240,000	7		
	300,000	8		
	340,000	9		
	380,000	10		
	425,000	11	Hoxnian	Warm – full interglacial
	480,000	12	Anglian	Cold – maximum extent southward of glacial ice in Britain; may incorporate interstadials that have been confused with Cromerian complex interglacials
	620,000	13-16	Cromerian Complex III and IV	Cycles of cold and warmth; still poorly understood due to obliteration of sediments by subsequent events
	780,000	1-19	Cromerian Complex I and II	
Late Early Pleistocene	1,000,000	19-25	Bavelian complex	Cycles of cool and warm, but generally not sufficiently cold for glaciation in Britain

Table 2.1: Major component stages of the British Pleistocene as outlined by Roe (1981)

		Colder periods	*Warmer periods*
HOLOCENE			Flandrian ('Postglacial')
PLEISTOCENE			
	Upper	DEVENSIAN	
			Ipswichian
		WOLSTONIAN	
	Middle		Hoxnian
		ANGLIAN	
			Cromerian
		Beestonian	
			Pastonian
	Lower	Baventian	
			Antian
		Thurnian	
			Ludhamian
		Waltonian	
PLIOCENE			

icant developments in our understanding of the climates of the Pleistocene and in particular of the number, duration and nature of the alternating series of warm and cold episodes we commonly call glacials and interglacials (Lowe and Walker 2015).

Since the late 1960s, with the discovery that the oxygen isotope record (Box 2.1) from deep sea cores could be used as a proxy record for climate (Shackleton and Opdyke 1973) and sea-level change (Shackleton 1987), it became apparent that the long-held assumptions about the number of warm and cold periods associated with the Palaeolithic archaeological record in the UK (Table 2.1; eg Roe 1981) were outdated and required re-evaluation (Wymer 1988). Prior to this, Palaeolithic archaeology was tied to a framework for climate change established using only terrestrial geological and biological proxies (Mitchell *et al.* 1973), which resulted in a limited number of warm and cold stages (Table 2.1) defined against a series of type sites. With the adoption of the oxygen isotope record (Box 2.1) more than 60 climate cycles (Marine Isotope Stages or MIS) have been identified during the last 1.8 million years. This record is now the commonly accepted framework that Quaternary scientists and Palaeolithic archaeologists use to order and correlate evidence from a wide variety of sources and situations (Table 2.2).

The key to understanding the Pleistocene climate record as we now know it (Table 2.2) is that,

Feature of the Palaeolithic archaeological record	*Palaeogeographic features*
Possible overlap of occasional Late Neanderthal populations with early modern humans	
Occasional presence of Neanderthal populations in Britain	
Absence of humans from Britain	Island Britain during much of interglacial
Absence of humans from Britain?	
Occasional proliferations of Levallois expression?	
Occasional proliferations of Levallois expression	
Incipient Levalloisian techniques alongside handaxe manufacture	
Continuation of quite common handaxe-based occupation	
Re-settlement of Britain, quite abundant evidence, mostly handaxe-based	
Absence of hominins in Britain	Major glaciation, 'old' river patterns disrupted, ?Weald/Artois ridge broken
Various, archaeologically diverse occupations of Britain: Boxgrove (handaxes); High Lodge (worked flakes)	
Sporadic flake/core-¬based settlement (Pakefield)	
Sporadic flake/core¬-based settlement (Happisburgh 3)	

although the major oscillations in temperature vary between warm (peaks) and cold (troughs) conditions, the evidence from individual marine isotope stages suggests that *within* the individual warm/cold episodes considerable variation in climate may have been experienced by animals (including humans). For example, in the warm episode between *c* 240,000 and 190,000 BP (MIS 7; Fig. 2.1) interglacial conditions were interrupted by cold intervals and associated low sea-level. By comparison, conditions within the 'last glacial' period (MIS 5d-2, the Devensian; Fig. 2.2) varied from near present day climates to periods of intense cold when ice expanded across much of northern and western Britain (Lowe and Walker 2015). However, this period of ice expansion was restricted to a period of about 10,000 years, between 25,000 and 15,000 BP, and therefore only represents a small part of a complex period of time.

More recently, work on cores taken from the ice sheets (Steffensen *et al.* 2008) in both northern and southern hemispheres suggest even greater and more rapid fluctuations in climate may have impacted the UK in the last 250,000 years. At present it is difficult to ascertain precisely the impact of such changes on Palaeolithic peoples in the UK but suffice to say that considerable adaptability would be required by hominin populations to cope with such changes.

The varying climatic cycles (of both long and short duration) will have impacted not only on humans but on the plant and animal resources available to humans, and on the physical environment through which they moved. Thus sea-levels rose and fell by up to 130m, rivers shifted between periods of erosion and periods of deposition (of either coarse gravels or fine silts and sands), vegetation fluctuated between steppic grasslands and mixed oak forests, and associated suites of animals came and went. These changes would have conspired to make Britain more or less attractive and accessible to hominins and consequently patterns of human occupation and 'extinction' would have occurred in tandem with the changing environmental conditions (Pettitt and White 2012).

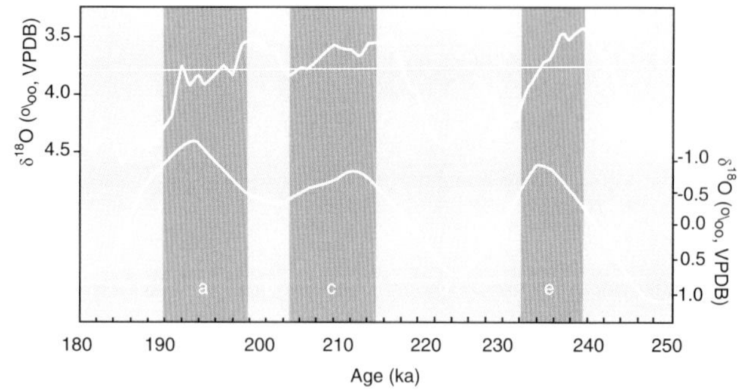

Fig. 2.1 Marine Isotope Stage 7 showing benthic $\delta^{18}O$ *isotope stack (after Lisiecki and Raymo 2005) (upper curve) and orbitally tuned pelagic O isotope stack of Bassinot* et al. *(1994) (lower curve). Note the fluctuations in these curves between warmer and cooler episodes, designated 7a-e*

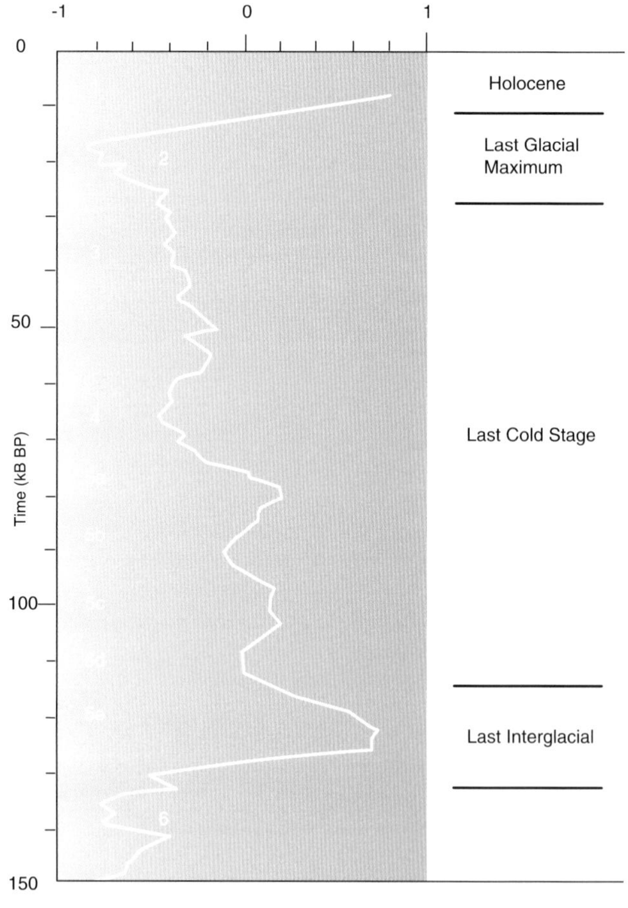

Fig. 2.2 The stacked marine oxygen isotope record for the last 130,000 years (after Martinson et al. *1987)*

METHODS FOR INVESTIGATION

The last decade has seen significant advances in the methodologies that can be applied to investigations of Pleistocene sequences and Palaeolithic archaeology. Many of these have been trialled through ALSF projects. The techniques utilised in these projects were typically developed outside archaeology, and adopted, adapted and applied as appropriate. They can be broken down into those applied in field investigations and those for post-excavation laboratory analysis.

Selecting appropriate methodologies for supporting Palaeolithic field and laboratory projects is in many instances a case of trial and error, and the successful deployment of a battery of techniques in one project does not guarantee success in another. Indeed, individual projects are unique, and appropriate methods need to be selected in order to address the archaeological questions posed and to reflect variation in bedrock geologies, superficial sediment types, etc. Consequently, projects need to be developed within the context of the individual site/area and any methods selected should be

OXYGEN ISOTOPE STRATIGRAPHY BOX 2.1

The different isotopes of oxygen preserved in the tests ('shells') of foraminifera (Fig. 2.1.1) have been instrumental in developing a framework for global climate change. Foraminifera combine oxygen in the calcite in their shells, and this is present in two different forms: the atomically heavier ^{18}O and atomically lighter ^{16}O. The precise isotopic composition of the foram test reflects the isotopic concentrations in the water from which the oxygen is derived, and these concentrations vary according to changes in the global volume of ice. So, because it is lighter, ^{16}O is preferentially evaporated from the ocean surface during periods of cold and, as much of this is subsequently precipitated as snow and retained on land as ice, marine waters become enriched in isotopically heavy oxygen. During warm periods the opposite happens, when the isotopically light water returns to the oceans (Fig. 2.1.2). By analysing foraminifera from samples taken from long cores, a history of ice build-up and decay can be inferred, showing peaks and troughs of isotope ratios that reflect cold and warm periods respectively.

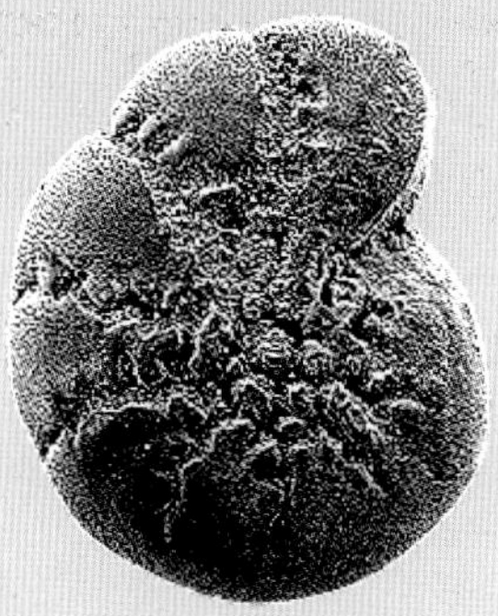

2.1.1 An example of a foraminifer: *Elphidium excavatum*

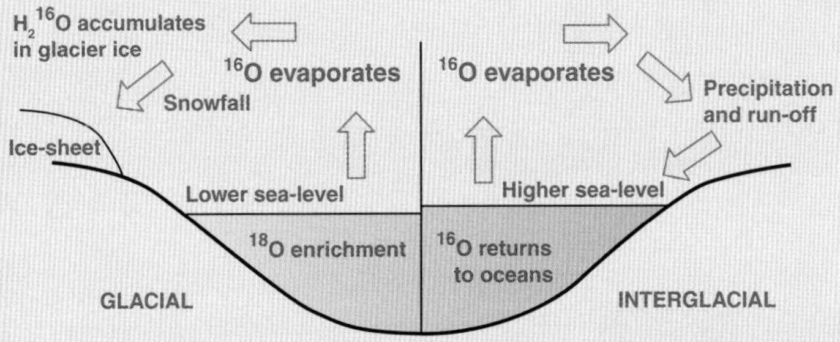

2.1.2 Effects of glacials and interglacials on the $^{18}O/^{16}O$ ratio of sea water

The first extensive application of this methodology was applied to a deep sea sediment core (V28-238) and the resulting graph of results showed that 23 peaks and troughs occurred in the last 800,000 years (Shackleton and Opdyke 1973). These periods have been numbered by counting back from the present-day interglacial or Holocene period (Marine Isotope Stage, MIS 1), with (usually) interglacial peaks (warm episodes) having odd numbers and glacial troughs (cold but not necessarily ice-dominated events) even numbers (Fig. 2.1.3).

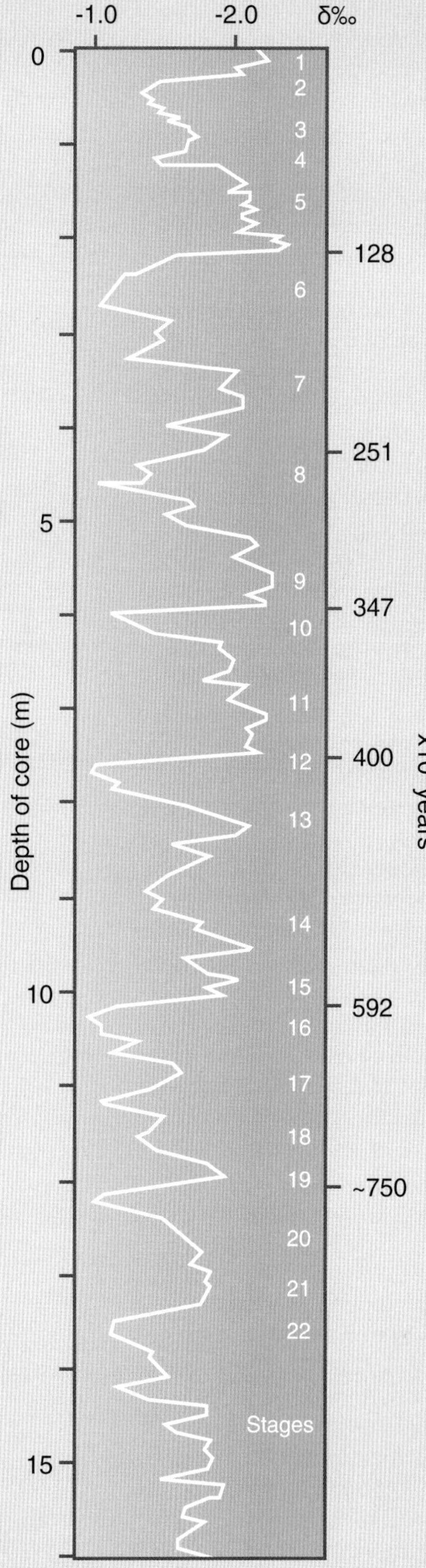

2.1.3 Marine oxygen isotope trace from deep-sea sediment core V28-238 (after Shackleton and Opdyke 1973)

USE OF BOREHOLES: TERRACES AND RAISED BEACHES

The work undertaken as part of the PASHCC project (*Palaeolithic Archaeology of the Sussex Hampshire Coastal Plain*) used a combination of extant borehole data from a wide variety of sources, coupled with purposive boreholes and test pits excavated to recover samples for palaeoenvironmental reconstruction and dating. The work was undertaken in order to provide the basis for a robust correlation for the river terraces of the Solent system (Briant *et al.* 2006; 2012) and to link the terraces with the marine raised beach sequences of the West Sussex Coastal Plain (Bates *et al.* 2010). Dating of these fluvial and marine terraces was achieved through OSL dating (Bates *et al.* 2004; 2007a; 2010; Briant *et al.* 2006; 2012).

River terraces are formed as a result of rivers downcutting through former floodplains in areas where uplift is ocurring. They are particularly important in providing a framework for understanding the Palaeolithic archaeological record and associated patterns of human occupation of the landscape (Bridgland 1996; 2006; Bridgland *et al.* 2006). Unfortunately the deposits remaining in the landscape today are fragments of these former floodplains and consequently the records are typically difficult to correlate up and downstream. Usually these remnants mirror the original geometry of the floodplain and dip in a downstream direction. By contrast, raised beaches usually form as spreads of sands and gravels at the inner margin of the former high sea-level event and form broadly horizontal sheets dissected by erosion.

In the PASHCC project a reconsideration of the previous mapping of the terraces of the Solent was undertaken (Fig. 2.2.1) and borehole data was inputted into a geological software system (Rockworks) to facilitate the plotting and correlation of fragments of former river systems. By contrast, marine sediments on the West Sussex Coastal Plain (Fig. 2.2.3) exhibit broadly horizontal distributions that allow a staircase of raised beaches to be reconstructed (Fig. 2.2.5).

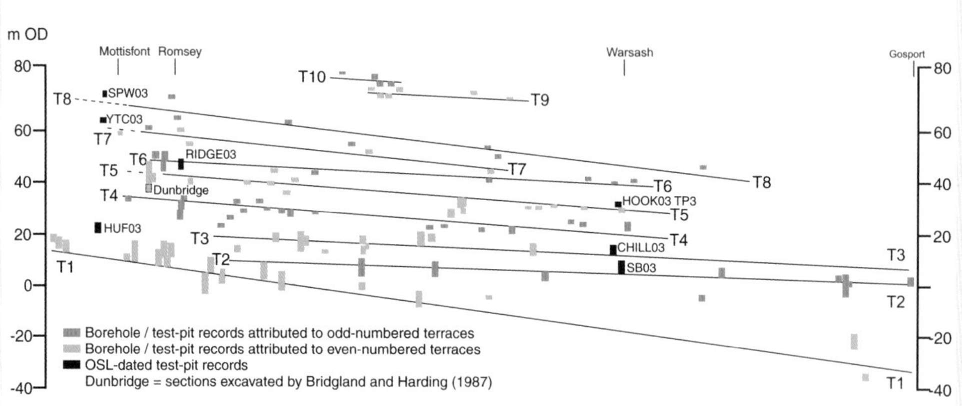

2.2.2 Long profiles of the eastern Solent terraces using the PASHCC scheme (from Briant *et al.* 2012)

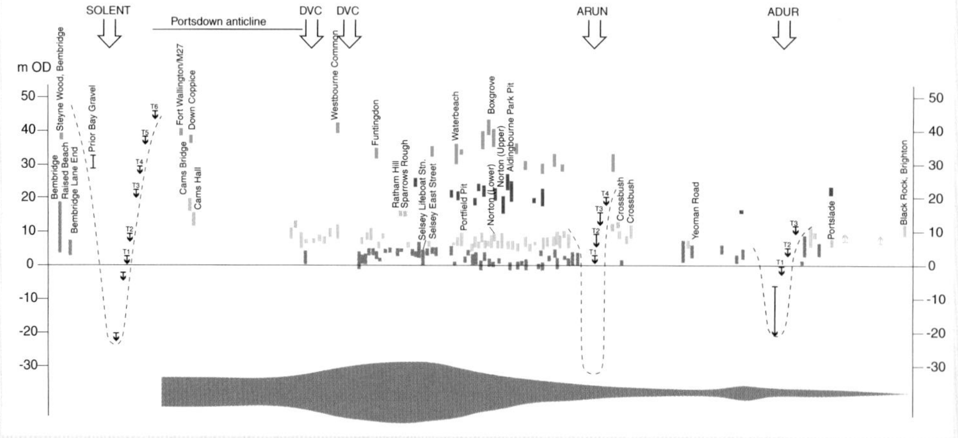

2.2.4 Elevation of marine sediments from selected sites in the PASHCC coastal plain study area (from Bates *et al.* 2010). Colour key: blue = Goodwood/Slindon Raised Beach; red = Aldingbourne Raised Beach; green = unknown; yellow = Brighton/Norton Raised Beach; brown = Pagham Raised Beach

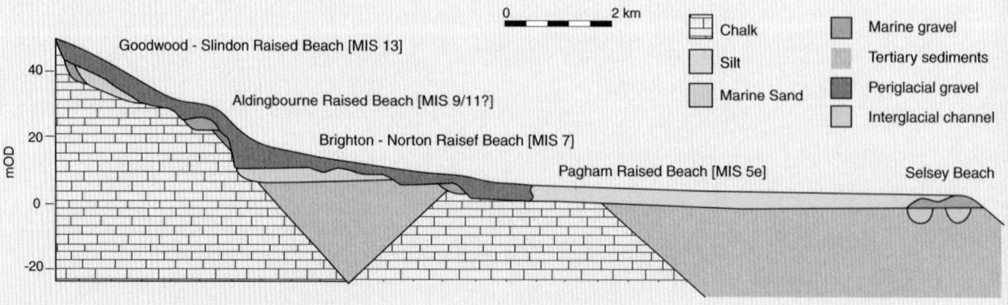

2.2.5 Schematic section through the West Sussex Coastal Plain showing the main stratigraphic units recognised today from integrated studies of boreholes and published records (from Bates *et al.* 2010)

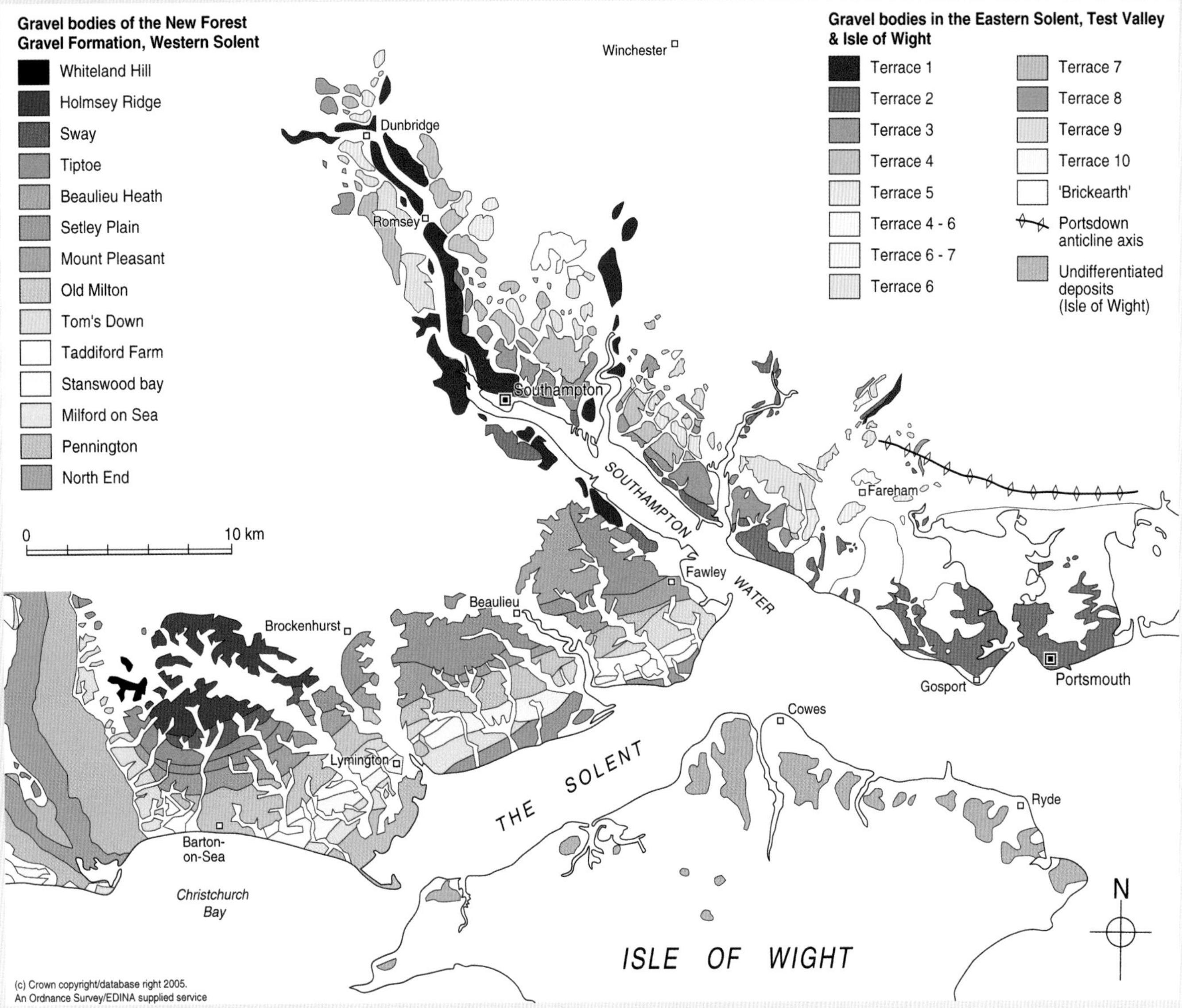

2.2.1 Distribution of gravel bodies in the eastern and western Solent (from Briant *et al.* 2012)

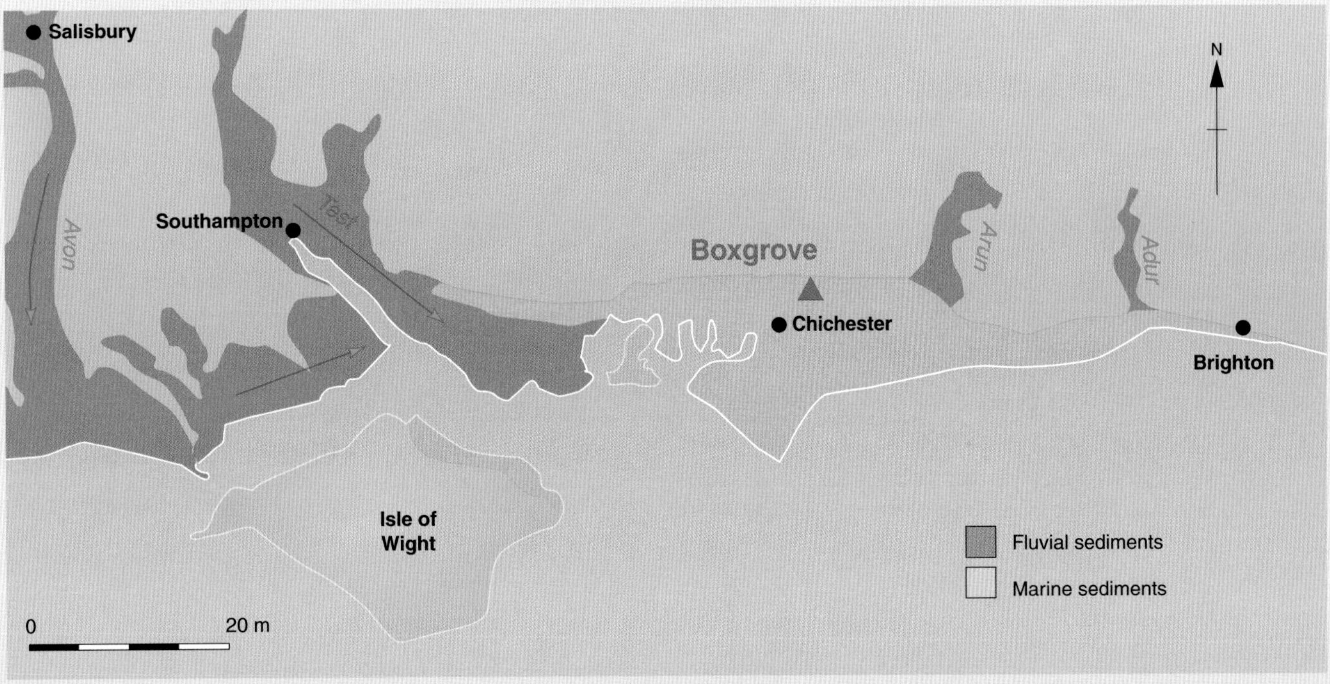

2.2.3 Distribution of marine and fluvial sediments in the PASHCC study area

trialled and deployed carefully. In most cases this is best achieved through the cooperation of specialists who are familiar with the nature of the Pleistocene record in that area. This combination of expertise and judicial selection of appropriate methods in the development of field projects is well illustrated by the success of the ALSF funded projects. Examples can be seen at the landscape scale – as shown by the *Trent Valley Palaeolithic Project* (TVPP: Bridgland *et al.* 2015) and *The Palaeolithic Archaeology of the Sussex/Hampshire Coastal Corridor* (PASHCC: Bates *et al.* 2004; 2007a; 2010; Briant *et al.* 2006; 2012) – to the site level, as seen at Lynford and the Valdoe (Boismier *et al.* 2012; Pope *et al.* 2009).

Field investigations

Field investigation of areas containing thick and complex sequences of Quaternary sediments – such as the Pleistocene river terrace sequence of the Thames (Bridgland 1994; Gibbard 1985; 1994) or raised beach and river gravels on southern England's coastal plains (Bates *et al.* 1997; 2003; 2010) – typically commences with the examination of published literature (both archaeological and geological) and extant borehole data (Box 2.2). This might be followed by field investigation involving mapping the surface expression of the deposits (Brown *et al.* 2008) and the recording and sampling of sequences exposed in quarry exposures, cliff sections etc (Box 2.3). Such an approach is often augmented by purposive boreholes and / or test pits in areas known or thought to include sequences likely to contain geological or biological data required for palaeoenvironmental reconstruction, correlation or dating.

The application of geophysical survey (Box 2.4) at this stage in a project may also be considered. Projects constructed in this fashion might address a number of issues. Firstly, where large quantities of extant material exist in archive collections such projects might usefully provide a context for that material enabling more to be made of historic collections – for example TVPP, PASHCC, *Medway Valley Palaeolithic Project* (MVPP: Wenban-Smith *et al.* 2007a and b), *Palaeolithic Rivers of Southwest Britain* (PRoSWeB: Brown *et al.* 2008). Alternatively, projects of this kind may be the precursor to searching for hitherto unknown Palaeolithic sites and are useful to facilitate development control within the HERs – for example the PASHCC project (Bates *et al.* 2007a), MVPP (Wenban-Smith *et al.* 2007 and b), and the *Middle Thames Northern Tributaries* project (MTNT: Bates and Heppell 2007).

As mentioned in Chapter 1, most of the sites we now think of as providing the key to our understanding the Palaeolithic human occupation of Britain are those that were found during quarrying

Fig. 2.3 Gravel quarrying in 19th/early 20th century; Galley Hill Pit. Note worker on left with shovel and barrow for aggregate removal.

in the late 19th and early to mid-20th centuries, when quarrying was undertaken by hand and artefacts were relatively easy to see during aggregate extraction and grading processes (Fig. 2.3). Sites such as Hoxne (Singer *et al.* 1993; Ashton *et al.* 2008), High Lodge (Ashton *et al.* 1992), Swanscombe (Conway *et al.* 1996), Clacton (Bridgland *et al.* 1999), Beeches Pit (Gowlett *et al.* 1998; 2005; Preece *et al.* 2006) and Barnham (Ashton *et al.* 1998) have been known for a century or more and have been re-excavated on a number of occasions following developments in methodologies as well as changes in accepted paradigms (see Fig. 1.1 for site locations). Typically these excavations have been undertaken by teams constituted from research-active scientists in the employment of universities or state-funded museums. By contrast, relatively few large, previously unknown sites have been found by prospecting in the last 20 years (Pettitt and White 2012). Those sites that have been discovered and excavated since the early 1980s, such as Boxgrove (Roberts and Parfitt 1999), Harnham (Whittaker *et al.* 2004), Southfleet Road (Wenban-Smith *et al.* 2006, Wenban-Smith 2013), Lynford (Boismier *et al.* 2012), Pakefield (Parfitt *et al.* 2005) and Happisburgh (Parfitt *et al.* 2010), have all been discovered either during investigation for later prehistoric archaeology or by chance.

Elsewhere, purposive strategies for locating Palaeolithic remains within sites of known archaeological potential have been successful at the Valdoe site (Pope *et al.* 2009), at Cuxton (Wenban-Smith *et al.* 2007a) and in Eastern Quarry, Swanscombe (Wenban-Smith pers. comm). Other projects that have set out to investigate landscapes for the specific purpose of locating Palaeolithic archaeology have met with spatially localised success; although not an ALSF project, a good example is the work in advance of construction of Ebbsfleet International Station in Kent (Wenban-Smith 2013). To the authors' knowledge only in one instance has purposive test pitting in an area of unknown archaeological potential produced artefacts and in this case, at Dartford in Kent, only a few, albeit potentially significant, artefacts were located (Wenban-Smith *et al.* 2010).

In the light of this discussion, we should, therefore, firstly note that in none of the ALSF projects were objectives set to find new Palaeolithic sites. Secondly, we should also take the time to consider why it is that so few projects have discovered Palaeolithic archaeology during their implementation and why we remain largely trusting to luck and chance to discover our new Palaeolithic archaeological sites. Because nearly all major Palaeolithic ALSF projects focused on better understanding of known archaeological occurrences, they concentrated on the application of new methodologies, the contextualisation of past finds within the landscape or the development of databases suitable for supplementing HER records and aiding development control. None of the projects focused on examining landscapes with the specified aims of locating new sites. For us, this is largely because:

- Opportunities to investigate new sites at the intensity needed to discover buried archaeology have been limited by changes within the terrestrial aggregates industry (relative to the late 19th and early 20th century). Therefore access to a large number of sites containing Pleistocene sands and gravels and associated archaeology was not possible
- Methods of investigation deployed through the projects include both direct observation of sequences through open sections, test pits, trenches and boreholes as well as indirect observations through geophysical surveys. These are either incapable of identifying artefact presence or are unlikely to do so where direct access to sediments is not possible (eg because trenches are shored), except in exceptional circumstances
- The significance of single reworked artefacts or single mint-condition artefacts in a test pit remains equivocal and experts in the discipline remain divided on the significance to be placed on such finds. This is particularly important in deposits that span the apparent lacunae in human occupation (cf Lewis *et al.* 2011). Even though individual finds in these sediments (eg Wenban-Smith *et al.* 2010) are rightly met with caution (eg Pettitt and White 2012), off-hand dismissals will only preserve the status quo and advance the discipline not a bit. Indeed, it is just as important, and at times more so, that such sediments are investigated as fully as areas that have already produced thousands of archaeological remains (see Chapter 1)

Therefore, it can be argued that the palaeogeographic approach to the Palaeolithic archive was adopted (knowingly or not) in projects where the combination of methods and approaches was to:

- Record sediment bodies that may contain archaeological remains
- Sample sediment bodies that are known to contain geologically important sequences (ie with faunal, floral, geochronological or archaeological properties)
- Recover artefacts from the sediment bodies (if possible)
- Sample sequences thought to be 'characteristic' of a mappable sediment body

Employing boreholes

The use of boreholes within Quaternary science and archaeology is well documented by Bates *et al.* (2000), and borehole data is routinely used to trace terrace long-profiles in river valleys such as the Thames (Gibbard 1985; 1994) and the Solent (Allen

QUARRY FACE RECORDING

Recording quarry exposures and sequences associated with Palaeolithic excavations can be time consuming and complex, particularly where sequences are laterally variable and where sections may run over tens of metres (Fig. 2.3.1). In such cases traditional approaches to recording are frequently utilised (Fig. 2.3.2) to produce long profiles and fence diagrams (Fig. 2.3.3). Today, however, new technology allows some of this time consuming work to be undertaken by laser scanning to produce accurate archives of the quarry faces and sedimentary successions at successive intervals in the quarry history.

Upper right 2.3.1 Long profile cut through a variety of sediments, Southfleet Road, north Kent

Right 2.3.2 Preparing section for traditional recording by drawing, Southfleet Road, north Kent

Below 2.3.3 Fence diagram showing deposit phases, Southfleet Road, north Kent (from Wenban-Smith 2013)

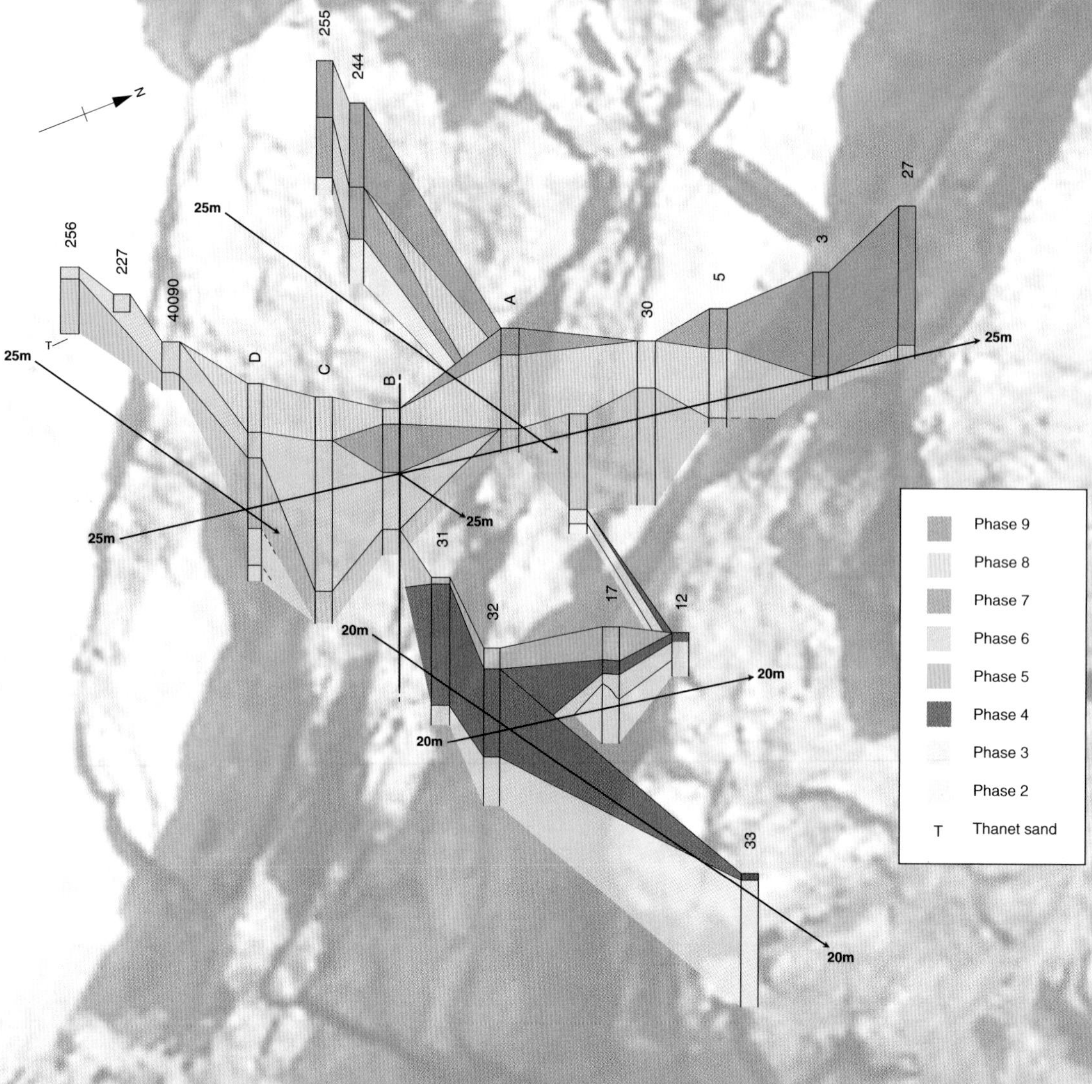

BOX 2.3

At Chard Junction terrestrial laser scanning (TLS; Fig. 2.3.4) has been used to rapidly record sections and is the first application of this approach to aggregate quarries. The data gathered during the survey has produced a 3D model (Fig. 2.3.5) of the quarry that allows both the finds and OSL dates to be displayed within a 3D volumetric model of the quarry (Fig. 2.3.6). Such approaches not only facilitate the long term recording of the site but help in planning, site monitoring and management.

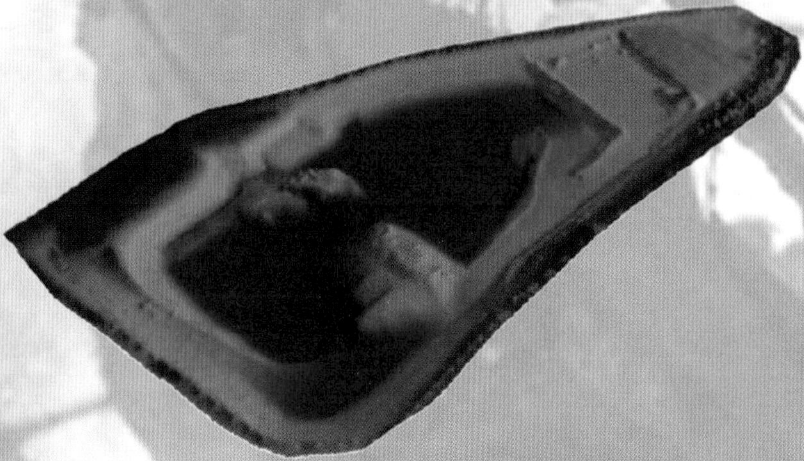

Upper right 2.3.4 Terrestrial laser survey at Hodge Ditch (from Brown 2012)

Right 2.3.5 Hodge Ditch 1, 2 and 3 point data interpolated in ArcMap 10 using inverse distance weighting and displayed in ArcScene in 3D using height values. Red=high and blue = low (from Brown 2012)

Below 2.3.6 A. Photograph of stepped face of Hodge Ditch I used for dating – note position of samples (arrows). B. Laser scanned image of stepped face in A (from Brown 2012)

ELECTRICAL GEOPHYSICS

Electrical techniques are used in terrestrial geophysics to record changes in the conductivity or resistance of the ground to electrical currents. Because different materials (solid rock, gravels, clays etc) show different responses to an electrical current these changes map differences in sediments beneath the ground. In general, sequences with high clay contents show higher conductivity. Conversely, sequences with low clay content, sands and gravel or bedrock such as limestones and chalks, show low conductivity or high resistivity.

2.4.1 DC electrical survey equipment laid out along a transect at West Wittering, Sussex

Two techniques have been used in the work of the PASHCC (Palaeolithic Archaeology of the Sussex Hampshire Coastal Corridor) and the MVPP (Medway Valley Palaeolithic Project):

• Direct current resistivity where an electrical current is put into the ground (Fig. 2.4.1)

• Electromagnetic techniques where an electrical current is induced in the ground by creating an electromagnetic field in a coil of wire located at the surface (Fig. 2.4.2)

2.4.2 EM31 electromagnetic survey at Allhallows in the Medway Estuary, K

Typical survey results for DC survey are electrical sections (Fig. 2.4.3), while for electromagnetic surveys they are contour maps of conductivity (Fig. 2.4.4). In the ALSF surveys these techniques have been applied to the sectioning of some of the intertidal channels beneath beach sands on the foreshore at West Wittering (Fig. 2.4.3) and mapping the extent of a channel at West Street, Selsey (Bates et al. 2004; 2009) (Figs 2.4.4 and 2.4.5) as well as Holocene and Pleistocene stratigraphies at the mouth of the Medway Estuary (Fig 2.4.6; Bates et al. 2007b; Wenban-Smith et al. 2007a).

The advantage of deploying such survey techniques is that they are rapid to undertake, can cover large areas and are useful in helping to site purposive test pits and trenches in areas deemed to be of high archaeological or palaeoenvironmental potential. They provide a flexibility in survey methodology and can be incorporated into project design where informed decisions are made in a step-wise fashion regarding the appropriate method and scale of investigation to be deployed (Bates and Stafford 2013).

2.4.5 Excavated edge of West Street, Selsey Channel as predicted from t
EM31 conductivity survey

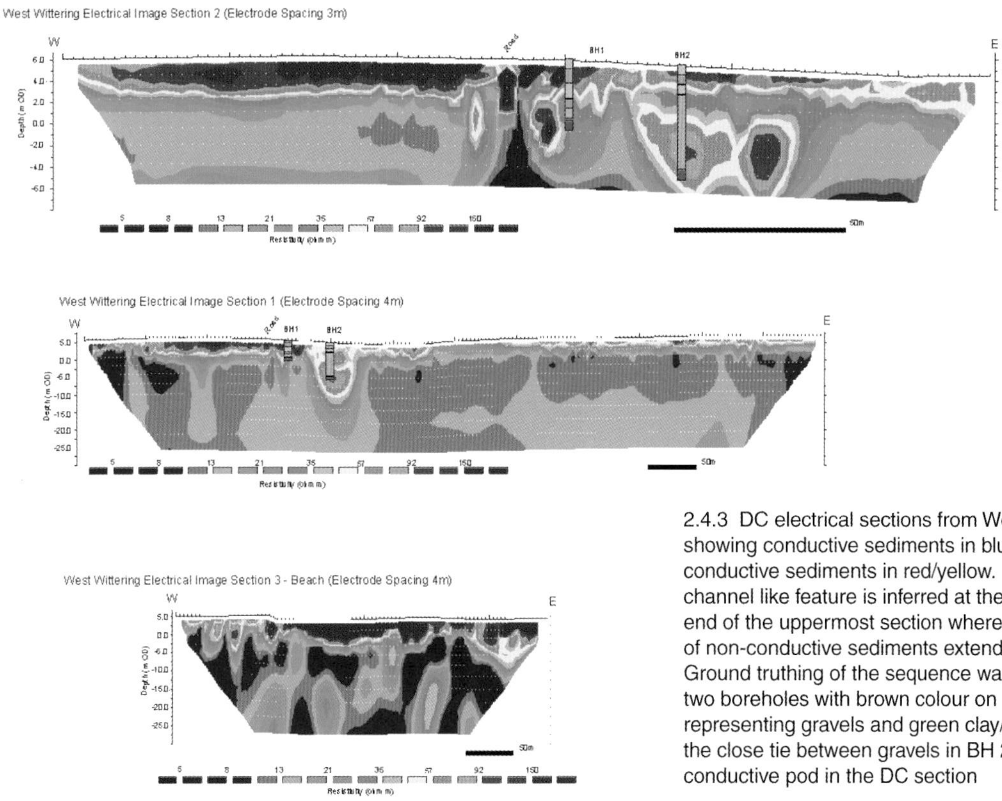

2.4.3 DC electrical sections from West Wittering showing conductive sediments in blue and non-conductive sediments in red/yellow. A large channel like feature is inferred at the right hand end of the uppermost section where a large pod of non-conductive sediments extends downwards. Ground truthing of the sequence was achieved by two boreholes with brown colour on borehole logs representing gravels and green clay/silt units. Note the close tie between gravels in BH 2 and the non-conductive pod in the DC section

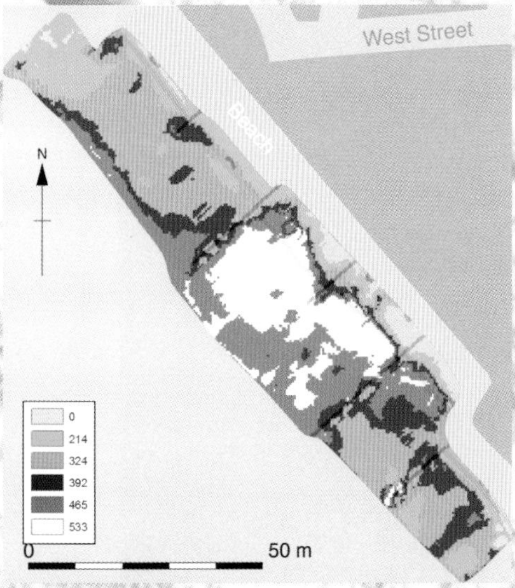

2.4.4 EM31 electromagnetic survey results from West Street, Selsey. Contour plot of conductivity values indicate a highly conductive zone equivalent with the position of the channel (Bates *et al.* 2009)

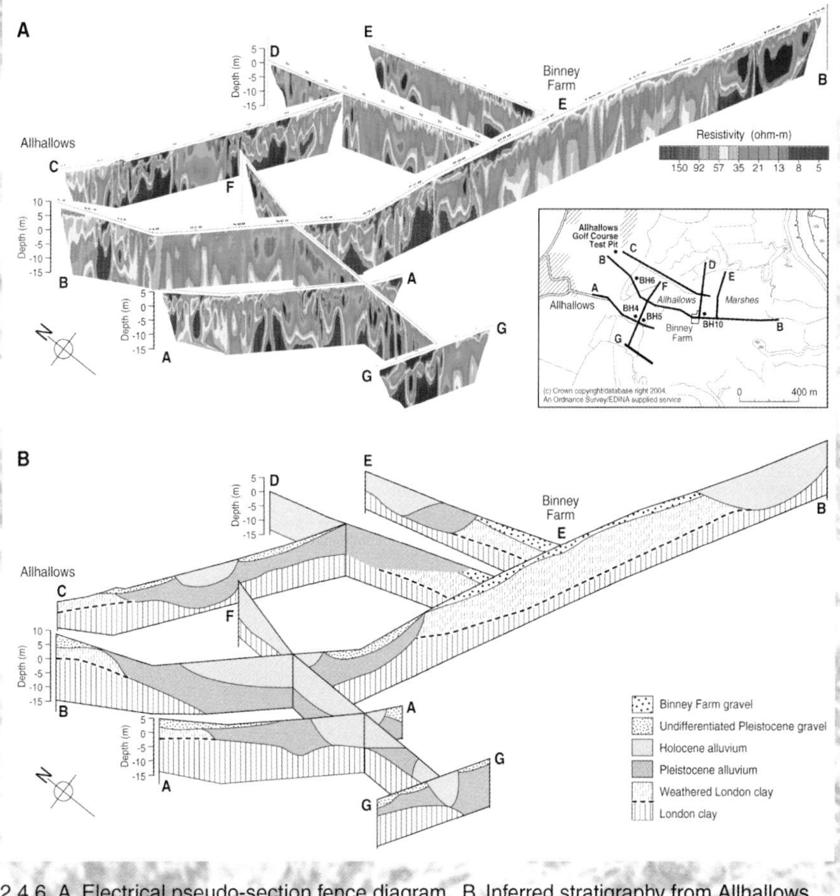

2.4.6 A. Electrical pseudo-section fence diagram. B. Inferred stratigraphy from Allhallows study area

and Gibbard 1993; Briant *et al.* 2006; 2012). Boreholes provide information on the lithology of sequences below ground that may be beyond the reach of conventional test pitting or where access to the site is limited, as is often the case in modern urban areas. Information from boreholes is often available in geotechnical reports and can provide data suitable for deriving predictions relevant to understanding the 3-D geometry of buried sediment bodies. However, it should be remembered that in the case of boreholes collected in advance of construction, for example, the distribution of the data across a given site (as well as the methods and techniques used) is typically dependent upon the type of structure and construction methods rather than any consideration relating to reconstructing the Quaternary geology.

A range of equipment is available for investigation of subsurface contexts from unpowered manually driven devices such as Hiller borers and

Fig. 2.4 Shell and auger drill rig at West Wittering, West Sussex

Fig. 2.5 Core samples from West Wittering. Cores are split to show stratigraphy. Fine grained sediments are estuarine deposits sandwiched between two cold stage gravels

Fig. 2.6 Section cleaning of a gravel quarry face at Badminston Farm Quarry, Hampshire

Fig. 2.7 Excavation of palaeolandsurface at CH2 Boxgrove, West Sussex in the mid 1980s

Fig. 2.8 Sampling at Corfe Mullen in a trench opened into the former quarry face

Russian (D-section) corers, which retrieve variably undisturbed sediment cores, to powered mechanical corers with a number of interchangeable coring heads (eg Eijkelkamp system), and small portable drill rigs including the Terrier 2000 self-propelled drill rig with a windowless liner sampling system and wireline percussive drilling (Figs 2.4 and 2.5; Bates *et al.* 2000; Clayton *et al.* 1995). Selection of appropriate drilling equipment varies depending on a number of factors including costs, site ground conditions, nature of the overburden (made ground), the type of sediment likely to be encountered in the subsurface, and the nature of the samples required for analysis.

Good examples of the use of large datasets in the construction of subsurface models include the work of Chen *et al.* (1996) on the North China Plain; Allen (2001) in the Severn Estuary; Berendsen and Stouthamer (2001) in the Rhine-Meuse delta region; Weerts *et al.* (2005) in the Netherlands; Culshaw (2005) in Manchester and the Neath/Swansea area of south Wales; and Hijma *et al.* (2012) in the southern North Sea. Within the ALSF projects extensive use of borehole data has been made in the PASHCC project (Box 2.2; Bates *et al.* 2004; 2007a).

Using trenches, test pits and quarry faces

To many archaeologists, quarries are intimately associated with the Palaeolithic, and images of section cleaning down quarry face exposures (Fig. 2.6; Box 2.3) or excavations in the base of quarries

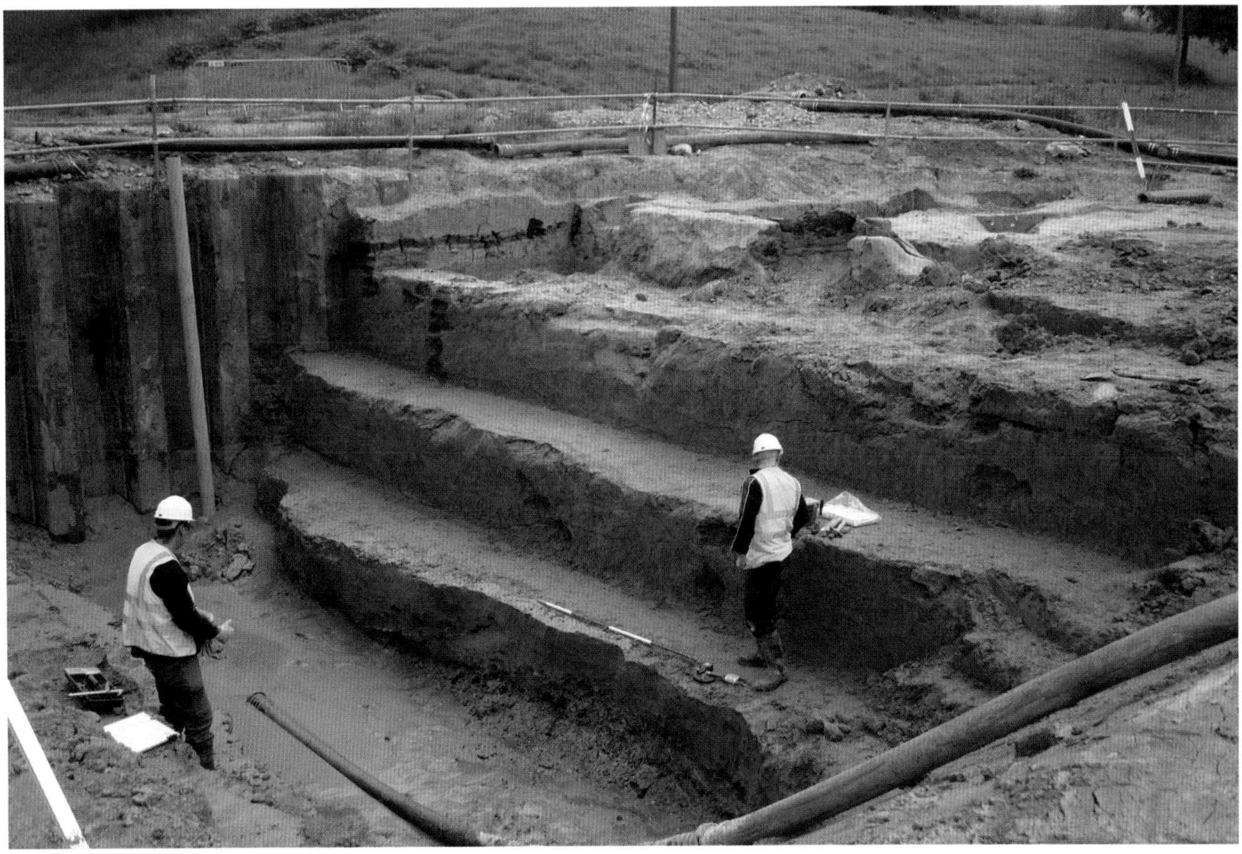

Fig. 2.9 Stepped trench at Northfleet Sewage Works during investigation of Devensian colluvial sediments

Fig. 2.10 Excavation of a test pit during the PASHCC fieldwork in the Solent system

Fig. 2.11 Long trench excavated in a stepped fashion through Devensian slope deposits at Dartford A2/A282 crossing

Fig. 2.12 Example of excavated test pit through gravels of the river Medina at Great Pan Farm, Isle of Wight

Fig. 2.13 Sieving sediment recovered from a test pit for artefacts

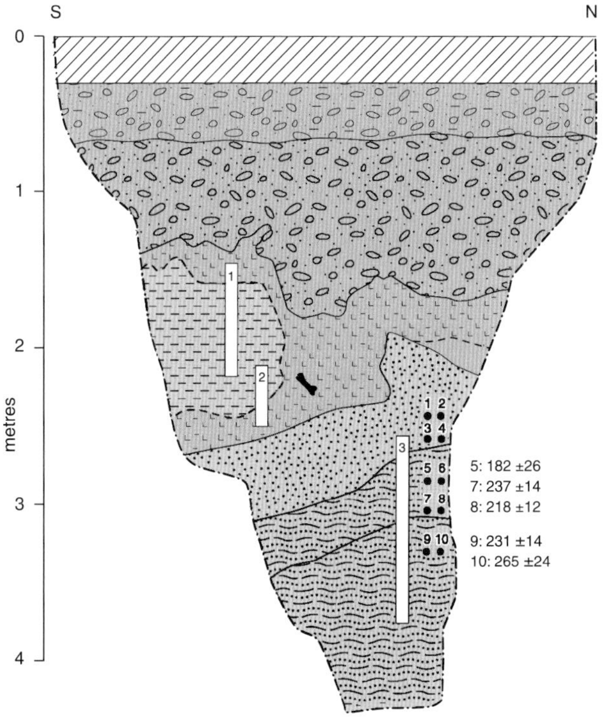

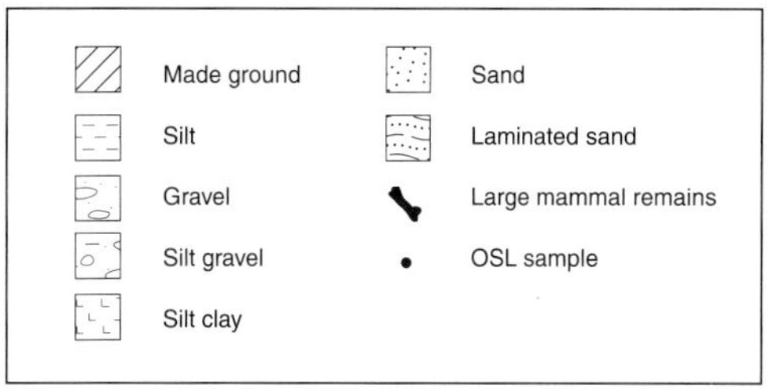

Fig. 2.14 Example of a stratigraphic profile and OSL sample points from Norton Farm in West Sussex. Boxes 1, 2, and 3 show the locations of monolith-tin samples; dates are ka BP (from Bates et al. *2010)*

(Fig. 2.7) are common to many. Indeed, most of the key sites that form our basic framework for the Palaeolithic are quarry sites (see Fig. 1.1), and access to sections is relatively easy even in quarries that have been abandoned for many years (Fig. 2.8), unless of course they have subsequently been infilled and developed. Consequently, the cleaning of faces, stepped where of excessive height (Fig. 2.9), the digging of test pits to evaluate stratigraphy (Fig. 2.10) and larger trenches for sampling and excavation (Fig. 2.11) are now common practices.

The varying approaches to the excavation of test pits, trenches etc dictates the type of information it is possible to retrieve from them. Single bucket-width test pits allow the stratigraphy to be recorded from the top, and where careful control of the excavation machine is possible spits 0.2m thick may

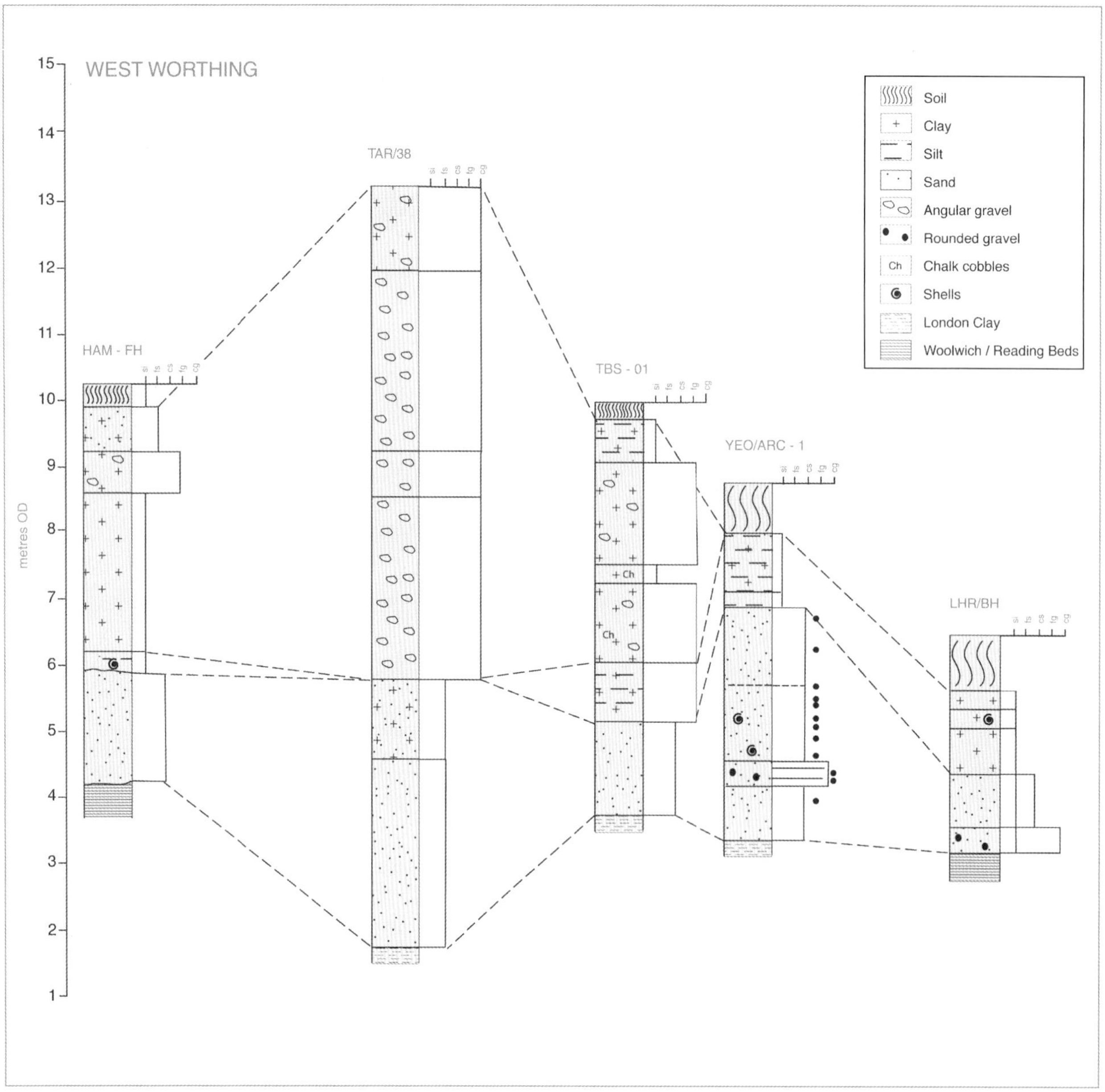

Fig. 2.15 Stratigraphic logs from boreholes and test pits used to form a site wide outline of sequences from the West Sussex Coastal Plain (after Bates et al. *2004, 2007a)*

be excavated and sampled for sieving for artefacts or palaeoenvironmental data (Figs 2.12-2.14). Such exercises can provide information on the broad stratigraphic framework at a site (Fig. 2.15), yet in order to fully understand the sequences, and in particular the context of any recovered Palaeolithic artefacts, larger trenches in which long profiles can be examined, drawn and sampled are a necessity (Fig. 2.16).

One of the hardest issues to deal with in Palaeolithic archaeological site evaluation is addressing the question, at an early stage in the project, of the number and location of interventions (be it test pits, trenches etc) to be used. In conventional archaeological evaluations, figures of 2-5% of total site area are considered appropriate to assess the archaeological potential of the site. In Palaeolithic archaeology it is rare for anywhere near that figure to be approached. Although no specific ALSF project tackled this issue directly, the problem was highlighted in the MVPP (Wenban-Smith *et al.* 2007a) where an intensive test pitting and sieving operation was undertaken at Roke Manor Farm, Romsey in the Test Valley in Hampshire. The site was chosen because of its proximity to the important Palaeolithic site at Dunbridge (Harding *et al.* 2012). More than 40 test pits, each 3m by 2m, were dug by Wenban-Smith *et al.* (2007a) on a closely spaced grid across 8 hectares (Fig. 2.17). The key aims of this project were to investigate the spatial concentration and vertical distribution of Palaeolithic remains within the

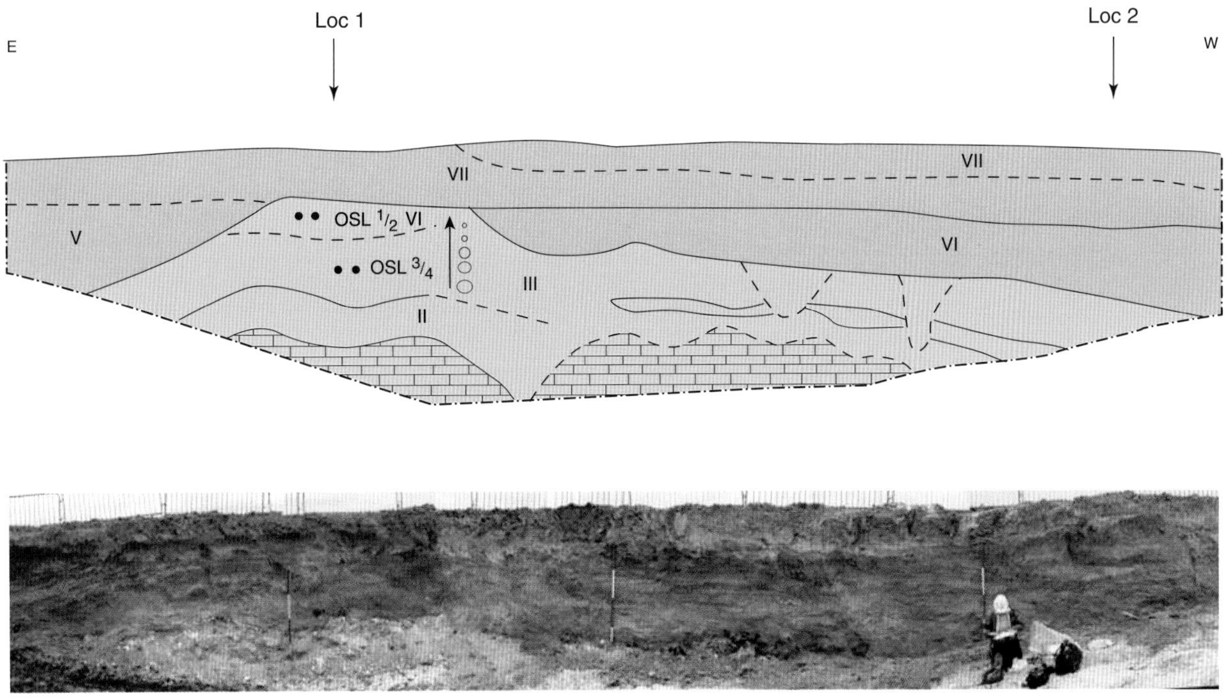

Fig. 2.16 Long profile from Pear Tree Knap site, West Sussex showing drawn and photographed section (after Bates et al. *2010, fig 5a)*

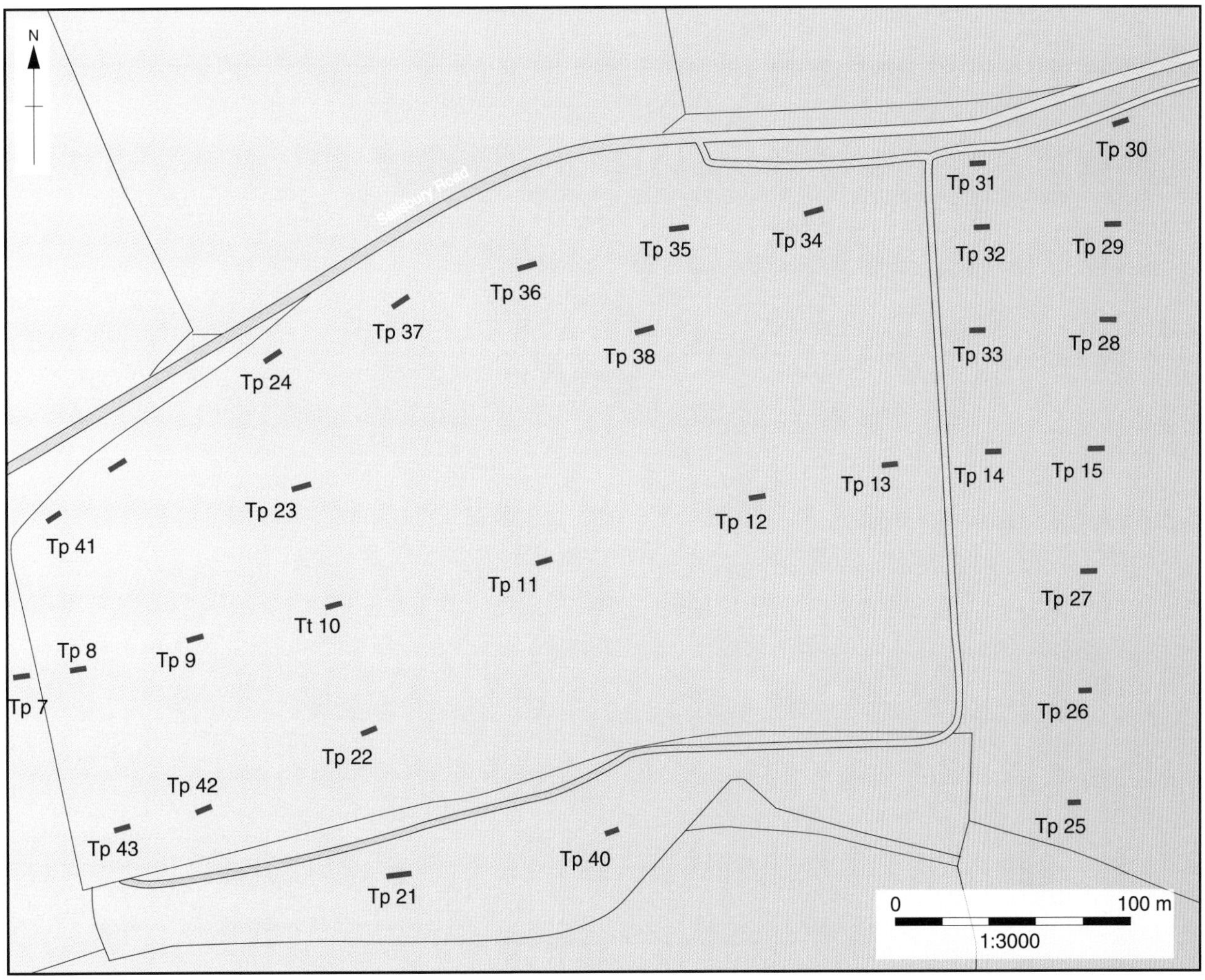

Fig. 2.17 Distribution of test pits at Roke Manor Farm, Romsey on a grid based pattern (after Bates et al. *2004, 2007a)*

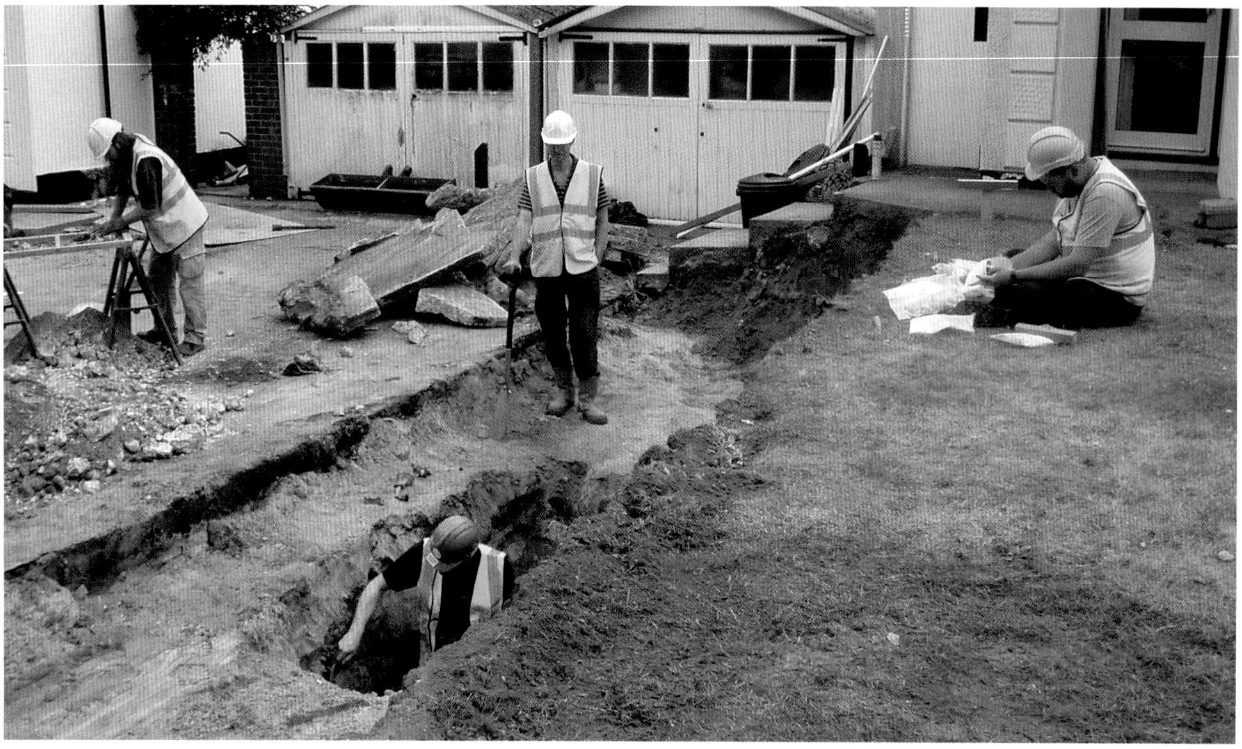

Fig. 2.18 Excavations at Cuxton (courtesy of Francis Wenban-Smith)

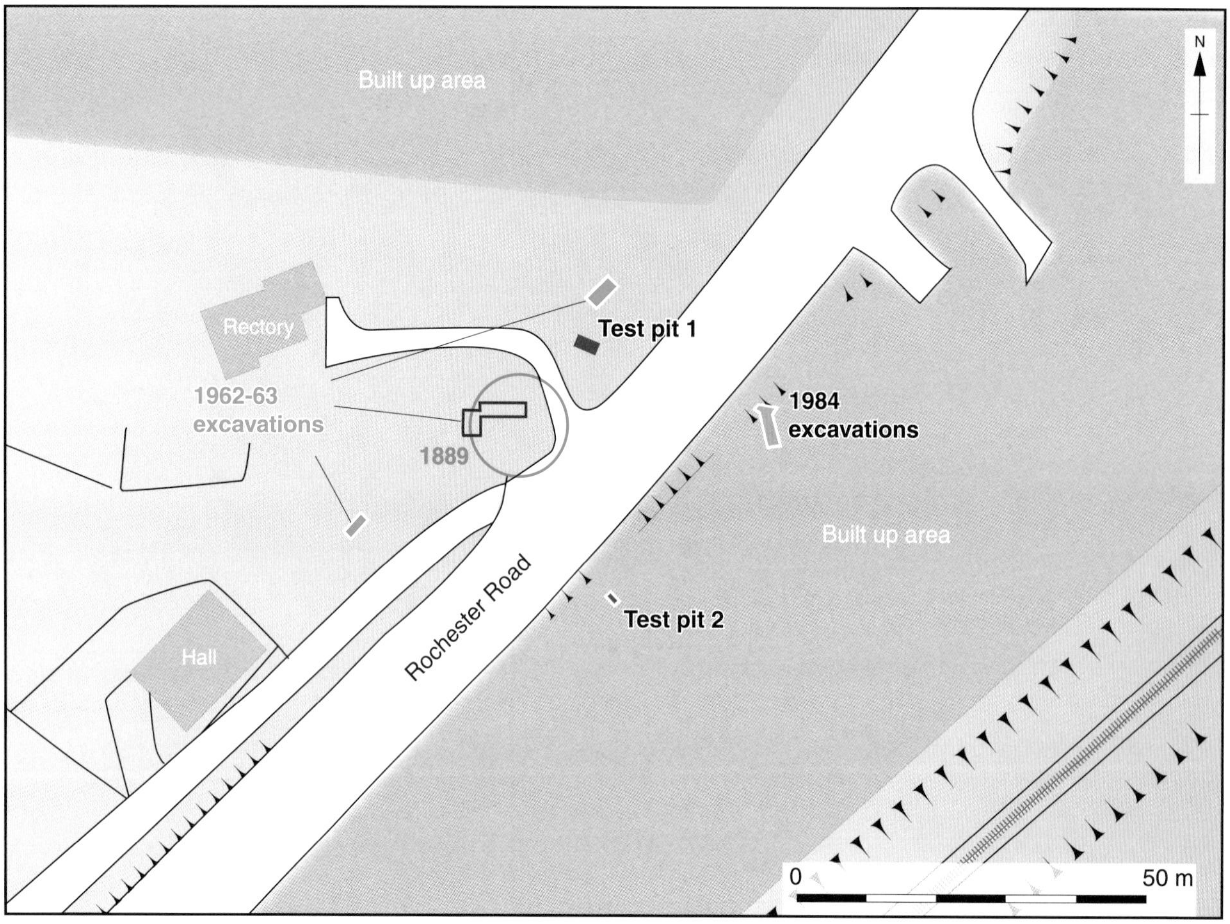

Fig. 2.19 Site location plan for past and recent work at Cuxton, with dates the trench was excavated (from Wenban-Smith et al. *2007)*

Fig. 2.20 Test pit excavated at Cuxton (Wenban-Smith et al. *2007a) showing fluvial gravels over Chalk bedrock*

gravel body, and to establish the most appropriate sampling volumes and test pit density for field evaluation and artefact recovery. The test pits were dug along the main east–west axis of the site, with a series of north–south transects (Fig. 2.17). Unfortunately, few artefacts were found in the sieved samples from the gravel deposits, despite two handaxes being found on the surface in one part of the site. The result of this investigation highlighted the difficulty of locating artefacts through test pitting even in proximity to sites of known potential.

By contrast, test pitting at Cuxton was spectacularly successful MVPP (Wenban-Smith *et al.* 2007a). Previous work at Cuxton indicated a site of considerable potential. For example, Tester (1965) recovered 210 handaxes from a thin seam of river gravel in three small test pits. Work on the

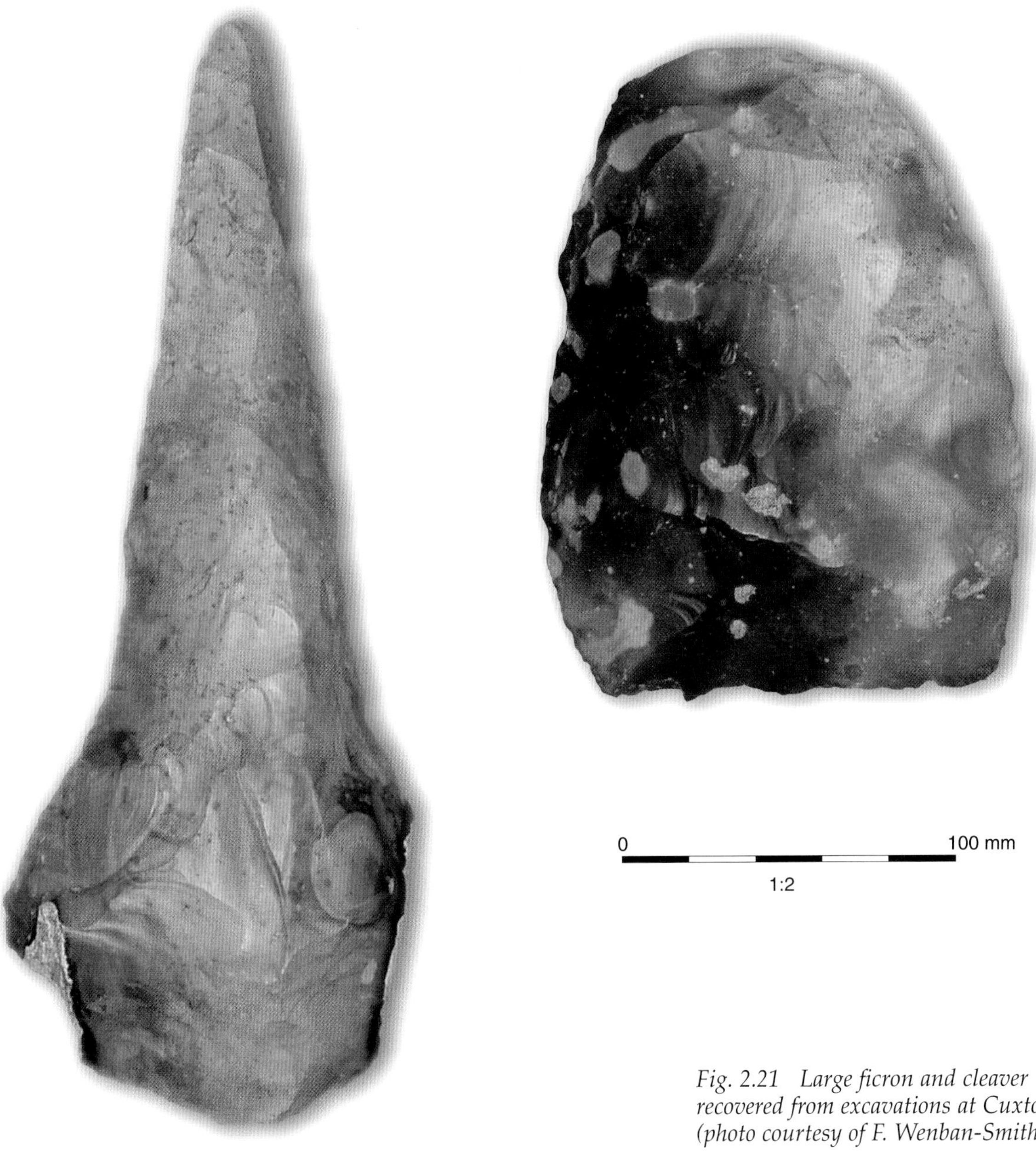

Fig. 2.21 Large ficron and cleaver recovered from excavations at Cuxton (photo courtesy of F. Wenban-Smith)

MVPP excavated a single test pit through a garden in Rochester Road that revealed a sequence of river gravels and a series of handaxes including a majestic ficron, a cleaver, cores, flakes and flake tools (Figs 2.18-2.21). The results of the work of the Medway Valley Project certainly suggest that the development of detailed methodologies and investigation strategies that are statistically significant depend on further work designed to address issues of sampling strategies and artefact taphonomy throughout Pleistocene landscapes.

Watching briefs

The use of watching briefs within the framework of Palaeolithic archaeology is well demonstrated by the works at Lynford (Boismier *et al.* 2012) and Dunbridge (Harding *et al.* 2012). The successful application of a watching brief will, of course, be dependent on the constraints set on the frequency of monitoring of the site as well as the nature of the impact and the experience of the monitors. Typically, where extraction of gravel from a relatively uniform, well-understood aggregate site is taking place, a

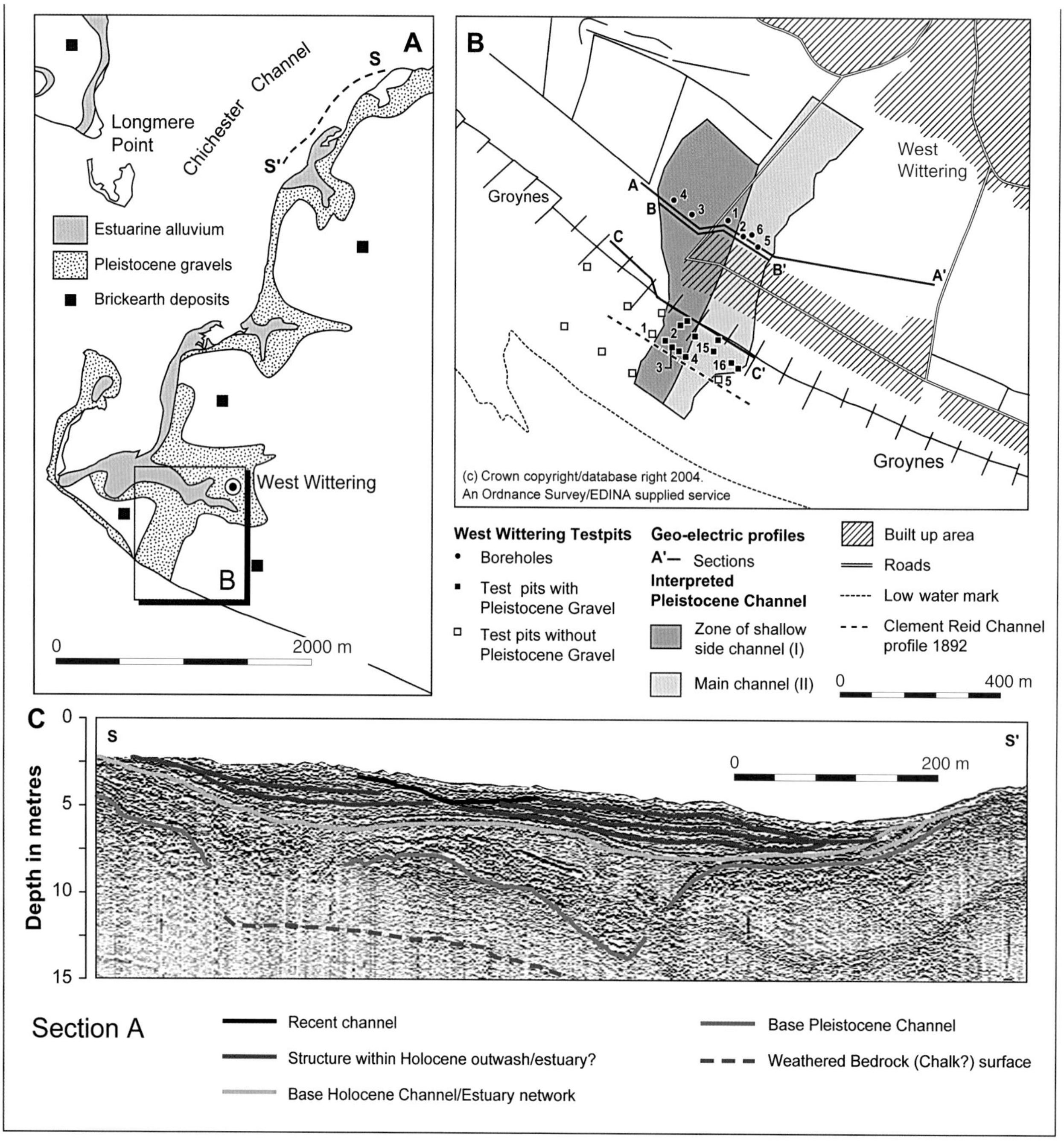

Fig. 2.22 West Wittering, West Sussex. A: site location plan for marine and terrestrial geophysics. B: West Wittering channel – terrestrial investigation and geophysics. C: sub-bottom profile data and interpretation from submerged channel in Chichester Harbour (from Bates et al. *2007c, fig 9)*

watching brief can usually be undertaken with a degree of precision provided that monitors are familiar with Quaternary geology and Palaeolithic archaeology. In the case of both Dunbridge and Lynford this was the case (Harding *et al.* 2012; Boismeir *et al.* 2012). The use of novel techniques for rapidly surveying and recording such as the terrestrial laser scanning (TLS) used at Chard Junction (Box 2.3) would significantly help in such processes.

In other situations, watching briefs are likely to be far more problematic. For example where Quaternary sediments at the margins of fluvial systems or in lacustrine contexts are being monitored, lateral variation in sediment types and consequently depositional context is likely and this may well be reflected in rapidly varying Palaeolithic archaeological potential. In such situations a considerably enhanced presence on site may be required in order to adequately monitor impact. Additionally, where gravel extraction is not the main aim access to sequences may also be problematic (for example, where narrow excavations are being undertaken for drainage).

Geophysics

The use of geophysics in Quaternary science has been increasing in recent years and although seismic profiling is commonly undertaken in the marine sector (Fig. 2.22), advances in radar and electromagnetic/electrical techniques have substantially enhanced our ability on land to see beneath the surface (Box 2.4). Marine geophysical survey was also undertaken as part of the ALSF in the English Channel area (Gupta *et al.* 2004) and in the southern North Sea (Wessex Archaeology 2008), which utilised a combination of seabed mapping techniques (Swath bathymetry) and sub-seabed mapping (seismic survey) to investigate the nature of the submerged landscapes in these areas (Fig. 2.23).

Discussion

There are problems when considering appropriate strategies for examining the Palaeolithic archive using these approaches. As previously noted, very few examples of direct discovery of a totally unknown Palaeolithic archaeological site have been made through an applied strategy of borehole/test pit investigation. The examples described in the MVPP (see above) illustrate the difficulties in investigating sites for Palaeolithic archaeological content by comparison with later prehistoric/historic archaeological investigations. Additionally, it is rare for investigations to adequately consider the impact that investigation strategy had on the

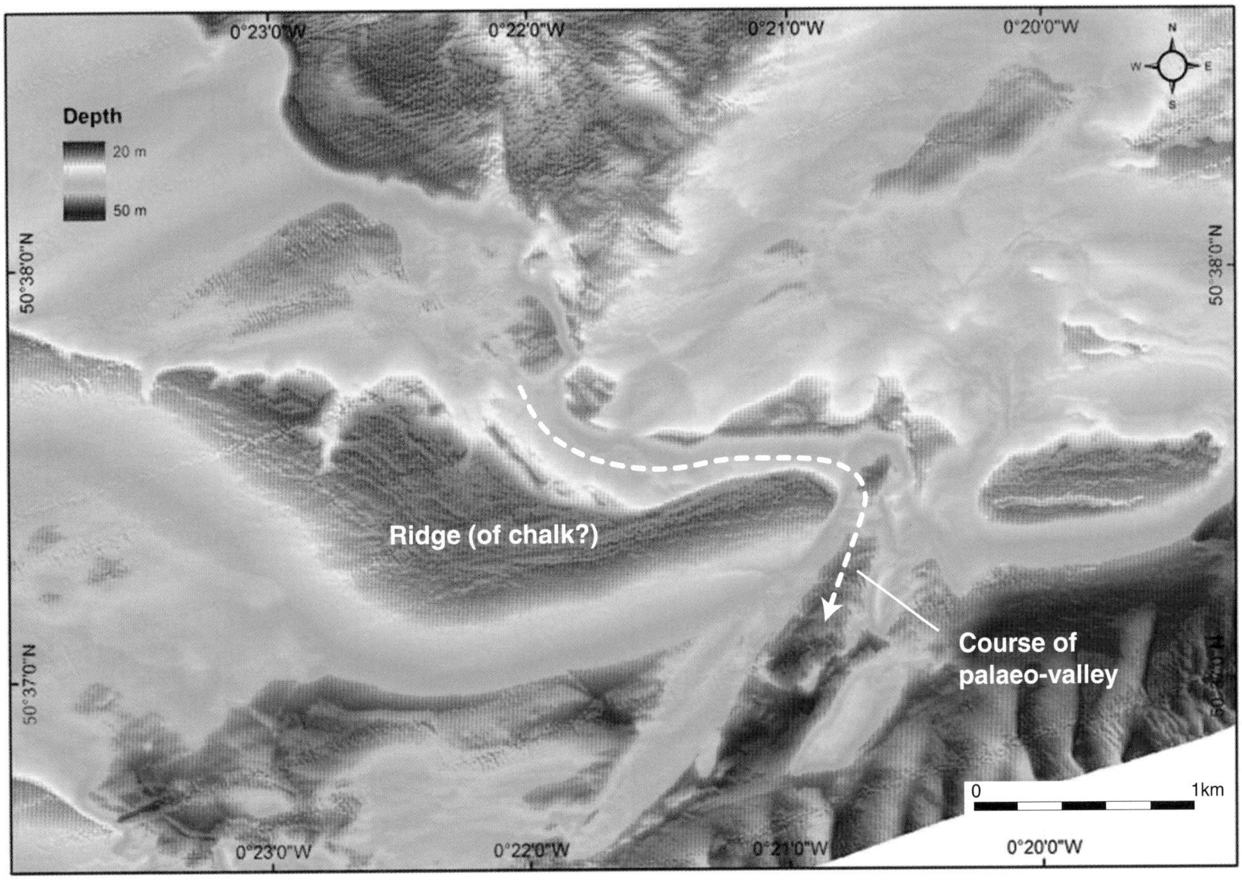

Fig. 2.23 Multibeam bathymetry for the lower segment of the submerged Arun valley displayed as a composite depth coloured and shaded relief image. Sun-illumination is from the north-west at an elevation of 45° (from Gupta et al. *2004)*

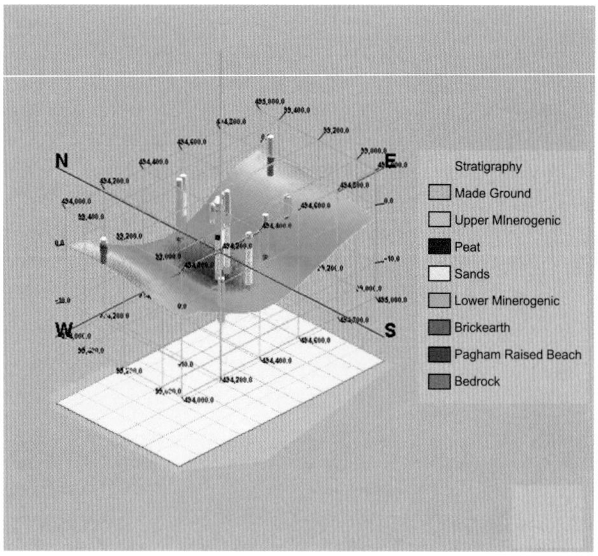

Fig. 2.24 Borehole logs and contoured bedrock surface from Bognor Regis, West Sussex illustrated through the Rockworks Software system

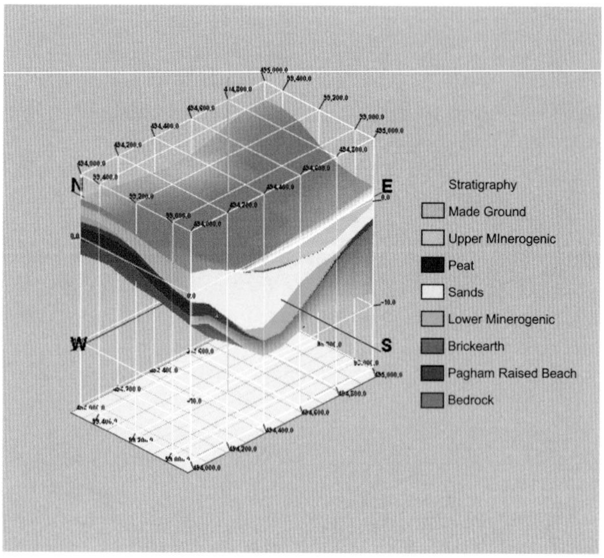

Fig. 2.25 Block model of major stratigraphic units from the boreholes at Bognor Regis, West Sussex

results of the project and the discovery, or not, of archaeological remains.

The rationale for the use of quarry section, borehole and test pit data (point specific data) recovered from regional terrestrial surveys (Barham and Bates 1994; Bates *et al.* 2000) as well as geophysical data (Bates *et al.* 2007c) is that such information may be used to model and understand the geometry and topography of these subsurface sediment bodies (ie reconstruct palaeogeographies within which the Palaeolithic archaeology resides). This means that the geometry and nature of the deposits themselves are being inferred mainly from the point-specific (ie borehole/test pit) data linked together by assumptions about litho- or chronostratigraphic correlations (Chew 1995).

Today, it is increasingly common to visualise these bodies using computerised geological modelling systems that provide the user (and reader) with pictorial images of the subsurface (Fig. 2.24; Culshaw 2005). The 3D geological models consist of a structural framework of 2D surfaces representing stratigraphic boundaries, chronostratigraphic horizons etc (Fig. 2.25). Such systems aim to produce a pseudo three-dimensional block model representation of subsurface deposits allowing the researcher the opportunity to investigate the relationships between deposits, and the ability to predict sequence occurrence away from known data positions (Jones 1992).

These are commonly used in developer-funded projects to understand the geoarchaeology of a site prior to investigation. However, the images produced from the models imply a robustness with respect to the 'hardness' of the surfaces being modelled, as well as the reliability of the relationship between data points. In many cases, the fact is that our understanding of these surfaces and correlations is based upon inadequate sampling intervals (of boreholes) and the use of facies models coupled with the understanding of the surface expression of the sediment bodies to make sense of our stratigraphies.

That said, one of the major outcomes of subsurface modelling is that the 2D/3D surfaces may be used to reconstruct palaeogeographies that subsequently form the basis for predictions and projections regarding Palaeolithic archaeological potential. This perspective is significant because when we adopt such an approach, information from both 'sites' (ie places at which artefacts have been recovered) and 'non-sites' (at which no artefacts but other sources of information may be present) become important to the archaeological picture as a whole at the landscape scale (see below). By comparison, marine data exists in the form of continuous profiles of seismic data that is only rarely ground truthed by point specific data (boreholes). Thus, direct comparison of marine and terrestrial data sets is impossible without interpretation of the results. Furthermore, no direct links between the terrestrial evidence and that from the marine sector exist in the British context, and nowhere can continuous profiles currently be demonstrated across the transition zone between marine and terrestrial domains (Fig. 2.26; Bates *et al.* 2007c). An attempt was made to understand the problems of such an approach through the Transition Zone Mapping Project (Bates *et al.* 2009) and attempts are now being made at Happisburgh.

Ultimately, an integrated approach to archaeological investigation using a range of geological, geomorphological and palaeoenvironmental perspectives derived from direct and indirect observations of subsurface stratigraphies is desirable, prior to developing a conceptual model containing palaeosurface information whether terrestrially or

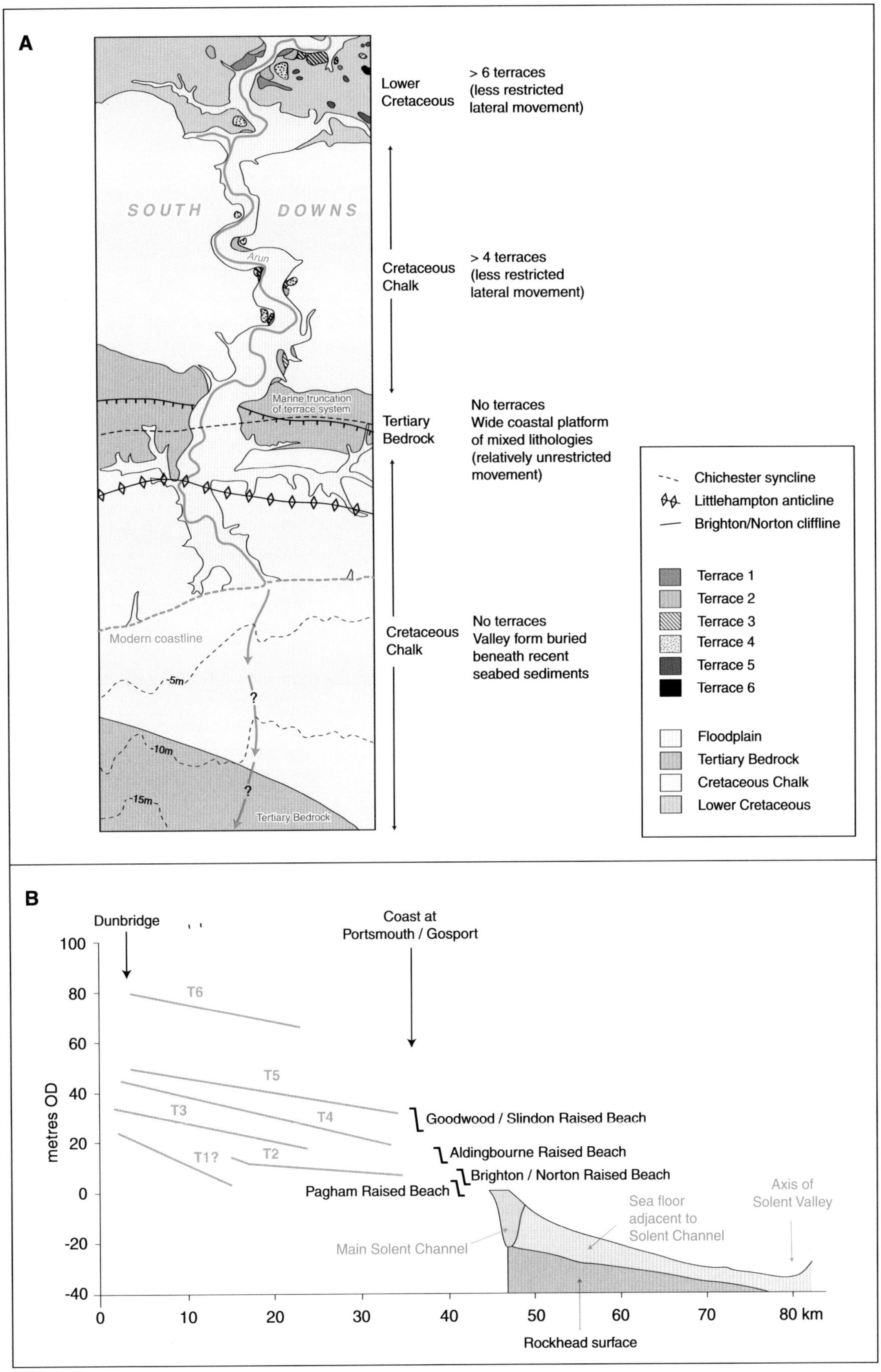

Fig. 2.26 A: On-shore to off-shore Arun Valley showing distribution of main geomorphological features. B: Terraces of the eastern Solent and Solent sea bed showing discontinuity between on- and off-shore sequences (from Bates et al. *2007c, fig 4)*

OPTICALLY STIMULATED LUMINESCENCE

2.5.1 OSL sampling and measurement of radiation from the surrounding environment from a raised beach at St Clement, Jersey

Luminescence dating is a chronological method that can be applied to a wide range of materials (sediment, burnt flint, pottery) that contain quartz or similar materials (Duller 2008). It is based on the emission of light (luminescence) by commonly occurring minerals, principally quartz. For ceramics and burnt flints the event being dated is the last heating while for sediments it is the last exposure of the mineral grains to daylight. The age range over which the methods can be applied is from a few to 300,000 years.

A simple analogy for luminescence is a rechargable battery, with the battery representing the mineral grains. Exposing mineral grains to light or heat will release the battery's energy so that when the mineral (battery) is incorporated into sediment it has no energy. The battery then begins to be recharged by exposure to radiation from the natural environment and over time the stored energy levels increase. A sample collected and measured in the laboratory releases the stored energy and light is created – the luminescence signal. The amount of energy in the battery being related to the brightness of the luminescence signal. Calculating the rate at which the battery was recharged (dose rate) from the radiation in the environment means we can determine how long it was recharging and thus the time since it was last emptied.

A

Sample	Depth	De(Gy)	Dose rate ($Gy.ka^{-1}$)	Age (ka)
GL06012	1.70	193.7 ± 11.0	1.97 ± 0.11	98 ± 8
GL06011	2.50	90.2 ± 6.8	0.96 ± 0.05	94 ± 9
GL06010	4.30	268.5 ± 22.0	1.54 ± 0.10	174 ± 18
GL06013	4.50	298.6 ± 19.2	1.09 ± 0.07	274 ± 25
GL06057	6.70	375.3 ± 24.6	1.02 ± 0.07	367 ± 35
GL06058	7.00	318.3 ± 33.3	1.12 ± 0.08	284 ± 36
GL08045	12.90	332.7 ± 23.8	1.26 ± 0.10	264 ± 28
GL08046	15.00	521.4 ± 41.5	1.56 ± 0.11	334 ± 36
GL08044	15.20	477.2 ± 45.1	1.63 ± 0.13	292 ± 37
GL08043	15.30	284.9 ± 31.9	0.80 ± 0.06	335+47
GL08047	15.50	736.8 ± 51.7	1.49 ± 0.10	494 ± 50

B

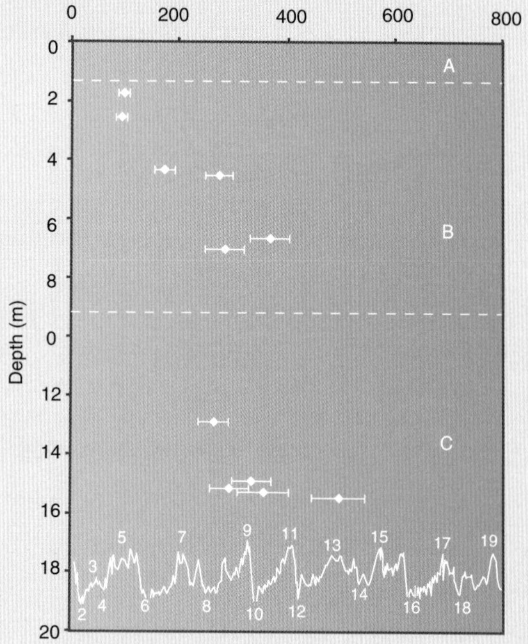

2.5.2 A: OSL age estimates from Hodge Ditch I, Chard Junction, listed in stratigraphic order (Basell *et al.* 2011). B. Age-depth plot for Hodge Ditch I Optical dating samples, Chard Junction. MIS curve from ODP 677 (Shackleton *et al.* 1990)

The most common used method for releasing the electrons stored within minerals is by exposing them to light. A stimulating light causes luminescence to be emitted by mineral grains and continues until the trapped electrons are emptied and the signal decreases – this is termed optically stimulated luminescence (OSL). Thermoluminescence produces a signal by heating a sample.

Luminescence dating in now widespread in Palaeolithic archaeology for dating artefacts (Preece et al 2006), artifact-bearing deposits (Hosfield et al 2011; Hosfield and Green 2013) and providing a chronology for landscape development (Bridgland et al 2014)

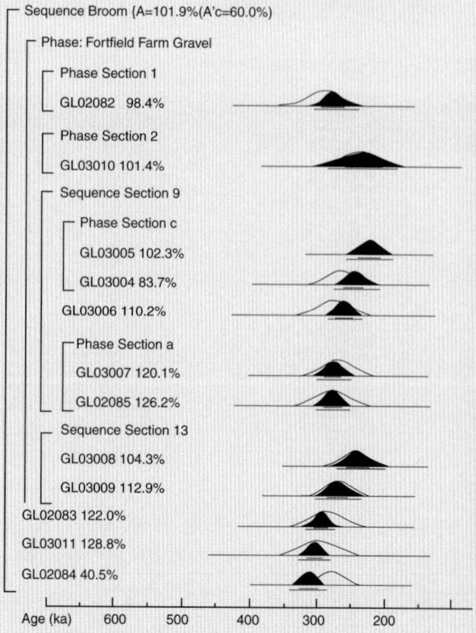

2.5.3 Bayesian modelling of accepted optical age estimates within the Broom Sand and Silt Bed (from Hosfield *et al.* 2011)

AMINO ACID RACEMIZATION

Amino acid racemization (AAR) has been applied to the correlation of Pleistocene sediments in the UK and NW Europe for some time (Bowen *et al.* 1989; Bates 1993) but for a variety of reasons (McCarroll 2002) has only recently been accepted as a routinely used approach for correlating Quaternary sediments (Penkman *et al.* 2011).

The technique relies on the fact that proteins are formed from 20 different types of amino acids, the majority of which can exist in different forms known as stereoisomers (Fig. 2.6.1). Most amino acids have two stereoisomers (an L-amino acid and a D-amino acid). The technique measures the extent of protein decomposition within shell material from material extracted from key geological or archaeological units. Because of metabolic reactions in living organisms only the L-amino acid is present in live specimens. After death, as the protein decomposes, the amino acids change and undergo isomerization (racemization) to produce a mixture of D-and L-amino acids that ultimately form an equilibrium. Samples are selected from material from sediment samples that have been washed through a sieve and picked from residues that have been air-dried.

From an early stage in the use of AAR in geochronology it was recognised that the rate of racemization varied between species (Fig. 2.6.2) and this species effect therefore limits the use of the technique. Samples can only be directly compared to other samples of the same species, so an aminostratigraphic framework must be developed for each species studied. Furthermore, changes in the ambient temperature that the samples have experienced since death also impact on the rate of racemization (increasing the temperature at which the samples have been kept since death will increase the rate at which racemization occurs). Consequently, equilibrium will be reached sooner where samples have been subject to higher temperatures. Thus comparison can only be made between samples for which it is likely that temperatures since death have been similar. In practice this means that samples can only be compared from geographical regions where temperatures are similar across the region.

Today, a principal focus of study is made on the amino acids obtained from the remains of the opercula from the freshwater gastropod *Bithynia tentaculata* (Penkman *et al.* 2011). Study has shown that analysis of D/L values of a range of amino acids from the chemically protected organic matter within the biominerals of the opercula provide a robust method of high reliability (Penkman *et al.* 2008). A combination of approaches including Reverse-Phase High Pressure Liquid Chromatography and bleach treatment has established a method that is now fulfilling the hopes of early researchers.

The results of Penkman's work on *Bithynia* opercula enables us to construct a chronological framework from different aggregate deposits in England that can be related to the marine oxygen isotope record, thereby independently validating the stratigraphic frameworks derived from terrace stratigraphy, mammalian palaeontology etc (Penkman *et al.* 2011; for example, compare the aminostratigraphy with the Thames terrace model: Fig. 2.6.3).

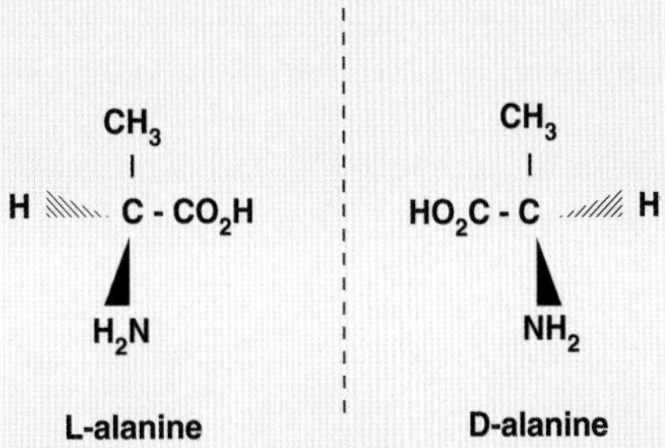

2.6.1 L- and D-amino acid structure (from Penkman *et al.* 2008)

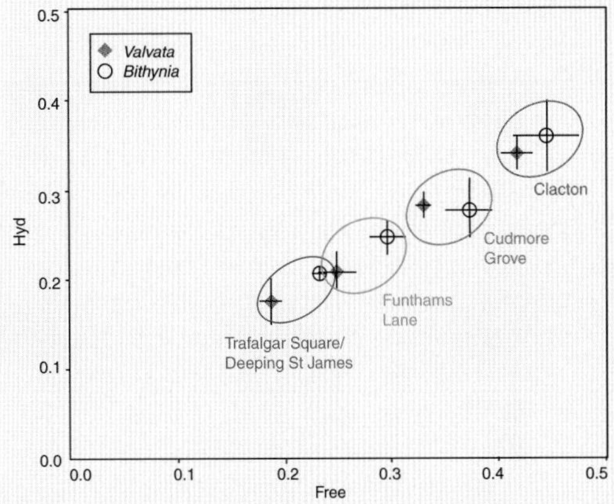

2.6.2 Plot of IcPD hydrolyzed vs IcPD free mean values, with 1 standard deviation, for shells of *Bithynia tentaculata* and *Valvata piscinalis* (from Penkman *et al.* 2008)

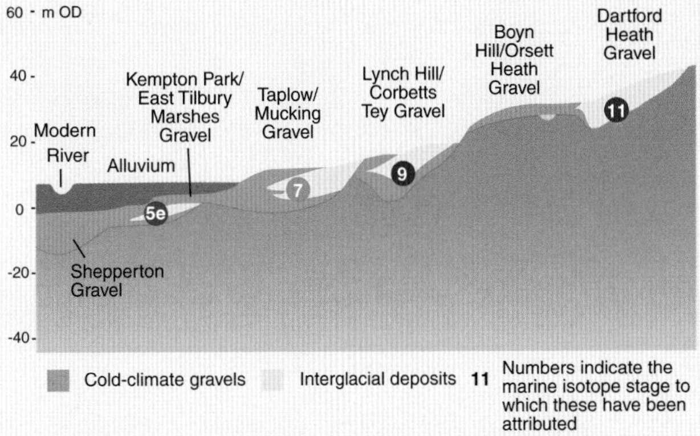

2.6.3 A. Lower Thames terrace stratigraphy (after Bridgland 1994)

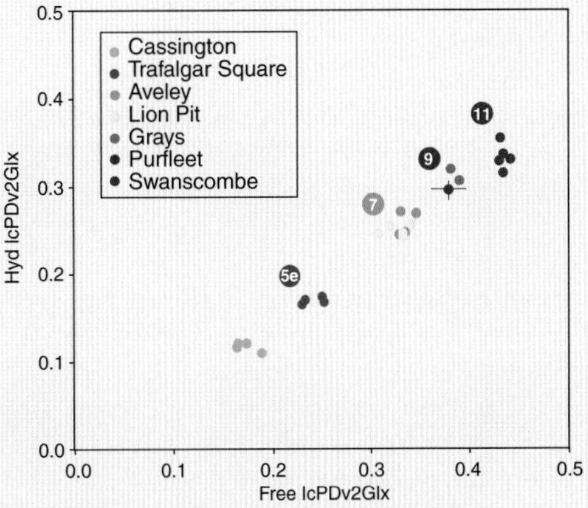

2.6.3 B. Hyd IcPD vs Free IcPD for the Thames aminostratigraphic sequence. Each point represents the overall extent of intra-crystalline protein decomposition from an individual *Bithynia tentaculata* opercula sample (from Penkman *et al.* 2008)

marine based. In some cases this information can then be used to place the archaeological site/area of investigation within a (pre)historical context as well as defining areas in which evidence of *in situ* activity by past human groups / environments may occur. In each case the mixed method approach needs to be structured in order to address the needs of the site/problem. An important element of the investigation is the clear articulation and discussion of the methodologies used, the limitations of the sampling approaches and the impact that that approach may have on the interpretation derived (in other words, the confidence limits that may be placed on the conclusions of the investigation that relate to the location of sample points and correlations made between sample points). Discussion of the sampling strategy utilised in a study as part of routine procedures practiced by Quaternary scientists is rarely documented in the published literature, although this is particularly important (in Quaternary science) where frameworks for site and sequence correlations may be based on individual classes of data (such as small mammals). In many cases complex frameworks may be erected on relatively few sites, and it is only rarely that the details of the sampling strategy (at a regional rather than site level) are considered in the discussion of the data and the confidence placed in the conclusions drawn from that information.

POST-EXCAVATION ANALYSIS

Analysis in the laboratory is one of the major cost factors in conducting Palaeolithic archaeological investigations where time-consuming and expensive investigations are necessary to tease out evidence about the past. These include palaeontological investigation of contained biological materials (Preece and Parfitt 2012), technological investigation of artefacts through refitting (Pope 2002), chemical and sedimentological investigation of sequences (Lewis in Boismier *et al.* 2012) and the dating of samples (Penkman *et al.* 2008; 2011). While traditional palaeontological investigations are now augmented by sophisticated investigations of isotopic signatures of the biological material, or study of DNA, key developments that aid field investigations have largely focused on dating and correlation with the marine isotope chronology (and through this between terrestrial sites).

Significant developments in the post-excavation analysis of field data have been made in the last 10 years through the application of new, or modified, dating techniques to enable more reliable and robust correlation to be made between sites and sequences (Walker 2005). These developments are most noticeable in the fields of radiometric dating where advances in the application of Optically Stimulated Luminescence (OSL) dating to fluvial and marine sediments in southern England have enabled hitherto undatable sequences to be ascribed ages (for examples see PASHCC, MVPP and TVVP and Box 2.5). Major advances have also been made in the application of Amino Acid Racemization (AAR) to the opercula of the freshwater species of mollusc *Bithynia tentaculata* (Penkman *et al.* 2008; 2011). This relative dating technique now provides a framework for comparing sites across the full time depth of the Palaeolithic record (Box 2.6).

APPROACHES TO LANDSCAPE AT A VARIETY OF SCALES

The range of projects undertaken in the ALSF include site-specific investigations such as the Valdoe (Pope *et al.* 2009), Lynford (Boismier *et al.* 2012) and Chard Junction Quarry (Brown *et al.* 2008; Basell *et al.* 2011) through to large-scale regional surveys (PASHCC, MVPP and TVPP). These projects reflect a wide range of scales, encompassing multiple drainage basins, single drainage basins and coastal plains, and spanning at least 500,000 years through the Middle and Upper Pleistocene. Selection of the appropriate scale of investigation is dictated by the nature of the questions being addressed by the archaeological team and, in the case of developer-funded investigation, the size of the area being impacted. Ultimately the scale of investigation will determine the sort of questions being asked of the project and the nature of the investigation strategy used to recover the information required in the project. Some of these issues have recently been considered by Bates and Wenban-Smith (2011).

Macro-scale

At this scale, issues such as palimpsest palaeogeography, ancestral rivers, the Channel link between Britain and Europe and the impact of glaciation are key issues (Box 2.7). In order to address big-picture questions regarding the likely migration routes into Britain, the impact of changing sea-levels on the ability of humans to colonise Britain, and possible reasons for human presence/absence in Britain at various times in the last 800,000 years, large scale palaeogeographies need to be examined. While no ALSF projects attempted to address such issues directly, work in a number of projects has indirectly addressed these problems – for example PASHCC (Bates *et al.* 2004; 2007a), the *Submerged Landscapes of the English Channel* (Gupta *et al.* 2004) and the *Pakefield/Happisburgh Marine Survey* (Wessex Archaeology 2008). Most recently these issues have been more directly addressed through the work of the *Ancient Human Occupation of Britain Project* (AHOB: Preece and Parfitt 2012) as well as the *North Sea Prehistory Research and Management Framework* (NSPRMF: Peeters *et al.* 2009; Cohen *et al.* 2012; Hijma *et al.* 2012). Of relevance here is the recognition that Palaeolithic investigation of a range of sites, at different scales of investigation, can provide relevant information for big picture questions even when the 'no result' scenario is attained during a site

The earliest human occupation of the British landmass (MIS 21-13) occurred during a period in the Pleistocene associated with a physical geography very different to that of the present (Fig. 2.7.1). Efforts to reconstruct the palaeogeography associated with this earliest phase of human occupation (Rose 2009) have focused on modelling the distribution of the contemporary river channels and the nature of the land bridge connecting southern Britain to the continent (Hijma *et al.* 2012). It should be noted that this model (Fig. 2.7.1) represents a combined period of time of nearly 500,000 years and consequently considerable variation (at the meso and micro scales) will have occurred throughout this time; this may be termed a palimpsest-palaeogeography. However, such coarse representations are useful not only for interpreting the local landscape setting of particular finds, but also in evaluating migration routes and associated sequences within which additional evidence for human activity may be preserved (Bates and Wenban-Smith 2011).

This earlier Middle Pleistocene geography, dominated by eastward or north-eastward draining major river channels originating in the Midlands and flowing across the area now occupied by the Fenland basin towards eastern Norfolk, lay north of a landbridge at the eastern end of the English Channel which formed a large embayment that included the embayment containing the important Palaeolithic site at Boxgrove (Roberts and Parfitt 1999). Disruption of this landscape is generally accepted as having occurred as a result of the advance of ice to the north London area around 450,000 years ago. This had a considerable impact on the geographical structure of the landscape resulting in major remodelling of the major drainage basins such as the Thames (Gibbard 1985), the loss of some systems (eg the Bytham River) and the creation of new rivers and basins (eg the Severn and Fen; Rose 1994). This event (or series of events) resulted in the destruction of much of the landscape associated with the earliest phases of human activity (Wymer 2001) and ALSF work in the English Channel (Gupta *et al.* 2004) provided some of the evidence used to suggest a two stage model for the erosion and loss of the old landbridge (Gupta *et al.* 2007).

The impact of creating the breach between southern England and northern France across the Straits of Dover would have been felt on human and animal access to Britain resulting from the intermittent flooding of this former land bridge (Gibbard 1995; White and Schreve 2000). The impact of these changes, at a regional level, has been examined in the PASHCC project (Bates *et al.* 2007a) which investigated how changes in the composition of foraminifera and ostracod assemblages from the different beaches reflect differences in regional palaeogeography related to open and closed channel geographies (Fig. 2.7.2).

Archaeologically, these landscapes operating at large scales (both temporally and spatially) are useful when attempting to understand the broad patterns of human movement across the landscape as well as temporal patterns at scales of 100,000 years (where perhaps crude changes in frequencies of occupation and technology may be mapped, Bates and Wenban-Smith 2011).

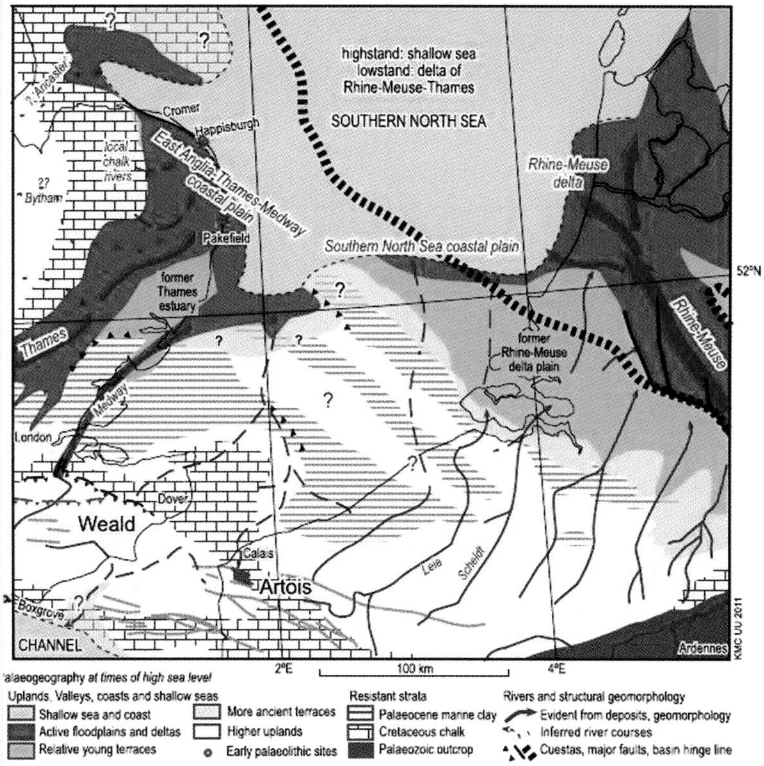

2.7.1 Palaeogeographic map for an interglacial during the early Middle Pleistocene between 0.5 and 1 million years ago (from Hijma *et al.* 2012)

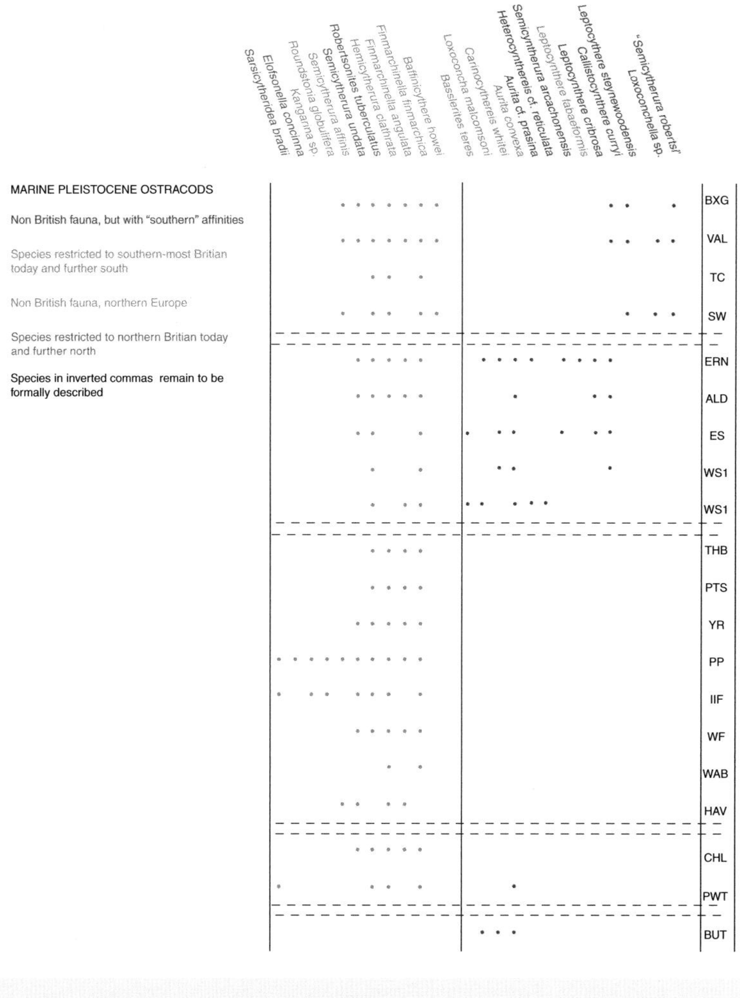

2.7.2 Ostracod range chart from the West Sussex Coastal Plain illustrating the main indicator species and their distributions

MESO-SCALE INVESTIGATIONS

Palaeolithic archaeology within the West Sussex area is best known for the important site at Boxgrove (Fig. 2.2.3; Roberts and Parfitt 1999). However, this site is associated with more extensive marine deposits at the northern end of a major coastal plain preserving sediments ranging in date from nearly 500,000 years old to recent Holocene deposits (Fig. 2.2.5) that were extensively studied in the PASHCC project (Bates *et al.* 2004; 2007; 2010). Understanding the distribution of potential sites and determining their age is significant in order to adequately address issues of probability and importance related to finds in the region.

Amongst the findings of the project was a significant revision of the age of the main raised beach sequences in the area. Traditionally (Roberts and Parfitt 1999) the Aldingbourne Beach (Fig. 2.2.5) has been assigned to the interglacial immediately following that of the Boxgrove sequences (ie MIS 11/Hoxnian). Artefacts are likely to be abundant in sediments of this age (Ashton and Lewis 2002), although in reality only relatively few, rolled artefacts have been recovered from this beach (Bates *et al.* 2004; 2007a). However, OSL dating and a reconsideration of other lines of evidence (Bates *et al.* 2004; 2007a; 2010) have suggested that

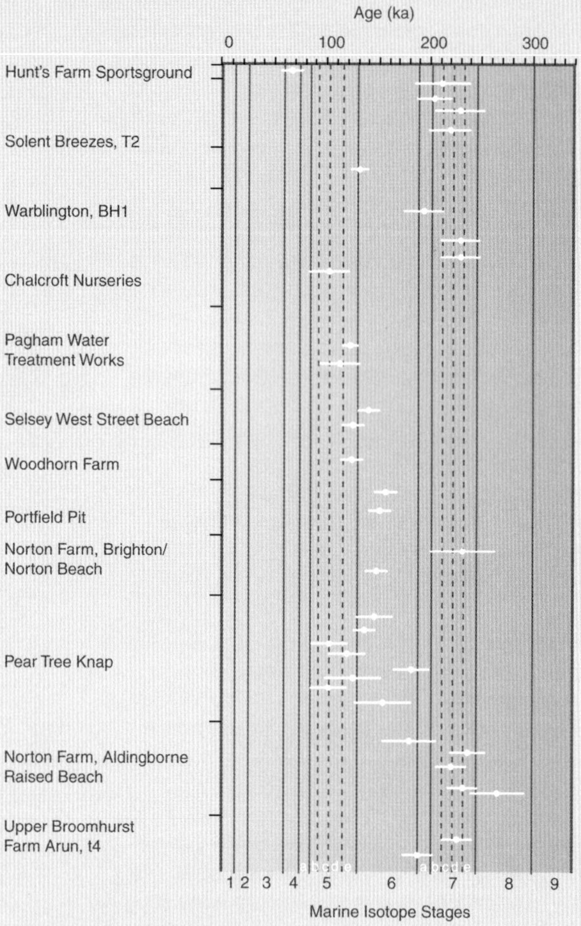

2.8.1 OSL dates from the West Sussex Coastal Plain area plotted against Marine Isotope Stages

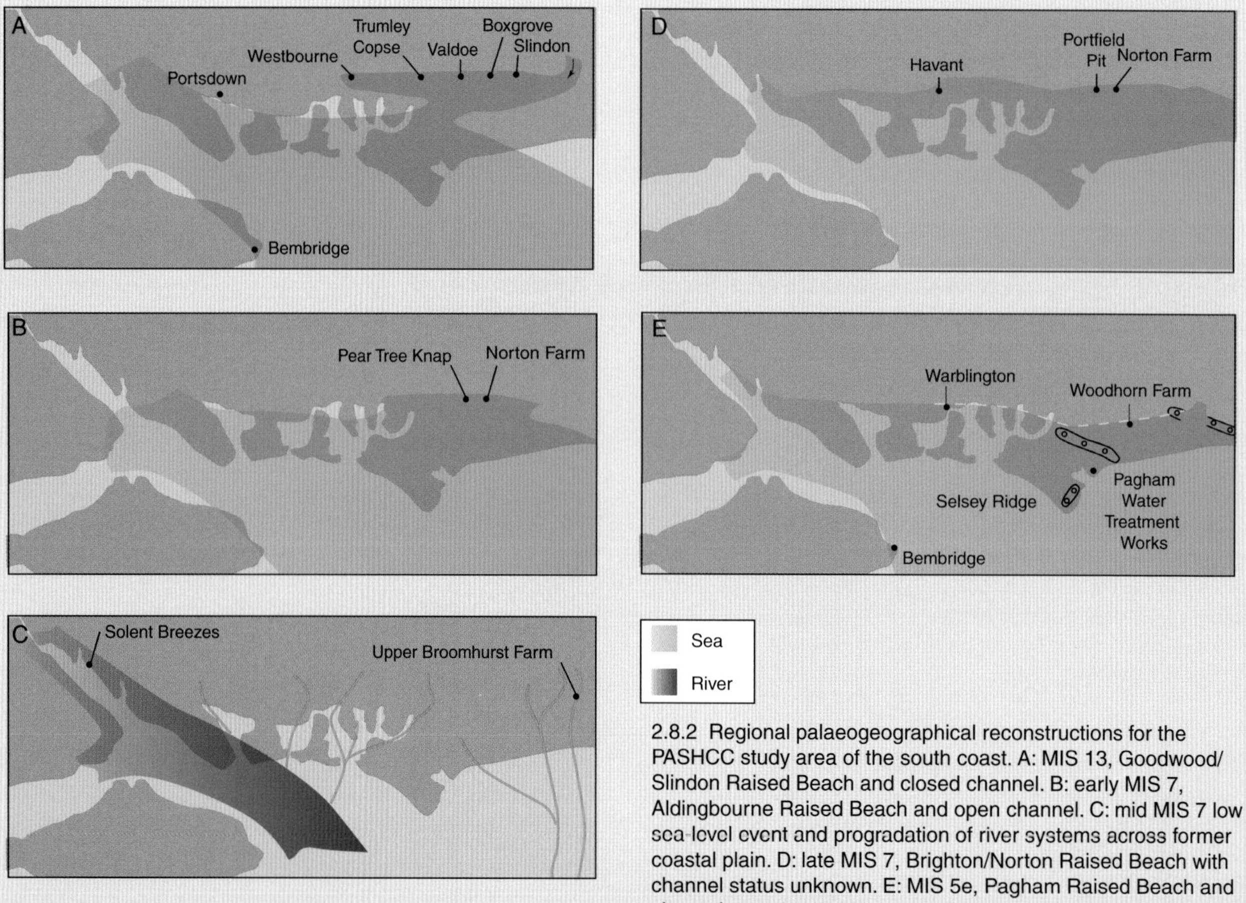

2.8.2 Regional palaeogeographical reconstructions for the PASHCC study area of the south coast. A: MIS 13, Goodwood/ Slindon Raised Beach and closed channel. B: early MIS 7, Aldingbourne Raised Beach and open channel. C: mid MIS 7 low sea-level event and progradation of river systems across former coastal plain. D: late MIS 7, Brighton/Norton Raised Beach with channel status unknown. E: MIS 5e, Pagham Raised Beach and channel open

the beach might be more likely to belong to the beginning of MIS 7 (Fig. 2.8.1). As Palaeolithic artefacts are likely to be much rarer in deposits of MIS 7 age (Ashton and Lewis 2002) this explains the relative paucity of artefacts recovered from the Aldingbourne Beach. Furthermore, it suggests (perhaps for reasons of local geography; Fig. 2.8.2) that sediments belonging to MIS 9 and 11 are going to be rare or absent in the area of the West Sussex Coastal Plain. This has significant implications for development control issues in the region (see below).

Elsewhere, regional projects such as the TVPP (White *et al.* 2009; Bridgland *et al.* in press) and the MVPP (Wenban-Smith *et al.* 2007 a and b) have played an important part in assessing and synthesising a regional record of archaeological and geological data. For example, in the Trent, survey of unpublished records (Fig. 2.8.3) was linked to a synthesis of the geological and chronological information from the river terraces to produce an integrated model of Palaeolithic distribution by terrace (Fig. 2.8.4).

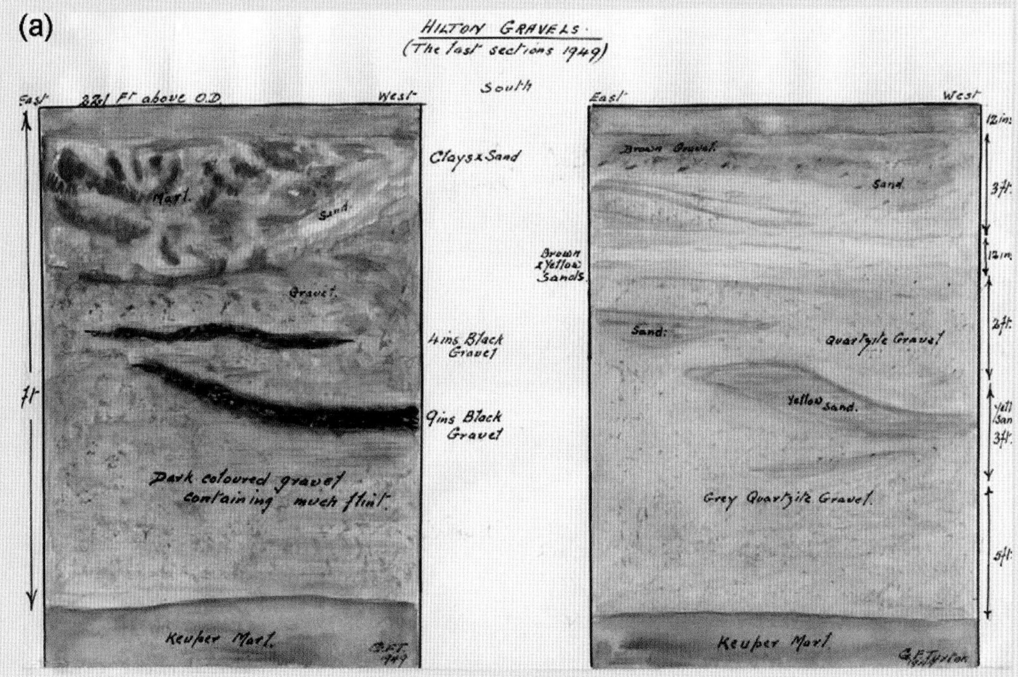

2.8.3 Mr George Turton's section drawing of the gravel deposits at Hilton, Derbyshire (reproduced courtesy of Derby Museum and Art Gallery)

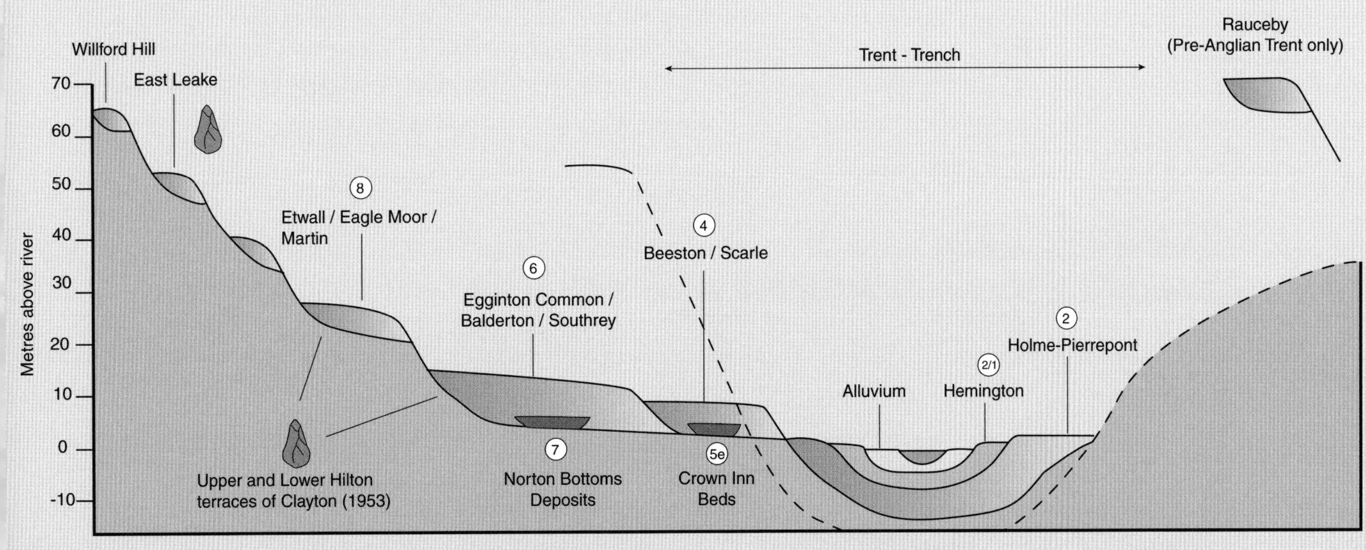

2.8.4 Modified transverse section through the terraces of the Middle Trent based on TVPP work showing the distribution of artefacts by terrace (White *et al.* 2009)

Because of the nature of the Palaeolithic, and in particular the problematic status of 'sites' in the Palaeolithic record, evidence recorded within the Historic Environment Record can be limited, and typically reflects only certain categories of information. Allied to this is the sometimes problematic nature of the baseline British Geological Survey mapping of superficial deposits at a scale reflecting that of the likely archaeological investigations (ie mapped boundaries of geological units may only be accurate to 50m or 100m, while smaller patches of Quaternary sediments may not be recorded at all). In order to address these issues and provide information suitable for incorporation into the HER and supporting GIS systems, a number of ALSF projects directly tackled these issues. Work on the TVPP (White *et al.* 2009; Bridgland *et al.* 2014) and PRoSWeB (Brown *et al.* 2008) provided detailed investigations of the study areas and supplied new and enhanced records for the HER.

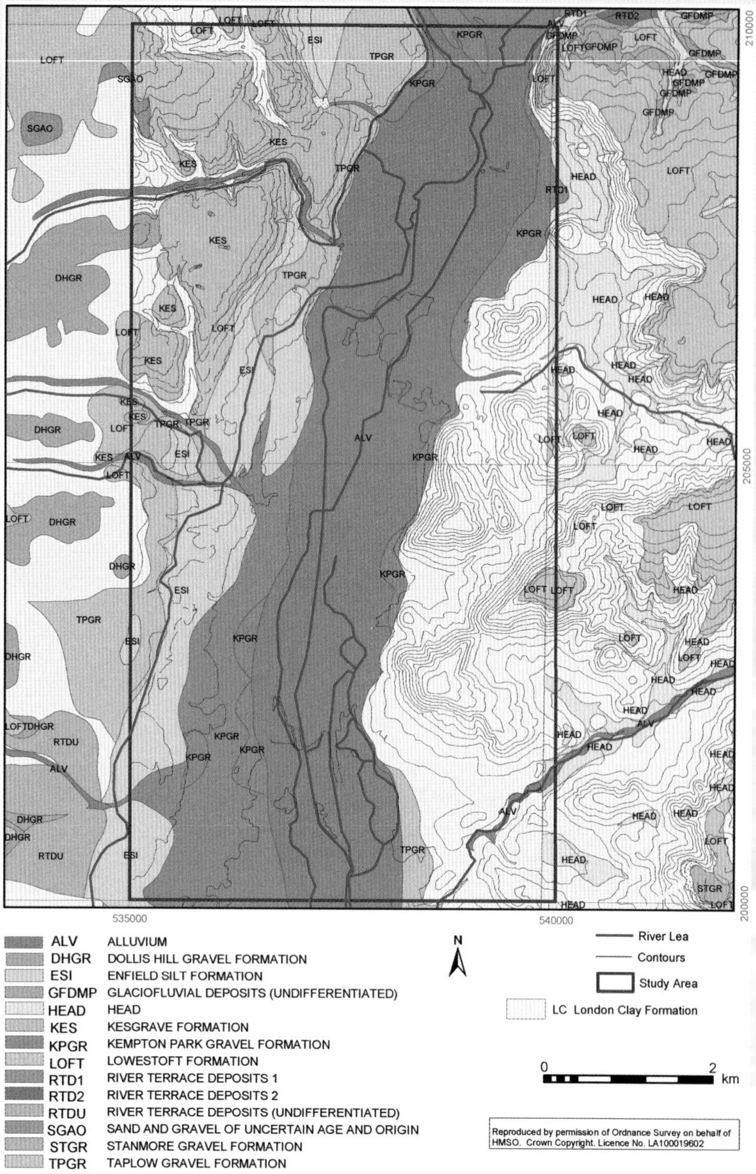

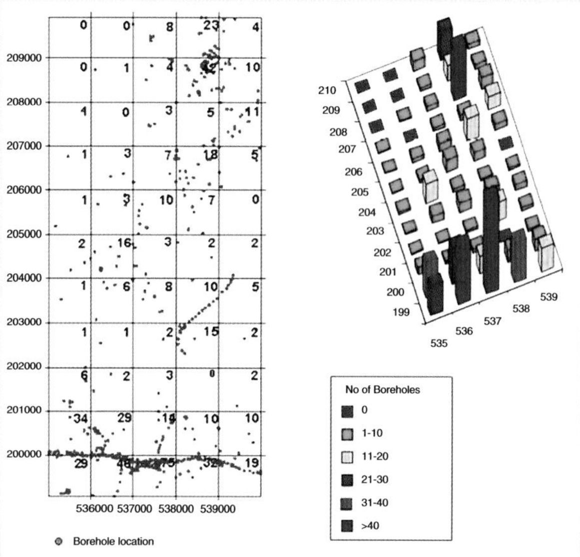

Above 2.9.1 GIS screenshot, superficial geology for the MTNT study area in the Lea Valley

Left 2.9.2 Distribution of boreholes across the MTNT study area

Below 2.9.3 Geoarchaeological model developed for MTNT study area

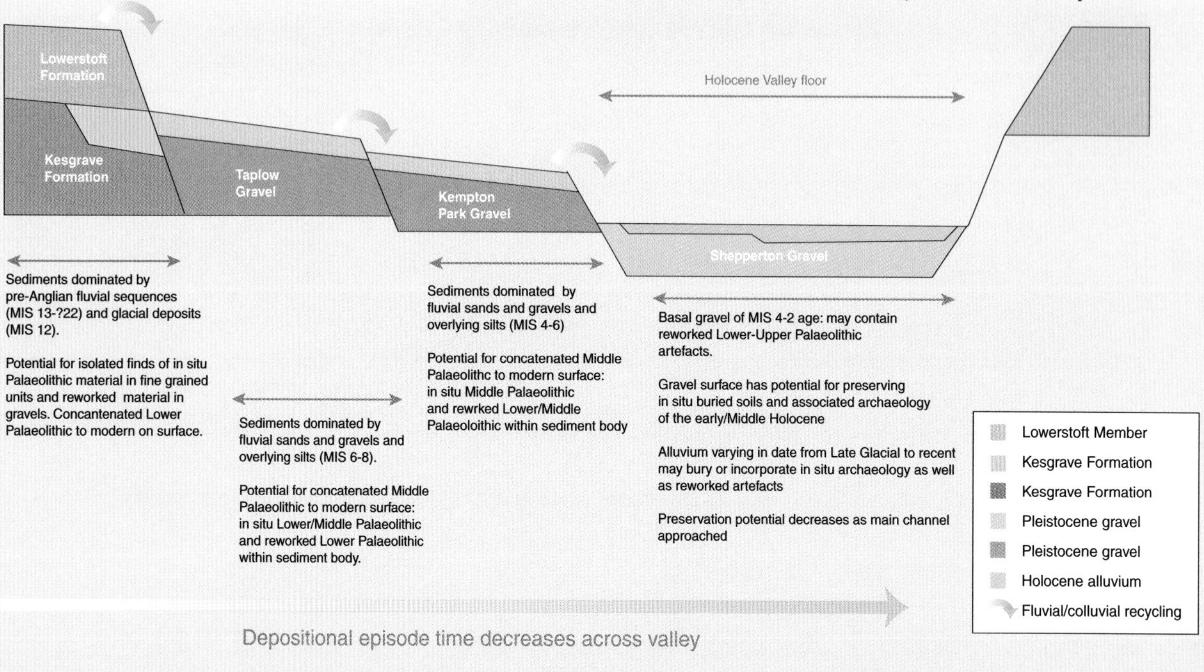

Lowerstoft Formation
Kesgrave Formation
Taplow Gravel
Kempton Park Gravel
Holocene Valley floor
Shepperton Gravel
Sediments dominated by pre-Anglian fluvial sequences (MIS 13-?22) and glacial deposits (MIS 12).
Potential for isolated finds of in situ Palaeolithic material in fine grained units and reworked material in gravels. Concantenated Lower Palaeolithic to modern on surface.
Sediments dominated by fluvial sands and gravels and overlying silts (MIS 6-8).
Potential for concatenated Middle Palaeolithic to modern surface: in situ Lower/Middle Palaeolithic and reworked Lower Palaeolithic within sediment body.
Sediments dominated by fluvial sands and gravels and overlying silts (MIS 4-6)
Potential for concatenated Middle Palaeolithc to modern surface: in situ Middle Palaeolithic and rewrked Lower/Middle Palaeoloithic within sediment body
Basal gravel of MIS 4-2 age: may contain reworked Lower-Upper Palaeolithic artefacts.
Gravel surface has potential for preserving in situ buried soils and associated archaeology of the early/Middle Holocene
Alluvium varying in date from Late Glacial to recent may bury or incorporate in situ archaeology as well as reworked artefacts
Preservation potential decreases as main channel approached
Lowerstoft Member
Kesgrave Formation
Kesgrave Formation
Pleistocene gravel
Pleistocene gravel
Holocene alluvium
Fluvial/colluvial recycling
Depositional episode time decreases across valley

By contrast, the MVPP (Wenban-Smith *et al.* 2007a and b), PASHCC (Bates *et al.* 2007a) and the MTNT (Bates and Heppell 2007) have all used field and desktop investigations to zone the landscape into differing zones of geoarchaeology/Palaeolithic archaeological potential. This is most clearly illustrated by the MTNT (Bates and Heppell 2007). Starting with the mapped superficial geology for the study area in the Lea Valley (Fig. 2.9.1) and a large data set of extant boreholes (Fig. 2.9.2), a framework geoarchaeological model relating bedrock and superficial geology to archaeology was articulated (Fig. 2.9.3). This enabled the study area to be divided into a series of zones of different potential (Fig. 2.9.4) with each zone supported by a table of data characterising that zone. Similar methods and results were obtained for both the PASHCC and Medway (Fig. 2.9.5) study areas.

Note: See Table 1.1 for project acronyms

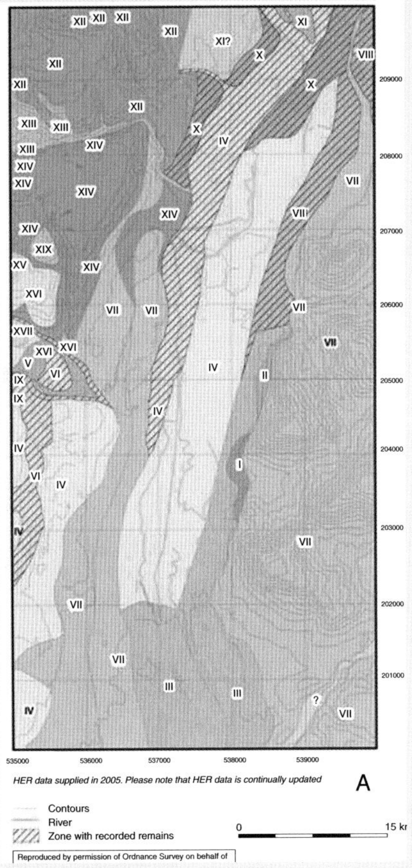

B

Zone descriptor	VI				
Total area of zone	3.79	Area of zone lost to quarrying:	km^2 / %	0.64 / 16.9	
Bedrock geology (defined)	London Clay				
Bedrock geology (description)					
Superficial geology (defined)	**Enfield Silt Formation.** Mid to Late Devensian silt probably overlying older gravels of the Kempton Park Gravel Formation				
Superficial geology (description)	Fine grained clays-silts.				
Geomorphological situation	Valley side, low lying topography (<3°)				
Age range of sediments	Early Devensian (c.90,000) to recent				
Number of boreholes in zone	54				
Number of palaeoenvironmental sites in zone					
Number of recorded sites in zone					
Paleolithic	1	*Mesolithic*	2	*Neolithic*	
Bronze Age	3	*Iron Age*	1	*Prehistoric*	
Roman		*Saxon*		*Medieval*	9
Post Medieval	5	*Modern*	1	*Unknown*	
Comments	Paleolithic (Levallois) artifact from Rikoff's pit Two Mesolithic occupation sites (C14 dates of 9350 BP +/- 120 and 6895BP +/-75) Bronze age entries refer to artifacts with possible uncertain provenance Medieval sites include Rye House moated site and associated entries, Cheshunt nunnery, a leper hospital and a derr park. Post medieval entries refer to the river and canal, a corn mill and a watercress bed				
Key research questions					
Investigation strategies					

Above 2.9.4 GIS screenshot of the MTNT study area subdivided into different Palaeolithic archaeological zones and example of supporting data table for the HER.

Below 2.9.5 GIS screenshot, zoned space in Kent for the MVPP

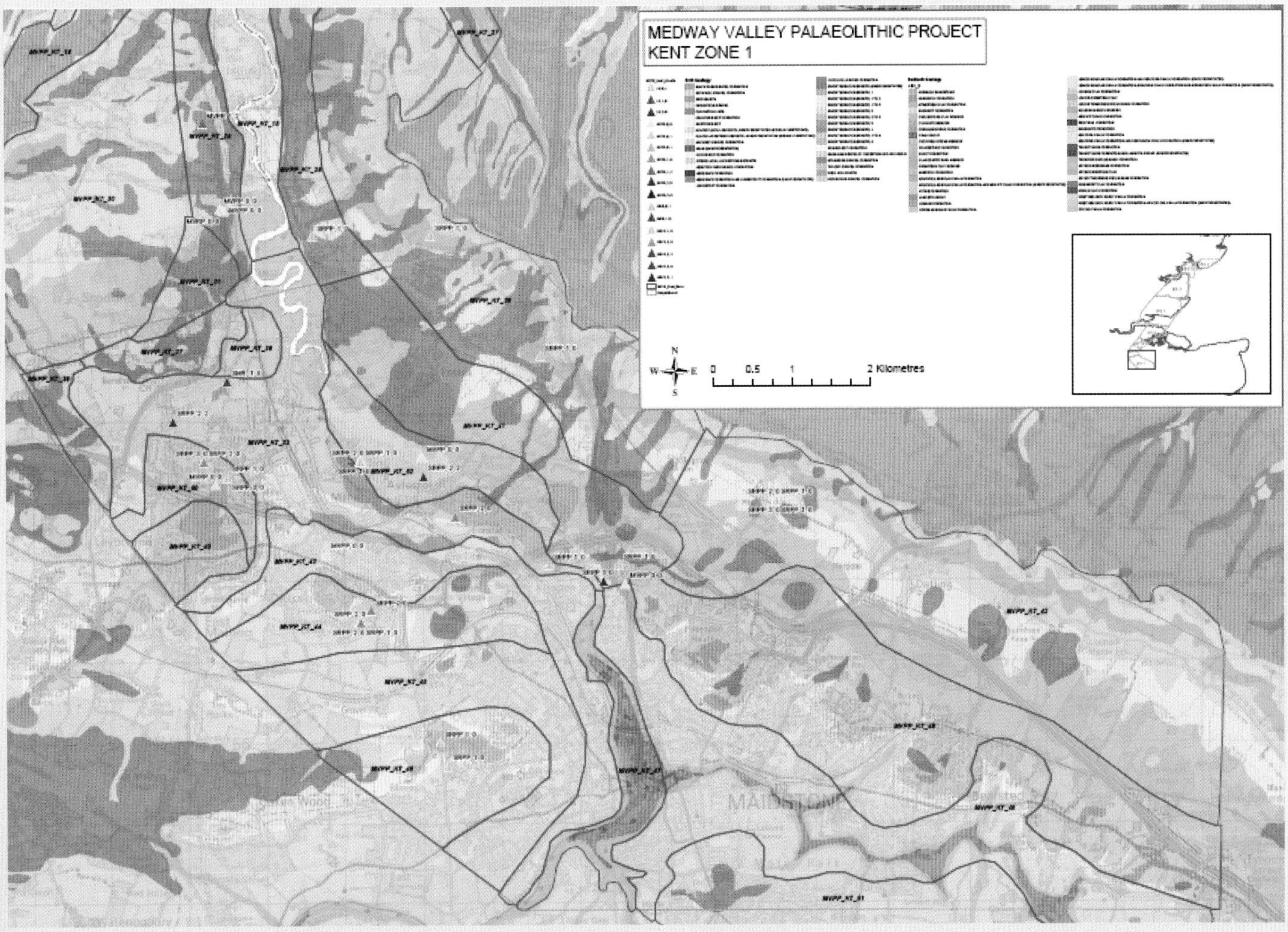

investigation. Thus sites that have been investigated and found to contain the Rhenish mollusc fauna (eg Bridgland *et al.* 2004) not only imply an age for that site in MIS 11 but also link to large scale palaeogeographic scenarios between the Thames and the Rhine (Bates and Wenban-Smith 2011).

Archaeologically, these temporally and spatially large-scale landscapes are useful when attempting to understand the broad patterns of human movement across the landscape as well as temporal patterns at scales of 100,000 years (where perhaps crude changes in frequencies of occupation and technology may be mapped).

Meso-scale

At this scale, ALSF projects (Box 2.8) have focused on discrete geomorphological systems such as the Chard Junction Quarry Project (Brown *et al.* 2008), the TVPP (Bridgland *et al.* in press), the offshore Arun (Gupta *et al.* 2004), the MVPP (Wenban-Smith *et al.* 2007a and b) and the PASHCC project (Bates *et al.* 2004; 2007a-c; 2010; Briant 2006; 2012). Typically these projects have attempted to:

- Contextualise extant collections of artefacts (eg the TVPP and PASHCC projects)
- Track and map individual bodies of sediment likely to contain archaeology or to provide marker horizons to help to date and correlate other sediments stratigraphically removed from these deposits (ie above or below the marker horizons). Examples of marker horizons within project study areas are the buried land surfaces associated with the Goodwood/Slindon and Brighton/Norton Raised Beaches in West Sussex (Fig. 2.27A/B). Sometimes the marker horizons or units can subsequently be dated directly (through OSL) or indirectly (through biostratigraphy or relative dating techniques such as AAR).

Fig. 2.27 A: Buried landsurface of the Goodwood/Slindon Raised Beach

Understanding these palaeogeographical changes helps explain the distribution of the archaeological resource, and allows us to make predictions regarding the location of sequences that elsewhere contain Palaeolithic archaeological remains. This scale of investigation is particularly useful for development control officers responsible for maintaining the HER or implementing strategies in advance of construction. This approach was pioneered in the PASHCC (Bates *et al.* 2004; 2007), MVPP (Wenban-Smith *et al.* 2007a and b), MTNT (Bates and Heppell 2007) and the *Fenland Rivers of Cambridgeshire Palaeolithic Project* (FRCPP: White *et al.* 2008a). These are projects where the ultimate goal was to provide the HER with additional information to aid the planning process (Box 2.9).

Fig. 2.27 B: Buried landsurface of the Brighton/Norton Raised Beach

MICRO-SCALE INVESTIGATIONS BOX 2.10

The Valdoe Quarry (Fig. 2.10.1) lies on the Goodwood Estate, near Chichester in West Sussex. Topographically, it occupies an almost identical position in the landscapes to the original Boxgrove site some 6km to the east, and it had been established that deposits of a similar nature existed in the pit. In 2006 a project, funded directly through the ALSF was established to assess the archaeological potential of areas of ongoing quarry expansion. The project developed an intensive and scaled approach to the assessment allowing for staged survey, geological mapping and targeted archaeological excavation as an understanding of the site developed. At the core of the project was the need to identity, isolate and excavate areas of an intact ancient landsurface (designated Unit 4c) identified at Boxgrove and known to extend more widely in the mapped palaeolandscape. This landsurface and its equivalent deposits preserved the highest resolution archaeology and associated hominin remains at Boxgrove.

2.10.1 A view of the Valdoe Quarry

2.10.2 Drilling on the Upper Coastal Plain

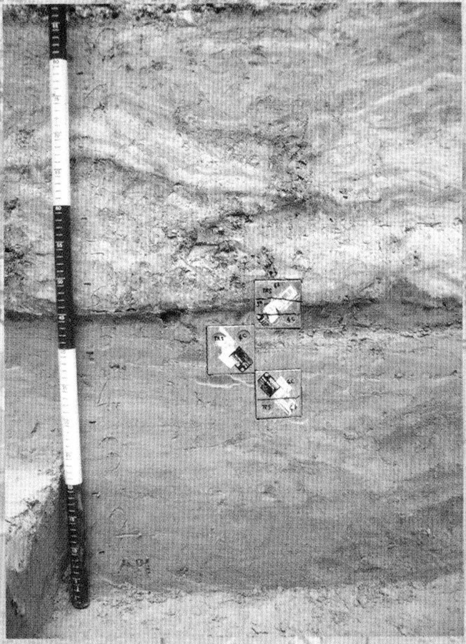

2.10.3 Excavated landsurface, Valdoe Quarry

The project also examined the wider distribution of the palaeolandsurface across the Goodwood Estate and into the Lavant Valley. This part of the county has produced a large quantity of Palaeolithic surface finds which may have largely derived from subcrops of the Slindon Formation.

Through geological mapping by percussion borehole (Fig. 2.10.2) the ancient landsurface was identified across the northern portion of the quarry site (Fig. 2.10.3) and test pits were dug to allow for hand excavation of its surface. The excavations recovered small scatters of handaxe sharpening flakes and, closer to the old cliff line, large flakes from the early stages of handaxe manufacture (Fig. 2.10.4).

The project produced the first clear evidence for *in-situ* archaeology within the wider Boxgrove palaeolandscape outside of the main Boxgrove site. In addition excellent palaeoenvironmental evidence was recovered, of a higher quality even to those preserved at the main Boxgrove site, allowing for nuanced reconstruction of ancient environments and landscape change at the Valdoe locality.

The project provides an example of how targeted funding through the ALSF worked alongside the aggregates industry to provide efficient evaluation and investigation methodology, taking a wider understanding of sedimentary context and ancient human behaviour to zero in on microscales of investigation within relatively extended landscapes.

2.10.4 Finds under excavation at the Valdoe Quarry

Table 2.3 Description of zones of Palaeolithic potential as defined in the PASHCC project for part of West Sussex Coastal Plain (see Fig. 2.29)

Zone	*Geomorphological context*	*Bedrock (as mapped by BGS)*	*Superficial sediments (as mapped by BGS)*
R5	Adur Valley floodplain floor	Upper and Middle Chalk	Alluvium with elements of Head, Raised Beach Deposits (1) and Storm Gravel Beach Deposits
R6	Lower coastal plain backing against steeply rising slopes of South Downs. Dry valleys enter from South Downs	Upper and Middle Chalk, Woolwich and Reading Beds and London Clay to southwest	Head, Raised Beach Deposits (1) and Alluvium
R7	Lower coastal plain.	Upper and Middle Chalk, Woolwich and Reading Beds and London Clay	Brickearth, Raised Beach Deposits (1), Alluvium
R8	Modern Storm beach coastal fringing strip	Upper and Middle Chalk	Storm Gravel Beach Deposits
R9	Lower coastal plain backing against steeply rising slopes of South Downs. Dry valleys enter from South Downs	Upper and Middle Chalk	Brickearth, Raised Beach Deposits (1), Alluvium
R10	Upper part of Lower coastal plain backing mouth of Arun Valley	Upper and Middle Chalk, Woolwich and Reading Beds and London Clay	Brickearth, Raised Beach Deposits (1), Alluvium
R11	Lower valley sides (east) of Arun Valley	Upper and Middle Chalk, Woolwich and Reading Beds and London Clay	Arun terraces 2/3/4
R12	Arun Valley/Upper Coastal Plain confluence	London Clay	Raised Storm Beach 2
R13	Arun Valley floodplain	Upper and Middle Chalk, Woolwich and Reading Beds and London Clay	Alluvium with elements of Head, Raised Beach Deposits (1, 2), Raised Storm Beach Deposits (1, 2) and Storm Gravel Beach Deposits
R14	Lower valley sides (west) of Arun Valley	Upper and Middle Chalk, Woolwich and Reading Beds and London Clay	Arun terraces 2/3/4

Superficial sediments (as mapped/ identified by PASHCC)	*Summary of Palaeolithic artefactual and zoological remains*	*Geological periods*
(may contain evidence of buried gravels of the Adur beneath alluvium)	Biological material expected in Holocene alluvium (pollen, plant macrofossils, insects, molluscs, foraminifera / ostracoda)	Mainly Holocene – some Devensian at depth. If elements of Raised Beach 1 present Saalian also
Chalky head deposits with a mixture of chalk and flint rich gravels overlying high energy storm beach gravels close to cliff. Away from cliff extensive sand sequences overlain by fine grained silts. Silts seal intact buried landsurface in places some evidence for palaeosols in Head deposits	Large, small mammal remains, molluscs, foraminifera / ostracoda reported from sands, silts and overlying chalky head	Saalian Devensian, Recent
Extensive sand sequences overlain by fine grained silts. Silts seal intact buried land-surface in places some evidence for palaeosols in Head deposits	Large, small mammal remains, molluscs, foraminifera / ostracoda reported from sands, silts and overlying chalky head	Saalian Devensian, Recent
–	None known	Recent Holocene
Chalky head deposits with a mixture of chalk and flint rich gravels overlying high energy storm beach gravels close to cliff. Away from cliff extensive sand sequences overlain by fine grained silts. Silts seal intact buried landsurface in places some evidence for palaeosols in Head deposits. High energy beach gravels replace sand in places in south of zone	Large, small mammal remains, molluscs, foraminifera / ostracoda reported from sands, silts and overlying chalky head	Saalian Devensian, Recent
Head deposits overlying high energy storm beach gravels close to cliff. Away from cliff extensive sand sequences overlain by fine grained silts. Silts seal intact buried landsurface in places some evidence for palaeosols in Head deposits	Large, small mammal remains, molluscs, foraminifera / ostracoda reported from sands, silts and overlying chalky head	Saalian Devensian, Recent
Fluvial gravel overlain by Periglacial Head / slope wash deposits	Occasional large mammal bone preservation	?Saalian / Devensian
Marine gravels over bedrock	None known	Saalian
(may contain evidence of buried gravels of the Arun beneath alluvium)	Biological material expected in Holocene alluvium (pollen, plant macrofossils, insects, molluscs, foraminifera / ostracoda)	Mainly Holocene – some Devensian at depth. If elements of Raised Beach 1 present Saalian also
Fluvial gravel overlain by Periglacial Head / slope wash deposits	Occasional large mammal bone preservation	?Saalian / Devensian

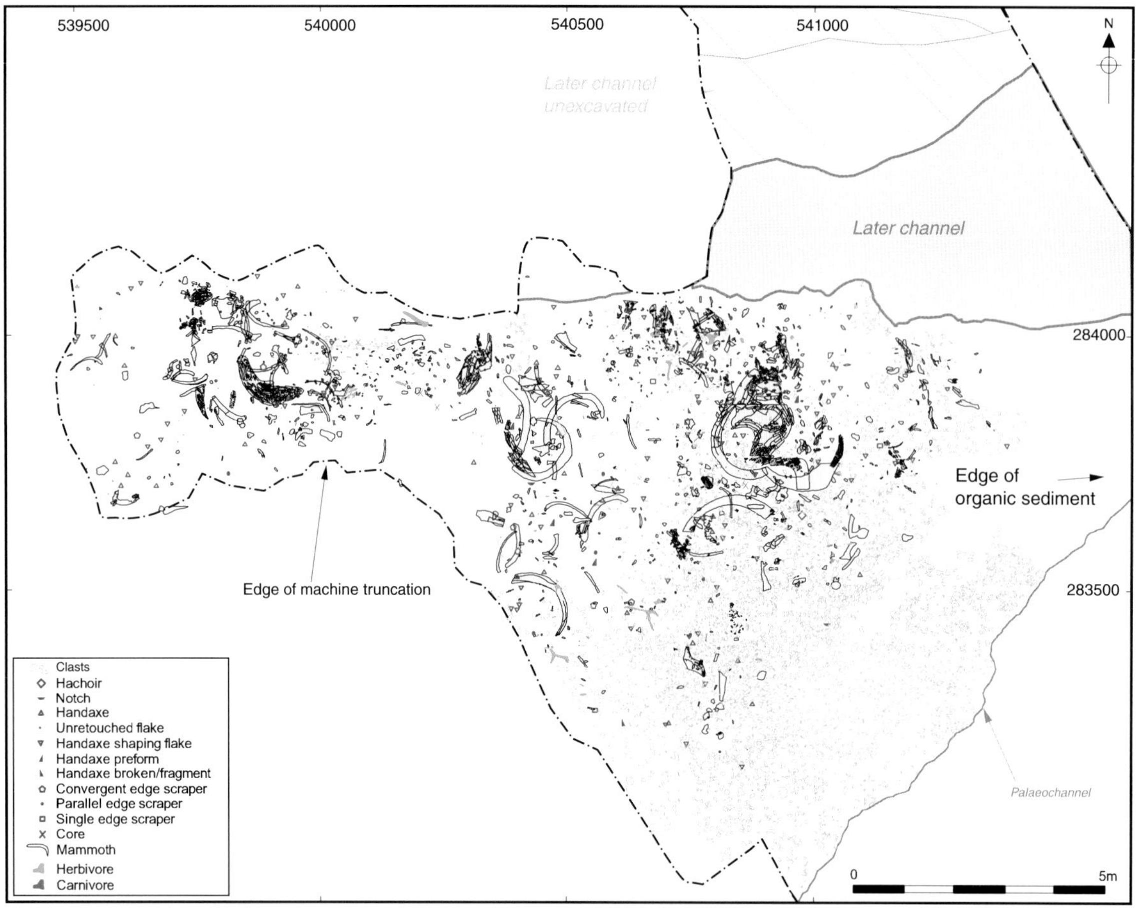
539500
540000
540500
541000
N
Later channel unexcavated
Later channel
284000
283500
Edge of organic sediment
Edge of machine truncation
Palaeochannel
0
5m
Clasts
Hachoir
Notch
Handaxe
Unretouched flake
Handaxe shaping flake
Handaxe preform
Handaxe broken/fragment
Convergent edge scraper
Parallel edge scraper
Single edge scraper
Core
Mammoth
Herbivore
Carnivore

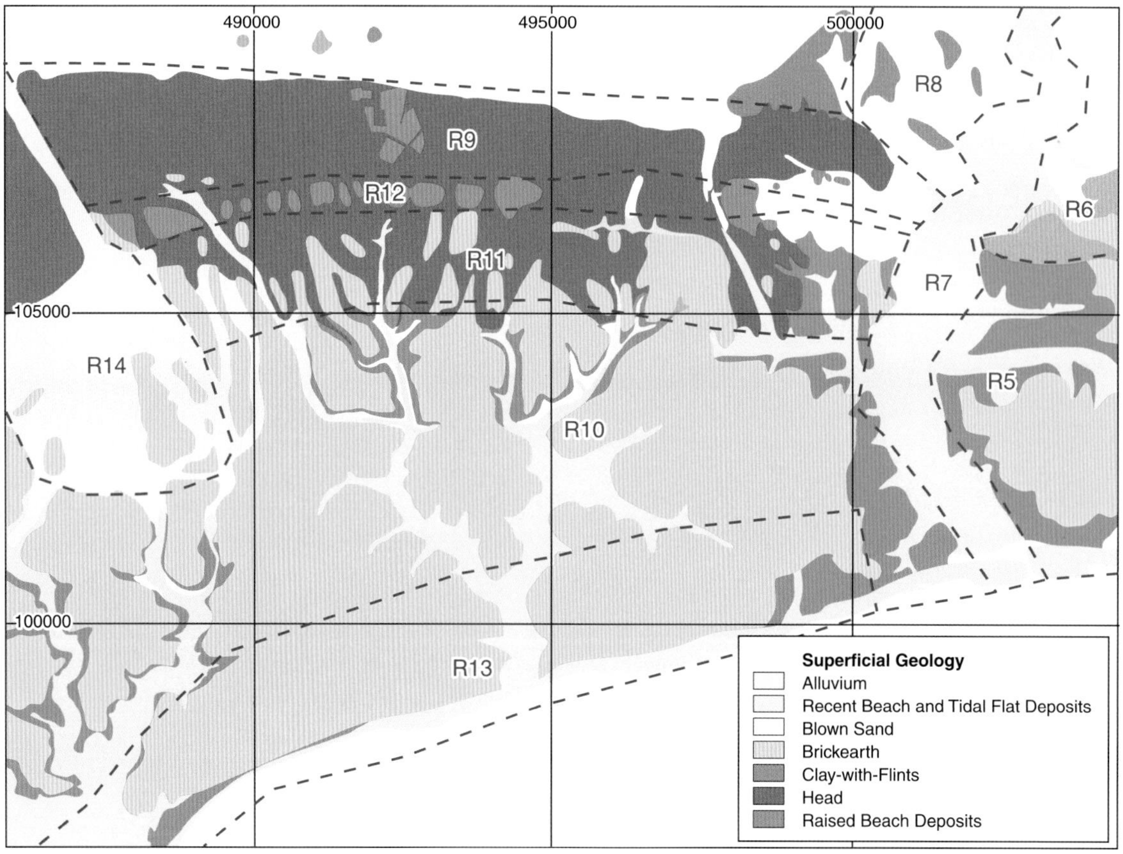
490000
495000
500000
105000
100000
R5
R6
R7
R8
R9
R10
R11
R12
R13
R14
Superficial Geology
Alluvium
Recent Beach and Tidal Flat Deposits
Blown Sand
Brickearth
Clay-with-Flints
Head
Raised Beach Deposits

Micro-scale

At this scale, examining the nature of the archaeology within a known site and in ideal situations addressing questions related to technology, mobility, and 'ethnographical' style hominin practices may be the focus of the investigation. Examples funded by the ALSF include the excavations at Lynford (Boismier *et al.* 2012) and the Valdoe (Box 2.10; Pope *et al.* 2009).

The excavations at the site of Lynford (Bosimier *et al.* 2012) demonstrate the problems often faced by Palaeolithic archaeologists even on sites where evidence of human activity and palaeoenvironmental data are recovered from the same deposits. Here, organic silts and sands filling a palaeochannel were found to contain a cold-stage mammalian assemblage rich in mammoth remains, and an associated Mousterian flint industry of some 2,720 pieces (Fig 2.28). The OSL dates place the filling of the channel at between 65,000 and 57,000 BP, at the transition between Marine Isotope Stages (MIS) 4 and 3. Unfortunately, there is no 'smoking gun' and the absence of cut-marks on the mammoth bones means that their relationship with human activity at the site remains circumstantial. There are, however, typically human patterns of breakage on the bones of horse and woolly rhinoceros; and given that the location was a still or slow-flowing backwater, at times stagnant and often boggy, one might reasonably argue that the Neanderthals were only there to exploit the carcasses of mammoths and other animals that had become trapped in the mire (through whatever agency).

DISCUSSION

The wide range of project types that have been undertaken in the guise of the ALSF have consistently attempted to contextualise sites and findings as well as to test new methods of investigation. The outcomes of the projects have been new or developed methodologies or novel applications of approaches used elsewhere but not previously applied in Palaeolithic archaeology. Most significantly, the projects all reflect the realistic application of techniques to problems that could, and should, be applied more widely. The approaches developed and illustrated by the ALSF projects do not reflect 'state-of-the-art' high-cost scientific techniques that may be applicable in one or two instances but are either limited in application or too expensive to routinely use. Rather, they are approaches that offer pragmatic methods to tackle the problems of our Palaeolithic past within a time and budget framework that is both practical and realistic.

The long term success and legacy of the Palaeolithic projects undertaken as part of the spectrum of ALSF funded works will ultimately be judged on their ability to inform non-specialist readers for whom the role of the Palaeolithic within development control is something of a 'dark art', practised by a few, and kept secret through the use of jargon and inaccessible terminology. It can be deemed to have been successful if, as a result of the projects that are synthesised in this volume, future Palaeolithic projects within the commercial sector take forward the findings and methods described and utilise them within the context for which they have been developed.

This educative process is perhaps best considered in the context of a better understanding of the fact that a 'no-return' on finding Palaeolithic artefacts does not negate the importance of a site – it simply modifies the information obtained from the study. Ultimately, Palaeolithic archaeology is not just about excavating the evidence for human behaviour – it is about that behaviour in a landscape in which the primary archaeological 'site' is just one node, and any information from that landscape has the potential to inform about the archaeology scattered across it. Perhaps in the near future we can hope that integration of results in the HER may include not only data on find spot distribution but also perhaps subdivision of the landscape into different zones of Palaeolithic potential (Table 2.3; Fig. 2.29; Box 2.9). This would provide curators with the tools to manage the resource in a proactive and informed fashion. If we achieve such an understanding, then the legacy of the ALSF will be cemented.

Fig. 2.28 (opposite, above) Distribution map showing mammal remains and stone tools from Lynford (from Boismier et al. *2012)*

Fig. 2.29 (opposite, below) Part of West Sussex Coastal Plain divided into zones of different Palaeolithic potential for integration with the HER (from Boismier et al. *2012)*

Chapter 3:
Coastal and submerged landscapes

by Matthew Pope and Martin Bates

THE CHANGING SHAPE OF BRITAIN

Britain is a landmass defined by its modern Holocene coastlines, situated on the edge of the continental shelf in the north-east Atlantic Ocean and separated from mainland Europe by the English Channel and the North Sea (Fig. 3.1). The long perspective offered by Palaeolithic archaeology and scientific study of Pleistocene sedimentation in the region demonstrates that this arrangement is simply the current geographical condition in a long and dynamic process of landscape evolution stretching back through the Pleistocene and into the later parts of the Tertiary (Gibbard and Lewin 2003). In order to reconstruct the long term development of Britain as a landmass, and to understand the human occupation record, it is necessary to understand the complex interplay of a number of long-term processes which include global climate change, changes in the relative and absolute height of solid rock formations, the short term processes of sedimentation/erosion, and fluctuations in sea-level.

Reconstructing the long term evolution of the British landscape and its relation to the sea is therefore critical in developing an accurate understanding of the prehistory of human colonisation of Britain in terms of connectivity or separation from the continent (Box 3.1). Recent research, heavily supported by English Heritage through the ALSF, has deepened

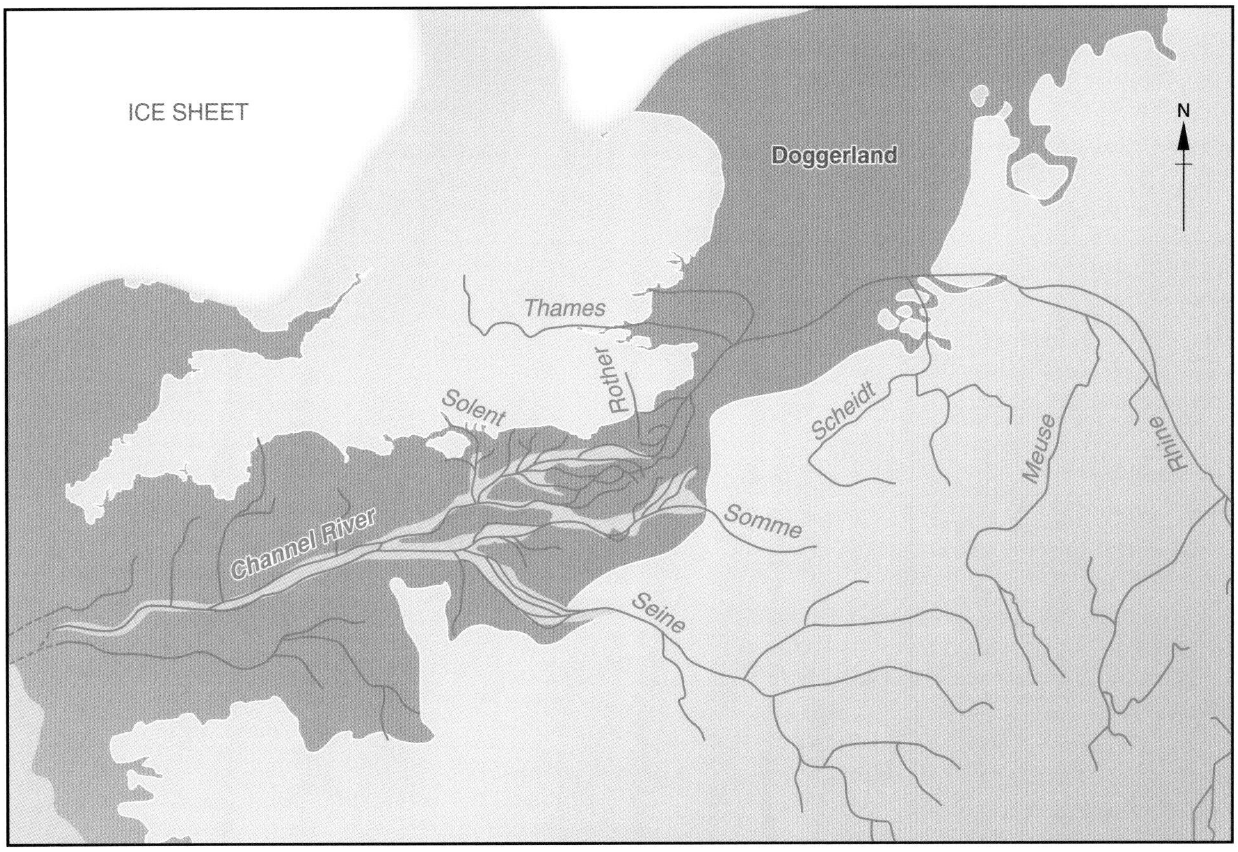

Fig. 3.1 Map showing the position and outline of Britain against landscapes of now submerged Doggerland and the La Manche/English Channel lowlands during the last glacial maximum (from Gibbard 2007)

ISLAND BRITAIN

Through tectonic uplift, much of Britain had emerged as a permanent landmass by the Early Pleistocene, effectively becoming a significant peninsula of north west Europe open to relatively easy colonisation by terrestrial plant, animal and human species. Its form defined areas of the continental margin such as the North Sea that was periodically subject to inundation during sea level high stands. It also saw the beginning of the English Channel (although at this stage this comprised simply a large embayment of the north east Atlantic). From this point on, the combination of long term climatic change and associated sea-level rise and fall began to shape the landscape of north west Europe and give shape to the British Isles as we know them today. The cycles of global warming and cooling intensified after 1 million years ago, ultimately forming 100,000 year cycles. With the on-set of each cold stage, sea-level falls would have occurred with the build-up and advance of the polar icecaps and peripheral ice sheets. During the shorter, more punctuated periods of global warming, meltwater lakes would have formed, which, when breached, would have released raging mega-floods. Interglacial periods would have also led to massive rises in sea-level to about the limit we see on the planet today. This would have led to the flooding of the lower reaches of our river systems and the continental margins and, as today, the resumption of erosion of the high sea-level coastline which over the millennia has defined the existence and shape of our island.

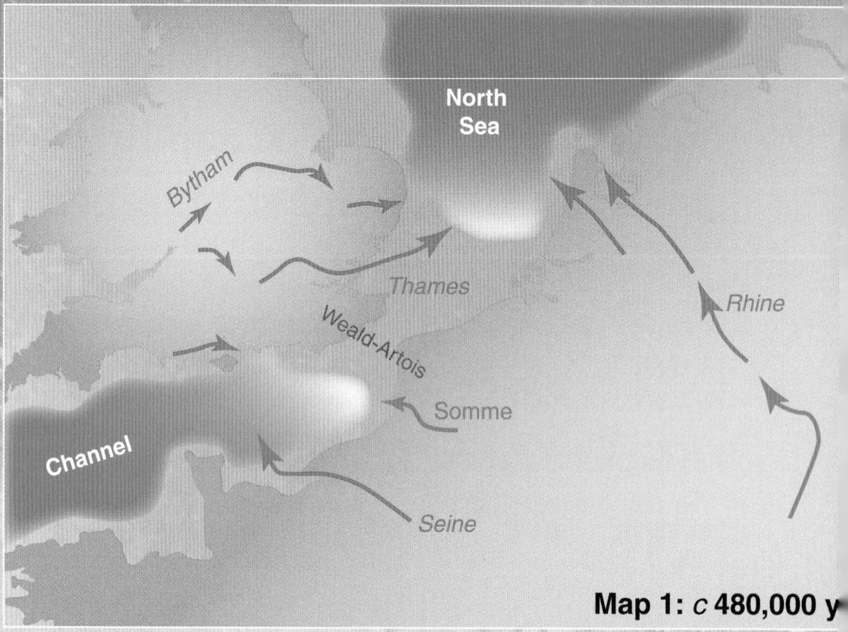

Map 1: *c* 480,000 y

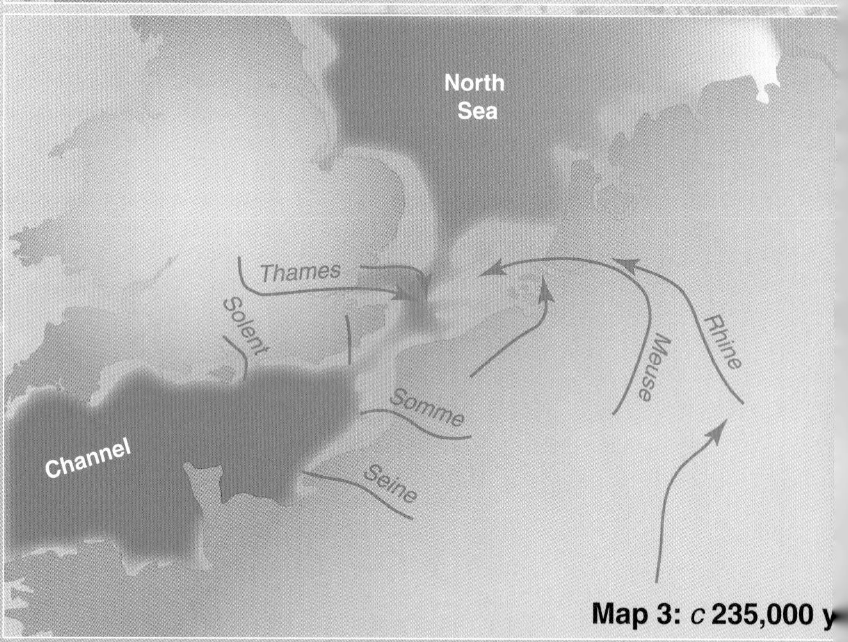

Map 3: *c* 235,000 y

Map 1 An early Middle Pleistocene interglacial: peninsula Britain, MIS 13

During a high sea-level interglacial period some 480,000 years ago, Britain's coastline broadly conformed to that we see today, although the coastline of south east England continued across to northern France. The River Thames and River Rhine emptied directly into a separate North Sea while the Seine, Solent, Arun and Rother flowed into the English Channel embayment. Access to the British landmass was relatively open, with a 110km corridor through the Weald-Artois anticline providing a permanent landbridge for humans (*Homo heidelbergensis*) and other Pleistocene fauna (White and Schreve 2000).

Map 2 An early Middle Pleistocene late glacial: formation of pro-glacial North Sea Lake, MIS 12

The Anglian glaciation was deep and prolonged and resulted in the furthest extension of the arctic ice sheet across Britain in the Pleistocene, as far south as Finchley in London. The course of the River Thames was effectively shifted into its current position occupying the London Basin, and much of the North Sea was covered by ice. It is thought that during the retreat of the ice sheet at the end of this glacial period meltwater from the ice, channelled also through the Rhine and Thames Valleys, accumulated as water in the southern North Sea. Eventually this meltwater would have spilled across the Weald Artois anticline (ridge) incising deep meltwater channels and beginning the process of breaching through the permanent land bridge connecting Britain to the continent.

BOX 3.1

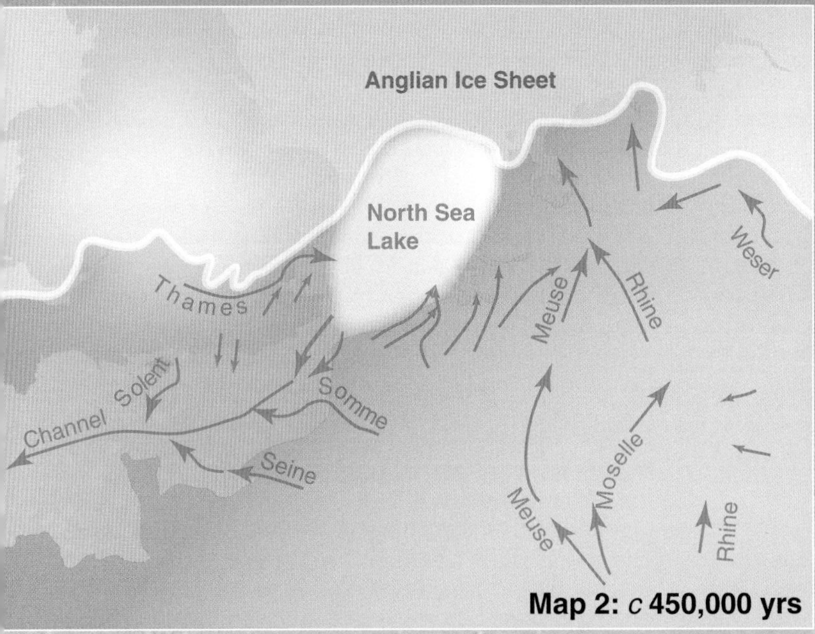

Map 2: ***c*** **450,000 yrs**

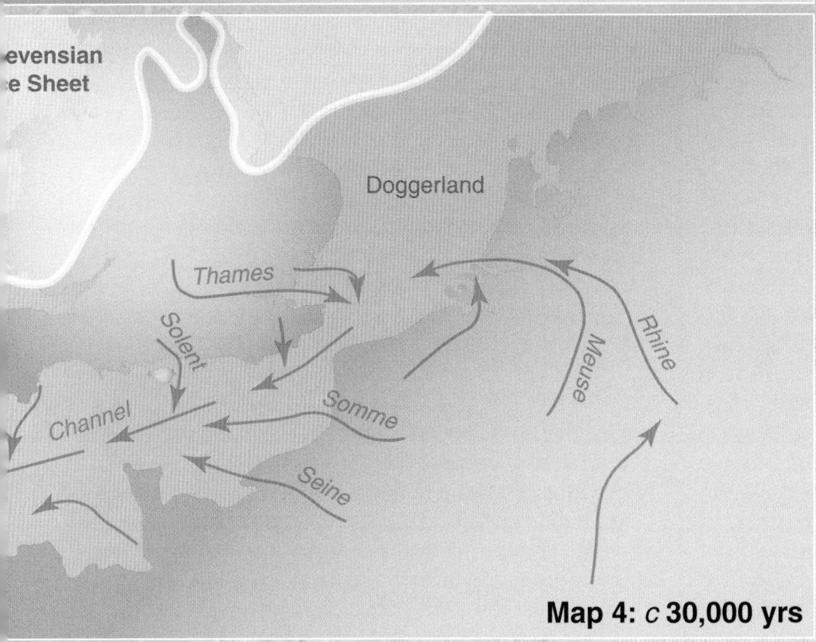

Map 4: ***c*** **30,000 yrs**

Sea floor survey undertaken by Gupta *et al.* (2007) have identified landforms in the submerged palaeo-valleys of the English Channel which appear to be a trace of the catastrophic mega-flooding caused by the formation and discharge of these melt-water lakes. At least two of these phases of catastrophic flooding appear to have occurred, one occurring during the end of MIS 12 as shown here, the other occurring during the closing stage of another later cold stage. Possibly MIS 8 or 10 (Gibbard 2012).

Map 3 Late Middle Pleistocene interglacial: the formation of island Britain

While it is not yet fully possible to determine exactly when Britain first became an island, it is highly likely that island Britain existed during parts of MIS 7. The English Channel may have been approaching something like its current configuration and was large enough, as climates cooled at the end of the interglacial period, to allow the movement of icebergs down the English Channel. The virtual absence of any evidence for human activity during the last interglacial period (MIS 5e), suggests that sea-level rise and the cutting off of Britain occurred rapidly during the onset of warm global conditions. During this period, in which global temperatures and sea level were slightly higher than those experienced today, there is good evidence for Neanderthal occupation of the continent, and for large mammals, including Hippopotamus, on the island of Britain. Traces of human activity which can be firmly tied to the period are, however, scant and controversial.

Map 4 Late Pleistocene Cold Stage MIS 2: landscapes of the English Channel River and Doggerland

This map shows the palaeo-topography for much of the last 100,000 years, prior to the sea-level rise of our own warm interglacial (the Holocene). During this time, Britain formed part of a large extension of the European continental landmass exposed by a sea-level fall of up to 125m. Areas exposed included the vast landscape of Doggerland, a series of river valleys and low plains occupying the southern North Sea, and the English Channel River system, the massive fluvial system left behind by the catastrophic events which breached the Weald-Artois anticline (ridge).

While Doggerland today is a relatively shallow area of sea, heavily exploited and impacted on by oil/gas and gravel extraction and fishing, much of the English Channel river system lies more deeply submerged with relatively few direct opportunities to explore its now flooded landscapes. Consequently, while Doggerland has revealed a great wealth of finds, including mammalian fauna, stone tools and even a portion of Neanderthal skull, finds from the English Channel River System are exceedingly rare. The English Channel River would have comprised the combined drainage of the Rhine, Thames, Seine, Solent and other tributaries making it potentially the largest river in Europe, and one of the great rivers of the world. Such a massive watercourse may have presented a significant barrier to human colonisation from the south compared to more easy access into Britain across the flatter and less broken Doggerland plains.

and widened this knowledge base. It has enabled earth scientists and archaeologists to develop a more accurate understanding of the distribution of ancient terrestrial deposits offshore and their potential to preserve traces of ancient human activity within both ancient landscapes now submerged by the sea and in deposits relating to past coastlines preserved high above the modern sea-level. In this chapter the unique record of these lost landscapes of human prehistory are considered in terms of their formation, current preservation and the potential they hold for documenting the colonisation and occupation of the British landmass over the past 800,000 years.

EVOLUTION OF THE BRITISH LANDMASS AND THE PREHISTORY OF HUMAN OCCUPATION

For much of the Pleistocene period Britain, as defined by the current limits of the landmass, was non-existent, it simply constituted the north-west extension of continental Europe projecting into the north Atlantic Ocean. Our understanding of the relationship between long term sea-level change and the Earth's climate has been radically accelerated in the past 40 years. Today, the starting point for understanding the chronology of sea-level fluctuations is the marine isotope curve discussed in Chapter 2 and Box 2.1 (Lislecki *et al.* 2005; Martinson *et al.* 1987; Shackleton 1987; Shackleton and Opdyke 1973; Shackleton *et al.* 1990; Steffersen *et al.* 2008). Simply put, during the cold stages and substages of the marine isotope sequence lowered sea-levels greatly increased the extent of the terrestrial landmass around what we currently know as the British Isles, exposing large areas of the continental shelf as open steppic environments. During periods of intense cold, permafrost tundra would have formed on the southern margins of these landscapes, while parts of northern Britain and the North Sea would have witnessed the encroachment of ice sheets. During the relatively brief warm stages and substages, sea-levels rose to submerge the low-lying continental shelf and the extensive river valley systems that flowed through them, thus drowning the landscapes of the English Channel and North Sea (see Box 3.1).

High sea-levels brought with them rapid transformations of the terrestrial landscapes through transgression of the coast and submergence of former dry landscapes. At the coast, erosion and deposition at the emergent zones formed active shingle beaches and new cliffs and estuarine environments identical to those that fringe the British Isles today. During the earliest phases of human occupation in Britain, even these periods of high sea-level did not always lead to isolation. For much of the Lower and early Middle Pleistocene, Britain remained connected to Europe across a substantial landbridge along the axis of the Wealden Anticline, a 60 mile wide neck of land which includes the South and North Downs and their equivalents on the French mainland (Gibbard 2007; Cohen *et al.* 2014).

This connecting peninsula was breached during one or more of the glacial periods of the last 500,000 years when large lakes, dammed on the northern side by the build up of ice (and at one point possibly moraine), catastrophically overflowed (Gibbard 1995; Gupta 2007; Gibbard 2007; Murton and Murton 2012). This initial erosional event was then augmented by more sustained marine erosion during the high sea-level stands of interglacials. After these processes of breaching, and certainly by 125,000 BP, we can finally begin to talk in terms of a definable island Britain, separated from the continental mainland during the high sea-levels of interglacial periods and defined as an upland zone by former coastlines during periods of sea retreat during the cold glacial stages.

Determining the details in terms of timing and process of this breaching of the Wealden Anticline, and the periods in which Britain was isolated from the continent, has been the focus of much work during the past 25 years and is absolutely critical to a true understanding of the British Palaeolithic record. The developing narrative of the hominin occupation of British throughout the Pleistocene relies entirely on a true appreciation of the dynamic palaeogeography of the landmass and the access points and obstacles at any given time (eg White and Schreve 2000; Conneller 2007).

Equally pivotal has been the unravelling of the story of the human occupation of the richest Palaeolithic landscapes in Britain: the Thames Valley (Bridgland 1994; 1996; Bridgland *et al.* 1999; 2004; 2006; Gibbard 1985; 1994; McNabb 2007; Mitchell *et al.* 1973; Pettitt and White 2012; Roe 1981; Wymer 1968; 1988). Detailed investigation of this occupation record by the Leverhulme-funded *Ancient Human Occupation of Britain Project* (AHOB) has attempted to develop and understand the macro-scale record of human occupation directly in terms of the interplay between hominin populations, sea-levels, climate and palaeogeography (Ashton and Lewis 2002). Current models rely on assumptions of what the archaeological record – in terms of density of artefacts – may tell us about palaeodemography, and how this in turn might relate to the accessibility of the British landmass in terms of environmental challenges during glacial periods and the gradual or sudden isolation of the landmass during the interglacials. However, the validity of this approach and the interpretations drawn from it are disputed by others (eg Pettitt and White 2012).

The importance of coastal exposures (see Pakefield and Happisburgh below and Fig. 3.2) and submerged landscapes for reconstructing the details of past coastline development has thrust the sedimentary archives preserved in both near-shore and offshore contexts into the spotlight during the past fifteen years. The identification of extensive and archaeologically important deposits associated with marine and intertidal deposits at Boxgrove in West Sussex drew attention to these sedimentary environments as offering preservation potential which

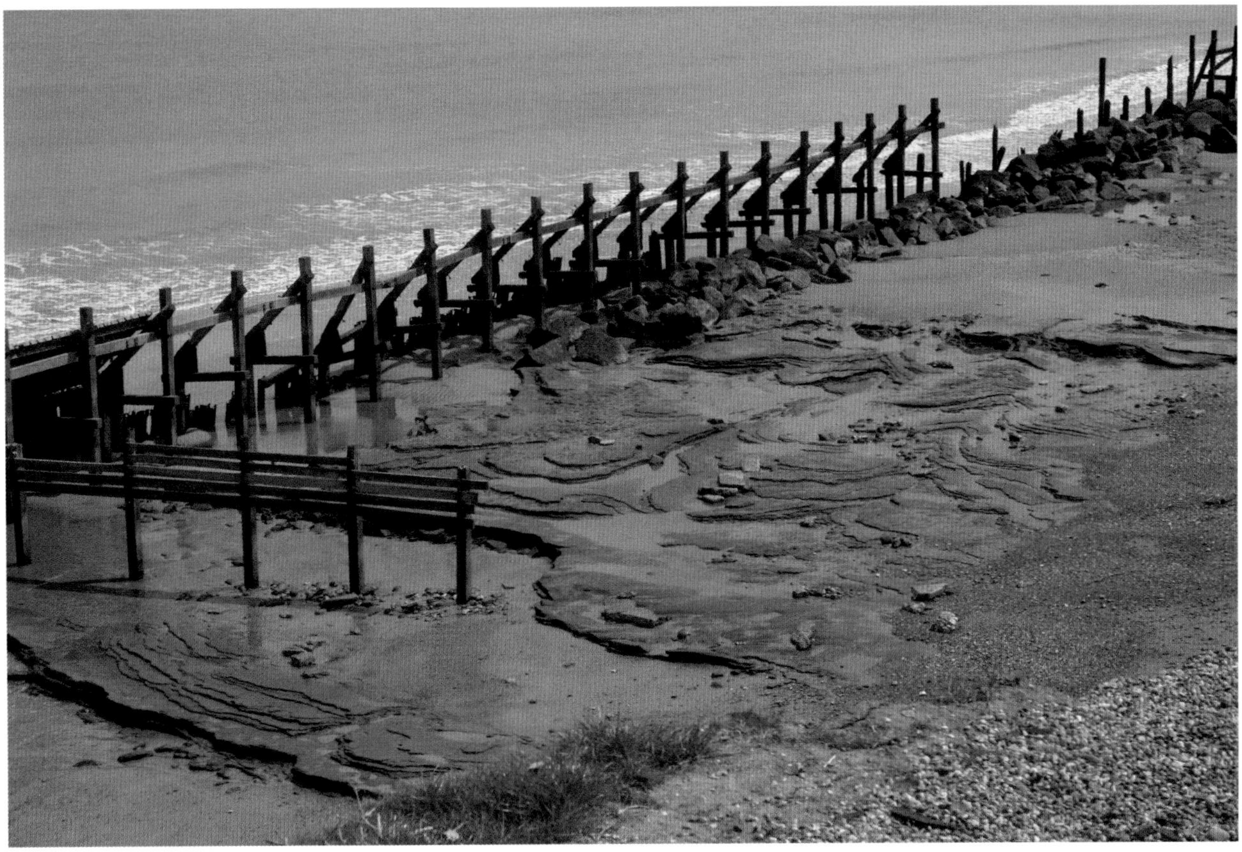

Fig. 3.2 Cromerian sediments exposed on the foreshore at Happisburgh, Norfolk

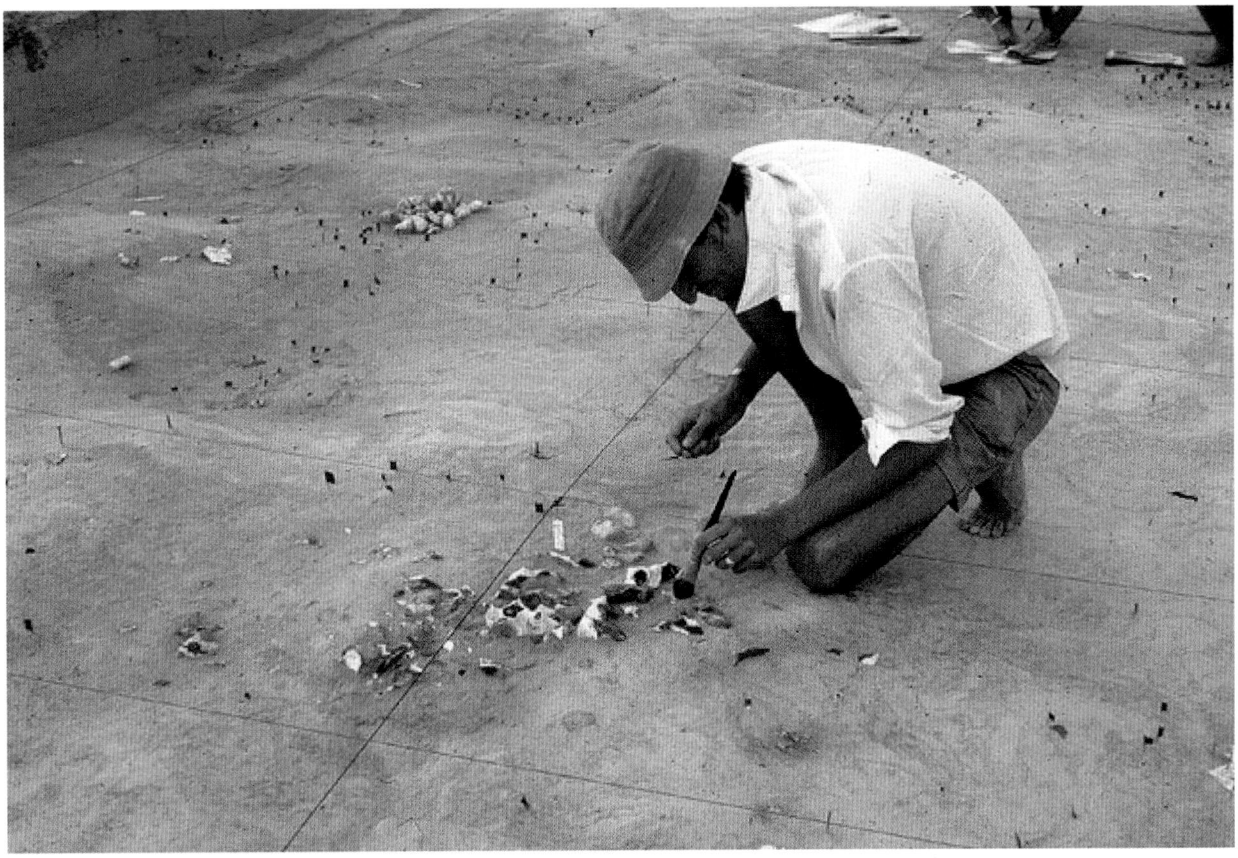

Fig. 3.3 Excavation of fine-grained deposits and in-situ *archaeology at the horse butchery site GTP17, Boxgrove*

matched, and sometimes exceeded, the level of detail from fluvial deposits that had previously contributed to our understanding of human occupation history (Fig. 3.3). With this recognition came an understanding that the connectivity and relative interplay of coastal and terrestrial resources necessitated an approach to Palaeolithic archaeology that was not confined by modern geographical boundaries. Marine and regressional deposits could be found inland at altitudes of up to 40m above modern sea-level, and terrestrial deposits were preserved at depths in the sea waters around Britain.

Rapid mechanised development of the aggregate extraction industry during the latter half of the 20th century – a recurring theme throughout this volume – impacted heavily on both near and offshore assets. Marine deposits preserved at elevations above sea-level were heavily exploited in both Sussex and Hampshire from the 1970s onwards and offshore dredging of gravel deposits increasingly actively targets submerged fluvial contexts (Wessex Archaeology 2008; Tizzard *et al.* 2015).

FLOTSAM OF THE ICE AGE: THE POTENTIAL OF THE SUBMERGED RESOURCES AS REVEALED BY FINDS

It has long been recognised that the fringes of coastal northern Europe were not as fixed as it might at first appear. The coastal and intertidal exposures of submerged forests (Reid 1913), peats (Hazell 2008) and bone-bearing channels revealed after storms and at low tides not only informed early scientific studies but had long fired the collective imagination of people deep in our medieval past and possibly earlier in prehistory. The occurrence of stone fish traps, tree stumps and other traces of apparent terrestrial activity has given rise to a deep, embedded mythological tradition of submerged lands and lost villages throughout the coastal areas of the continent. These include the Tír na nÓg of Irish mythology, Cité d'Ys of Breton mythology and the Welsh equivalent – Cantre'r Gwaelod – a legendary drowned kingdom in Cardigan Bay (Kavanagh and Bates in press).

In the 20th century, the intensification of seabed trawling, private collection from the foreshore and the development of professional archaeology and Quaternary science, started to lead to an understanding of the reality behind these myths. Fishermen's nets gave rise to abundant finds of ice age and early Holocene fauna, stone and bone artefacts and palaeoenvironmental remains including tree stumps. Despite the unsystematic nature of this collection, it

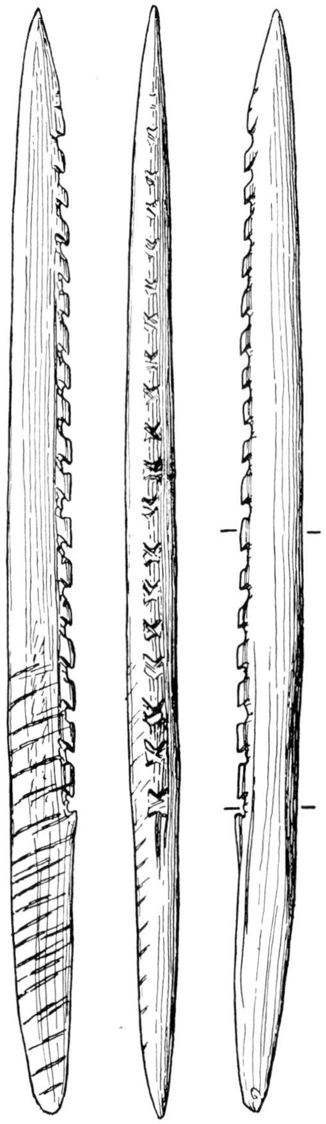

Fig. 3.4 Barbed antler point, discovered by the trawler Colinda from the surface of the bed of the North Sea in 1931(from Clarke and Godwin 1956)

Fig. 3.5 A large commercial trawler. These vessels, along with marine extraction activities, are undoubtedly having a damaging effect to the offshore record. Through proper management under the NSPRMF, this destruction is monitored, controlled and utilised to provide investigations of the deeply submerged archaeological record (Wessex Archaeology)

firmly demonstrated that deposits preserving stone tools and organic material in remarkable condition were widespread across the bed of the North Sea (Gaffney *et al.* 2009). The find, in 1931, by the trawler Colinda was instrumental here. The skipper, Captain Pilgrim E Lockwood, recovered a barbed antler point dating to the Mesolithic period from a block of peat 25 miles off the Norfolk coast (Fig. 3.4). The find demonstrated that there lay, preserved in submerged organic deposits, exceptional archaeology of a type that was to take British archaeology a couple of decades to equal on land, with Clark's Star Carr excavations. Today we know the area of former submerged landscape as Doggerland, after the shallow bank of the same name known to millions through the shipping forecast, a term first used in this context by Bryony Coles (1998).

Today, trawling is still the most effective way of recovering faunal and artefactual material from the sea, given the practical difficulties of using divers or submersibles to search large areas. Specialist trawlers have been in operation for the past 20 years as a result of partnerships between Dutch fishermen and museums to undertake controlled trawls of the seabed and systemic study of the recovered material (Fig. 3.5; Peeters *et al.* 2009). While an improvement on the *ad hoc* nature of previous studies of submerged material, these trawls produce material for which it is still difficult to ascertain information on time-depth, association and context. The trawls are also destructive to underlying deposits, not to mention marine life, and represent a level of fieldwork standards that would not be tolerated in terrestrial contexts. But perhaps this sacrifice is worth making, given our low levels of understanding and logistical issues surrounding other methods of recovery, the widespread threat and damage occurring through uncontrolled commercial activities and unregulated trade in fossils from the same deposits. The loss to what appear to be extensive deposits seems minimal in comparison to the information and awareness being gained by such studies. It will be up to future researchers to judge whether the cost was worth it. That will be dependent upon us now capitalising on

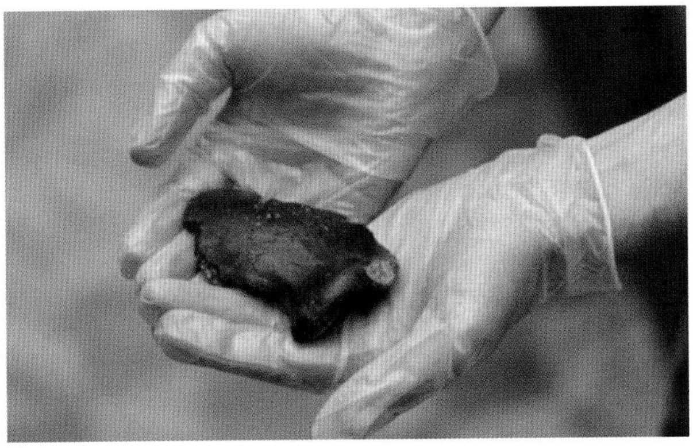

Fig. 3.6 Portion of frontal bone from the skull of a Neanderthal, dredged from the Zeeland Bank off the Dutch coast

these early gains in understanding through coarse investigation methods and evolving a fully mature investigative and management approach to the submerged record.

The collections of fauna recovered thus far are overwhelmingly dominated by cold-stage mammals of the last glacial, representing a cool period of low sea-level when Doggerland was last fully exposed as a terrestrial land surface. Finds of woolly rhinoceros (*Coelodonta antiquitatis*), mammoth (*Mammuthus primigenius*), bison (*Bos bison*) and reindeer (*Rangifer tarandus*) attest to cool, open environments of the mammoth steppe that dominated here during the 90,000 years of the last glacial. However the fauna also contains species that hint at different environments, ranging from marine mammals from previous high sea-level interglacials, through to warm terrestrial mammals such as straight-tusked elephant (*Palaeoloxodon antiquus*), aurochs (*Bos primigenius*), red deer (*Cervus elephas*) and hippopotamus (*Hippopotamus sp.*). Early Pleistocene faunas representing diverse environments are also present, including the southern mammoth (*Mammuthus meridionalis*), musk ox (*Ovibos moschatus*) and beaver (*Castor fiber*). Part of the explanation for the presence of deposits of different ages close to the sea floor in the southern North Sea is that the area is part of a structural basin, sinking in the middle and infilling with sediments primarily derived from the river Rhine. At the edges of this basin older sediments lie close to the sea-bed while towards the middle of the basin older sediments lie deeply buried beneath more recent ones.

The finds also include two very significant and rare species. In 2008, the Dutch trawler TX-1 collected the partial leg bone of a large scimitar-toothed cat (*Homotherium latidens*) usually thought to have been absent from northern Europe after 600,000 BP. This and other dated finds (Reumer *et al.* 2003) are significant in suggesting that large cats might have either continued to occupy northern Europe through the Middle and Late Pleistocene, albeit in low numbers, or had a range which occasionally extended into the Doggerland region. Amongst the bones dredged from the Zeeland Bank, an area that has also produced many handaxes, a frontal bone of a Neanderthal has recently been reported (Fig. 3.6; Hublin *et al.* 2009). Although lacking information about the original context of the find, which could have had an origin as diverse as a formal burial or a hyena den bone accumulation, the find indicates the potential of the submerged deposits to preserve scientifically important human fossil material. The bones of Neanderthals and other human species will undoubtedly be rare, as will those of the sabre-toothed cats, since top level predators occur in lower numbers than herd mammals like bison. But research may develop to allow future researchers to home in on suitable areas, especially by targeting the concentrations of human artefacts that might indicate occupation sites.

It should, however, be noted that the scenario presented for the southern North Sea (Doggerland) is but one facet of our submerged landscapes, and that the English Channel region presents a very different set of features and problems for investigation (Gupta *et al.* 2007). The prime reason for the preservation of stacked sequences of sediments in the southern North Sea rests, as has just been mentioned, on the fact that it is a geological basin that is subsiding over time. During the Pleistocene this basin was periodically filled by sediments (primarily) derived from the Rhine system. These buried older sediments beneath thick sequences of deposits in the centre, but left those same deposits closer to the seabed at the margins. In contrast, conditions in the English Channel are essentially defined by uplift, meaning that erosion rather than deposition dominates and only in incised river valleys, such as those of the Arun or Seine, are sediments preserved. This means that across much of the Channel bedrock dominates close to the seabed. The result of these very different sets of geological and geomorphological conditions means that not only are differences seen in the nature and types of sequences present but that preservational potential will vary between the areas and different methodologies will be needed to investigate the sequences.

Through developments in research frameworks and a truer picture of threats and potentials, archaeologists and Quaternary scientists have developed an impetus towards greater understanding in the North Sea and English Channel (Coles 1998; Flemming 2002; 2004). As part of this drive, the first decade of the 21st century saw significant research funding through the ALSF aimed at increasing our understanding of these resources, and developing tools for their effective management and preservation. Today we can recognise that there are a number of different elements to the 'marine' archaeological resource:

- Elements of erstwhile terrestrial landscapes, formed during low sea-level stands (colder climatic episodes), that are now submerged beneath the sea
- Elements of terrestrial landscapes that were submerged due to subsidence of formerly dry ground or when topographic features may have prevented flooding of low-lying areas during sea-level high-stands (warm, interglacial periods)
- Elements of marine sedimentary sequences preserved as ribbons of deposits around our coastlines as raised beach/marine sequences from erstwhile high sea-levels

While challenging, the present day terrestrial components of these marine records (see above) could be dealt with using a range of existing techniques of geological survey and mapping. However, the offshore record presents real challenges to effective understanding: its depth, relative inaccessibility and vast spatial distribution requiring the application of cutting edge science-based investigation, costly technology and a new breed of highly skilled marine Palaeolithic archaeologists. While very much in its infancy as a discipline, significant developments have been made through ALSF-funded research. These have resulted in a new and exciting perspective on ancient landscapes as dynamic, transitional and continuous surfaces that require an approach that can fully integrate terrestrial and marine assets of the ancient human occupation record. The examples presented here give an account of how the submerged resource provides opportunities to examine established and emerging ecological niches of critical importance to ancient hunting and gathering populations.

FIRST EUROPEANS AND DYNAMIC COASTS: PAKEFIELD/HAPPISBURGH MARINE SURVEY

The confirmation in the first decade of the 21st century that genuine artefacts were present beneath Middle Pleistocene tills (perhaps in excess of 750,000 years old) transformed our understanding of the colonisation of the British Isles. Leading this new understanding of human presence in Britain was the Leverhulme-funded AHOB Project, with some landform work also carried out under the auspices of ALSF.

The first important finds were from the site of Pakefield, on the Suffolk coast, where a collection of struck flint artefacts was found in sedimentary deposits relating to an ancient river, draining into what was to later become the North Sea (Parfitt *et al.* 2005; Preece and Parfitt 2012). Environmental evidence suggests that temperatures at Pakefield during the time of human occupation were as warm, if not warmer, than they are today. Beetle fauna indicate July temperatures between 18 and 23°C and mean January/February temperatures between -6 and +4°C. The combined assessment of forest composition, temperature range and the presence of carbonate nodules within the deposits indicated a seasonally dry woodland environment, such as that found in today's Mediterranean zone. The tools were also found alongside the remains of well-preserved fauna that included rhinoceros (*Stephanorhinus hundsheimensis*), hyena (*Crocuta crocuta*), mammoth (*Mammuthus trogontherii*), and sabre-toothed cat (*Homotherium sp.*). The site was dated on the basis of palaeomagnetism and biostratigraphy as early as MIS 19 (*c* 750,000 BP).

In 2005, investigations were undertaken by the AHOB team on the Norfolk coast at Happisburgh some 30 miles north of Pakefield. Here artefacts were recovered from deposits that seemed superficially similar to the context at the former site: freshwater and terrestrial sediments underlying Anglian glacial till. Initially the team investigated a set of deposits exposed on the foreshore at low tide that

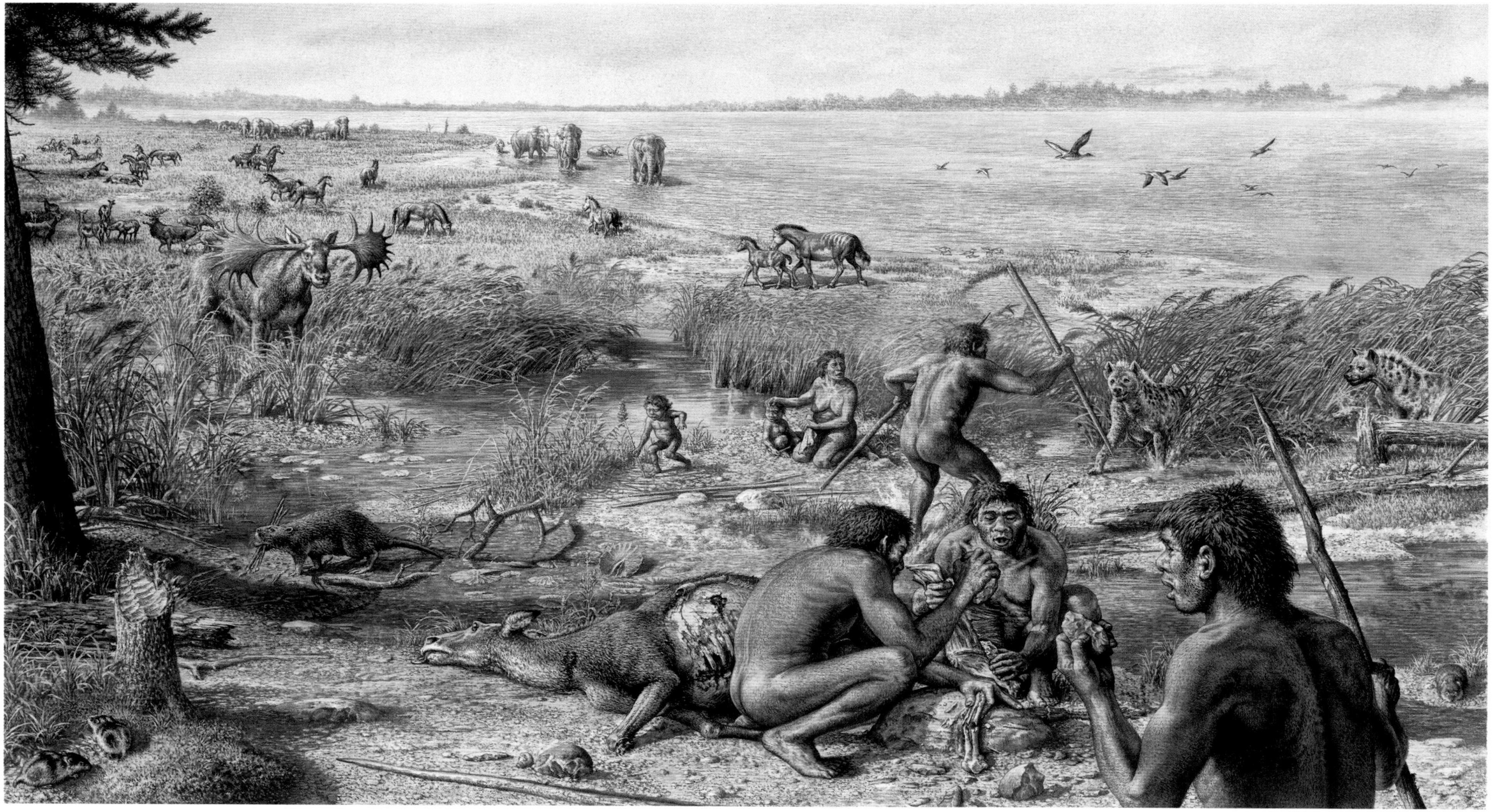

Fig. 3.7 Artist's reconstruction of the boreal woodland environment of Happisburgh. Early Homo *utilised a simple stone tool technology to butcher mammals. It is not known whether these were secured through direct hunting or scavenging of other carnivore kills. Copyright John Sibbick*

produced a single handaxe and other sparsely distributed flakes. When, however, attention was turned to fluvial gravels a few hundred yards to the north of the handaxe site, a different archaeological signature was encountered. Here, 78 simple flint artefacts were recovered from deposits relating to the estuary of a significant river – on the basis of the geological origin its gravels. This river was draining a large portion of lowland Britain including the Midlands, south-east England and possibly parts of Wales (Parfitt *et al.* 2010).

Palaeoenvironmental analysis on sediments from Happisburgh indicated a different climatic profile to that found at Pakefield. At Happisburgh, pollen evidence pointed to a more open woodland of pine and spruce, with the beetle fauna attesting to cooler mean summer temperatures in the range of 16–18°C and winter temperatures averaging 0–3°C. Taken together, the evidence suggests a more continental climate with ecology and temperatures equivalent to those of southern Scandinavia (Fig. 3.7). The dating evidence is based on palaeomagnetism (Bassinot *et al.* 1994) and the presence of Early Pleistocene flora and fauna, including the ancestral mammoth (*Mammuthus meridionalis*), archaic horse (*Equus suessenbornensis*) and *Tsuga* (tree hemlock). These have been used to claim either an MIS 21 age (*c* 860,000–810,000 BP) or an MIS 25 age (*c* 970,000–930,000 BP), although this has been disputed (Westaway 2011).

Unlike the other two key resources for Palaeolithic archaeology to be examined in this chapter (raised beaches and submerged landscapes), the Pakefield and Happisburgh sites point to an exciting and problematic context for evidence of lost landscapes and extinct humans. Both sites presented evidence for hitherto unknown episodes of early human occupation, separated widely in time from each other and later sites in Britain (which show more established human populations after 600,000 BP). Both sites, however, are located on rapidly eroding and retreating coastlines, parts of the coast of Britain that are being reshaped and redefined with almost every passing tide. The rapid erosion on the East Anglian coast is part of a pattern of increased erosion rates that can be seen around the beaches and cliff of many areas in Britain. Partly this appears to be a response to patterns of climate and maritime change that have developed in our own lifetimes, as sea-levels gradually rise and the climatic system gives rise to increasingly common storm events. However, in recent years erosion has been accelerated at sites at some vulnerable coastal locations through a change in costal management policies. For example, the rapid erosion at Happisburgh comes from the abandonment of beach defences maintained for many decades as part of widespread and relatively effective coastal defence measures. The adoption of policies involving managed retreat have seen coasts that were previously 'tamed' and inactive abandoned to the full transformative force of the sea, the relatively soft sediments of the Pleistocene and early Holocene exposed to erosion, and the archaeological evidence preserved within both brought to the surface and at great threat of loss. The archaeology of this intertidal zone faces a clear and present danger. Parts of these precious Pleistocene landscapes are lost every year and without organised responses and assessment it is left to fate alone whether tools or faunal remains are discovered before surf and sediment remove or cover them.

Investigating the offshore record of the North Sea

One response to the discovery of significant sites like Pakefield and Happisburgh on the North Sea coast has been to focus attention on the offshore continuation of the deposits preserved at these sites as part of the near shore seabed and into deeper waters. Between 2004 and 2007 the ALSF funded the *Seabed Prehistory* project (ALSF 3876, 4600, 5401, 5684). Round 2 of the *Seabed Prehistory* project comprised a further 3 years of work again funded by the ALSF through both English Heritage and the Minerals Industry Research Organisation (MIRO) (Tizzard *et al.* 2015).

This ground-breaking project aimed to push existing methodologies to their limits within the marine environment and allow the development of new techniques and protocols for the management and investigations of the off-shore resource. Through the project, methodologies would be developed for characterising deposits and determining the presence or absence of prehistoric archaeology within marine sands and gravels as well as providing guidance to industry.

English Heritage funded four phases of research as part of the *Seabed Prehistory* project:

- Geophysical and geotechnical survey off the coast of Great Yarmouth, Norfolk (Area 240)
- Geophysical and geotechnical survey just offshore from Happisburgh, Norfolk and Pakefield, Suffolk
- Grab sampling survey in the palaeo-Arun, off the coast of Sussex (described later in this chapter)
- A project synthesis, which provided an overall interpretation of the results from each phase, including phases commissioned by MIRO

Area 240 Survey

The background to the project was the long history of seabed gravel extraction as part of the aggregate industry but the specific impetus was the discovery of stone tools and mammal bones within gravels being washed at the SBV Flushing Wharf in Holland. Here, Dutch palaeontologist Jan Meulmeester recovered 75 flint tools, including handaxes, and the remains of mammoth, bison, reindeer and rhinoceros. The gravel producing this rich assemblage of tools and fauna was traced back to a specific area of

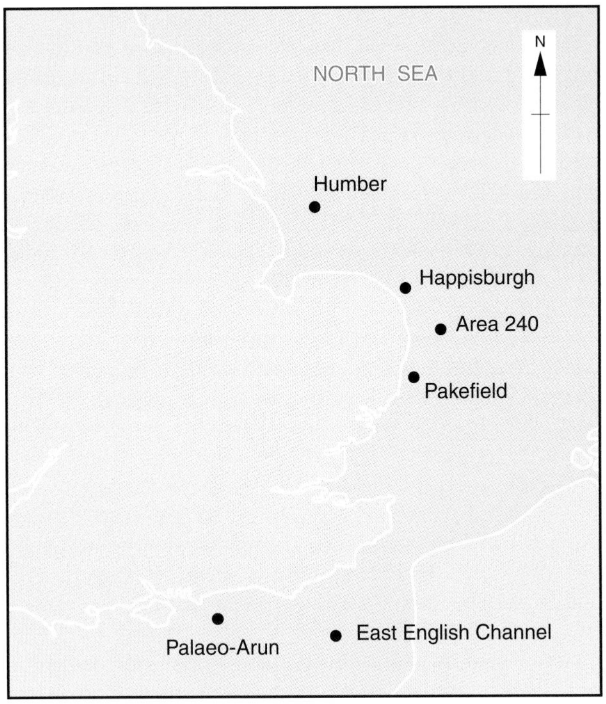

Fig. 3.8 Map of the North Sea showing localities of gravel extraction monitored through ALSF surveys

the seabed: Area 240 situated just 13km off the coast of Great Yarmouth in the southern North Sea (Fig. 3.8). While the original collection of tools was studied by Dutch archaeologists at the University of Leiden, English Heritage commissioned the mapping of the 3 x 1km area of sea floor comprising gravel extraction Area 240 (Wessex Archaeology 2008).

Initially the project sought to collate existing data, bringing together the results of 158 vibracores sunk into the sediments below the sea by the main gravel-extracting contractor Hanson Aggregates Marine Ltd. In addition to this, some 400km of subsurface geophysics were undertaken including side-scan sonar, single beam echo sounders and magnetometer survey. Taken together this allowed the Wessex Archaeology team to build up a picture of the sediments preserved below the sea floor, identifying changes in the sedimentation, and determining the distribution and topography of key deposits. In this way, the team was able to target areas which were likely sources for the dredged artefacts found in the gravels taken to Holland. From the virtual 3D model of the offshore geology target areas were noted and the second phase of the project could allow for focused assessment of sediments during further phases of extraction. This took the form of sieving of up to 17 tonnes of sediment yielding 10 possible flakes but no further handaxes.

Pakefield and Happisburgh Offshore Survey

In response to the exceptional finds made within the intertidal zone at Happisburgh and Pakefield, English Heritage commissioned Wessex Archaeology to assess the possible survival of related deposits in the near-shore zone. Initially, sediment sequences known to contain archaeology exposed in the intertidal zone and cliffs of Pakefield and Yarmouth were mapped and traced offshore using high-resolution geophysical survey followed up with samples taken using a geotechnical vibracore. While the survey was easily able to identify deposits relating to the underlying Wroxham Crag Formation (ancient marine and estuarine deposits), the archaeologically important Cromer Forest Bed Formation (alluvial/terrestrial deposits) appeared entirely absent, having been apparently removed by either glacial or marine erosion. The geophysical survey did not rule out the possibility that these deposits survived close to the shore, but determined that survival was not extensive across the seafloor. The Vibracore survey, comprising 5 cores into the seabed (Fig. 3.9) did, however, confirm that the upper parts of the Wroxam Formation, which contain possible artefacts, were present as part of the submerged offshore record. Dating and palaeo-

Fig. 3.9 Vibracore survey undertaken at Area 240 to map the sea floor off the Yarmouth Coast

environmental samples were taken from these cores to provide an archive of detailed scientific data for further analysis of the age and context of these early archaeological levels.

The survey at Happisburgh was hindered by the remains of offshore coastal defences – the remains of wooden groynes now submerged by the inundating sea. These obstructions prevented the operation of the survey close to the shore and required positioning in deeper, safer water. Perhaps as a consequence, the survey revealed only deposits that were older than the archaeological levels, the sea-bed being below the depth of the river channel that preserved the flakes and fauna in the intertidal site. However, the likelihood is that deposits do survive immediately offshore here, although there is obviously the danger of erosion, a fact which might be corroborated by the occasional finds of organic deposits and fauna rolled amongst the beach material after storms on the Happisburgh shore.

PRESERVED ANCIENT COASTLINES: MAPPING RAISED BEACHES IN SUSSEX AND HAMPSHIRE

The Raised Beach Mapping Project (RBMP)

Historically, a number of sites in the region surrounding Boxgrove have produced Acheulean archaeology. Some of these were known to be associated with identical suites of marine and terrestrial deposits at a similar altitude to the Boxgrove site, about 40m above sea-level (Roberts 1986; Roberts and Parfitt 1999). In the late 1990s Boxgrove was shortlisted for status as a UNESCO World Heritage Site, but it was considered prudent to first establish the true extent of the Boxgrove deposits so that the whole palaeolandscape could be included with the designated area. To this end, a geological survey was initiated in 2001 with the aim of mapping the limits of preserved land surfaces, characterising differences in local sedimentary sequences, and prospecting for future archaeological potential (Pope 2005). The mapping project incorporated reassessment of historical records with trial pitting and borehole surveys across the northern extent of the coastal plain of Sussex and eastern Hampshire. Through 42 field investigations, a full picture of the Boxgrove palaeolandscape became apparent for the first time (Fig. 3.10). The marine deposits and associated cliff line have now been traced for some 26km, between the towns of Westbourne to the west and Arundel to the east. Within this area, some 13km of intact fossiliferous land surface have been identified (Fig. 3.11). These deposits are very similar to those discovered at Boxgrove and have the potential to preserve similar high-resolution behavioural and social information. One horizon, designated the Unit 4c palaeosol, is a single isochronous land surface which has been shown to have developed over a period of 10-50 years. This important unit represents a developing grassland habitat and preserves *in-situ* human activity over the broad time-span of a single hominin generation (Roberts and Parfitt 1999). The realisation that this horizon is now traceable for over 10km opens the possibility that patterns of variation in human activity across a huge spatial area, within a relatively limited timeframe, can now be explored.

The survey also revealed some local environmental variation and has allowed the reconstruction of the topographic setting of the palaeolandscape in finer detail (Pope 2005). The saltmarsh and grassland environments that developed as the interglacial sea retreated appear to have been partially enclosed by two pronounced chalk ridges. These have now been lost to later marine erosion. The two

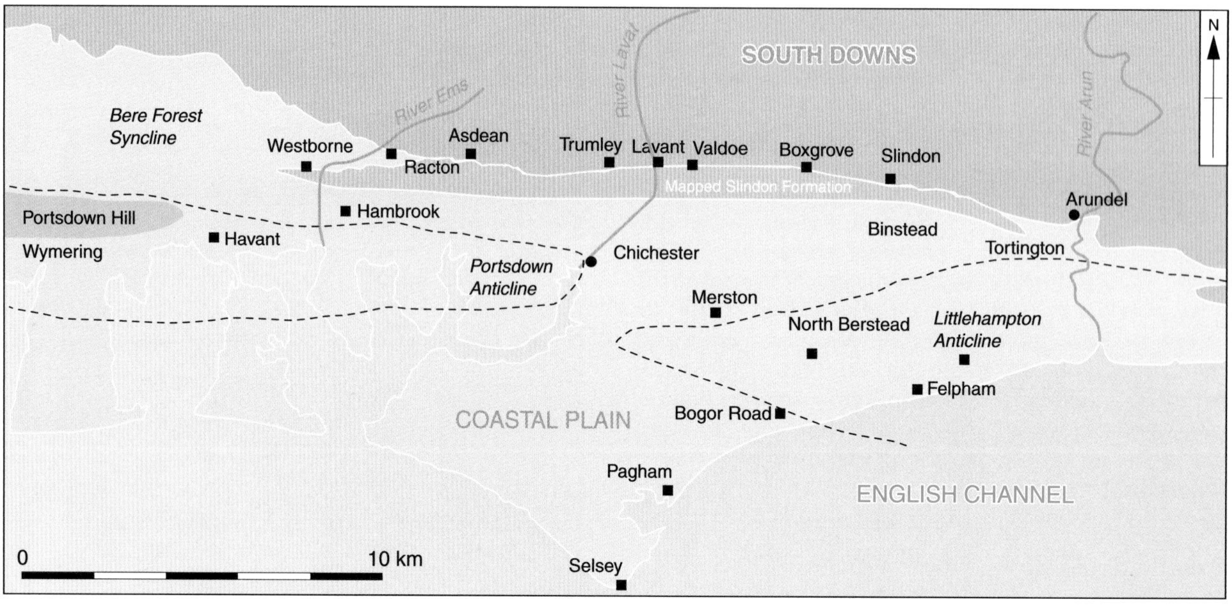

Fig. 3.10 Map showing the 26km extent of the Boxgrove palaeolandscape as mapped through the Raised Beach Mapping project. The dashed lines show the position the chalk bedrock beneath the coastal plain

headlands defined an embayment backed by the imposing 80m chalk cliffs traced along much of the course of the raised beach (Fig. 3.12; Roberts and Pope 2009). A series of spring-fed chalk streams appear to have emptied into this embayment, forming gravel fans at their estuarine mouths, and the project was able to explore the interface of these gravels with the grassland palaeo-land surfaces. In addition, beds of preserved organic remains were identified with potential to help in the reconstruction of local vegetation. At the margins of this embayment, where unfortunately preservation was less good, areas have been located where the cliffs were lower in height and cut into the clay geology

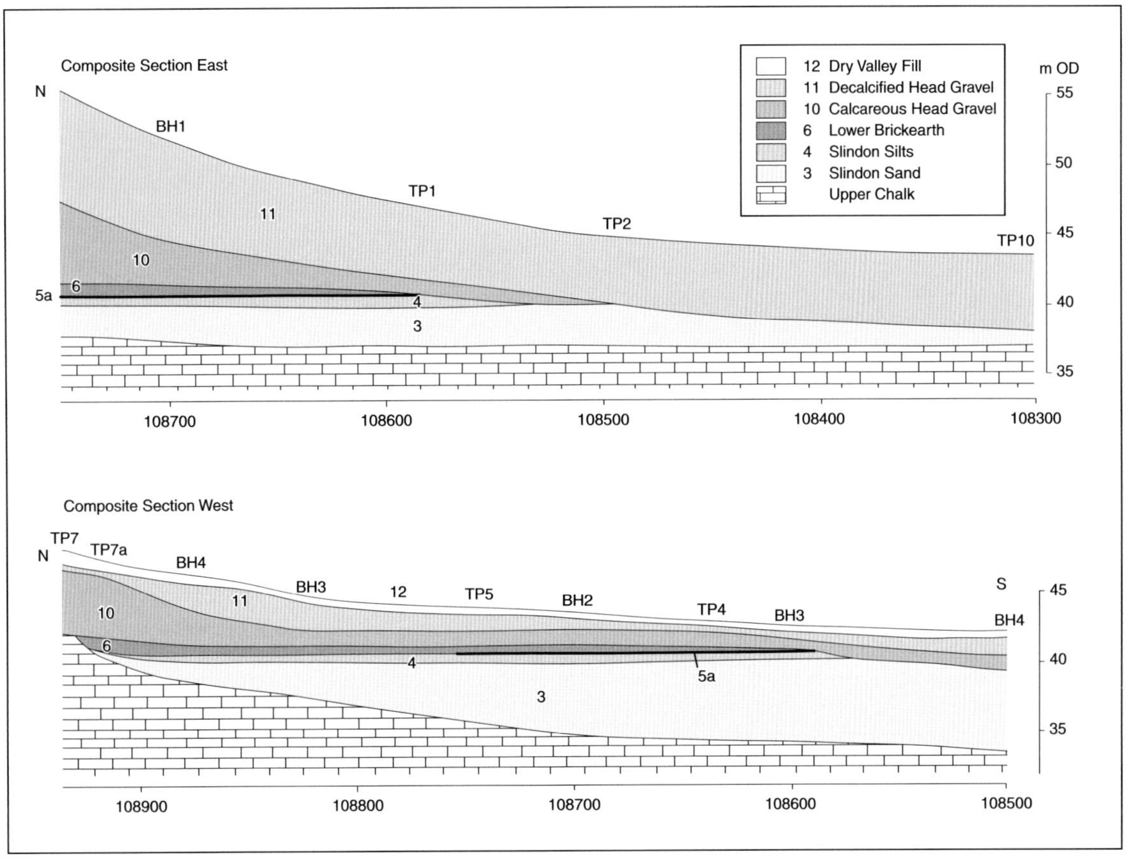

Fig. 3.11 Cross section through the archaeologically important Slindon Silts at the Valdoe, West Sussex. This site presented a direct continuation of the sedimentary sequence observed at the main Boxgrove site but lay some 6km to west (Unit 5a is the ferric manganese layer representing marshy conditions, also found at Boxgrove)

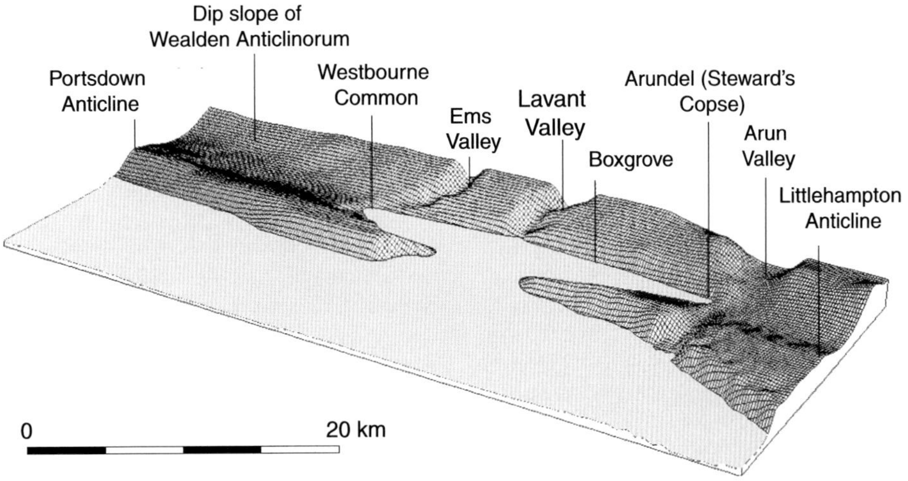

Fig. 3.12 Reconstruction of the partially enclosed marine embayment defining the Boxgrove Raised B each during the MIS 13 interglacial

of Tertiary bedrock rather than chalk. These varying local environments may have produced different local ecologies and provoked different behavioural responses among the human groups occupying them. Further prospective excavation – small test pits as described in Chapter 2, for example – may help to isolate some of these behavioural differences. One testable hypothesis is that human groups would have curated and reused stone tools more extensively in these marginal areas away from local raw material sources (Pope *et al.* 2009).

The results of the RBMP clearly show that it is no longer valid to consider Boxgrove a single, isolated site. Instead, it sits at the heart of a vast, preserved prehistoric landscape buried between 2 and 20m below the modern soil horizon of the Sussex coastal plain. While quarries such as those at Boxgrove still provide the best chance of getting at extensive tracts of this landscape, the discovery of a number of valley-side locations, where the deposits rest close to the surface, holds open the possibility of discovering new locales rich in the traces of human activity.

The Palaeolithic Archaeology of the Sussex/Hampshire Coastal Corridor (PASHCC)

Directly complementing the RBMP was the ALSF research initiative aimed at understanding Pleistocene sedimentation of the lower coastal plain in West Sussex and Hampshire. Like the RBMP, it aimed to map and characterise marine, intertidal and terrestrial sequences associated with raised beach landforms dating from the more recent parts of the Quaternary record of the area. The *Palaeolithic Archaeology of the Sussex/Hampshire Coastal Corridor* (PASHCC) project ran between 2005 and 2007. It was the culmination of almost 20 years of field and desk-based research in the West Sussex coastal plain by Martin Bates and other workers (Bates 1993; 2001; Bates *et al.* 1997; 2000; 2003; 2004; 2007a; 2007b; 2007c; Bates and Wenban-Smith 2011). As with the RBMP it took a multi-disciplinary approach to landscape investigation, building a team comprising archaeologists and earth scientists from a number of institutions throughout the United Kingdom.

While an understanding of the nature and distribution of Pleistocene deposits relating to the Middle and Late Pleistocene has been developed over a period of nearly 150 years, until recently there had been little formal work aimed at integrating the range of existing datasets into a single coherent model of sediment distribution and archaeological potential. The PASHCC offered the possibility of understanding the relationship between sea-level change, climate cycles, tectonic processes and human activity across 400,000 years of the Pleistocene, and formed a record contiguous with submerged deposits to be investigated by some of the same team in the Transition Zone Mapping Project (see below).

The key objectives were straightforward: to obtain a better understanding of the distribution of sediments likely to contain Palaeolithic archaeology, the nature of the archaeological materials, and the ages of the sediments containing the archaeology. To do this, it focussed on integrating and assessing existing datasets, which could later be tested and ground-truthed through targeted fieldwork. This methodology was different to that used in the RBMP because an extensive body of commercial and research data already existed, resulting from the more urbanised and industrial nature of modern landuse on the lower coastal plain compared to the relatively unspoilt landscape of the Westbourne-Arundel Raised Beach (where prior knowledge was minimal). For the lower coastal plain the project aimed to develop a more detailed understanding of the distribution of key sedimentary sequences, constrain the age through dating of key sedimentary sequences, and determine the potential for the survival of Palaeolithic archaeology across a range of timescales. The area examined was also highly significant, comprising the eastern margins of the Solent river system and the extensive suites of preserved fluvial terrace gravels rich in Palaeolithic archaeology, the main body of the Sussex Raised Beaches of the lower coastal plain (including the key localities of Aldingbourne, Brighton-Norton and Pagham) as well as the rivers Arun and Adur.

For the West Sussex coastal plain, large archives of borehole data were collated from work previously undertaken through mineral assessment surveys by the BGS (Lovell and Nancarrow 1983). These were integrated with other archives of borehole observations and use to create a subsurface sediment model using geological modelling software. Investigations utilising geophysical survey, borehole drilling and test pitting were then undertaken as part of a programme of fieldwork, allowing the development of mapped transects for the geological sequence across the West Sussex coastal plain. Sediment bodies were sampled for indicators of past palaeoenvironmental conditions, including detailed analysis of microfossils (foraminifera and ostracoda), and dating work was undertaken using OSL (Huntley *et al.* 1985; Murray and Wintle 2000; Rhodes 1988; Bates *et al.* 2010) and Amino Acid Geochronology (McCarroll 2002; Penkman *et al.* 2008; 2011).

Alongside the identification and study of marine and intertidal sequences relating to earlier interglacials, the research located an extensive distribution of non-marine sediments associated with cold climate and low sea-level events. The added complexity raised the possibility of more complete sequences of climate and landscape change being preserved as part of the overall sediment body on the coastal plain, offering the potential for better reconstructing the interplay between marine and terrestrial phases of sedimentation than had been previously thought possible. Perhaps among the most surprising results of the study was the fact that the team's preconceptions regarding the range of deposits present in the area were quickly demonstrated to be wrong. It soon became apparent during the fieldwork phase that extensive bodies of previously unrecognised sediments were present in the area, radically modifying our understanding of the landscape history and demanding a rethink of the archaeological potential of the area (Fig. 3.13).

In the west of the study area, the nature of sedimentation and the formulated response were different. The Eastern Solent and Test Valley (previously studied by Allen and Gibbard 1993) differed from that of the West Sussex coastal plain in presenting a far more restricted corridor for investigation, associated with narrow ribbons of river terrace sediments. The area was also more substantially developed, being largely covered by the urban areas of Portsmouth, Gosport and Southampton. This restricted the scope for field research, so the project focussed on integrating the detailed records that existed in archives rather than developing new datasets through fieldwork.

This work confirmed the continued validity of existing schemes of terrace mapping and allowed previous understanding to be refined and built upon, through dating work (Briant *et al.* 2006) and reconstruction of river development (Briant *et al.* 2012). Beyond the academic output from the project, the evidence recovered has been integrated into a GIS model in which both river valleys and the coastal plain have been divided into a series of mapped zones that characterise the nature of the sediments within the zone and define the potential for Palaeolithic archaeology. These zones were then utilised as the basis for eventual integration with the offshore record as part of the subsequent Transition Zone Mapping Project (see below), and now form the basis for an enhanced HER within parts of West Sussex and Hampshire.

THE LOST RIVER: SUBMERGED LANDSCAPES OF THE ENGLISH CHANNEL

Out of the wide-ranging work funded through the ALSF, few projects brought the topography of the submerged Pleistocene landscapes to life as clearly as the detailed offshore mapping of the submerged Palaeo-Arun River. This project concentrated on a clearly defined marine landform that had a relatively well-understood onshore continuation and demonstrated archaeological potential. Led by Sanjeev Gupta from Imperial College, it aimed to integrate multiple datasets into a detailed landform model of the submerged Palaeo-Arun Valley system (Fig. 3.14) and assess from sediment samples the palaeoenvironmental and archaeological potential (Gupta *et al.* 2004; 2007; Wessex Archaeology 2008).

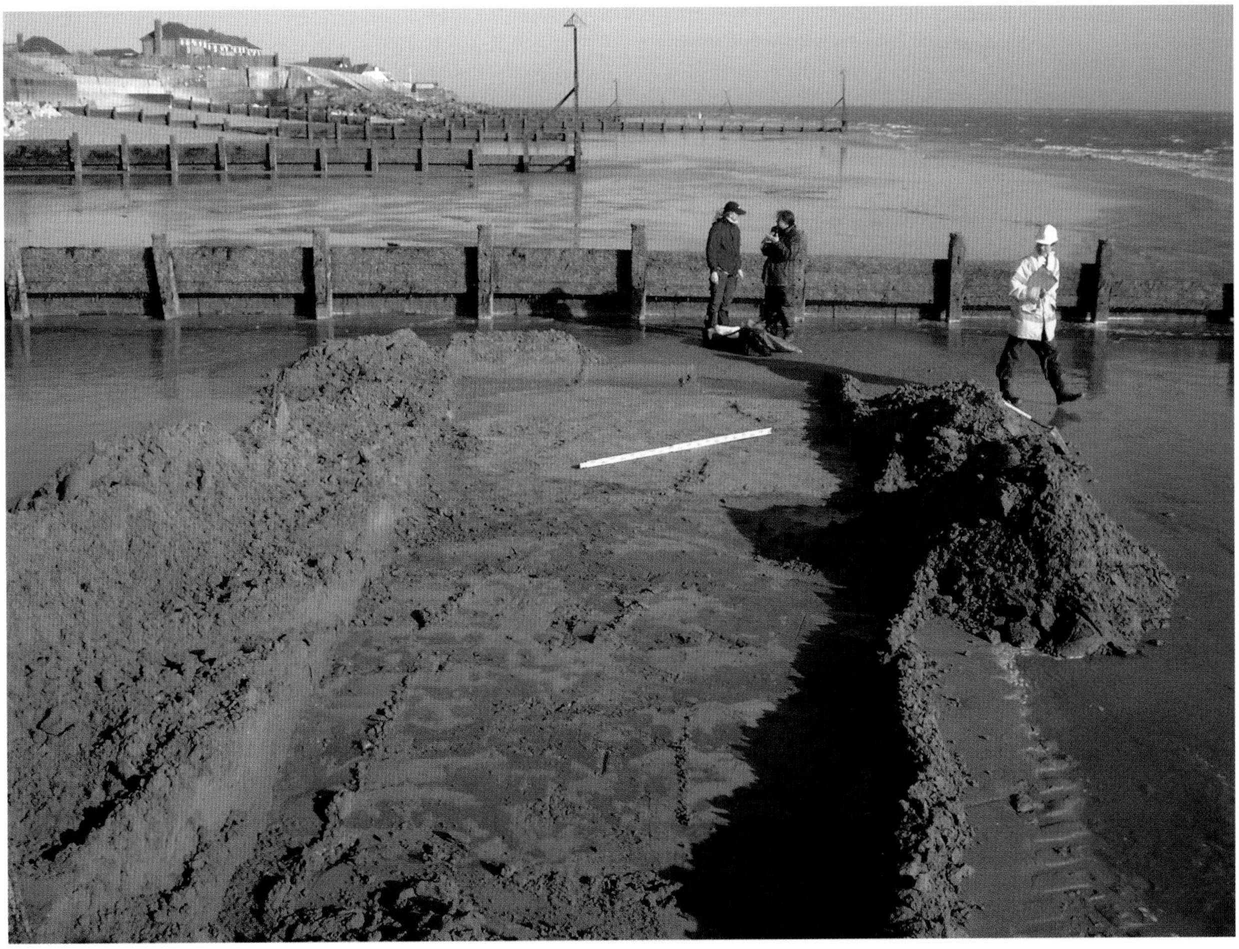

Fig. 3.13 Mapping of marine, intertidal and terrestrial deposits undertaken by the PASHCC project

The results led to the emergence of a highly detailed and focused dataset comprising a level of terrain mapping normally limited to terrestrial contexts. This allowed details of the submerged topography to emerge in high resolution, allowing the identification of specific features of the Palaeo-Arun Valley landform, including terraces and details of the submerged floodplain. Vibracore sampling established not only the presence of well-developed Pleistocene and early Holocene environmental sequences but also the presence of human activity (evidenced by collections of apparently humanly struck stone artefacts). The project provides perhaps the most vivid example of translation from understanding of terrestrial prehistoric assets to the targeting of likely offshore potential, with dedicated mapping of the distribution of significant sedimentary contexts and recovery of apparently archaeological material. The success stemmed from the scale of enquiry aimed at understanding a key landform rather than a wide area of seabed. As such it perhaps provides a research model for how exploration of the submerged landscape around Britain might proceed, and an indication of the resources involved in progressing from desk-based assessment and research design to recovery of archaeology.

There are, however, a number of problems with offshore work that need to be addressed. The nature of the identified and discussed features do not fit into the normal terrestrial models used by scientists to understand geochronology (eg the Thames terrace sequence: Bridgland 1994). Interpreting archaeological evidence such as stone artefacts can also be problematic as we are not able to carry out the usual range of analysis of material in context, which can help us determine the role of natural processes in the formation of these assemblages. However, as increasingly high-resolution datasets are collected from onshore and offshore, attempts can be made to understand this evidence at increasing levels of complexity. Central to future work will be the development of strategies that can help establish the nature of site formation processes in forming archaeological assemblages found offshore, and developing methodological approaches, such as transition zone studies described below, that can link the better understood terrestrial deposits with their offshore counterparts.

CONTIGUOUS PALAEO-LANDSCAPE RECONSTRUCTION: TRANSITION ZONE MAPPING

Another project aimed at taking a fully integrated approach to linking offshore sedimentation with the terrestrial record was undertaken by the ALSF-funded *Transition Zone Mapping Project* (TZMP), led by Dr Richard Bates. The transition zone is that part of the coastline between low water mark and deeper offshore waters in which geophysical surveys are safely undertaken. The nucleus of the TZMP was a comprehensive review of the methodologies available to enhance our understanding of the relationship between onshore and offshore records. These included seismic, sonar and electrical seabed and subsurface mapping techniques and ground truthing using borehole data from commercial and public borehole records of both the onshore and offshore records. Information from all these datasets was evaluated and integrated, leading to the development of a continuous zoned map of Pleistocene sedimentation and topography across the West Sussex Coastal Plain and extending some 12 miles out under the sea floor.

This project focused on the Sussex coast between the mouth of the River Arun at Littlehampton and Chichester Harbour, a modern marine inlet some 12 miles to the west. In between these points sits a low-lying peninsula coastline known as Selsey Bill, a projecting triangle of largely Tertiary solid geology overlain by Pleistocene Head and raised beach

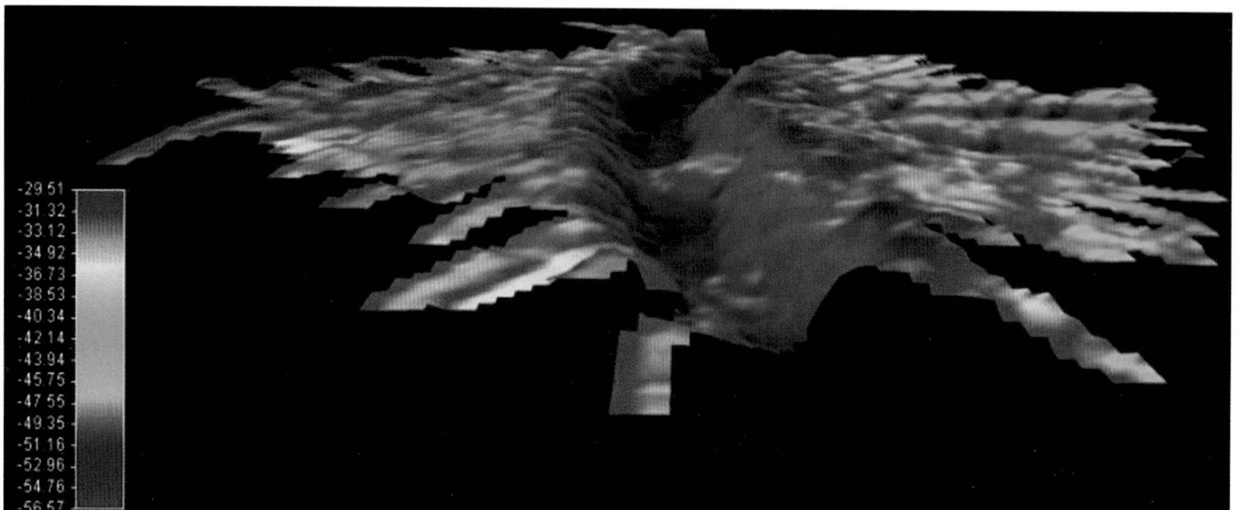

Fig. 3.14 Bathymetric survey of the palaeo-Arun Valley mapped by Gupta et al. *(2004)*

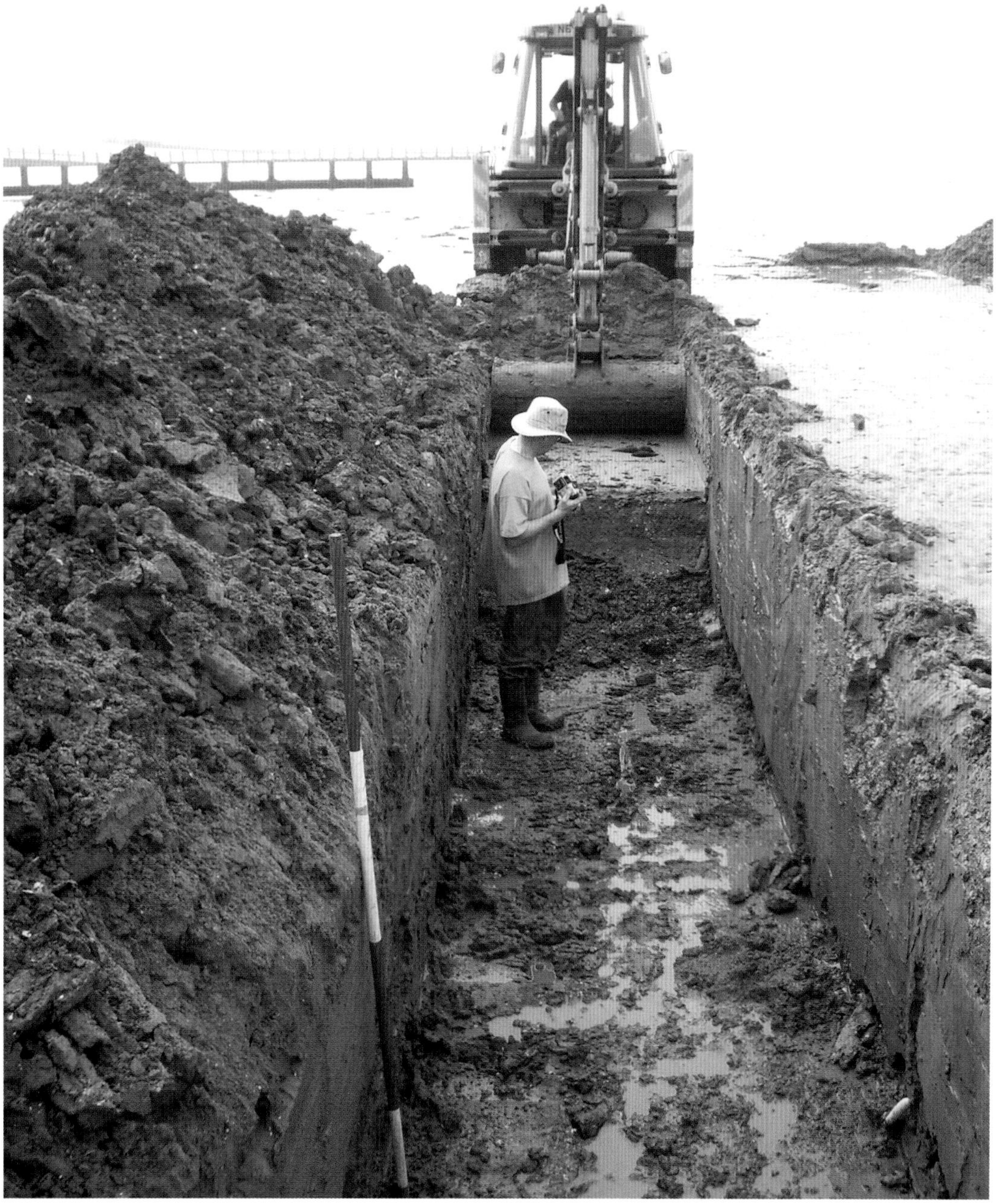

Fig. 3.15 Excavating fluvial deposits from the Middle Pleistocene Earnley Channel on Selsey Bill, West Sussex

deposits and dissected by Pleistocene fluvial channels and mostly infilled Holocene marine inlets. The Pleistocene geology of the coastline and its immediate terrestrial hinterland has been intensively studied since the late 19th century, from early work by Reid (1904) through West and Sparks (1960) to a substantial body of research and commercial geoarchological recording led by Martin Bates and augmented by other researchers including Chris Pine, Mark Roberts and Matt Pope (Bates *et al.* 1997; 2010; Roberts and Pope 2009).

The work characterised the nature and extent of raised beach formation across the Selsey peninsula, which forms a substantial portion of the West Sussex lower coastal plain. The modern topography lies at less than 30m OD, and constitutes two clearly defined raised beaches:

- The Pagham Raised Beach, which has its wave cut bench at 0.5m OD
- The older Brighton Norton Raised Beach at 8m OD

In between these two beaches further raised beach deposits outcrop at intervening altitudes, possibly comprising a continuous, if patchily preserved, record of sea-level and climate change between 250,000 and 120,000 BP.

Preserved both under and over this record of marine level change are north-south orientated alluvial sequences that appear to be the antecedents of drainage systems that once flowed across the coastal plain draining the South Downs escarpment to the north. These channels are best seen after storm events on the foreshore around Selsey Bill where scour exposes the alluvial sedimentation at low tide. Discrete channels can be seen displaying a range of depositional regimes from high energy fluvial gravels through to organic channel margin deposits and estuarine/marine sediments. They range in date from perhaps 500,000 BP through to the early Holocene, and contain excellent records of organics, fauna and occasional lithic artefacts (Fig. 3.15, Box 2.4 and Fig. 2.22; Bates *et al.* 2009). These channels provide an excellent record of palaeoenvironments, and are undoubtedly also preserved further inland, where they are covered by depths of Pleistocene Head deposits, and out to sea where they are submerged and buried beneath marine sediment.

The TZMP successfully met its primary objective, which was to create a seamless model characterising Pleistocene sediments from the dry terrestrial zone, through intertidal and nearshore contexts and into the offshore, submerged record (Bates *et al.* 2007a; Bates *et al.* 2007b; Bates *et al.* 2009). Rather than simply attempt to develop isolated models of offshore sedimentation, or correlate sub-bottom samples with the geological sequence of the shore, this approach aimed to create contiguously mapped datasets that fully encompassed the transition zone. The project was important in both methodological terms, where a new paradigm and standard was established for the mapping of offshore and transition zone records, and also in integrating pre-existing datasets and extending understanding directly aimed at the recovery of archaeological material. The first step in these explorations is a multibeam survey, which provides detailed information of the seabed topography and, at a broad scale, can be taken to represent the landscape at the time of occupation (minus any sandwave fields etc). This would be followed by sub-bottom profiling to ascertain where any bodies of sediment exist in pockets in the landscape or as river terrace sequences associated with major drainage. The final stages involve coring, remotely operated vehicles (ROV) and diving work.

In the test area the project was able to identify clearly where gaps in data existed, allowing for future targeted surveys. It also identified areas where the preservation of fluvial terraces was likely to be better, generally in deeper water where sea-level change may have proceeded more quickly at the beginning and end of interglacial periods. The project also flagged up the need for access to datasets from the oil and gas industry and offshore dredging and was able to develop clear statements regarding Palaeolithic and palaeoenvironmental potential, likely levels of significance and key research questions. This represents a significant first step in developing a basis for future targeted fieldwork both as mitigation of offshore industrial impacts on the Pleistocene aggregate resource and as strategic research projects.

To date, the TZMP represents the most comprehensive attempt to integrate onshore and offshore data, and provides a benchmark model for how the offshore record can begin to be integrated with the terrestrial component. This raises our overall understanding of both as a single depositional system, and installs the Pleistocene sedimentary configuration as the significant boundaries rather than modern coastlines. Transition zone mapping at Happisburgh is now underway following the lines outlined in the TZMP.

THE 21ST CENTURY EXPLORATION OF DOGGERLAND AND THE SUBMERGED ENGLISH CHANNEL: NORTH SEA PREHISTORY RESEARCH AND MANAGEMENT FRAMEWORK

The culmination of the strands of research discussed above is not yet, unfortunately, a mature and developed archaeology of the submerged landscapes of northern Europe. We must consider this a discipline and exploration area that, having emerged from infancy, is still only taking tentative steps towards an effective methodological approach. While the resources and sophisticated techniques exist to assess potential, it is still trawling which provides the source of most recovered artefacts and faunal material.

The exploitation of offshore gravel deposits is now being brought under national and international management through resource protection and exploitation strategies (Peeters *et al.* 2009) and the marine licensing system brought into force in April 2011 under the auspices of the Marine Management Organisation. Yet it is arguably still the case that where high potential is determined neither the resources nor the methodologies are in place to adequately assess it, let alone recover high quality archaeological and palaeoenvironmental information. Indeed, actually ascertaining potential (high or low) remains difficult where research questions remain unarticulated. Without an effective moratorium on marine gravel extraction – which is not likely to happen in the current or any other economic climate – it is not possible to say that we have anything more than a degree of oversight and awareness of the potential destruction to the records of these drowned ice age and early Holocene landscapes.

But great leaps have been made in developing a coherent, and necessarily international, consensus that strategies and research methods need to be developed, and that the resource requires urgent protection and continued improvements in assessment and research. Perhaps the most concrete and hopeful outcome of this focus has been the *North Sea Prehistory Research and Management Framework* (NSPMF), a document funded and produced by international bodies and researchers including

English Heritage. First published in 2009 and conceived of as a living document to be updated as new finds are made and understanding develops, the NSPMF is an agreed international statement on the prehistoric potential of the submerged record and a commitment to developing research and protection of the resource. The initiative began with meetings in the Netherlands and led to the formation of a network of heritage managers and researchers from countries fringing the North Sea and English Channel, taking regional understanding and attempting to correlate across records (eg Fischer 2004; Fitch *et al.* 2005; Gibbard and Cohne 2008; Gijessel 2006; Hijma *et al.* 2012; Laban 1995; Laban *et al.* 1984; Roep *et al.* 1975; 2005). It took as its scope the entire chronological period from the earliest occupation of Europe (Cohen *et al.* 2012) through to the final flooding of the North Sea by 7,500 BP. It thus covers the entire Palaeolithic, Mesolithic and (on the continent) early Neolithic (Behre 2007; Bell 2007; Bell and Walker 2005; Bos and Janssen 1996; Bos *et al.* 2005; Cohen 2005; Jelgersma 1979; Kiden *et al.* 2002).

Through further international meetings and consultation, the NSPMF stands as a comprehensive management document, identifying research agendas, the significance of the resource, threats from commercial activities, and providing a methodological framework for improving understanding. This mirrors the level of engaged and joined-up strategic thinking that up till now has only characterised the heritage management approach to the terrestrial resource across western Europe. The parity in approach shows that for the first time the submerged resource has been placed on an equal footing, even if we cannot yet deliver parity in terms of actual field investigation.

EMERGING MISCONCEPTIONS

Although significant works have been undertaken in the marine sector during the last ten years many issues remain to be addressed and the concept of the 'archaeological potential of our shallow seas' remains difficult to address. Much of the focus of current works stems from the 'Doggerland syndrome', where vast tracts of submerged landscapes have been mapped in the subsiding/infilling basin of the southern North Sea. These sequences have been quietly adopted as the norm for comparison and are typically rated 'high potential' areas in much the same way '*in situ*' archaeological remains are rated high potential in terrestrial situations. By contrast those areas such as the English Channel where erosion dominates are often considered as lower potential in much the same way that secondary context artefacts from river gravels are graded at a lower scale in terrestrial situations. However, this somewhat simplistic association fails to take into account the nature of the questions being asked of the sequences and the ability of the sequences to provide answers to archaeological questions.

Another area of emerging consideration concerns the approaches to investigation within such diverse situations. Methods adopted by Gaffney *et al.* (2007; 2009) for the southern North Sea are not applicable in erosional situations. Although a coherent set of methods for the Palaeolithic has not been put forward for bedrock-dominated landscapes, Bates *et al.* (2012) have published methodologies for investigation of later prehistoric landscapes in such situations (based on fieldwork in Orkney).

The emerging issue that appears at the present time is, therefore, one of heterogeneity within the marine sector. Although perhaps treated until now as an area in which terrestrial ideas can be applied, we might today argue that just as a range of methods and techniques are necessary in terrestrial situations to address the key questions, so too tailored approaches need to be applied to the marine sector. We cannot, and should not, simply see our marine resource as an extended British landmass just like the current one. Archaeologies of the (modern) sea-bed are likely to be as diverse and specific as those in terrestrial situations, and we should expect novel archaeologies to exist beneath the sea floor that require tailored approaches to their understanding.

SUMMARY

The submerged landscapes around Britain truly represent Lost Landscapes of deep prehistory. They deserve this title because they offer a distinctive record of extensive and well-preserved terrains that have so far been inaccessible to archaeological research. Despite great improvements in mapping and seabed profile modelling, the actual characterisation of preserved palaeoenvironments is still coarse. The collection of material by trawler and private individuals may have been brought within wider networks, but it still provides the overwhelming majority of finds, both faunal and artefactual, from the seabed. In this sense, we are still very much standing on the shoreline of these lost worlds and are reliant on flotsam and chance finds to inform our understanding of the potential which might lie there. That these finds include Neanderthal human remains, well-preserved tools and fresh, undisturbed archaeological signatures, has made scientists aware that the record is not simply a great jumble of scoured and disturbed debris, but rather contains extensive tracts of sediment in primary context and with immense potential, perhaps equalling that of contemporary sites such as Lynford in Norfolk (Fig. 3.16; Boismier *et al.* 2012; Wymer 2001).

There remain numerous challenges to investigating these environments in terms of methods and in working in such locations, but also in developing frameworks for investigation. The assessment of potential in the marine zone remains a contentious and largely ignored facet of the debate. High potential is typically assigned to those areas of the seabed

Fig. 3.16 Crossing Doggerland. Excavation of Middle Palaeolithic archaeology and mammoth remains at Lynford, Norfolk showed that the southern North Sea was an important seasonal migration route for Neanderthal hunters during MIS 3 © Nigel Larkin

in which deposition outweighs erosion. However, recent work around the British coastline has demonstrated that even in those parts of the seabed thought to be erosional in character, important information may be preserved on the seabed (Bates *et al.* 2012). Additionally, and something that has not generally been articulated through the ALSF projects, is the difficulty in projecting terrestrially based archaeological knowledge into the marine zone. Although fluvial sediments do exist in the submerged zone they do not necessarily represent contexts analogous to those in present-day terrestrial situations, and consequently assigning significance to these offshore bodies of sediment may require additional consideration. Perhaps we need to be looking to develop an offshore framework for Quaternary sediments that reflects the fact that our submerged landscapes are not simply extensions of the modern landscape beneath the sea but areas in which processes reflect the unique nature of landscapes at lower elevations, subject to frequent transgressions and regressions, and in which large river systems operate at scales rarely, if ever, seen in the terrestrial UK today.

What we cannot know, from the perspective of our glimpse of these Lost Landscapes, is how important they were to people in the past. Were they marginal, undifferentiated and difficult landscapes through which hunter-gatherers moved, or were they core areas of prime importance for which out terrestrial landscapes served as only marginal hinterlands? Answering these questions for different periods and climatic conditions will become one of the great research drivers of the next century. The possibility exists that parts of the record of the behaviours of hunter-gatherers not represented in the terrestrial archives might exist in the landscapes of the English Channel river and Doggerland. Given the methodological advances and suitable resources, we may soon be in a position to deliver a fully integrated archaeology of north-west Europe, where the transition between these records is seamless, in terms of research, methodological effectiveness and understanding.

Chapter 4:
Terrestrial fluvial landscapes

by Danielle Schreve

INTRODUCTION

As noted elsewhere in this volume (see Chapters 1 and 6), the investigation of the Pleistocene fluvial archive for Palaeolithic and Pleistocene information has a long and rich history in Britain, beginning in earnest back in the mid 19th century when antiquarian collectors would tour active sand and gravel pits, making finds themselves or remunerating the workmen for their recovery of artefacts and faunal remains (Fig. 4.1). Hand-extraction and sorting of the aggregate resources provided unparalleled opportunities for the recovery of fossil and artefactual remains, leading to the creation of an exceptional repository of such finds, still preserved today in regional and national museum collections across Britain. Spanning nearly 100 years, this period saw the tremendous florescence of both antiquarian and wider public interest in what is now known as Quaternary Science, coinciding with new understanding of human antiquity, past geomorphological processes and biological evolution.

This chapter outlines the range of ALSF-funded investigations into Pleistocene fluvial deposits (ie those laid down by rivers), and discusses the

Fig. 4.1 The 19th century antiquarian Worthington George Smith indicates the position of Palaeolithic artefacts from the site of Gaddesden Row, Bedfordshire (courtesy of Luton Museum Service)

evidence they provide for past climatic and landscape reconstruction at different spatial scales. By their very nature, since river deposits comprise sands and gravels that are frequently of economic interest, this type of deposit is the single most important context for the preservation of Palaeolithic and associated Pleistocene palaeoenvironmental evidence, both in terms of sheer numbers of sites and assemblages and also the geographical scope of ALSF projects. As explained in Chapter 1, the commercial exploitation of fluvial aggregates deposits presents something of a double-edged sword for those interested in deeper archaeological time. It is clear that without quarrying activities, such deeply buried sites will only rarely come to light, but equally, there is no statutory protection for this precious resource, and thus far, exceptionally limited opportunities for archaeological mitigation in comparison to traditional 'surface' archaeology.

In contrast to the past, opportunities today for 'preservation by record' have been made extremely difficult by the advance of mechanised, large-scale quarrying. Thus, as recognised in English Heritage's 2008 *Research and Conservation Framework for the British Palaeolithic* (funded by the ALSF), the very process of modern aggregates extraction can destroy both sites and material unseen (see Chapter 1). Given the voracious exploitation of aggregates by today's society and constant development pressures, these risks are only likely to increase. In the Thames Gateway area alone the archaeological and geological resource has experienced sustained pressure from industrial development over 150 years, and the construction of High Speed 1 (the Channel Tunnel Rail Link) with further threats implicit in the government's strategic plan identifying north Kent and south Essex as priority spots for regeneration, as well as in the mooted expansion of Stansted airport. The situation is compounded by the issues outlined in Chapter 1 regarding the frequent misunderstanding as to the very different nature of Palaeolithic and Pleistocene remains and how these might be most effectively and economically recorded and investigated (see Chapter 2). In consequence, a number of the projects described here specifically focussed on raising public and professional awareness of the Palaeolithic and Pleistocene in order to stimulate interest in, and increase knowledge of, the distant archaeological past in a diversity of stakeholders. These audiences naturally include those who work in the aggregates industry and who therefore may be closely involved in any new discoveries. In a period where recognisable archaeological features are minimal (or more usually completely absent), it is critical to accept that investigation of our Palaeolithic archaeological heritage should include not only anthropogenic artefacts but also study of deposits that may be archaeologically sterile but which contain chronological or palaeoenvironmental data. Only through this holistic and interdisciplinary approach can more light be shed on past human behaviour.

As noted throughout this volume, one major benefit of ALSF funding has been the opportunity to revisit often poorly known collections and to place them within an updated chronological, stratigraphical and palaeoenvironmental framework, thereby maximising 'added value' to the museum resource, and providing new educational and outreach opportunities. Equally important, however, is the need to assist the curatorial and professional archaeological community in managing the Palaeolithic and Pleistocene resource contained in the contemporary aggregate extraction landscape. This is imperative since nationally both original Sites and Monuments Records (SMRs) and more wide-ranging Historic Environment Records (HERs) are notably poor in basic, verifiable information concerning the Palaeolithic and its palaeoenvironmental context. Urgent enhancement of these resources is therefore required, and indeed was one of the desired outcomes of many of the fluvial ALSF projects described here. The generation of both site-specific and valley-wide datasets therefore not only allows the characterisation and predictive modelling of the Palaeolithic resource in individual river systems but also facilitates the identification of particular areas of significance, which can then inform future research priorities. Finally, the range of fluvial projects provided an opportunity to highlight to archaeological professionals the range and applicability of appropriate methods for evaluating and excavating Palaeolithic and Pleistocene sites. ALSF funding thus provided an important opening not only for contextualising knowledge gained from past aggregates extraction but also for exploring new sites and creating a new predictive resource to enable planning authorities and the aggregates industry to minimise the impact of extraction on the historic environment in future.

THE POTENTIAL OF FLUVIAL SEQUENCES FOR RECONSTRUCTING PAST LANDSCAPES AND HOMININ OCCUPATION

The importance of fluvial sequences to Palaeolithic archaeology lies in their role as an archive for the preservation of both artefactual and multi-proxy Pleistocene palaeoenvironmental evidence, including a range of biological proxies as well as the sediments and soils themselves. River valleys are not only believed to have acted as important conduits through the landscape for early hominins (Ashton *et al.* 2006) but also to have provided the essential raw material for stone tool manufacture, as they erode through bedrock and accumulate gravel deposits, thereby further influencing patterns of movement around the landscape. Rivers therefore acted as focal points in the distant past, providing valuable raw material as well as other resources in the form of fresh water, plants and animals. Although stone tools in secondary contexts are often clearly transported from their point of origin, potential equally exists within fluvial sequences for the recovery of refitting material from discrete knapping episodes and (rarely) for elucidation of hominin subsistence patterns and behaviour, through the recovery of butchered or otherwise humanly modified faunal material. Even when archaeology may not be present, it is increasingly recognised that the study of geological sequences is of great value for its own sake, not only for the direct information concerning the past climates and environments that hominins inhabited but also for dating the Palaeolithic record, through lithostratigraphy, biostratigraphy and geochronology (see also Chapter 2).

Pleistocene river terrace sequences are present all over the world but are particularly well preserved in temperate latitudes (cf. Bridgland and Maddy 2002). They are interpreted as relict fragments of former floodplains, which are left perched above the river's level by subsequent fluvial downcutting, a process known as rejuvenation. In the majority of cases the downcutting is progressive, leaving behind a 'staircase' of bench-like terraces that increase in age with height above the river. In recent years, it has been accepted by many workers that river terrace formation occurs as a combined response to two forces: climate change and tectonic uplift (Bridgland 1994; 2000; Bridgland and Allen 1996; Maddy 1997; Maddy and Bridgland 2000; Bridgland and Westaway 2007).

Climatic change is a key driver of fluvial activity, triggering the depositional and erosional events preserved in terrace sequences and acting both directly, for example through variability and mode of precipitation, seasonally increased discharge associated with permafrost melt, and indirectly by influencing vegetation and its effect on slope stability and sediment supply (Bull 1991; Bridgland 1994; Vandenberghe 2003; 2007; Westaway and Bridgland 2010). During the last 3 million years, while the south of England has been uplifted, the southern North Sea Basin has been subsiding, with the hinge line for this movement lying on a roughly north-south axis close to the present coast of Suffolk and Essex (Rose *et al.* 1999). The rate of uplift has been calculated at around 0.07 m ka^{-1} in the west of the region (eg Maddy 1997) while over the same period the southern North Sea basin has subsided at an average rate of 0.15m per thousand years. This pattern of uplift and tilting has been a major factor in the formation of the terraces.

Debate continues about the formation of depositional river terraces. Previous workers (for example, Zeuner 1945; 1959) believed that terraces in the lower reaches of rivers were aggraded in response to sea-level rise, itself climatically influenced during the Quaternary. River terrace aggradation was also believed to happen as a single event during one temperate climate episode, on account of the large quantities of warm-climate fossils that were seemingly found in the gravel. More recently, however, the observation that typical river terrace gravels have accumulated under conditions of extreme cold, often associated with permafrost features (for example, Rose and Allen 1977; Green and McGregor 1980; Gibbard 1985) has overturned this view. In Britain, evidence from the exceptional record in the Lower Thames (see below) provided corroboration that both cold- and warm-climatic episodes could be recorded within terrace sequences, and that their disposition could help explain the relation between terrace formation and climatic fluctuation (Bridgland 1994; 2000; 2006). The modified paradigm of climatically-triggered terrace formation, driven by progressive uplift, has been widely accepted in the Quaternary fluvial community (see, however, Kiden and Tornqvist 1998; Gibbard and Lewin 2008; Lewin and Gibbard 2010). Based on empirical evidence from the Lower Thames (see below), a climatic model for terrace formation is now envisaged, in which the major incision event is believed to have coincided with warming transitions in the climate cycle (Fig. 4.2; Bridgland and Allen 1996; Bridgland 2000; 2006; 2014). Gravel aggradations thus occur mainly under cold, periglacial conditions and river terrace deposits form over multiple climatic stages.

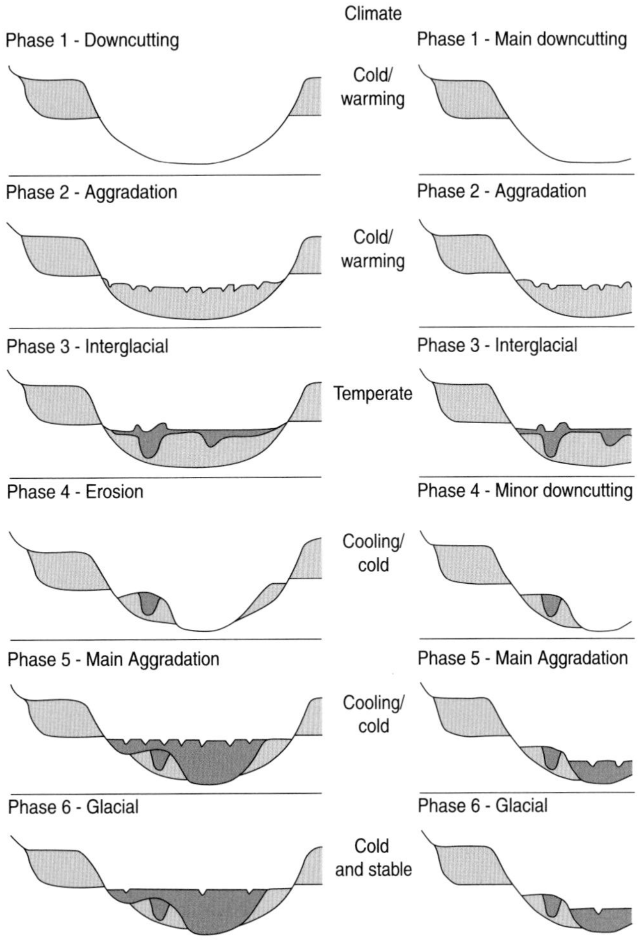

Fig. 4.2 Phased model of fluvial aggradation in synchrony with climatic change (from Bridgland 2014)

Within this scheme, fossiliferous deposits are generally laid down during periods of temperate climate between gravel aggradations, comprising finer-grained sediments of silt, clay and peat, thereby creating a cold-warm-cold 'sandwich' of deposits.

The Pleistocene deposits of the river Thames and its tributaries are of international importance, since they form a chronostratigraphical framework for this part of the geological record in Britain, linking the glacial stratigraphy of East Anglia, the fluvial stratigraphy of the Rhine and Seine, and global climatic stratigraphy (Morigi *et al.* 2011). Although other English rivers possess long terrace sequences, they do not contain as rich an archaeological and palaeontological record, particularly for the last half million years. The Thames is therefore used here as a powerful example of the potential information that can be derived from fluvial sequences. As well as preserving a long stratigraphical record through the Pleistocene, the Thames deposits are also blessed by good preservation of vertebrate and molluscan remains, on account of the calcareous groundwater conditions and Chalk bedrock in this part of the country. Finally, the Thames has a long pedigree of archaeological collection, prospection and excavation, meaning that its extensive Palaeolithic collections can be fully integrated with state-of-the-art chronological and palaeoenvironmental information.

In the Thames Valley, there are about eighteen different terraces along the pre-Anglian course of the ancient Thames, although they are not all present in any one section of the river valley. The best-preserved flight of terraces is in the Middle Thames between Reading and Rickmansworth where up to thirteen terraces have been recognised. However, it is the Lower Thames (that part of the river's course through and downstream from London), which possesses one of the best archives globally of climatic events since the Anglian glaciation, *c* 450,000 BP. The Thames has flowed in its present course through London only since the Anglian ice sheet blocked its former valley in the Vale of St Albans, ultimately leading to catastrophic overspill from ice-dammed lakes and diversion of the river into the pre-existing Medway-Darent drainage basin to the south (Gibbard 1977; 1979; Bridgland 1988; 1999; Bridgland and Gibbard 1997). Four post-Anglian terraces can be recognised, with the lowest of these buried beneath the modern floodplain downstream from London (Fig. 4.3). In the case of the Lower Thames, the process of terrace formation has led to the creation of approximately one terrace per 100,000 year climatic cycle, with interglacial sediments in the Lower Thames correlated with MIS 11, 9, 7 and 5e (Bridgland 1994; 2000). This chronological model has been applied as an interpretative tool in sequences lacking the empirical palaeoclimatic evidence, such as the Bytham River in East Anglia (Lee *et al.* 2004), although not without controversy (Banham *et al.* 2001). Indeed, the Lower Thames record may be atypical, even within the wider Thames system as a

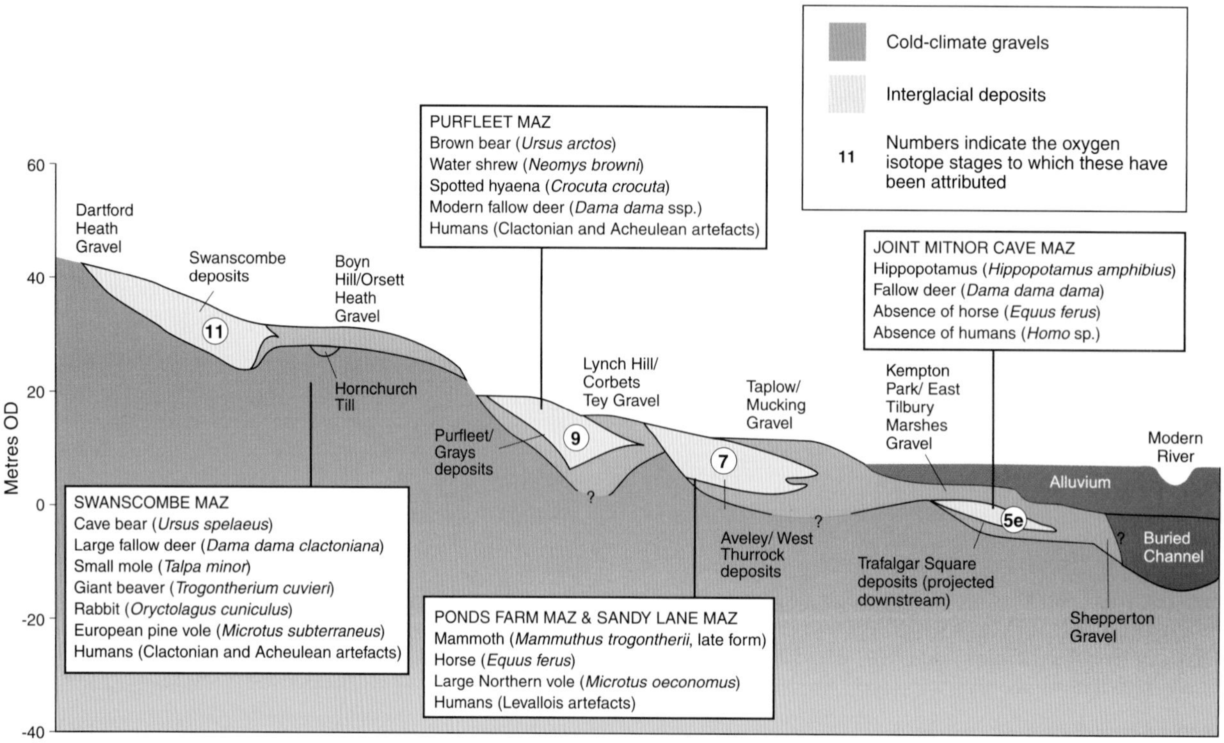

Fig. 4.3 Schematic cross-section through the Lower Thames terraces, showing four post-Anglian terraces. Proposed correlations with the marine oxygen isotope record are shown, together with mammalian biostratigraphical characteristics (MAZ = mammalian assemblage zone)

whole. Many rivers have formed terraces less frequently than one per cycle and some (more rarely) display more than one terrace per climate cycle, as indeed occurs in one of Britain's most extensive records, that of the River Solent in southern England (Fig. 4.4; Westaway *et al.* 2006). Major advances in the dating of the Lower Thames, through the application of terrace stratigraphy (Bridgland 1994), mammalian (Box 4.1) and molluscan biostratigraphy (Fig. 4.3; Keen 2001; Schreve 2001) and geochronology (Penkman *et al.* 2011; Bridgland *et al.* 2012) have now permitted detailed understanding of the timing and environments under which sediments, fossils and archaeology were deposited, allowing the landscapes of early hominins, patterns of settlement and abandonment, and technological and behavioural changes to be reconstructed and interpreted.

As outlined in Chapter 2, the fluvial archive can be examined on a range of spatial scales, from the macro-scale (whereby questions concerning the palaeogeography of ancestral rivers or connections to the continental mainland, for example, can be explored), through the meso-scale (investigation of individual geomorphological systems such as river valleys), to the micro-scale (site-specific studies). Since no ALSF projects have directly addressed the first of these, the information presented below focuses on the second and third categories, which formed the main corpus of Palaeolithic and Pleistocene studies funded since 2002. The following description of projects is not intended to be exhaustive for the entire range of funded studies but rather to provide an illustration of relevant examples and their outcomes.

THE BIGGER PICTURE: MESO-SCALE INVESTIGATION OF RIVER VALLEYS

In accordance with the overarching research themes later formalised in the 2008 *Research and Conservation Framework for the British Palaeolithic,* a core goal of many of the ALSF projects was to generate up-to-date and integrated chronological and stratigraphical frameworks for individual geomorphological systems in order to explore patterns of hominin occupation, cultural change and responses to palaeoenvironmental oscillations. A number of projects therefore focussed on generating new information for selected river valleys through examination of borehole records and reappraisal of museum artefact collections, as well as targeted fieldwork combined with new geochronological and palaeoenvironmental analyses (see descriptions of methods employed in ALSF projects in Chapter 2). Although opportunities occasionally presented themselves for detailed site-specific investigations as part of these valley-wide projects (see below), the main emphasis was on the understanding of 'bigger picture' questions concerning palaeogeography, geochronology and palaeoenvironmental change, as well as the generation of landscape-scale deposit models and GIS maps as predictive tools.

Developing predictive modelling – Mapping the Sub-Surface Drift Geology of Greater London project

A typical example of this approach comes from the *Mapping the Sub-Surface Drift Geology of Greater London* project (also known as the *Lea Valley Mapping Project,* LVMP) undertaken by the Museum of

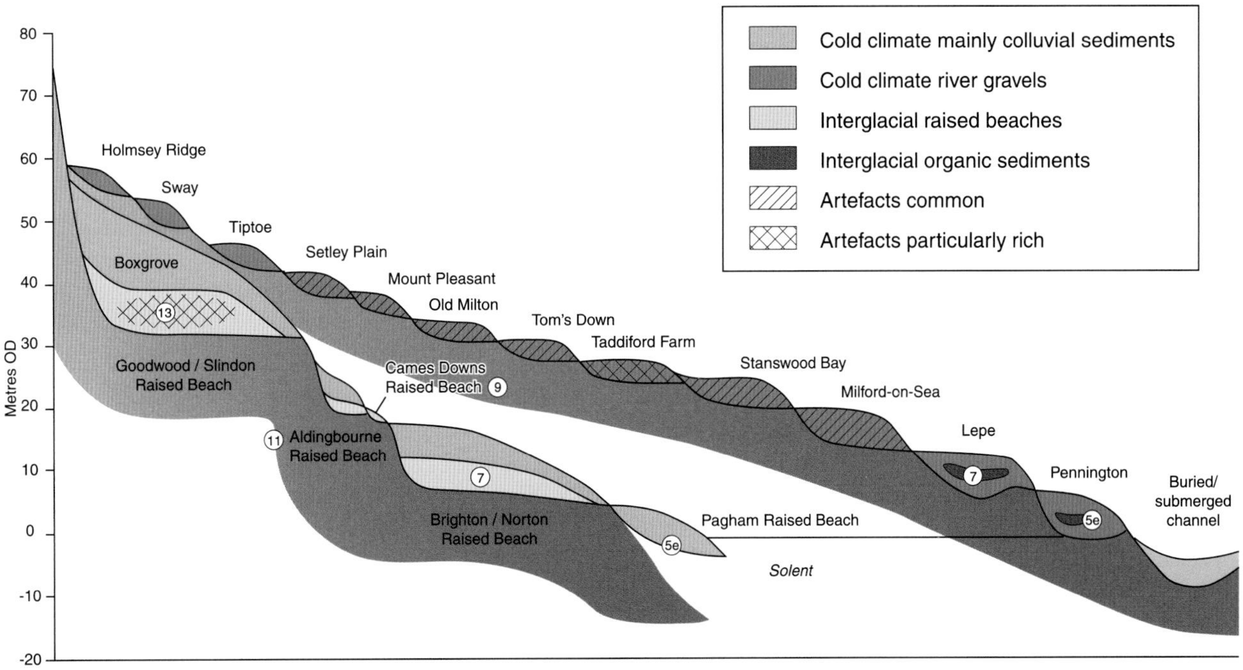

Fig. 4.4 Schematic cross-section through the terraces of the Solent Valley and correlation with the raised beach sequence of the Sussex coastal plain (after Bridgland 2000)

LATE PLEISTOCENE MAMMALIAN TURNOVER IN BRITAIN

BOX 4.1

The mammalian faunas of the British Late Pleistocene demonstrate an exceptional degree of turnover, in response to the sharp climatic fluctuations of the period. This has led to the recognition of a succession of discrete Mammal Assemblage-Zones (MAZ) based on evidence of faunal replacement, evolutionary trends and extinction events.

The Late Pleistocene covers Marine Oxygen Isotope Stages (MIS) 5-2 inclusive, comprising the Last (Ipswichian) interglacial (MIS 5e, the first temperate substage in the oxygen isotope record of MIS 5) and a complex last glacial, the Devensian Glaciation, which covers MIS 5d-2. The Last Interglacial is well represented in both cave and open sites across Britain. Its mammalian fauna (Joint Mitnor Cave MAZ) is of typically temperate, woodland character, reflecting mean summer temperatures around 5°C warmer than at present, including fallow deer (*Dama dama*), bison (*Bison priscus*), straight-tusked elephant (*Palaeoloxodon antiquus*), narrow-nosed rhinoceros (*Stephanorhinus hemitoechus*) and a highly characteristic element, in the form of hippopotamus (*Hippopotamus amphibius*). No faunal records are known from the very earliest cold-climate phase of the Early Devensian (MIS 5d, nor indeed from the later MIS 5b), although the MIS 5c interstadial (a short episode of relatively mild climatic conditions) is represented by the Bacon Hole MAZ of the Gower peninsula in south Wales. The mammalian assemblage from MIS 5c is of temperate character, with straight-tusked elephant, but has lost hippopotamus, the most thermophilous (warm-loving) element.

4.1.1 *Palaeoloxodon antiquus*

The mammals from the final part of the Early Devensian are attributed to MIS 5a, a correlation supported by Uranium-series dating on flowstones from caves encasing bones. This faunal grouping (the Banwell Bone Cave MAZ) is formed by a very distinctive group of cold, maritime species, indicative of high snow cover. Biodiversity is low, possibly reflecting island isolation at this time, with only reindeer (*Rangifer tarandus*) and bison (*Bison priscus*) represented in any great numbers. The major predator is a brown bear (*Ursus arctos*), of exceptionally large body size; indeed, early findings of this bear were initially misidentified as polar bear. Reconnection to the continent occurred around 65,000 years ago, in conjunction with the broad climatic amelioration of MIS 3 (the Middle Devensian, 65-25,000 years ago). The mammalian fauna of the Pin Hole Cave MAZ, of which the Lynford and Whitemoor Haye assemblages are typical examples, reflects the extensive spread of a non-analogue grassland environment, often referred to as the Mammoth Steppe, an arid but exceptionally rich habitat that could support many tons of large herbivore biomass. Although reindeer and bison were still present, the fauna is dominated by woolly mammoth (*Mammuthus primigenius*), woolly rhinoceros (*Coelodonta antiquitatis*), horse (*Equus ferus*), spotted hyaena (*Crocuta crocuta*). MIS 3 also witnesses the reappearance in Britain of Neanderthals after a protracted absence of around 100,000 years, and their subsequent replacement by modern humans. This period, although the warmest part of the last glaciation is characterised by multiple abrupt climatic oscillations on a submillennial scale. It is also at this time that many of the Pleistocene megafauna begin to go extinct, at least partly because of climatically-driven ecological stress.

The ensuing dramatic climatic deterioration of the Last Glacial Maximum, around 22,000 years ago, is characterised by a restricted fauna including reindeer, woolly mammoth and musk ox (*Ovibos moschatus*). Later, the brief initial warming of the Late glacial Interstadial (Bølling interstadial,14,800 years ago) caused the return of a temperate fauna (the Gough's Cave MAZ), this time comprising mostly wild horse, red deer (*Cervus elaphus*), mountain hare (*Lepus timidus*), rare records of saiga antelope (*Saiga tatarica*) and modern humans. Faunas of the later parts of the interstadial (Allerød interstadial) include red deer and elk (*Alces alces*) and reflect the spread of birch woodland in Britain, before the climatic deterioration of the Younger Dryas (12,900 years ago) brought about the return of reindeer, arctic fox (*Alopex lagopus*) and other cold-climate species. These species enjoyed a brief reign before the climatic warming of the Holocene (11,500 years ago) and the spread of woodland led to the formation of Britain's modern mammal fauna.

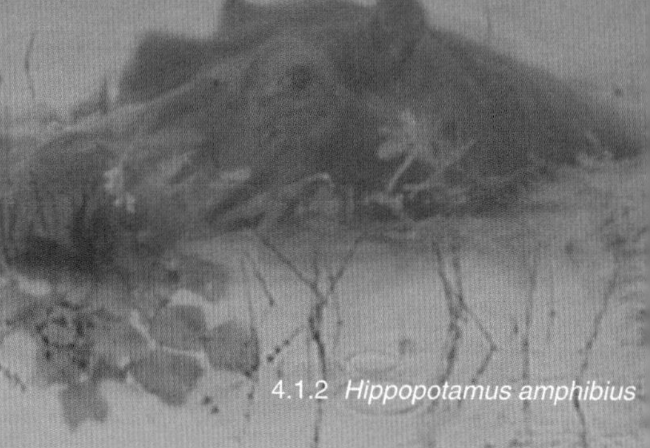

4.1.2 *Hippopotamus amphibius*

London Archaeology Service (Corcoran *et al.* 2011). This project focussed on the Quaternary deposits of the lower Lea Valley, an area of regionally significant large-scale aggregate extraction, and one where the combination of a built-up urban location, deeply-buried deposits and lack of previous major archaeological excavations presented particular challenges to the understanding and interpretation of the fluvial sequence. Extending across the six London boroughs of Enfield, Waltham Forest, Haringey, Hackney, Tower Hamlets and Newham, as well as part of Epping Forest in Essex, the study area covered 80.64 km^2 in its northern part and 30.50 km^2 in the south (Fig. 4.5), as five mapped areas, encompassing the Lea floodplain and pre-Holocene terraces in the north and the floodplain and lowermost adjacent valley sides in the south.

The project drew on over 3000 British Geological Survey (BGS) borehole logs and archaeological records from small-scale excavation and evaluation studies in order to create a digital geoarchaeological database, a gazetteer of finds and subsequently, an integrated GIS for the lower Lea Valley and its confluence with the Thames. This was then used to generate a series of deposit models and maps with the aim of reconstructing the topography and palaeoenvironments of the lower Lea Valley during the late Pleistocene and Holocene, so as to be able to predict areas of archaeological potential and future risk. As a core objective (and in common with the majority of similar landscape-scale fluvial ALSF projects), the LVMP undertook to engage with a broad audience and specifically to engage with a diversity of professional archaeological, industrial and non-professional stakeholders to provide 'meaningful information about a range of issues of relevance to the understanding and management of the past landscape and archaeological resource…' (Corcoran *et al.* 2011, 4).

As Corcoran *et al.* (2011) indicate, arguably the single most useful concept and product of the LVMP project was the formulation of a pre-Holocene Digital Elevation Model (DEM) for the study area (Fig. 4.6), which creates a lattice of known elevation points in order to form a palaeogeographical visualisation of the height of a given surface. This enables borehole profiles and transects to be accurately placed within their past topographical context, thereby forming the template upon which alluvial/colluvial deposition subsequently occurred during the Holocene. The irregular nature of the topography can then be examined in order to assess differences in archaeological potential. For example the presence of topographic 'highs' and 'lows' on the floodplain might indicate islands, promontories, pools or channels, all of which might have been attractive to past inhabitants and be focal points for future archaeological investigation. Although the DEM created presents the situation at the start of the Holocene (and hence offers insight into the landscape of the earliest Mesolithic occupants of the Lea Valley), the result nonetheless provides a snapshot of the complex land surface present at the end of the Pleistocene and clearly demonstrates applicability to more distant Palaeolithic time periods. The irregular surface of the gravel on the river terraces noted by Corcoran *et al.* (2011) may be partly the reflection of erosion during the Pleistocene (since such processes are likely to have been much more active than during the Holocene). However, in an area such as the Lea

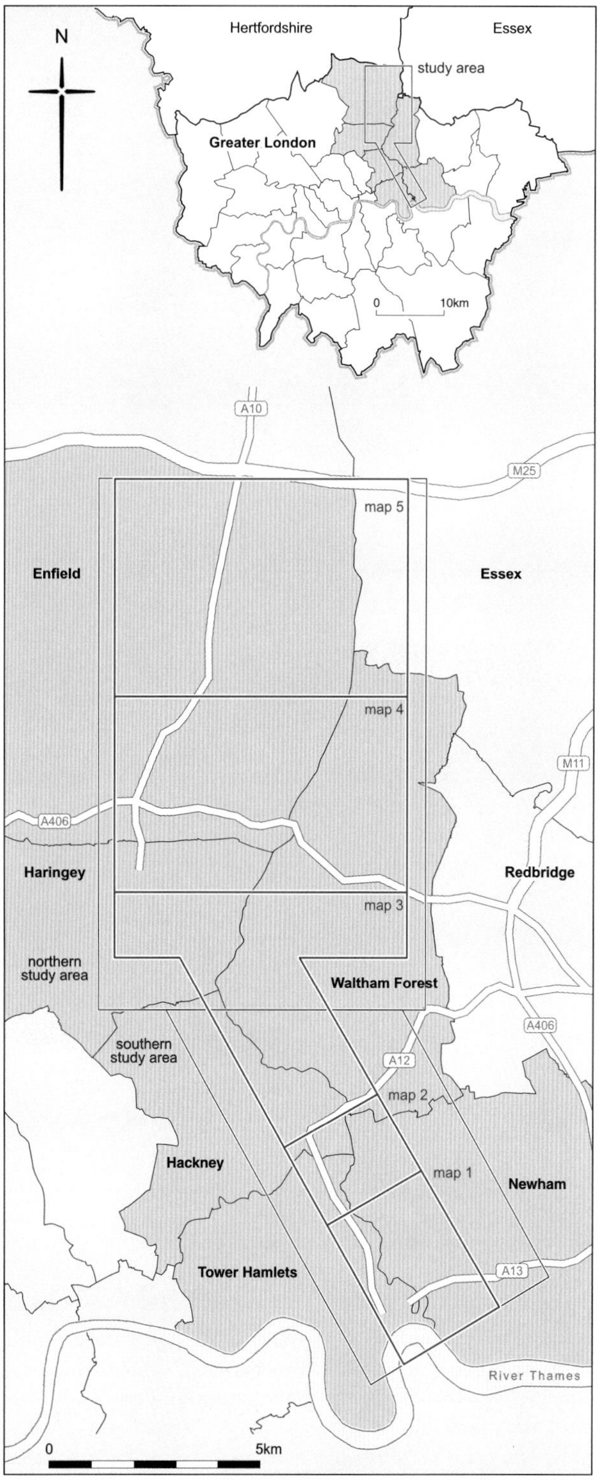

Fig. 4.5 Location map of the Mapping the Sub-Surface Drift Geology of Greater London project study area

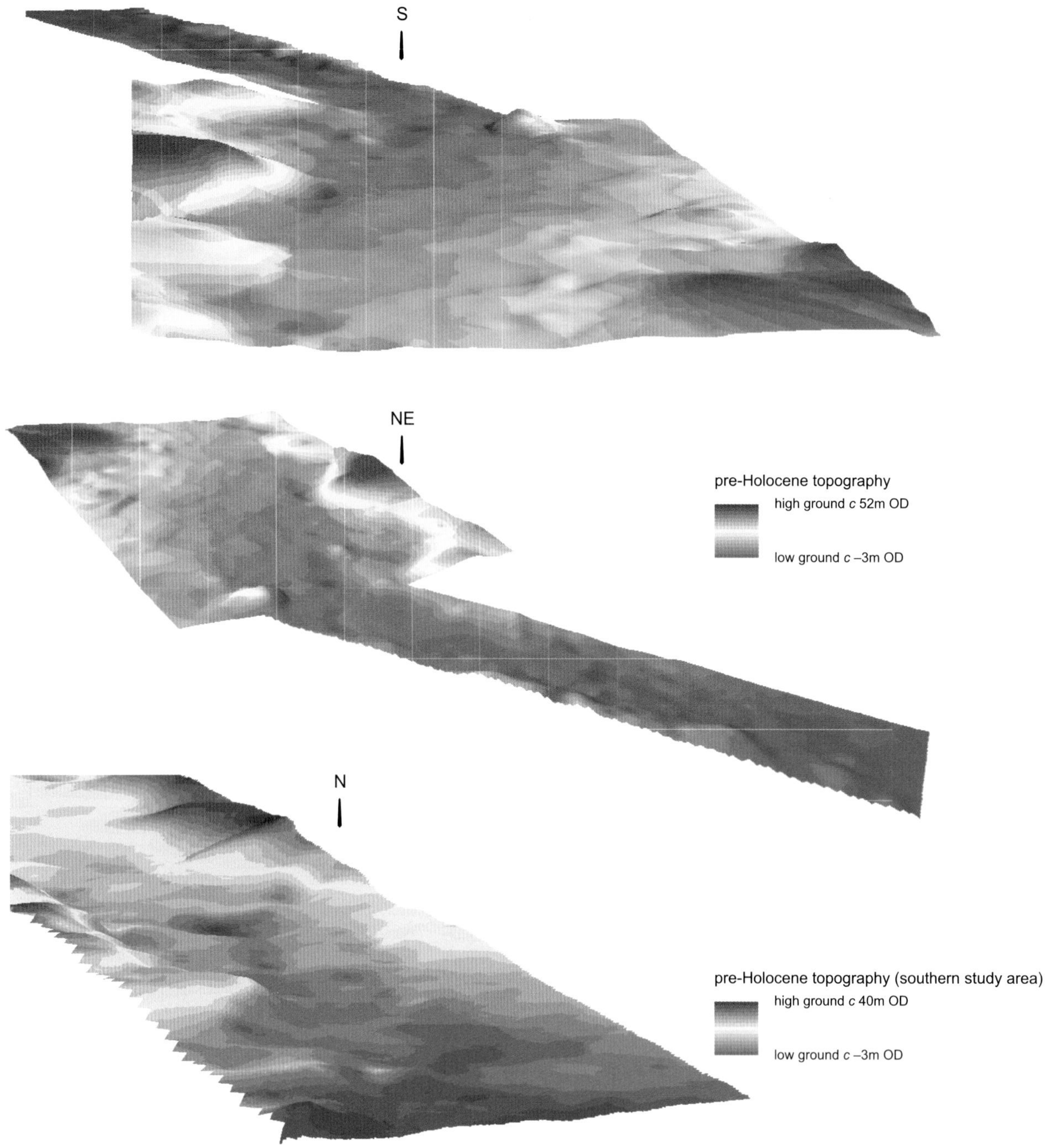

Fig. 4.6 3-D plots of the 'pre-Holocene' landsurface (vertical exaggeration x 4) (from Corcoran et al. *2011)*

Valley, where there has been extensive landscaping and quarrying, much of the irregularity may be down to human activity. Thus, in many cases, the pre-Holocene gravel surface is likely to have been higher than as modelled currently.

Borehole transects and contour maps were then combined to provide an overview of pre-Holocene landscape and deposit characteristics (Fig. 4.7) and the area subdivided into buried 'landscape zones' (Fig. 4.8). This approach allowed the recognition of six 'terrain' types, which could then be traced across individual mapped areas and used to address wider questions beyond any single development site. Terrain 1 represents the main part of the river channel and valley floor (floodplain), at the base of which (in the study area) are Pleistocene gravels. Terrain 2 represents the marginal zone at the peripheries of the floodplain, characterised by the frequent presence of colluvial deposits, the preservation of archaeological and palaeoenvironmental remains in abandoned floodplain-edge depressions and the presence of infilled scour features representing the mouths of tributary valleys. Terrain 3 is represented by a low terrace of Devensian (last cold stage) age, frequently dissected by fluvial channels, lying immediately above or just below the flood-

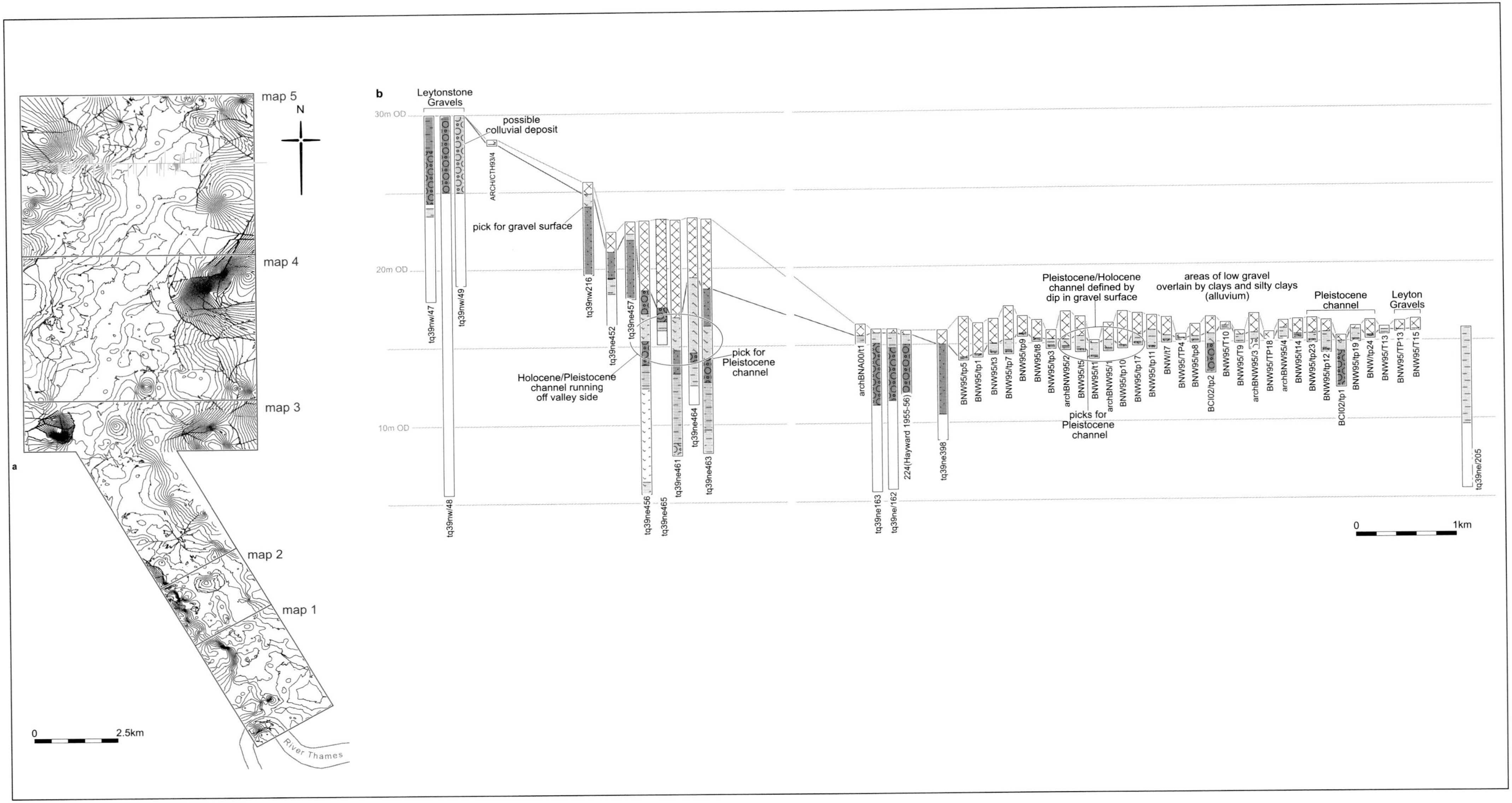

Fig. 4.7 Combining deposit characteristics and pre-Holocene topography for Map 5 of the Mapping the Sub-Surface Drift Geology of Greater London project study area (from Corcoran et al. *2011)*

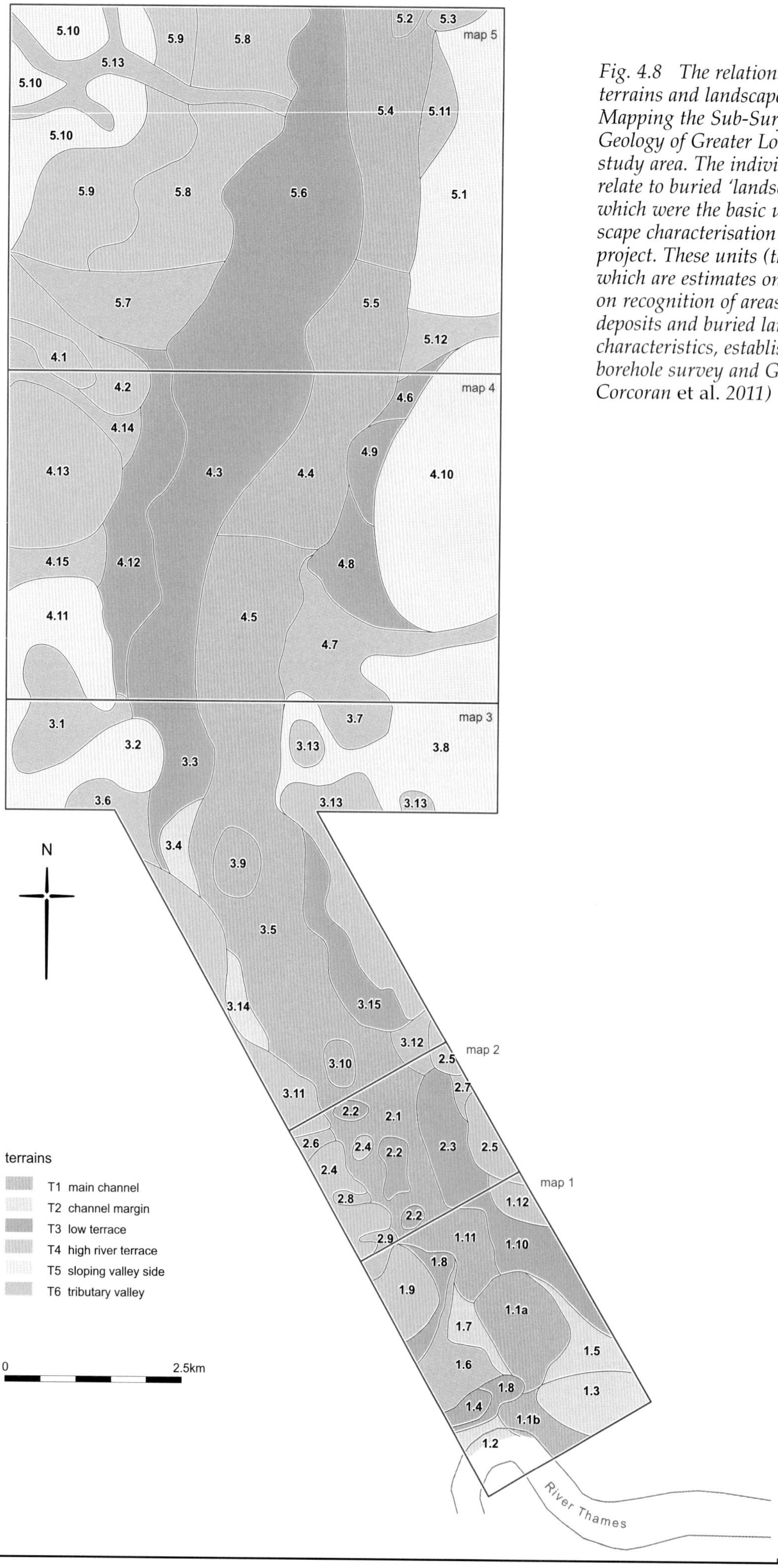

Fig. 4.8 The relationship between terrains and landscape zones in the Mapping the Sub-Surface Drift Geology of Greater London project study area. The individual numbers relate to buried 'landscape zones', which were the basic units of landscape characterisation defined by the project. These units (the limits of which are estimates only) are based on recognition of areas of similar deposits and buried landscape characteristics, established through borehole survey and GIS (from Corcoran et al. *2011)*

Fig. 4.9 BGS mapping of the Mapping the Sub-Surface Drift Geology of Greater London project study area (from Corcoran et al. *2011)*

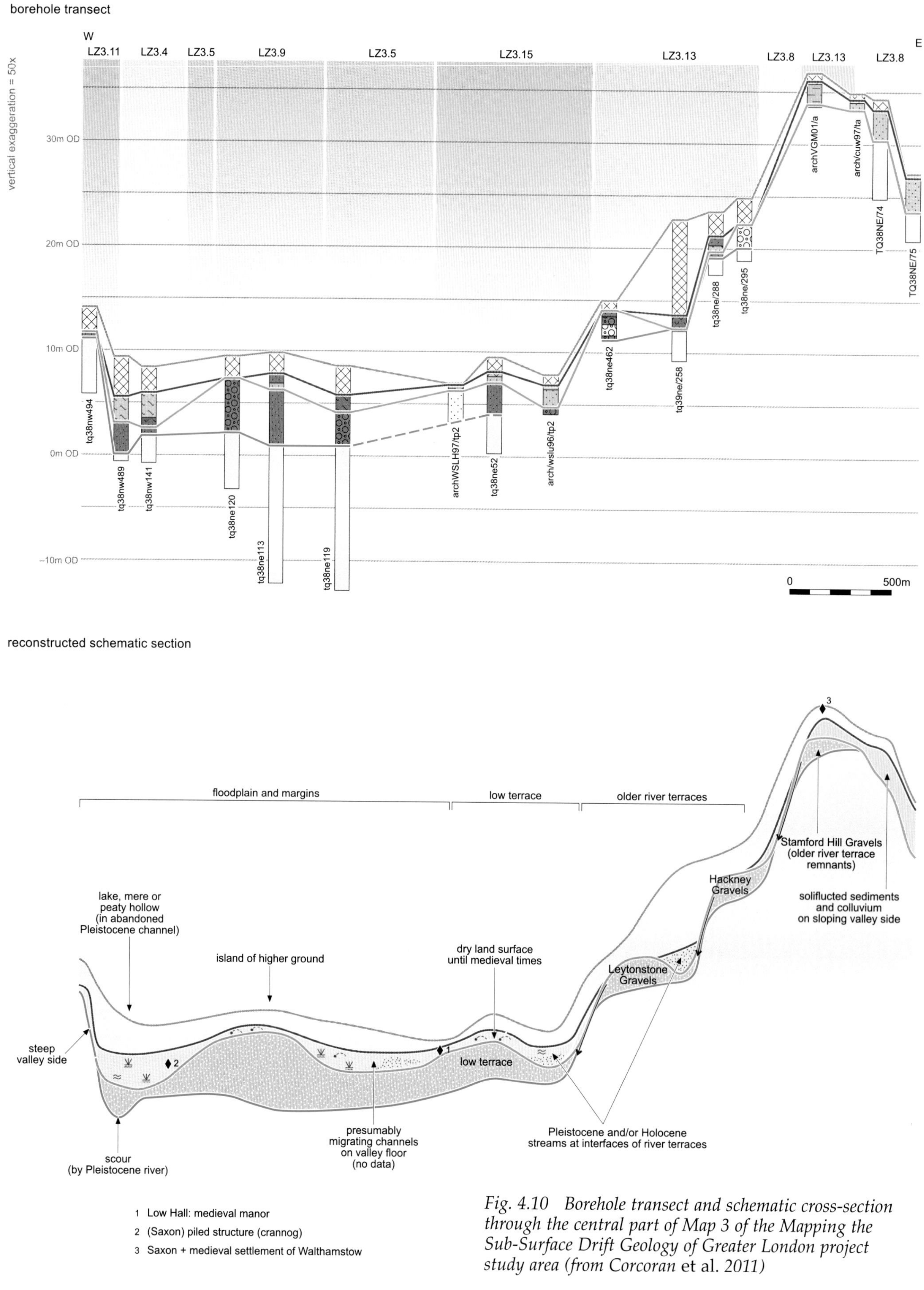

Fig. 4.10 Borehole transect and schematic cross-section through the central part of Map 3 of the Mapping the Sub-Surface Drift Geology of Greater London project study area (from Corcoran et al. *2011)*

plain and variably underlain by either the Leyton Gravels or the Lea Valley Gravels (= Kempton Park Gravel of the BGS; Fig. 4.9) depending on the mapping area. Terrain 4 represents higher (and older) river terraces, today lying around 20m OD, well above the modern floodplain. These terraces are typically underlain by the Leytonstone Gravels (= Taplow Gravel of the BGS) laid down in the late Middle Pleistocene between Marine Oxygen Isotope Stage (MIS) 8 and MIS 6, *c* 280,000–128,000 BP and by the Hackney Gravel, the latter most recently considered to be of MIS 8 age, since it

Fig. 4.11 Lea Valley Arctic Beds (a-e) in the Angel Road ballast pit, north London (from Warren 1912)

overlies fossiliferous interglacial silts attributed to MIS 9 (Green *et al.* 2006). Occasional remnants of higher, older terraces such as that formed by the Stamford Hill Gravel, are also noted (Fig. 4.10). Terrain 5 represents sloping valley-side areas, usually associated with exposed London Clay bedrock and overlain by colluvium and solifluction deposits, whereas Terrain 6 represents tributary valleys, often dating back to the Pleistocene and typified by alluvial sediments.

The characteristics of each landscape zone were noted in terms of the typical sequence of deposits (with anticipated depths and thicknesses) and inferred formation process and then integrated with any available archaeological and palaeoenvironmental evidence. Although there is archaeological potential for the recovery of Late Glacial remains from the 'pre Holocene' land surface of Terrain 1 (for example, palaeoenvironmental evidence preserved within topographic lows on the floodplain), the terrains with the greatest potential for preservation of Palaeolithic and Pleistocene palaeoenvironmental evidence are Terrains 3, 4 and 6. At any given point in time, older terrace remnants, lying just above the valley floor wetlands, would have enabled good access to water sources and to patches of higher ground, thereby creating an attractive location for hominin activity and resource exploitation. Historical accounts noted the presence of Lower Palaeolithic handaxes and rarer Middle Palaeolithic material from the low terrace of Terrain 3, although these are likely to have been *ex situ* within later Holocene deposits. Upstream of the study area, the gravels of the low terrace preserve organic deposits rich in mosses, dwarf birch and dwarf willow, associated with a cold-climate mammalian assemblage, including woolly mammoth (*Mammuthus primigenius*), woolly rhinoceros (*Coelodonta antiquitatis*), collared lemming (*Dicrostonyx henseli = torquatus*) and reindeer (*Rangifer tarandus*; Warren 1915). These deposits are known as the Lea Valley Arctic Beds (Fig. 4.11; Warren 1912; 1915) and have been radiocarbon-dated to the Late Pleistocene, 28,000–20,000 BP, immediately prior to the Last Glacial Maximum (LGM). In places, these former floodplain deposits are thought to have been locally reworked as frozen blocks of peaty sediment, under cold climate conditions, as the river continued to incise after the LGM (Gibbard 1994). Analysis of insect remains by Coope and Tallon (1983) suggested the presence of a sparsely vegetated landscape with meltwater puddles and the proximity of large herbivores, as indicated by the dung beetle genus *Aphodius*. The beetles indicated a comparable climate to that of modern arctic Russia, with mean summer temperatures of 9.5°C and mean winter temperatures of -10.9°C. On the basis of observations and deposit modelling, the LVMP study further identified zones with considerable potential for preservation of these important organic beds within Terrain 3, along both banks of the main channel.

For Terrain 4, deposits in the Stoke Newington area of north London have long been known for their exceptional assemblages of Lower Palaeolithic archaeology (Prestwich 1855; Smith 1883; 1884; Harding and Gibbard 1983). At the nearby Nightingale Estate in Hackney, rich palaeoenvironmental evidence from the Highbury Silts and Sands (preserved within a palaeochannel) has indicated interglacial conditions with elevated summer temperatures, correlated with MIS 9 (Green *et al.* 2006). Although many historic records of handaxes from Terrain 4 are unstratified, deposits of archaeological and palaeoenvironmental potential are thus highly likely to occur within the fine-grained sediments that overlie and are sandwiched between the Pleistocene gravels of Terrain 4. These represent areas either within or marginal to the river channels of the Middle Pleistocene valley and would be expected to have been prime spots for animal and hominin activity. Equally, the overlying brickearth and colluvial deposits that cap the Pleistocene gravels of Terrain 4 are likely to have potential for both *in situ* and redeposited Palaeolithic archaeology.

Testing predictive models: the Medway Valley Palaeolithic Project

A recurring element of the study of past fluvial deposits concerns the migration of rivers through time, sometimes resulting in the preservation of sediments and contained archaeology and palaeoenvironmental evidence at distance from the modern river, or in other cases associated with a now extinct fluvial system such as the Bytham River (Rose 1994). One such project, the Medway Valley Palaeolithic Project (MVPP), focused on the investigation of aggregate deposits in north Kent and south-east Essex associated with the River Medway (Wenban-Smith *et al.* 2007a and b). Today, the Medway is an exclusively Kentish river, flowing northwards from its source in the Weald, through Maidstone and joining the Thames Estuary at Chatham. However, earlier in the Quaternary, the drainage pattern was rather different, with the Thames occupying a more northerly route than today and the Medway flowing across southeastern Essex to its confluence with the Thames. The path of the early Medway is therefore traced via substantial sand and gravel aggregate deposits in southern and eastern Essex, as well as northern Kent.

Amongst others, the MVPP built on an earlier ALSF-funded *2003 Greater Thames Survey of Known Mineral Extraction Sites* (TEMES) undertaken by Essex and Kent County Councils (Essex County Council/Kent County Council 2004). This project was the first to create a GIS map and database for both banks of the Lower Thames estuary to the east of London, examining past, present and proposed aggregate extraction sites and related historic environment features in order to document important archaeological and geological sites within the area. The very high number of mineral extraction sites (*c* 1600) initially documented in the study area

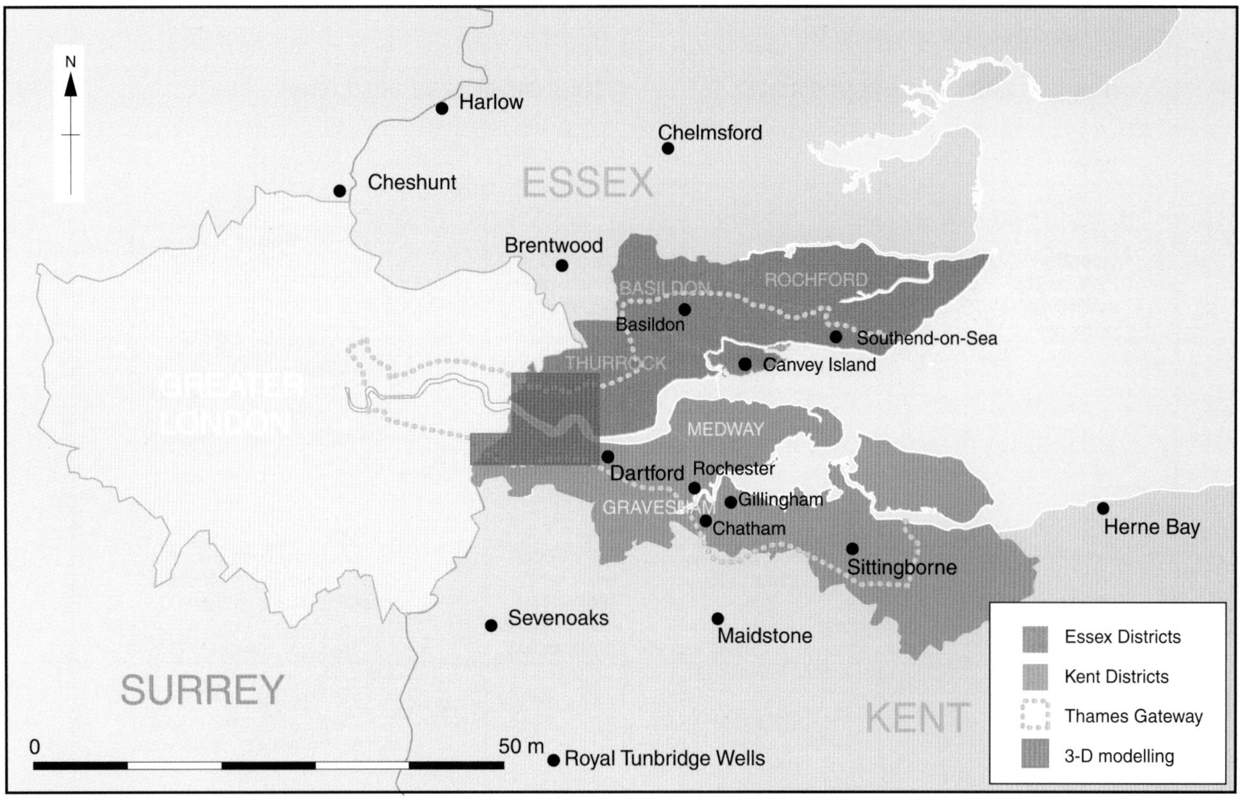

Fig. 4.12 The Greater Thames Survey of Known Mineral Extraction Sites project study area, showing zone of 3-D modelling in red

underlines the increasing development pressure in this region and emphasises the urgent need for protection and better management of this important archaeological and geological resource. From there, a smaller pilot study was developed for parts of the boroughs of Dartford and Gravesham in Kent and the unitary authority of Thurrock in Essex (Fig. 4.12). 3D modelling of deposits, based on borehole logs, was undertaken by the British Geological Survey, and each identified site in the revised study area was examined for Pleistocene and Holocene deposits, Palaeolithic and post-Palaeolithic archaeology and mineral-extraction related industrial archaeology, through a combination of desk-top survey and/or site visits to assess geological, palaeoenvironmental and Palaeolithic archaeological potential (Fig. 4.13).

Subsequently, the MVPP provided the opportunity to expand upon a part of the TEMES study area – that which related specifically to Medway deposits of Essex and Kent – by re-examining over 1300 borehole and other sedimentary records and carrying out fieldwork at over 40 sites. This was combined with a number of specialist analyses on exposures, in particular Optically-Stimulated Luminescence (OSL) and Amino Acid Racemization (AAR), in order to improve the geochronological framework of the Medway deposits. Within eastern Essex, a particular aim was to resolve the stratigraphical relationships between the various Medway gravel aggradations and the spatially-restricted fine-grained channel deposits reported in the region (see Brown 1840; Lake *et al.* 1977; 1986; Roe 1999; 2001; Roe *et al.* 2009) by providing a series of dated tie-points within this sequence. The results confirmed the attribution of all 'high level' channel deposits to MIS 11, as previously suggested by Bridgland (1988; 2003) and Roe (2001), and all 'low level' channel deposits, together with the intermediate Rochford Channel, to MIS 9 (Bridgland *et al.* 2001; Roe *et al.* 2009; 2011; see Briant *et al.* 2012 for discussion), in addition to the well-constrained Last Interglacial channel deposits from the East Mersea Restaurant Site (Bridgland *et al.* 1995) and Hippopotamus Site (Bridgland and Sutcliffe 1995). In Kent, the MVPP proposed additional terrace sequences for both the Maidstone and Hoo areas. These might potentially represent depositional phases within temperate MIS stages, although the lack of interglacial deposits and the problems of incorporating estuarine sediments in the Hoo area into a terrace framework leave this matter unresolved.

A limited amount of palaeobiological data was recovered during the course of the MVPP. Most notable were samples from East Hyde borehole and Bradwell Hall, from the Tillingham palaeochannel previously described by Roe (2001) and considered to have accumulated during the late temperate substage of the Hoxnian interglacial, correlated with MIS 11 *c* 400,000 BP. The analyses confirmed the presence of an unusual molluscan assemblage (following Roe and Preece 1995), the so-called

Site visit pro-forma GV

ALSF THAMES GATEWAY PROJECT **GEOLOGICAL SITE VISIT (GV)**

Date

SITE

Visit by

GV1 **Quantity of Pleistocene sediments present**		0 - None/unknown	GV2 **Location of Pleistocene sediments**		0 - None/Unknown
		1 - Small amount			1 - On site/quarry floor
		2. - Moderate amount			2 - In quarry sides/walls
		3 - Abundant sediments			3 - At land surface adjacent to quarry, within or contiguous with property boundaries

GV3 **Potential of sediments (physical environmental information)**		0 - None	GV4 **Potential of sediments (biological environmental information)**		0 - None
		1 - Limited potential for sedimentological information (stone counts, heavy minerals)			1 - Limited potential for bio-environmental information (microfossils e.g. pollen)
		2 - Medium potential (some measurable features, e.g. x-beds)			2 - Medium potential (e.g. possibility of microvertebrates
		3 - High potential (many measurable features, e.g. x-beds, clast fabrics, deformation structures)			3 - High potential (e.g. macrovertebrates, molluscs, beetles, plant macros)

GV5 **Stratigraphic value of site**		0 - None	GV6 **Accessibility**		0 - No deposit
		1 - Limited (e.g. cold stage gravels only)			1 - Poor: covered by roads or housing; no faces or very inaccessible faces
		2 - Medium (sediments with limited stratigraphic indicators)			2 - Moderate; faces with limited potential for cleaning; restricted or difficult top access
		3 - High potential (e.g. sediments of more than one stage with clear stratigraphic indicators)			3 - Good; direct unrestricted access to face and from above

Notes

Fig. 4.13 Example of a proforma for recording geological characteristics for The Greater Thames Survey of Known Mineral Extraction Sites project

'Rhenish fauna', which entered Britain during a period of confluence of the Thames and Rhine drainage systems and is equally known from the classic Lower Thames sites of Clacton-on-Sea (Essex), Barnfield Pit at Swanscombe and Dierden's Pit at Ingress Vale (both Kent; Kennard 1942; Kerney 1971). The molluscan and ostracod assemblages from these sites also provided significant palaeoenvironmental evidence, in particular revealing brackish conditions (corresponding with high sea-levels), as attested by the presence of hydrobiids such as *Helebia* sp (= *Paladilhia radigueli* auctt.) and other marine taxa such as *Cerastoderma glaucum* at Bradwell Hall and barnacles at East Hyde), as well as the brackish water ostracod *Cyprideis torosa* (Preece, in Wenban-Smith 2007b).

In addition, all known Palaeolithic material in the study area was documented and two particular highlights are singled out. These include the discovery at Cuxton (Kent) of two contrasting types of handaxe, a cleaver and a ficron, within the same archaeological horizon. In addition, new OSL dating of the Cuxton site to *c* 230,000 BP (the onset of MIS 7) makes it the youngest site in the UK with an almost exclusively handaxe-focused material culture, at a time when Middle Palaeolithic Levalloisian assemblages were beginning to become common elsewhere in southern England. The re-dating of the site and the presence within a single assemblage of two very different types of handaxe thus has important implications for understanding the cognitive capabilities of early hominins and regional cultural variation. At the other end of the study area, in Essex, a single small flint waste flake was recovered from the Clinch Street/Canewdon Gravel at Westcliff High School for Girls. With an assumed age for the gravel of *c* 600,000 BP, this artefact represents the earliest evidence of hominin presence in proto-Medway deposits in either Essex or Kent.

In contrast to the archaeologically and palaeontologically rich river terrace deposits of southern England, other meso-scale studies concentrated on areas where the investigation of early hominin occupation and Quaternary palaeoenvironmental change had been relatively neglected, such as the Fenland rivers of Cambridgeshire, the rivers of south-west Britain and the river Trent in the English Midlands. The *Fenland Rivers of Cambridgeshire Palaeolithic Project* (FRCPP) was conceived as a short collaborative project between Durham University, the University of Cambridge and Cambridgeshire County Council, in recognition of the fact that Cambridgeshire has received scant attention compared to the well-studied Palaeolithic landscapes of the neighbouring counties of Norfolk and Suffolk, despite having a diverse archaeological record dating back *c* 500,000 years. The project provided the first review of Lower and Middle Palaeolithic artefacts from sites across the county and synthesised lithostratigraphic and palaeoenvironmental records from the deposits of the major rivers flowing across the Cambridgeshire Fenland towards the Wash (the Great Ouse and Nene, as well as important tributaries such as the Cam; White *et al.* 2008a). The final product not only significantly enhanced the HER for this part of East Anglia but also determined the impact of past aggregates extraction and provided a reference point for establishing potential in the face of future extraction.

Closing the lacunae: Palaeolithic Rivers of Southwest Britain project

In similar vein, the *Palaeolithic Rivers of Southwest Britain* project (PRoSWeB) and (in part) the *Archaeological Potential of Secondary Contexts* project (APSC), tackled another region where baseline information was extremely sketchy and a geochronological framework for Pleistocene fluvial deposits was largely absent. Unlike other regions, the aggregates threats in the south-west were viewed as distinctive, comprising small, episodically exploited quarries, prohibition order sites and local 'borrow' pits. The project, led by the Universities of Exeter and Reading, provided the first up-to-date statement of the known archaeological materials from the region's fluvial aggregate deposits, an assessment of the archaeological and geological potential of those deposits and guidelines for the management and mitigation of aggregates extraction (Hosfield *et al.* 2007). The study area focussed on the Rivers Axe, Otter and Exe and on the palaeo-Washford at Doniford Cliffs, modelling the evolution and development of these river systems, partially underpinning the resultant terrace models with OSL and integrating the poorly-known Lower and Middle Palaeolithic archaeological record. The PRoSWeB project also included a detailed programme of public outreach and dissemination activity, which is discussed further below.

The clear disparity with south-east England (where the Palaeolithic resource of counties such as Kent and Essex is comparatively well documented) was apparent at an early stage of the project, when desktop data collection and museum visits succeeded in increasing the number of known archaeological findspots by almost 50%. Although overall numbers are still small in comparison with south-east England, Palaeolithic artefacts were recorded in association with Terraces 5 of the River Exe, 2 and 5 of the River Otter, and the fill terraces of the River Axe, confirming a Lower Palaeolithic occupation in the Axe Valley and a Middle (and probably also a Lower) Palaeolithic occupation west of the Axe (Hosfield *et al.* 2007). Field investigations utilised new remote sensing methods, such as ground penetrating radar (GPR) and interferometric synthetic aperture radar (IFSAR), as well as OSL dating, fieldwalking of terrace landform surfaces, and coring/trenching of suitable fluvial deposits in order to map and characterise deposits with archaeological potential. The results of the fieldwork highlighted the fill terrace nature of the Axe sediments and the contrasting deposit types present, including extensive sequences of fluvial, colluvial and debris deposits of potential interest to the aggregates industry at sites such as Broom and Chard Junction. At the same time, the Axe was particularly identified as a system where fine-grained units may be present, in which artefacts may be concentrated with minimal reworking, together with organic channel deposits for palaeoenvironmental recovery. In contrast, the landforms and deposits from the Exe and the Otter river valleys were characterised by strath terrace systems (ie those resulting from the river downcutting through bedrock), with relatively thin sediments (in comparison to the Axe terraces), frequently heavily cryoturbated and/or truncated in some locations. These deposits are unlikely to be of high priority interest for aggregates extraction and equally, any contained archaeology is thought likely to have been either significantly disturbed or reworked (Hosfield *et al.* 2007).

The extensive programme of OSL dating undertaken during the PRoSWeB project revealed that the modern north-south drainage patterns of the Exe, Otter and probably also the Axe are of relatively recent origin, post-dating a major realignment of palaeo-drainage systems sometime after MIS 9 (around 300,000 BP). As well as providing a more secure dating context for Palaeolithic sites such as Broom in the Axe Valley, the new geochronological framework had further implications for the archaeological record, implying that any pre-MIS 9 artefacts were likely to have been substantially reworked, resulting in single artefact or low concentration findspots.

One can hope that as predictive estimates of potential move beyond simple counts of known finds and towards such reconstructions of palaeogeography, curatorial decisions will become better informed, and the hopes for predictive tools expressed in Chapter 1 will be fully realised. However, another issue of scale is at work. Even the most prolific historical sites rarely yield major new riches, even from developer-funded projects over relatively large areas. Modern scholars rarely have the luxury of unlimited time or access to the vast expanses of deposits available to previous generations. Apparent abundances may have been highly localised or entirely illusory, as highlighted at the site of Sturry in the Kentish Stour, where the 500 plus handaxes in museum collections were estimated to have occurred at the rate of just one per six tons of gravel (Dewey 1926). This is not always the case though, as shown by the recent spate of work at Purfleet, which produced hundreds of new finds and completely revised our understanding of the MIS 9 human landscape (Schreve *et al.* 2002; Bates *et al.* 1999; Bridgland *et al.* 2012).

Investigating the northern boundaries: Trent Valley Palaeolithic Project

The final case study presented here also focussed on what might previously have been considered to be a more marginal area for Lower and Middle Palaeolithic settlement, at the northern edge of hominin territories. The *Trent Valley Palaeolithic Project* (TVPP), a collaborative project by Durham University and the University of Birmingham, aimed to reveal the Palaeolithic archive of the Trent Valley, to establish a robust geological, chronological and palaeoenvironmental context for these assemblages and to provide an informed basis for future resource management. This was achieved through exhaustive study of museum and private artefact and fossil collections, combined with extensive fieldwork in operational quarries, palaeoenvironmental sampling, a programme of OSL and AAR dating and novel mathematical modelling of fluvial incision as recorded by the river terrace deposits. Significant new data were generated, including the discovery of new sites of archaeological and palaeoenvironmental importance, evidence for a hitherto unrecognized late Middle Pleistocene glaciation and previously unrecognized fluvial deposits, the results of which are presented in an extensive series of publications including a monograph (Bridgland *et al.* 2014), a field guide (White *et al.* 2007a) and various journal articles (Howard *et al.* 2007; 2011; White *et al.* 2007b; 2008b; 2009; 2010).

The Trent sedimentary sequence spans around a half a million years, with its earliest deposits known to pre-date the Anglian glaciation, *c* 450,000 BP. It plays an important role in the wider reconstruction of Pleistocene palaeo-drainage in Britain, and in particular its previous contribution to the headwaters, in the west Midlands, of the Bytham River (also referred to as the Baginton–Ingham river system), which existed prior to the Anglian glaciation (cf Rose 1994; Bridgland 2010). Furthermore, the Trent is the largest of the British rivers that combined to create the post-Anglian Fen Basin fluvial network, a major northward-flowing system now submerged beneath the North Sea and which doubtless formed an important corridor for animal movement and human migration. Over the last 500,000 years the course of the Trent has changed significantly, probably as a result of glaciations, and indeed the Trent is unique amongst the major English rivers in that it has flowed in close proximity to (and has sometimes been over-ridden by) ice sheets during several glacial episodes (White *et al.* 2007a; 2010; Bridgland *et al.* 2010).

The Palaeolithic record of the east Midlands has traditionally been viewed as patchy and uninspiring compared to that from East Anglia, despite attempts to raise its profile by several review articles (Posnansky 1963; McNabb 2001; McNabb 2006; Graf 2002). The issue has been compounded by the absence of high-quality flint in the area, a problem that would have been equally significant for early hominins in the landscape. As a result, the majority of artefacts have been made on quartzite, a raw material that rapidly becomes abraded by fluvial transport (tested by the TVPP in taphonomic experimentation), is difficult to spot against a quartzite-rich gravel (in contrast to flint) and often difficult to differentiate from natural material even when fresh. Although few find-spots have yielded more than a handful of stone tools, careful prospection by local collectors has amassed significant assemblages (by Trent Valley standards) from the villages of Hilton and Willington in Derbyshire, at Beeston in Nottinghamshire and the beach deposits at Kirmington in north Lincolnshire. These, and all other documented finds, are comprehensively reviewed in Bridgland *et al.* (2014). Little can be stated unequivocally about the earliest human occupants of the Trent system, with only the Waverley Wood lithic assemblage, including spectacular examples of volcanic andesitic handaxes (Lang and Keen 2005a and 2005b; Keen *et al.* 2006) and other scattered finds from the Baginton–Thurmaston Sands and Gravels providing any evidence for pre-Anglian hominin settlement in the wider Midlands region. The immediate post-

Anglian period (MIS 11-9) is equally obscure archaeologically, a fact that has previously been attributed to the Anglian extinction of the Bytham River, removing the main conduit into the Midlands (Keen *et al.* 2006), or to the greater proximity of the Trent region to the ice margins of the MIS 10 and 8 glaciations (Bridgland *et al.* 2014). However, the TVPP has revealed that little remains of the fluvial deposits laid down during MIS 11–9 so the absence of an archaeological signature from this period may be entirely explicable in terms of the paucity of terrace deposits of this age. In addition, large collections of heavily rolled artefacts in the MIS 8, 6, 4 and 2 terrace deposits doubtless reflect periods of earlier hominin occupation rather than their contemporaneous presence. The majority of artefacts are derived into the MIS 8 terrace, leading to the conclusion that the bulk of the assemblages probably belong somewhere in the period MIS 11–8, even if the gravels that contain them are much younger.

As with its Palaeolithic archive, the Pleistocene fossil record of the Trent is similarly poorly known compared to equivalent records from the Thames and many of the East Anglian rivers. Much of this may be down to the acidic groundwater conditions of the East Midlands, which do not favour long-term preservation of bone and shell, although there are notable exceptions such as the Whitemoor Haye woolly rhino site (see below). In addition, the more recent commercial aggregates exploitation history of the Trent, when compared to the Thames, has been through mechanical excavation as opposed to hand-digging, so the scant palaeontological material present is likely to be destroyed, missed or simply not collected. As noted in Bridgland *et al.* (2014), the mechanisation of aggregate extraction in the Trent has also created a bias against all but the largest vertebrate remains being collected by a sharp-eyed machine operator or emerging onto the reject piles of over-sized material at the processing plant and hopefully picked up by collectors.

The TVPP undertook a complete review of the palaeoenvironmental evidence, including the compilation of a gazetteer of the most significant collection of Pleistocene vertebrates from the Trent valley, the Brandon collection, now housed in the National Museum of Scotland in Edinburgh and the University Museum of Zoology, Cambridge. This collection comprises *c* 2000 bones, teeth and antlers from a number of localities between Newark and Lincoln. Additional assemblages of molluscs, pollen, plant macrofossils and insects were also generated through sampling at field sites, thereby adding substantially to the body of palaeoenvironmental knowledge from the Trent system. With the exception of localities such as Waverley Wood (Shotton *et al.* 1993), Brandon (Maddy *et al.* 1994) and Brooksby (Stephens *et al.* 2008), little is known of pre-Anglian palaeoenvironments in the Midlands, the vast majority of sites yielding palaeobiological proxies are from MIS 7 and later. Of particular note from the TVPP are the discovery of an important new MIS 7 site at Norton Bottoms in Lincolnshire (White *et al.* 2007b) and re-evaluation of the rich MIS 7-6 vertebrate assemblages from the Balderton terrace (Bridgland *et al.* 2014). The integration of the available palaeobiological datasets not only provides important contextual information for the archaeological assemblages but also assists, from a biostratigraphical perspective, in constraining the terrace age model proposed.

MICRO-SCALE: NEW SITE-SPECIFIC INFORMATION FROM THE FLUVIAL RECORD

As well as the landscape-scale fluvial studies described above, which occasionally revealed opportunities for more detailed investigation of individual sites, a number of ALSF projects focussed exclusively on single localities, either where archaeological evidence was discovered in association with palaeoenvironmental proxies, or where artefacts were absent but where other sources potentially provided valuable contextual climatic, environmental, biochronological or geographical information related to hominin occupation. With respect to the latter, it is important to recognise here the input of funding from a second ALSF provider, namely English Nature (now Natural England), since investigation of purely palaeontological sites fell more comfortably within their geodiversity remit. Almost without exception, every one of these investigations was undertaken as a rescue excavation in active quarries, where short-lived opportunities existed to salvage exceptional material at short notice.

Norton Subcourse

English Nature was able to fund a number of important projects, including rescue excavation at Norton Subcourse Quarry, Norfolk, led by Queen Mary, University of London. The site lies within the Crag Basin, which contains Early and early Middle Pleistocene marine sediments of the Norwich Crag and Wroxham Crag Formations, overlain by an extensive deposit of fossiliferous organic muds (the Cromer Forest-bed Formation, of early Middle Pleistocene age) and fluvial gravels of the Bytham River, the whole capped by Anglian glacigenic deposits. Although purely palaeoenvironmental in focus, the site is broadly coeval with some of the oldest evidence for hominin occupation in Britain, such as that at Pakefield, Suffolk (Parfitt *et al.* 2005), and as such can provide significant new information on early human environments and the landscapes of the early Middle Pleistocene in Britain. The pollen spectra indicate a temperate climate, spanning at least half of an interglacial. Molluscs, ostracods, fish and rare bird remains were also recovered, together with small mammals including an extinct water vole (*Mimomys savini*), extinct horse (*Equus altidens*), a cluster of large hyaena coprolites and remains of hippopotamus

(Lewis *et al.* 2004). The combined evidence appears to indicate that the site reflects a previously unrecognised temperate episode in the British early Middle Pleistocene. This obviously offers a prime example of sites where archaeology may be absent, but where the potential for understanding the landscapes of human presence and absence is immense (see Chapter 2).

Aylesford Gravel Pit

ALSF rescue investigations were also carried out on deposits of the Second Medway Terrace at Aylesford Gravel Pit SSSI (Kent) by the Kent RIGS (Regionally Important Geological and Geomorphological Sites) Group. A component of the project included the appraisal of the Aylesford vertebrate assemblage housed in Maidstone Museum (Schreve unpubl.), which complemented the stratigraphical, geochronological and archaeological investigations undertaken by the MVPP described above. The faunal analysis revealed a predominantly cold-climate (but taphonomically mixed) assemblage dominated by woolly rhinoceros (*Coelodonta antiquitatis*) with smaller numbers of woolly mammoth (*Mammuthus primigenius*), wild horse (*Equus ferus*), wild boar (*Sus scrofa*), giant deer (*Megaloceros giganteus*), red deer (*Cervus elaphus*) and large bovid. Pits in the Aylesford area have also produced a relatively rich but evidently derived Lower Palaeolithic handaxe assemblage, as well as some Middle Palaeolithic Levalloisian material that may or may not be contemporary with the faunal material. The age of the Aylesford Gravel Pit SSSI deposits remains inconclusive. The deposits were OSL dated to *c* 250,000–270,000 BP as part of the ALSF project (E Jarzembowski pers. comm., in Wenban-Smith 2007a). However, the presence of younger terrace deposits in the southern side of the quarry and of extensive solifluction gravels capping the fluvial sediments (Wenban-Smith *et al.* 2007a) potentially obscures the relationship of the date to the faunal assemblage, little of which bears any stratigraphical information. An additional complicating factor is the presence of both a lower and upper gravel member in the Aylesford terrace, separated by an interglacial 'brickearth' (the Kingsnorth Member) attributed to MIS 5e by Bates *et al.* (2002) although the attribution has yet to be confirmed on biostratigraphical or geochronological grounds (Bridgland 2003). The Aylesford gravel deposits appear to 'sandwich' these interglacial sediments and thus apparently cover both a pre-Ipswichian period of cold climate conditions, equated with MIS 6 and parts of the Devensian (last glaciations). It is not known from which part of the Aylesford Gravel Formation (ie pre- or post- the Kingsnorth interglacial Member) the fossil mammal remains come, and certainly, on the basis of the limited stratigraphical data preserved on the specimens, they could easily come from both.

Welton-le-Wold

Similar chronological issues were faced by the project *Towards an Understanding of the Ice Age at Welton-le-Wold*, undertaken by the Heritage Trust for Lincolnshire (Aram *et al.* 2004). This site, near Louth in Lincolnshire, exposes a complex glacial sequence, including up to 13m of glacial tills overlying *c* 10m of silts, sands and flint-rich gravels. Three distinctive till units (Welton Till, Calcethorpe Till and the Marsh Till, the last of Devensian age) are visible in the quarry, although in no place do all occur in stratigraphical superposition and the dating of the lower two tills has long been controversial. The importance of the site lies in the fact that it was for many years considered to provide evidence in support of a 'Wolstonian' glaciation in eastern England, stemming from the presence of mammalian remains and Palaeolithic artefacts in gravels underlying two generations of till, the younger of which was attributed to the Devensian (Alabaster and Straw 1976; Wymer and Straw 1977; Straw 2005). In the 1970s, prior to the widespread recognition of pre-Anglian hominin settlement in Britain, the artefacts and fauna were generally regarded as being of Hoxnian (late Middle Pleistocene) age. The ALSF project undertook a re-evaluation of artefact and faunal assemblage to gather fresh information about the date and context of the material, a programme of borehole survey to re-assess the stratigraphical context of the 1960s finds, and examination of the entirety of the Pleistocene sedimentary sequence. At the same time, a parallel series of outreach activities was designed to enhance immediate and long-term intellectual access to the geological and archaeological resource (Aram *et al.* 2004).

Re-examination of the limited faunal assemblage by Schreve (in Aram *et al.* 2004) confirmed the presence of a minimum number of two straight-tusked elephants (*Palaeoloxodon antiquus*), a single individual each of horse (*Equus* sp.) and red deer, as well as two large bovids, previously misidentified as giant deer (Alabaster and Straw 1976). The assemblage can be subdivided into two parts: a derived component (horse, red deer and large bovid) and a relatively fresh component (straight-tusked elephant). The former is not diagnostic of any particular climatic conditions, although the presence of horse indicates the availability of open grassland habitats. Equally, age determination is difficult, other than the fact that the occurrence of horse precludes a date within the Last Interglacial and the Early Devensian. The derived component may therefore represent any interstadial, interglacial or period of cold climate prior to the Last Interglacial. The fresh component consists only of straight-tusked elephant, an animal found solely in association with temperate-climate episodes during the Pleistocene. Although it is not age-diagnostic (occurring from the early Middle Pleistocene until the Last Interglacial in the UK), its presence

Fig. 4.14 The Whitemoor Haye woolly rhinoceros shortly after its discovery (photo @ Birmingham Archaeology)

indicates that the sands and gravels were laid down during an interstadial or interglacial episode. New OSL age-estimates undertaken by Aram *et al.* (2004) place the entire sequence between MIS 10 and 6. However, this is challenged by the findings of the TVPP described above, which assert that at least one of the two lowermost tills could be Anglian (if not both), making the faunal and archaeological assemblage not only pre-Anglian in age but if true, the most northerly evidence of pre-Anglian occupation in Britain yet discovered. The artefacts from Welton are discussed further in Chapter 5 (Box 5.2).

Whitemoor Haye Quarry

One of the most spectacular palaeontological finds to be made during the course of the ALSF lifetime was the recovery of the front half of a skeleton of woolly rhinoceros from deposits of the River Tame (a Trent tributary) at Whitemoor Haye Quarry, near Alrewas in Staffordshire. Follow-up investigations led by the University of Birmingham (project number IW/2002/127; Buteux *et al.* 2003) were funded by English Nature, following the chance find in a single scoop of a machine operator's bucket (Fig. 4.14). The bones were in excellent condition and represent the finest example of a woolly rhino found in Britain this century, and one of the most important finds of a Pleistocene fossil mammal skeleton made in the UK in the last 100 years. The full results of the project are reported in Schreve *et al.* (2013). Thirty-three separate skeletal elements of the rhinoceros were recovered, predominantly associated elements, including a magnificent cranium with complete dentition (Fig. 4.15), strongly suggesting that these were originally in articulated (or near-articulated) position in the ground. Based upon additional material collected, the remains of at least four adult woolly rhinoceroses are preserved at the site (the most abundant species within the vertebrate assemblage), together with reindeer (*Rangifer tarandus*), woolly mammoth, horse, bison (*Bison priscus*) and wolf (*Canis lupus*). Preservation of Pleistocene vertebrate remains is extremely unusual in this part of the Midlands, given the absence of calcareous groundwaters. However, the undulating surface of the Mercia Mudstone bedrock would have provided opportunities for localised ponding and stagnation of water and organic debris, leading to a near-neutral pH and a reducing environment more favourable to bone preservation. Analysis of pollen, plant macrofossil and arthropod (beetle, chironomid and caddisfly) remains suggests that the rhinoceros was rapidly buried on a braided river floodplain surrounded by a predominantly treeless, herb-rich grassland. Comparative calculations of coleopteran and chironomid palaeotemperatures suggest a mean July temperature of 8–11° C and a mean December temperature of between -22° C and -16° C. Radiocarbon age estimates on skeletal material, supported by OSL ages from surrounding sediments, indicate that the rhinoceros lived at around 41,000-43,000 BP (Schreve *et al.* 2013).

Lynford Quarry

The final example illustrated in this section can be described as a flagship site for our understanding of Middle Palaeolithic technology and Neanderthal

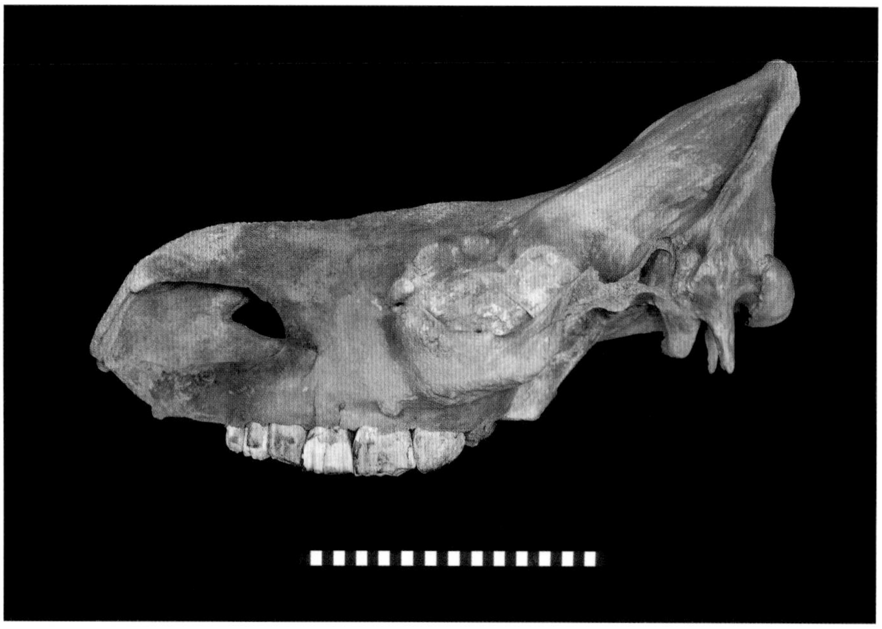

Fig. 4.15 Skull with complete dentition of the Whitemoor Haye woolly rhinoceros Coelodonta antiquitatis *(scale bar in cm)*

environments in Britain. This is the site of Lynford, in the valley of the River Wissey in Norfolk, which was discovered during active quarrying in 2002 and subsequently excavated, with support from the ALSF, by the Norfolk Archaeological Unit and associated specialists. During quarrying, a palaeochannel containing *in situ* faunal remains and a rich associated Mousterian flint assemblage was revealed (Boismier 2003; Schreve 2006; Boismier *et al.* 2012; see also Chapter 2, Figs 2.28 and 2.29 and Box 5.8). With the exception of a handful of mammalian remains from gravels underlying the palaeochannel, all of the fauna comes from the palaeochannel itself (Fig. 4.16), and is thought to represent an accumulation within a former meander cut-off. The age of the site was established by geochronology and biostratigraphy. Radiocarbon dating of woolly mammoth bone and molar

Fig. 4.16 Excavation of the Lynford site (courtesy of the Norfolk Museums Service)

KILLING THE MAMMOTH

BOX 4.2

The Lynford vertebrate assemblage not only sheds light on Middle Devensian palaeoenvironments and mammalian faunal history in Britain but also contributes to our understanding of Neanderthal diet and subsistence behaviour in a marginal environment. The richness of the faunal vertebrate assemblage is mirrored by that of the archaeological assemblage, including more than 2700 artefacts, of which 47 are handaxes, mostly in mint-fresh condition (White, in Boismier *et al.* 2012). The faunal assemblages represent a palimpsest of material, with some specimens deposited rapidly under very still water conditions, and others laying on the land surface for variable amounts of time before being incorporated into the channel fill through debris flows, bank collapse or overbank flooding, over a period of perhaps tens of years. Although there is abundant evidence of fragmentation, particularly of mammoth crania and tusks (probably the result of trampling), the general lack of abrasion, root-etching and evidence of fluvial winnowing on the fauna, together with the presence of refitting lithic pieces, suggests that the assemblages can be interpreted as a coherent whole.

Direct evidence of faunal exploitation comes from horse, reindeer and woolly rhinoceros teeth and bones that appear to have been deliberately smashed during marrow extraction activities.

Evidence for mammoth utilization is harder to establish, although the predominance of prime individuals, the absence of the meatiest limb bones (despite other large elements being present), the paucity of carnivore gnaw marks and evidence for tool resharpening and damage on the tips of the handaxes collectively support the view that Neanderthals were coming to the site deliberately to exploit, if not to hunt, mammoth. The site itself presents certain advantages for this endeavour, since Neanderthals could have actively 'shepherded' mammoths into the swampy channel, tiring them out before moving in for the kill, a strategy developed by early hominins in Britain as long ago as 500,000 years BP. Interestingly, the Lynford mammoth remains also present an exceptional number of pathologies, much higher than has been seen in other mammoth assemblages where occasional damage is usually the result of inter-specific fighting. Here, the pathologies are clustered in key, vital areas of the body, leading to speculation that they may result from previous, failed hunting attempts. Clear evidence for the exploitation of large and dangerous megafauna by Neanderthals exists elsewhere in Europe; there is no reason to suspect that British populations were any less proficient.

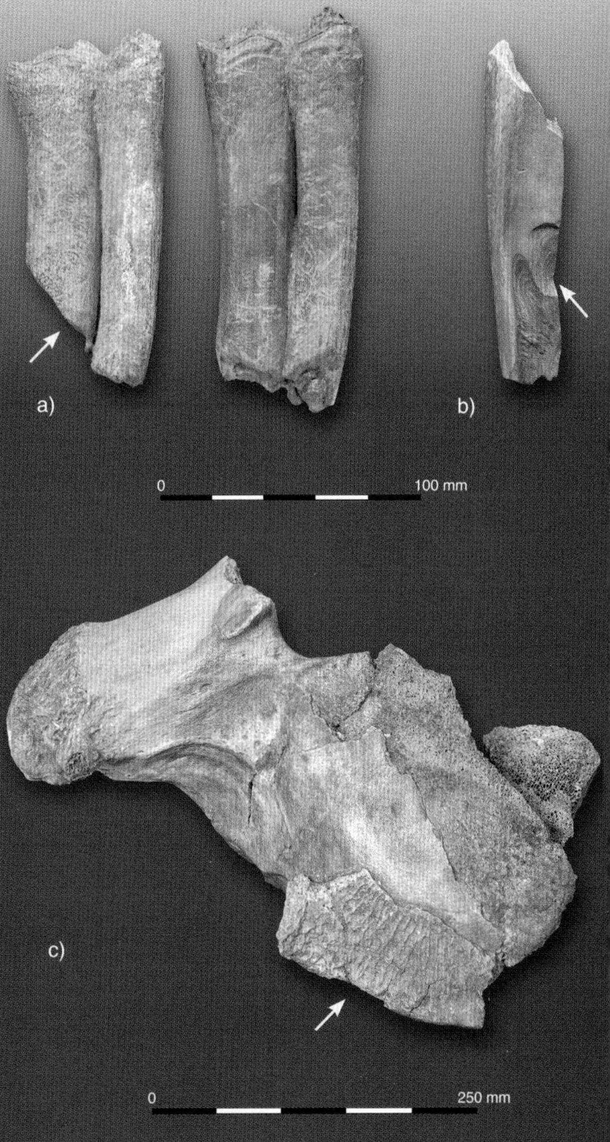

4.2.1 Modified bones from Lynford

a) Horse molars broken during extraction of marrow from the mandibular cavity (arrow)

b) Reindeer tibia fragment showing impact scars from marrow extraction (arrow)

c) Partial mammoth vertebra showing attached fragment of adjacent vertebra (arrow), broken while being prised apart

fragments from the main channel yielded age estimates of 53,700 ± 3100 BP (OxA-11571) and > 49,700 BP (OxA-11572), indicating an age for the site in excess of 50,000 years, whereas OSL ages of 64,000 ± 5000 and 67,000 ± 5000 BP place the deposition of the channel sediments at the transition from MIS 4 to 3. In terms of its species composition, the Lynford mammalian assemblage is typical of the Middle Devensian in Britain, correlated with MIS 3 (Currant and Jacobi 2001). This period overall represents a modest climatic amelioration but is characterised by numerous abrupt climatic oscillations occurring on a submillennial scale.

The vertebrate faunal assemblage comprised just over 2000 individually-numbered large mammal finds (1300 of which could be identified to species, genus or Family level), together with over 2000 microvertebrate remains and other fragments from wet-sieved bulk samples taking for palaeoenvironmental analysis. In addition, one quarter of all excavated spoil was sieved for the recovery of faunal remains, yielding over 26,400 specimens from dry-sieved soil residues and over 17,400 from wet-sieved spoil residues. Twelve mammalian taxa (including *Homo*, represented on the basis of the artefacts), four fish taxa, one amphibian taxon and one bird taxon were recorded. The mammal assemblage is dominated by remains of eleven woolly mammoths (Fig. 4.17), all prime adults apart from a single calf and mostly male where determinable, followed by reindeer, woolly rhino, bison, horse, wolf, red fox (*Vulpes vulpes*), brown bear (*Ursus arctos*), spotted hyaena (*Crocuta crocuta*), ground squirrel (*Spermophilus* sp.) and narrow-skulled vole (*Microtus gregalis*). The remaining vertebrates comprise pike (*Esox lucius*), three-spined stickleback (*Gasterosteus aculeatus*), a member of the carp family (Cyprinidae sp.) and perch (*Perca fluviatilis*), together with crake (*Porzana* sp.) and common frog (*Rana temporaria*). The combined palaeoenvironmental evidence from plant remains, pollen, molluscs, insects and vertebrates indicates open conditions dominated by grasses, sedges and low-growing herbaceous communities with small stands of birch or scrub, acid heath or wetlands, adjacent to a source of slow-flowing permanent water. Beetle remains suggest that the mean temperature of the warmest month (July) lay somewhere between 14°C and 12°C, with the mean temperature of the coldest months (January/February) at or below –15°C (Boismier *et al.* 2012). The implications of the faunal assemblage in terms of interpreting Neanderthal subsistence behaviour are discussed in Box 4.2.

WIDER ENGAGEMENT

One of the most important roles of the ALSF involved the raising of awareness and strengthening of contacts between those working in the aggregate extraction environment. These include quarry companies, planning authorities, geologists, archaeologists, Quaternary scientists, other specialists and members of the public whose local landscape has been impacted by past or present quarrying. With this in mind, ALSF funding was directed towards a major public exhibition that highlighted the Palaeolithic and Pleistocene record and emphasised the role of aggregates extraction in enhancing our knowledge of early prehistory. The

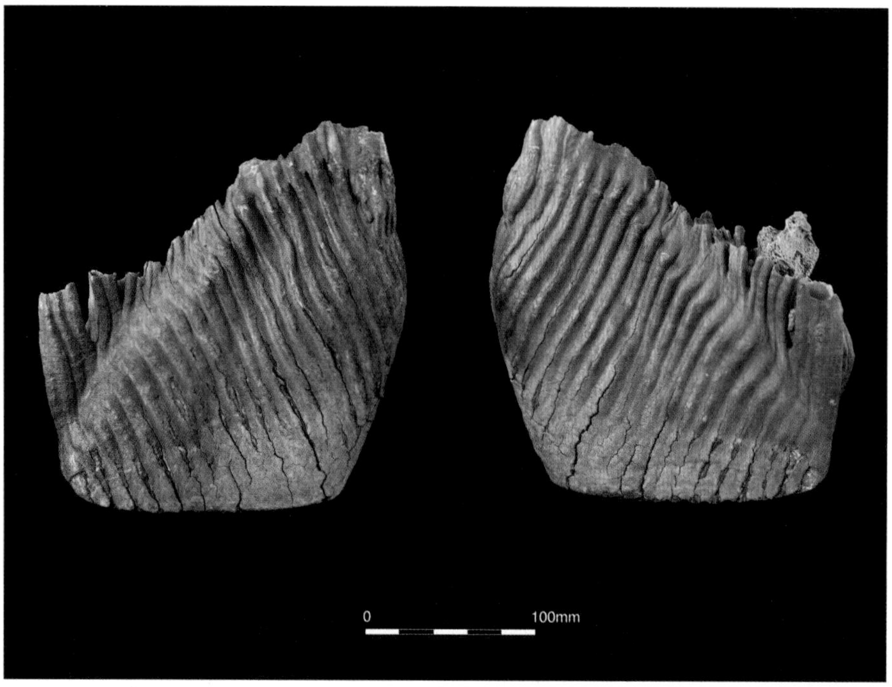

Fig. 4.17 Associated upper molars of Mammuthus primigenius *from Lynford, Norfolk (scale bar in cm)*

Museum of London's 'London Before London' gallery tells the story of the Lower Thames Valley from the arrival of the earliest hominins during the Middle Pleistocene to the founding of Roman Londinium in the mid 1st century AD. The gallery provided a unique opportunity in the UK to engage the public by showing off over 1500 specimens of superb fossil and artefactual material, many of them from excavations associated with gravel extraction.

Dissemination of Palaeolithic and Pleistocene research findings in Britain was also promoted through the funding of a major monograph publication, 'The Thames Through Time' Volume 1, by Morigi *et al.* (2011), which formed the first of a four-part series coordinated by Oxford Archaeology. The monograph series focussed on the archaeology of the Pleistocene gravel terraces of the Upper and Middle Thames Valley, which were intensively worked for gravel extraction during the 19th and 20th centuries. The region remains a major focus for aggregate operations today, with primary extraction set to continue at a high level for the foreseeable future engendering some of the most intensive archaeological activity in England in recent years. The series was particularly devised to facilitate intellectual access to excavation results for professional practitioners (benefitting heritage management and curation, informing professional practice, advancing the regional research agenda, and supporting the teaching of archaeology) as well as being tailored for the informed non-specialist reader, including especially the voluntary archaeological sector and a diverse range of non-archaeological organisations with convergent interests in the protection and management of the river and its surrounding landscape.

Several of the meso-scale projects described above contained elements of public engagement, such as the provision of public information leaflets and talks to specialist interest societies. In many of the regions outside East Anglia and the South-East, however, where historically interest in the Palaeolithic has been comparatively limited, the importance of building networks between stakeholders, and of regional 'champions', becomes all the more important. In this respect, the Shotton Project: a Midlands Palaeolithic Network led by Birmingham University identified the key role played by the late Professor Frederick Shotton, who for more than fifty years maintained a regional network of local enthusiasts who worked with quarry companies to discover and record the Pleistocene geology and archaeology of the Midlands. With the death of Professor Shotton in 1990, much of the research momentum was lost. The ALSF-funded *Shotton Project* (based in the counties of Herefordshire, Leicestershire, Rutland, Shropshire, Staffordshire, Warwickshire and Worcestershire) was therefore designed to forge new links between aggregates

Fig. 4.18 Palaeolithic geoarchaeology walk at Ottery St Mary (Devon), 2006, by PRoSWeB

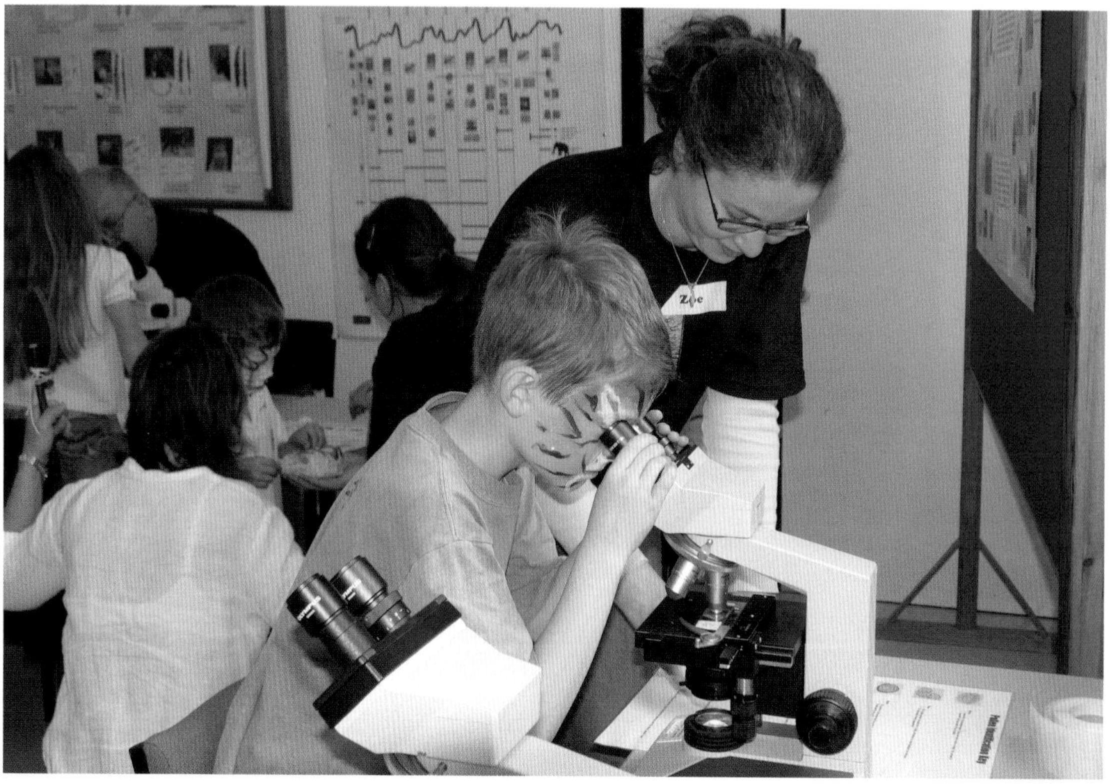

Fig. 4.19 Montage of images from the Royal Holloway 'Day In the Ice Age' (19a-d), showing flint knapping, pollen analysis, demonstration of vertebrate fossils and spear-making and cave painting activities for children

companies and their employees, archaeologists, palaeontologists, geologists, local societies, museums and schools, in order to recreate a network dedicated to systematic and regular monitoring of sand and gravel workings for finds and deposits of significance, while investigating and promoting interest in the Palaeolithic. The PRoSWeB project in south-west Britain was equally successful in developing new networks to promote Palaeolithic and Pleistocene research in the region, including (amongst other activities) the provision of geoarchaeology walks (Fig. 4.18), schools activity days and teaching resource boxes, containing replica Palaeolithic stone tools and resource cards, thereby ensuring a maintainable resource that could continue to promote interest in the Palaeolithic archaeology and Pleistocene geology of the south-west region beyond the lifetime of the project.

Following on from the success of the Shotton Project in the Midlands, this integrated approach was extended to the macro-scale through the flagship *National Ice Age Network* (NIAN) project, operating from four regional centres based in the Universities of Birmingham, Royal Holloway University of London, Southampton and Leicester and uniquely co-funded through the ALSF by

One of the most successful examples of public engagement came from the National Ice Age Network project (NIAN) which designed and distributed a series of four bespoke 'recognition sheets', covering stone tools, sediments, vertebrate fossils, and molluscs, insects and plant remains. The leaflets were pitched in such a manner that they would appeal and be of interest to as wide an audience as possible, including but not limited to quarry personnel, commercial archaeologists and the general public. Distribution was widespread, including collaboration through the PRoSWeB project and downloads through the NIAN website, as well as an invitation from the Council for British Archaeology to supply 7500 packs of the four recognition sheets in the February 2007 edition of British Archaeology magazine. Their widespread distribution has brought information regarding Ice Age evidence to a huge audience. At the time of writing, over 42,500 stone tool recognition sheets and 32,000 copies of the other three sheets have been distributed and distribution is still ongoing. Sheets have been used by Finds Liaison Officers, for AS Level and undergraduate teaching and by the general public to help spot and identify Ice Age remains and artefacts. The project further worked closely with museums across England, reviewing the Palaeolithic and Pleistocene collections and developing a travelling display of museum panels, tailored for the individual regions, and produced a handbook for the recognition and recording of remains in quarries (Buteux *et al.* 2009).

4.3.1 National Ice Age Network project's "Digging up the Ice Age"

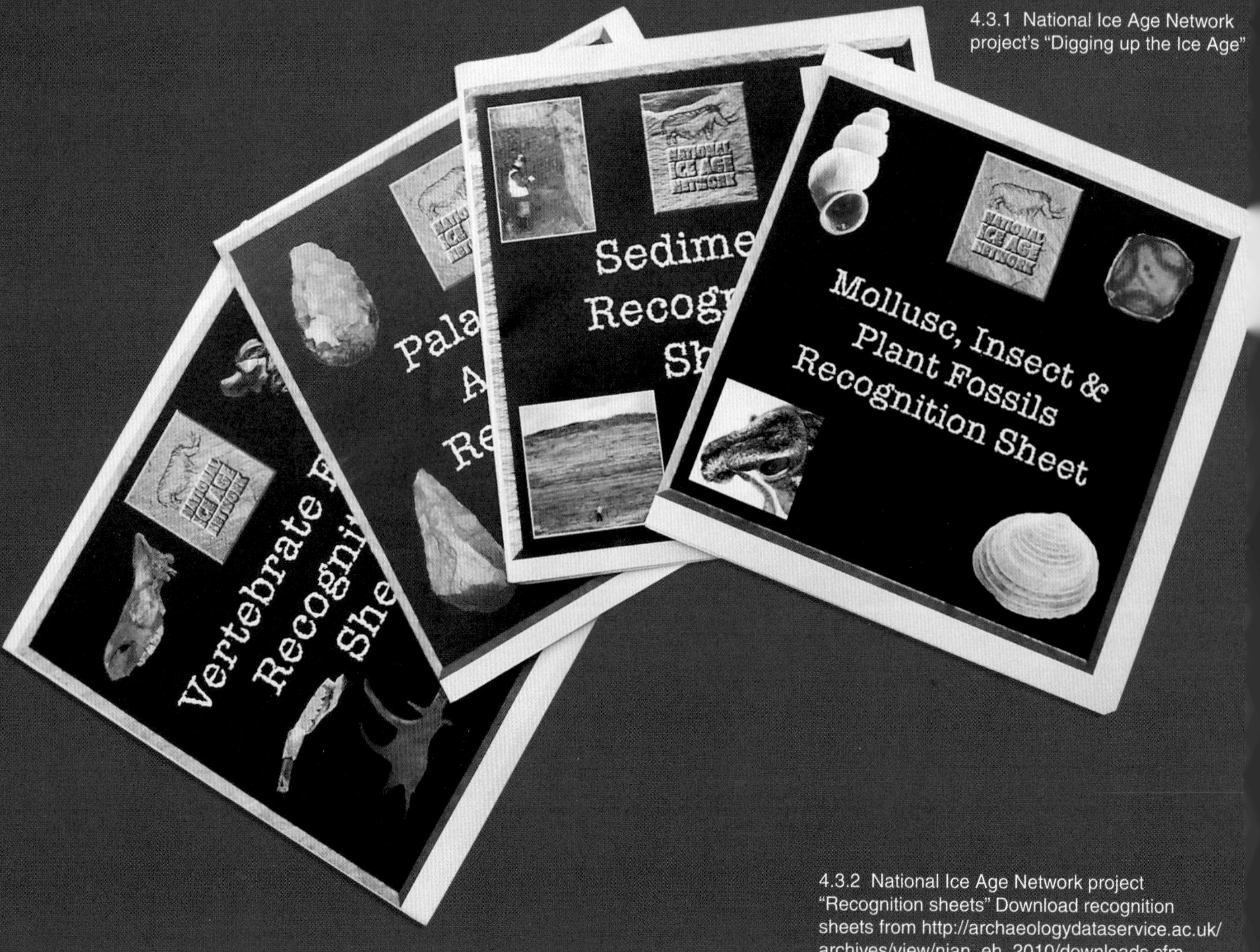

4.3.2 National Ice Age Network project "Recognition sheets" Download recognition sheets from http://archaeologydataservice.ac.uk/archives/view/nian_eh_2010/downloads.cfm

English Heritage (now Historic England) and English Nature (now Natural England). The overarching goals of the project were threefold:

- To develop a national network of stakeholders and other interested participants to raise awareness of Palaeolithic archaeology and Pleistocene geology
- To undertake a detailed programme of outreach and dissemination activities
- To create an infrastructure throughout England to promote the regular and systematic monitoring of sand and gravel workings in order to assess their potential for providing Palaeolithic and Pleistocene finds that can be used to reconstruct past environments.

Through the NIAN project website, a database of nearly 1100 participants was established, including museum staff, local government archaeologists, academic departments and researchers, local archaeological and geological societies and members of the public. This network later performed an important consultation role when NIAN coordinated preparation of English Heritage's National Research Framework for the Palaeolithic/Pleistocene. Over 100 outreach events were carried out, including public lectures, society presentations and hands-on training sessions, as well as major 'Day In the Ice Age' public events in the four regional centres (Fig. 4.19). Twenty five thousand copies of an A4 colour duplex leaflet on the Ice Age were produced and distributed to museums, commercial archaeologists, academic departments, local societies and relevant conferences, together with a number of 'recognition sheets' for the identification of different remains (Fig. 4.20; Box 4.3).

Dealing appropriately with significant Ice Age remains uncovered during sand and gravel quarrying is a very important aspect of environmentally sustainable aggregate extraction. Although quarrying provides the opportunity to bring such remains to light, because of its ultimately destructive nature, there are no second chances. It was a premise of the NIAN project that these issues were not sufficiently appreciated both by those in the aggregates industry and by those in charge of regulating the industry – the minerals planners and their advisors. For this reason, the NIAN project was funded to tackle an issue that goes to the heart of sustainability and the aims of the ALSF.

However, the extent to which the importance of Palaeolithic and Pleistocene remains uncovered during quarrying was not appreciated was underestimated at the outset of the project. This was compounded by widespread misapprehension on the part of some quarry companies that the recording and recovery of significant remains would entail significant disruption to aggregates extraction, a view heavily coloured by their experiences with developer-funded surface archaeology preservation by record. As well as the outreach aspects of the NIAN project, a significant element was to have been a field-based survey of all active quarries in England to assess their potential to yield significant Ice Age remains, combined with GIS modelling of this potential. In this respect, NIAN adopted the same methodology as projects described above but sought to apply it at a national level, in the hope of developing a 'light touch' procedure for future monitoring, agreed in collaboration with the aggregates industry. Very many in the industry were sympathetic to and supportive of this aim, which built on a long tradition of voluntary collaboration between the industry, geologists and amateur collectors. Unfortunately, in the course of negotiations with the larger companies in the industry, ultimately at the request of the quarry companies through the Quarry Products Association (QPA, now the Mineral Products Association), a consensus developed that such collaboration was not currently in the interests of the QPA's members and would not be until required by future legislation.

The QPA expressed concerns that Pleistocene remains uncovered within and beneath the 'aggregate body' was a new responsibility for the industry to assume, presenting the possibility of significant disruption to extraction, health and safety concerns, and the possibility of further planning constraints in the future. The argument that the long tradition of successful collaboration between quarry companies and researchers at the local level showed that this was not the case, was not accepted. Despite support from English Nature and English Heritage in these negotiations, the proposed national audit of the 'Pleistocene potential' of active quarries had to be largely abandoned. Many aggregates companies fully appreciate that taking responsibility for the significant Ice Age remains uncovered during quarrying is something that, in their goal of achieving environmentally-responsible extraction, they should be concerned with. The door was left open to continue negotiations on the matter once other pressing matters facing the industry, including the increasing costs of archaeological mitigation, had been satisfactorily resolved. Such renewed negotiations could not take place within the duration of the project, however, and remain a matter for the future. The hope is that these negotiations have laid a foundation for a more positive approach to be developed in due course. Revealing the mysteries of our distant ancestors and past environments through quarrying has major potential benefits for science and society, but the industry as a whole needs to capitalise on this.

Chapter 5: Site and artefact studies

by Andrew Shaw and Beccy Scott

LOST IN TRANSLATION: COMMUNICATING THE PALAEOLITHIC RECORD

The Palaeolithic record often appears to be simply composed of dots on maps. This is certainly the form in which it has been translated through into Historic Environment Records – single points where one or more artefacts have been found. Barring the issues of incompleteness that attend such records for any period, this enthusiasm for pointillism actually serves to distort the record as understood and interpreted by Palaeolithic archaeologists. As emphasised throughout this volume, the Palaeolithic is a period investigated and accessed on a variety of contrasting and complementary scales. This chapter aims to return to the nuts and bolts of this record – sites and artefacts – and to explain the scale and texture of the information that can be extracted from them. Such detail is often lost within specialist literature and archive reports, and it is a failing of the academic Palaeolithic community as a whole that, when attempting to communicate our findings to a wider audience, we too often retreat into clichéd stories, or frame our findings in the language of later prehistory. It is precisely this issue of incomplete translation that the ALSF – and this volume in particular – sought to address.

As explained in earlier chapters (see Chapters 2 and 4), a large portion of the Palaeolithic record actually comprises archives (frequently fluvial) of changing climate and landscape. Humans are not necessarily represented within these. In this chapter, we explore specifically what Palaeolithic sites are, emphasising key differences between such sites, and those more familiar to curators, consultants and contract units. As elsewhere in this volume, the key point here is the question of working on an appropriate scale, and asking the right questions of different datasets. In particular, we deal with 'secondary context' sites – a topic that illustrates many of the difficulties encountered when translating the importance of Palaeolithic research between academic archaeologists and other stakeholders. To term a whole group of sites and assemblages 'secondary' context implies that they are of lesser significance than a whole group of other sites – and thus perhaps not worth dealing with. In Chapter 1, we put ourselves in the developers' shoes and asked the obvious question: 'if you already have a large collection of rolled handaxes from this spot, why bother to collect any more?' We here address the different scales of questions which such collections (which make up the vast bulk of the British Palaeolithic record) can be used to answer, and present ways in which ALSF projects have shown how this can be achieved, both in terms of research and fieldwork.

To the non-specialist, most Palaeolithic archaeologists might seem a little obsessed with stone tools. The temptation, when translating research from an academic to a broader context, is to concentrate on the most aesthetically appealing artefacts, and to gloss over the seemingly arcane details of the lithic assemblage. We here present a broad overview of the changing technologies of the British Palaeolithic record, as currently understood, whilst emphasising this picture is always open to adjustment in the light of new sites, discoveries and dates. Using examples drawn from ALSF projects, we explain the varied ways in which Palaeolithic archaeologists use the information gleaned from stone tools to understand site formation processes, technical decision making, and how whole landscapes were exploited. This latter point is significant; whilst the aggregate archives of Britain have produced the vast majority of the Palaeolithic resource, it is important to look away from the river valleys to the other places where Palaeolithic lives were lived.

WHEN IS A SITE NOT A SITE?

Having spent some time traversing the perhaps unfamiliar landscapes of the Palaeolithic, readers whose specialism lies outside Quaternary studies might draw some comfort at reaching, finally, a chapter that deals with the twin archaeological certainties of sites and artefacts. These, after all, are the bread and butter of archaeology and, in a curatorial context, what we seek to protect. Sites and artefacts are the raw material from which Historic Environment Records are wrought – findspots reflecting the physical evidence of how humans modify their world, through digging, building, and making things. In HER terms, in fact,

Although frequently offered up as a flagship site (Gamble 1996), Boxgrove exemplifies the problem of trying to extend the concept of the 'archaeological site' to the Palaeolithic record. Even though the exceptionally well-preserved archaeology it has produced allows the reconstruction of hominin behaviour on an individual, and ethno-historical timescale, it is better described as a palaeolandscape than a site (Chapter 2). The deposits making up the Boxgrove palaeolandscape have been mapped over 26km, situated at the point where the uplifted chalk and coastal plain intersect. They comprise a sequence of fine-grained sediments of marine, terrestrial and lagoonal origin, dated to around 480,000 BP on biostratigraphic grounds (Roberts and Parfitt 1999).

5.1.2 Handaxes from Boxgrove

Since 1982, more than 90 separate areas within the Boxgrove palaeolandscape have been investigated; half of these have produced artefacts (largely reflecting the use of handaxes) and a number are intimately associated with butchered animal carcasses. The archaeology derives from two primary units: a palaeosol (Unit 4c; estimated to have formed over 20-100 years) overlying a series of exceptionally well-preserved landsurfaces established for short periods on inter-tidal silts (Unit 4b). Pope and Roberts (2005) describe the archaeology contained within these units as spanning a variety of preservational gradients – from momentary snapshots of individual action in the lower landsurfaces, to spatially extensive, more time-averaged patterns, whereby the *in situ* record of the palaeosol scatter coalesce into local concentrations ('patches'; cf. Isaacs 1989) through repeated hominin action.

The behavioural evidence preserved within the Boxgrove palaeolandscape is informative at a variety of scales, ranging from the micro-, meso- and macro-scales. The Q1/A knapping scatter captures the moment and movements of an individual thinning one area of a bifacial roughout (Austin 1994), whilst the dynamics of technology and butchery are captured within accumulations such as the GTP17, where eight refitting scatters were associated with the butchered remains of a single horse (Roberts and Parfitt 1999). Whilst handaxe manufacture dominated, no handaxes were actually discarded in this area, instead being carried away for use elsewhere (Pope 2002, Pope and Roberts 2005). Combining such instances with the longer-view temporal focus permitted by material from the palaeosol, however, allows these snapshots to be reshuffled to fit into the panorama provided by the whole landscape setting. All tool-using behaviour was essentially organised in relation to the degrading chalk cliff that backs the northern edge of the palaeolandscape (Roberts and Parfitt 1999), and from which high quality nodular flint was available. Material was tested and selected from this, then carried back away from the cliff, primarily to be reworked into handaxes – frequently at butchery sites (Pope 2002; Pope and Roberts 2005).

The spatial and temporal structure of the hominin world is also accessible at Boxgrove; the Q1/B locality represents a seasonally wet waterhole associated with the palaeosol. Excavation and investigation of this locale was

5.1.1 The chalk cliff backing the Boxgrove palaeolandscape, as exposed in GTP 25a

funded by English Heritage (Boxgrove D) These freshwater deposits were rich in butchered animal remains and lithic material, and formed a repeated focus for human action. The artefact assemblage here differs markedly from that recovered from throughout the contemporary palaeosol, being rich in handaxes, flake tools, and antler hammers for flint working (Pope and Roberts 2005, 89). Detailed taphonomic analyses demonstrate that this predominance of handaxes is a behavioural, and not a preservational pattern (Pope 2002). Thus Q1/B represents a position in the landscape repeatedly visited by humans who routinely discarded handaxes. This can be contrast with situations like GTP17, where humans carried their tools away from a single episode butchery site. Overall, handaxes were discarded most frequently close to the cliff and freshwater (Pope 2002; Pope and Roberts 2005). The association of increased handaxe discard near raw material sources and fresh water has been frequently commented upon on a coarse scale, usually based on coarser secondary context patterns and framed in terms of habitat preference (eg Ashton 1998). Critically, Pope's detailed work reintroduces the concept of hominin agency to interpreting such patterns, through investigating them on an ethnohistorical scale (Pope 2002; Pope and Roberts 2005). Within the generational envelope of these time-averaged contexts, hominin behaviour can be seen as having a structuring effect upon subsequent actions.

The flagship individual scatters preserved at Boxgrove are therefore equally informative when viewed either from the ground upwards, or in long shot (repeated behaviour over 20-100 years) and wide view (the structure of the palaeolandscape). Even when dealing with such well-preserved archaeological signatures, it is essential to take account of the different scales over which particular assemblages accumulated. The Boxgrove palaeolandscape represents an exceptional setting within which such relationships can be investigated.

5.1.3 The Q1/A knapping scatter, Boxgrove

5.1.4 Q1/B waterhole, Boxgrove

an artefact can become a 'site' – a single discovery transformed to a dot on a map where somebody in the past dropped something. Most archaeologists would be comfortable, moreover, with accepting the definition of a site as somewhere in the landscape where artefacts and other evidence of occupation (whether actually dwelling, or undertaking other activities) occur together, allowing what people did to be reconstructed on an ethnographic and historical scale. In practical terms, we often think of sites as defined by the presence of cut features and the material contained within them. Such traces are what we are used to dealing with in later prehistoric and historic periods (for instance, pits, ditches, buildings and post holes) and their evaluation and investigation is routine practice.

Simply extending the same definition of sites to the Palaeolithic record becomes problematic. Cut features are rarely left by any hunter-gatherer group and are particularly uncommon in the Lower and Middle Palaeolithic, when evidence for any sort of structure is ambiguous at best. Another way of thinking about sites might be to consider them as places where humanly modified material (stone tools and worked bone) is concentrated. Such material may occur sporadically throughout Pleistocene sediments, but it is only where many such artefacts are concentrated that we can talk about a site in a sense equivalent to how we think about them in more recent prehistory. However, in the Palaeolithic, such concentrations may not be a direct reflection of repeated human behaviour in the past, but of other taphonomic and collection factors – for instance, different fluvial dynamics in different stretches of a river, or the indefatigable nature of particular dedicated collectors who, by their very activities, create clusters of finds within their collecting ambit. Sites where artefacts and evidence of occupation and other activities are preserved in such a way to allow human behaviour to be reconstructed at an ethnographic or historical scale are extremely uncommon, and these isolated occurrences are the flagships around which a flotilla of interpretations coalesce (cf. Gamble 1996).

Palaeolithic archaeology, perhaps even more than any other period, demands an approach that considers human activity within its entire landscape context. A broad distinction can be drawn, then, between two different types of site: those from which humanly worked artefacts have been recovered, and those which do not contain direct evidence for a human presence, but which allow the detailed reconstruction of the environments within which they were active. Reconstructing both the landscapes through which early humans moved and those that they avoided is crucial for understanding hominin adaptations, behaviour, and capabilities (see Chapter 2). Thus, a Palaeolithic site might contain no evidence that humans were ever there and yet be critical to reconstructing the non-analogue environments (in terms of climate, vegetation and animal biomass) of the Palaeolithic. These 'ghost ships' provide the environmental cargo necessary to float broader behavioural interpretations. Perhaps more importantly, building up a picture of the types of environment that humans could not survive in, or periods in which they were not present, allows us to look at their adaptive capabilities, and especially, in the case of Britain, the conditions necessary for colonising a landmass that fluctuated between island and peninsula.

In Palaeolithic terms, then, an archaeological site is a location that provides evidence upon which inferences about past environments can be built, and which thus can contribute to our overall understanding of changing hominin adaptations. Most deposits encountered within the context of aggregate extraction would fit this broad definition. However, different types of deposit – and the humanly modified material that is sometimes contained within them – are appropriate for addressing different scales of question.

SPACE, TIME AND SCALE

Clive Gamble (1996) suggested that the Palaeolithic artefactual record is made up of two main types of site: 'Flagships' and 'Dredgers'. The first group comprises sites that provide detailed information that can be related to an ethnographic scale of analysis – for instance, refitting lithics and cut-marked animal bones, that have been minimally reworked since their deposition. Dredgers, which are far more common, are sites at which reworked artefacts derived from the wider landscape have become associated within a geological deposit. Most of the Palaeolithic artefacts recovered in the context of aggregate extraction could broadly be termed dredgers, although Gamble's intention was not to denigrate the value of the record but to demonstrate that *both* types of site are important. Building up a picture of hominin adaptation and behaviour involves 'tacking' between the scales of analysis appropriate to each preservational scale. Flagship sites are few and far between, but feel familiar to most archaeologists because they allow interpretations to be offered that operate at the historical or ethnographic level – the level of interpretation that we are used to dealing with in later periods. However, relying only on these flagship sites would result in a very partial picture of the Palaeolithic world; isolated snapshots, such as those we can reconstruct from parts of the Boxgrove palaeo-landscape (see Box 5.1).

Since most sites from aggregate sources could fall within the dredger category, it is often difficult to communicate the level of inference they allow, and how these complementary scales allow us to build up a picture of the Pleistocene world. Certainly they are in 'secondary context' and represent clusters of material that was not originally discarded in the place from which it was recovered, but has been deposited by subsequent natural processes: river action, slope processes and the like. But does this justify Palaeolithic specialists, curators and, especially, stakeholders working in development archaeology who do not want to upset the apple cart of preferred client status, writing them off as mere palimpsests? Are they really associations of reworked artefacts of different ages, associated with a particular deposit simply by chance and possessing limited interpretative potential, or do they have value? We would argue the latter.

Dealing with artefacts from secondary contexts of course demands that two fundamental caveats be always borne in mind:

- That the associated materials might originally have been eroded from much older sedimentary envelopes
- That these artefacts might have been originally manufactured, used and discarded long before the deposits within which they are associated were laid down (Hosfield and Chambers 2004, 39)

Certainly, such assemblages are not appropriate for answering fine-grained questions but, as Clive Gamble has pointed out, the problem lies with the appropriateness of the questions posed, and not with the data themselves (Gamble 1996, 65).

The different interpretative scales at which Palaeolithic archaeologists are forced to think operate in a nested fashion. Roughly speaking, artefacts and ecofacts that have become associated within a geological deposit (eg a gravel river terrace) over a very prolonged period of time allow the 'hard framework' of hominin adaptation to be reconstructed. For example, a collection of handaxes brought together within a gravel over many hundreds and thousands of years might indicate only one type of raw material was used, and that this relates closely to the nature of the local solid geology. A change in the physical nature of the local environment (such as a river downcutting into a different type of solid geology) might be indicated by a change in the types of artefacts present, or the raw material used to produce them. Thus, assemblages that have been brought together over long periods of time often allow us to reconstruct the material limits within which more flexible, individual hominin choices were made.

Deposits and assemblages that have been brought together over shorter and shorter periods, then, allow insight into increasingly fluid choices, from the choice (or ability) to colonise a particular region, or manufacture a particular type of tool, down to the level of the individual knapper in the case of a refitting sequence. Not all sites that could be described as dredgers are therefore informative at the same scale of analysis, emphasising again the importance of understanding how particular deposits accumulated before dealing with any artefacts they may contain. This question of scale is key and it is important to understand what timescale a particular site reflects, before offering any interpretative statements based on the artefact collection.

The ALSF commissioned *The Archaeological Potential of Secondary Contexts* project (APSC) in 2002 specifically to assess the value of the secondary context resource for addressing current and future research objectives. Critically, the project emphasised that archaeological assemblages derived from secondary contexts are unique not only in terms of the time over which they accumulated, but also in terms of the catchment from which they derive. Thus some secondary context sites combine artefacts and ecofacts drawn from spatially distant sources (such as an entire region, or river valley), whilst others (where many tools are found together) may reflect the reworking artefacts that have travelled minimally from the place where they were originally discarded (but see Hosfield 1999). Therefore, the three key questions that need to be posed when dealing with archaeology from a secondary context are:

- Between what dates did the deposits containing the archaeology accumulate?
- Where were the artefacts associated with a secondary context originally discarded?
- When were the artefacts associated with a secondary context originally discarded (ie have they been reworked from an older deposit)?

Significantly, the APSC emphasised that in order to ask questions appropriate to the secondary context in question, it is important to recognise the mechanisms through which it accumulated (Hosfield and Chambers 2004). Using models drawn from well-dated Late Glacial/early Holocene fluvial sequences, they emphasise the following temporal characteristics of the fluvial record which affect the composition of assemblages from secondary contexts:

- Rivers are most active, and therefore most likely to rearrange archaeology from the floodplain, during periods of climatic instability – for instance, the transition from glacial to interglacial conditions, but also in response to smaller scale oscillations in climate
- Fluvial sediments are not deposited at the same rate throughout glacial/interglacial cycles, and so archaeology is likely to be preferentially incorporated into fluvial sediments during more rapid phases of deposition (eg Late Glacial/early interglacials). The fine grained nature of interglacial deposits and their position in the terrace 'sandwich' also mean that they are generally more vulnerable to erosion. Furthermore, sediments laid down early in a cycle will be more deeply buried when a river starts to cut-down, and may have a greater chance of survival. This means that the record is naturally biased towards

REFLOATING DREDGERS 1 BOX 5.2

Two handaxes were recovered during ALSF funded investigations in the Hodge Ditch area of Chard Junction Quarry, located south of the River Axe, where a variety of techniques have been used to monitor and record changes in the sedimentology of the gravel deposits exposed during aggregate extraction (see Chapter 2). The sequence comprises over 20m of sands and gravels (predominantly fluvial in origin) alternating with fan gravels and solifluction deposits originating from the valley sides. The gravels make up a 'stacked' sequence, reflecting ongoing reworking of floodplain sediments and increasing in age the deeper they occur. Although three other handaxes are recorded as coming from the Chard area, these are the first to have been recovered in the context of modern geoarchaeological investigation (Brown and Basell 2008).

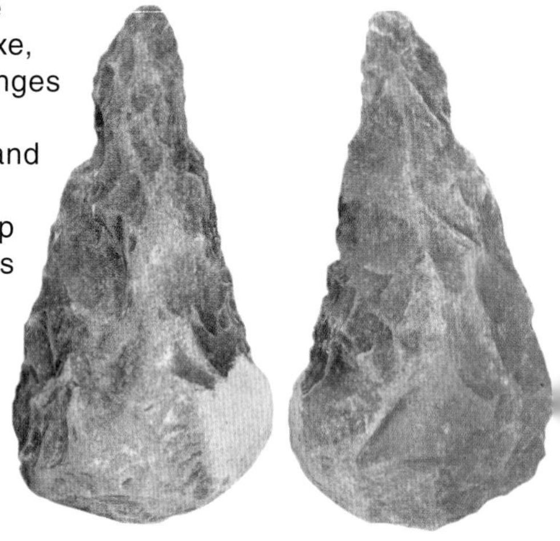
5.2.1 Handaxe from Chard Junction (courtesy of Laura Basell)

The two handaxes were picked up from the quarry floor at a depth of 18m, towards the base of the gravel sequence. They are made of Greensand Chert and are moderately-heavily abraded, suggesting that they have been reworked, although they may not have travelled far. OSL dates from throughout the gravels show a consistent and logical progression, with the oldest dates indicating the aggradation of lower gravel units at 367± 35 ka (MIS 10). This date was obtained on a deposit some 6m above the level from which the handaxes were recovered, which means these artefacts must be older; their condition might further indicate that they were derived from an existing, older, and hence reworked, terrace deposit.

On face value, it is easy to dismiss the importance of two rolled handaxes from a secondary context site; however, these represent the earliest and best-dated evidence for hominin occupation of south-west England. Even the least heavily laden 'dredger' can thus contribute to reconstructions of regional colonisation and landuse.

preserving evidence from early interglacial contexts, if at all

- Because of the imperfect resolution of geochronological tools (ie OSL dating), the internal geochronology of river terraces is a floating sequence. Secondary context assemblages may thus be placed 'early' or 'late' in stratigraphical relation to unequivocal interglacial sediments, but further resolution is currently contentious
- Fluvial activity in Late Glacial/early Holocene British contexts seems to have operated on a c. 3000 year cycle; thus secondary contexts may combine artefacts derived from the floodplain every few thousand years, although not necessarily in the same stratigraphic position

This last point is significant. Whilst an entire river terrace may have accumulated over a 70,000 year glacial-interglacial cycle, the artefacts within it may reflect the punctuated sweeping of the floodplain surface every few thousand years or so. In such a situation, it might be possible to identify change over time in behaviour, as reflected by stratified artefacts, and to relate this to changes in material conditions, such as climate and environment. However, given that secondary context accumulations conflate material from the ground surface with that reworked from older deposits, careful consideration must be given to how secondary contexts accumulated, and what impact these specific mechanisms had upon the composition of the assemblage contained therein. It is only on this basis that an appropriate level of analysis can be selected, and the right questions asked.

Historically, secondary context sites have rarely been used to do any more than attempt to build typological sequences (see McNabb 1996b; O'Connor 1997). However, the very fact that they reflect time- and space-averaged behaviour actually means that they are the only sources of data capable of answering particular macro- and meso-scales of question. As Gamble (1996) has pointed out, the fact that repeated patterns are visible in the secondary context record (ie repeated use of particular places, or choice of tool making technique) reflects the fact that these behaviours are selected for. In fact, secondary contexts sites as a category can allow us to investigate processes that operate on an evolutionary timescale.

Through the APSC Hosfield and Chambers (2004, 302) propose a framework for considering what

REFLOATING DREDGERS 2

BOX 5.3

The site of Welton-le-Wold was one of the first reinvestigated through the ALSF in 2003. Archaeology and fauna had been recovered from a series of sand and gravel quarries around the village since the 19th Century. The sequence was first described by Straw, following fieldwork between 1969 and 1972 when a 30m section was cleared, which recovered three handaxes, a retouched tool, and mammalian fossils (see Chapter 4). All came from gravel, 3.25m below till. Straw subdivided this gravel into two units (Upper and Lower Welton Members) and the till into three units – from bottom to top, Welton Till, Calcethorpe Till and Marsh Till. It was suggested the Marsh Till was Devensian in date.

The ALSF funded project aimed to reassess the extant excavation archive, to undertake further investigations of the surviving deposits, and to use these investigations as the basis for outreach work and wider public engagement. In particular, the project sought to establish the age, depositional context, and taphonomy of the artefacts and fauna, through reanalysis of the material and resampling of Straw's section. Reanalysis of the artefacts showed the three handaxes and a flake (unretouched) to be in variable condition; one handaxe is significantly more rolled than others. Interestingly, one handaxe shows evidence that it has been resharpened and re-shaped.

5.3.1 Handaxe from Welton-le-Wold

5.3.2 Excavating the elephant molar from the western quarry face in 1969 (Photo Alan Straw)

Limited fieldwork (boreholes) generally confirmed the sequence recorded by Straw and Alabaster (1976); the Welton Till is separated from the underlying gravels by a thick bed of silt and the gravels subdivided into an Upper and Lower unit. Archaeology was restricted to the Upper gravels – a fluvial deposit some 6 metres thick, reflecting the activity of a small braided river. The silts result from loess deposition within standing water, whilst the basal gravels were laid down during a cold period; diamictons are present towards the base of the sequence, interpreted as having been reworked from the valley sides by solifluction. Provisional OSL dates obtained from throughout the sequence suggest an MIS 8 attribution for the Lower gravels and an early MIS 6 attribution for the lower (Welton) Till, as well as a tentative date of 150,000 BP (i.e. late MIS 6) for the lower part of the Marsh Till, sampled in the Lincolnshire Wildlife Trust Reserve adjacent to Straw's section. This suggests that all the tills at Welton-le-Wold are in fact attributable to MIS 6, and the subjacent gravels to MIS 8/7. The handaxes, being rolled, probably date to an earlier period. The work at Welton-le-Wold demonstrates how comparatively little, surgically targeted (and thus cost effective) fieldwork can actually add an enormous amount of value to existing collections.

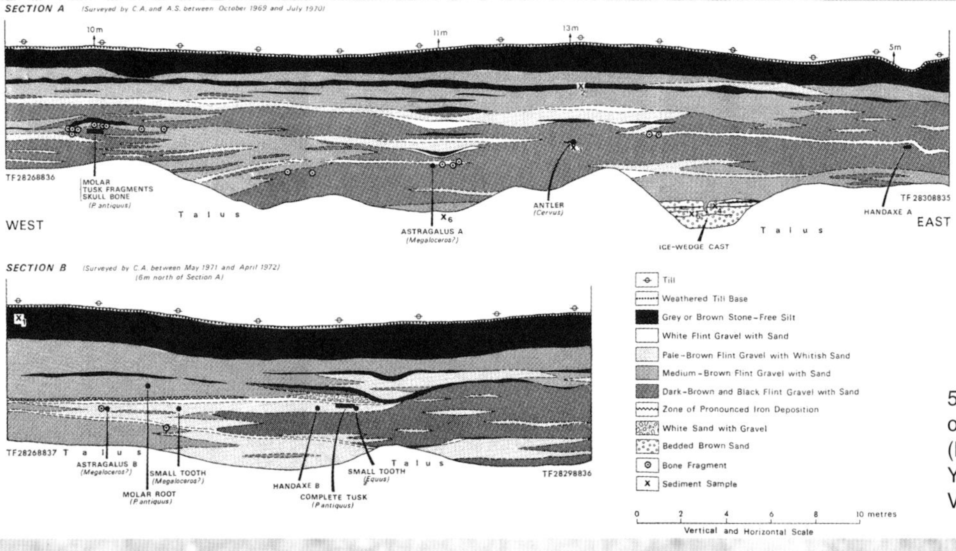

5.3.3 Alabaster and Straw's original recorded section (From the Proceedings of the Yorkshire Geological Society, Vol 41)

information can be derived from secondary context sites that takes account of differing spatial and temporal scales of research question. The temporal scale over which a context accumulated and artefacts became incorporated is related to different scales of fluvial process. Thus, short-term accumulations are those which are incorporated within fluvial structures that form over periods of hundreds or thousands of years; conversely, examples of long term accumulations include those which accumulate over a whole glacial-interglacial cycle (ie everything from a particular river terrace). Spatially, they break the catchment from which associated archaeological material is drawn down to three levels, all of which in the terms utilised throughout this volume would (unless combined into regional syntheses) probably fall within the meso-scale of analysis (Hosfield and Chambers 2004, 302):

- On-site – evidence of human activity has been rearranged over distances < 100m
- Off-site – evidence of human activity has been rearranged over distances between 100m and < 1 km
- Basin-wide – evidence for human activity is drawn from the entire upstream catchment of the river (> 1km)

Even the broadest of these spatio-temporal groupings, however, can be used to answer particular scales of research question, and thus are important evidence for building up an understanding of how humans engaged with the Pleistocene world. Recent attempts to use artefacts from river terraces to reconstruct hominin demography on the basis of the number of artefacts contained within different river terraces illustrate this (Ashton and Lewis 2002; Ashton *et al.* 2011). In these studies, *The English Rivers Project* (TERPS) data on the numbers of handaxes and Levallois flakes were extracted for the Middle Thames (Ashton and Lewis 2002) and Solent (Ashton *et al.* 2011). The number of artefacts from each river terrace was considered to act as a proxy for population density in that region (river valley) when the terrace aggraded, with variations in duration of accumulation and collector bias ostensibly taken into account by reference to a 100,000 year base-line and modelling the extent of urbanisation and quarrying (see above for problems with both these assumptions). Because each terrace is dated in relation to others in the same sequence, a rough model of population density through time can be suggested. Whilst there are problems involved in building such models, secondary contexts can be used to provide a rough measure of how frequently artefacts are discarded. Whether this reflects number of people, or a change in how stone tools were treated by hominins, however, remains a moot point. The data drawn from the aggregate record as a whole, therefore, as recorded by the TERPS, can be used to investigate broad questions of demography and colonisation. However, asking appropriate research questions of individual secondary context sites requires careful assessment of the age and history of each assemblage. The potential of these secondary contexts for developing our understanding of the Palaeolithic has been repeatedly demonstrated through ALSF projects, most notably Chard Junction (Box 5.2), Welton-le-Wold (Box 5.3) and Broom (APSC) (Box 5.4).

COLLECTIONS AND COLLECTORS

The Palaeolithic archaeological record is slightly peculiar in comparison with that of later prehistoric periods. As noted many times in this book, by far the majority of the artefacts that fill British museums, and upon which most of our analyses are based, were collected by non-professional archaeologists before the widespread adoption of mechanised aggregate extraction after the First World War. Indeed, the chances of a Palaeolithic artefact ever reaching a museum were dramatically altered after 1918: mechanisation drastically reduced the chances of a workman or collector even noticing an artefact, whilst the drive to build 'homes fit for heroes' rendered many of the gravel spreads in West London and North Kent archaeologically inaccessible.

Following the widespread acceptance of the antiquity of the human species in 1859 (Evans 1860; Prestwich 1860), Sir John Evans, the pre-eminent Palaeolithic archaeologist of his day, urged those with an interest in such matters to go out and seek artefacts and bones equivalent to those they had viewed on the continent at St Acheul in the Somme Valley. His call was heeded by a plethora of local collectors – most typically, those with an existing interest in the natural world, and especially fossil animals. This was the age of the great Victorian polymath, marked by the formation of many local learned societies of catholic tastes – for instance, the West Kent Natural History, Microscopical and Photographic Society – and the appearance of popular publications (McNabb 2012) targeted at the 'learned man' (and he was almost without exception a man!).

These late Victorian and Edwardian zealots were a disparate group, and the different ways in which they undertook their collecting impacted upon both what was collected and the information that can still be extracted from their collections. Indeed, the records kept by some were extremely detailed, allowing many intricacies of geological and depositional context to be reconstructed. In fact, the careful work of particular local collectors means that their archive material still has much to contribute, both to modern academic research and the protection of the historic environment. For instance, the west London archaeologist John Allen Brown collected from a variety of small gravel pits in Acton and Ealing, as well as taking the occasional foray out towards Slough on the newly constructed Great Western

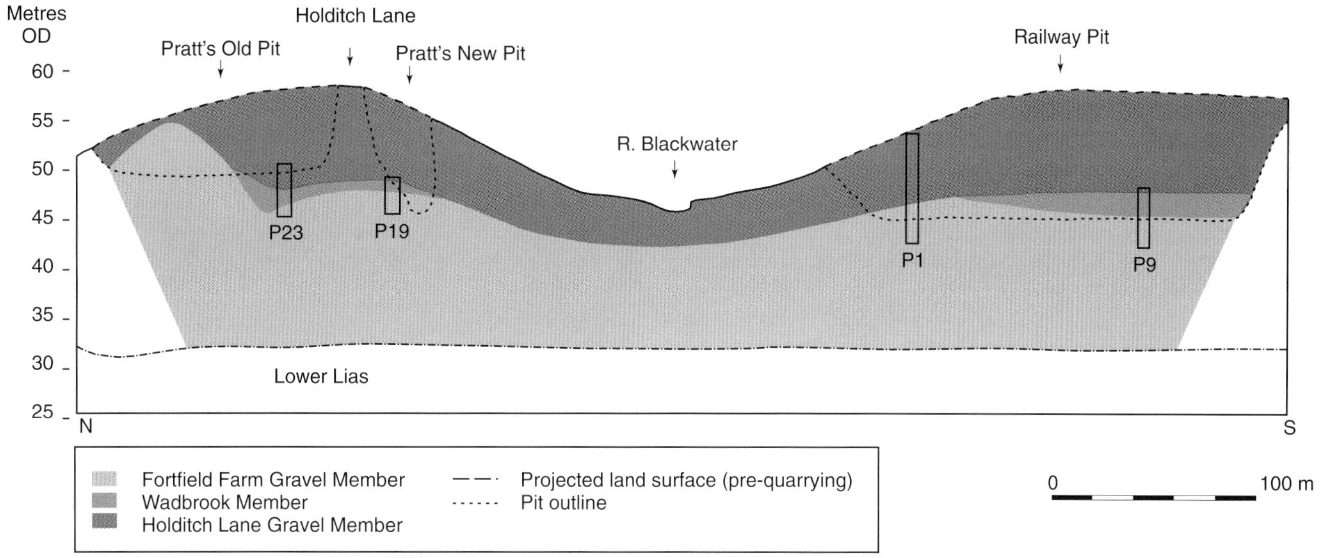

5.4.1 Schematic section illustrating the Broom Pleistocene deposits (Hosfield and Green 2013, fig 4.1)

The Broom gravel pits are located in the Axe Valley, some 3km downstream of Chard Junction. Artefacts have been recovered from the locality since at least the 1870s, principally from three pits: Railway Ballast, and Pratt's New and Old Pits. Most were amassed by C.E. Bean of Sherborne in the 1930s. At least 2301 artefacts are still extant, predominantly handaxes (1903) or handaxe fragments and roughouts (77). The fluvial sequence exposed in the Broom quarries is up to 20m thick and divided into three units, comprising a basal, flint-rich gravel, surmounted by finer beds of gravel and sand, with a chert-rich gravel capping the sequence.

The reinvestigations of Broom undertaken as part of the APSC project (Archaeological Potential of Secondary Contexts) were multi-faceted, and directed towards establishing the temporal interval over which the artefacts were brought together, the processes which led to the formation of this secondary context assemblage and the size of the catchment from which the archaeology was drawn. On this basis, the Broom assemblage could be used to examine questions relating to handaxe variability within Britain during the MIS 9-8 transition — a time when, in other areas, Levallois flaking was entering the technological repertoire.

5.4.2 An asymmetrical handaxe from Broom (see Hosfield and Chambers 2009; handaxe no. 234, C.E. Bean collection, Dorset County Museum [DORCM 2005.35.AB820])

Fieldwork at Broom indicates three primary periods of aggradation; lithostratigraphy shows the upper (Fortfield Farm) and lower (Holditch Lane) gravels to reflect cold climate deposition, separated by temperate deposits (Wadbrook Member). A sequence of OSL dates taken indicates a mid MIS 9 - mid MIS 8 date for the Wadbrook Member and a MIS 8-7 date for the Fortfield Farm gravels. Bean maintained careful notes of where and how he obtained his artefacts, allowing artefact position within the gravels to be reconstructed; the assemblage came predominantly from the Wadbrook Member, though material also came from the Fortfield Farm gravels above.

Reanalysis of the extant artefact collection suggested that they represent a locally derived, secondary context accumulation — material brought together by the periodic reworking of the adjacent floodplain and contemporary with the Wadbrook Member. Some were then reworked into the overlying Fortfield gravels — there is an erosional unconformity at the top of the Wadbrook gravels. Thus it seems likely that Broom was subject to a single, continuous phase of occupation, perhaps extending over several generations, and restricted to this warm period, but with a complex albeit local post-depositional history. Many of the Broom handaxes are assymetrical; reanalysis suggests that this relates to a short-lived, local tradition, although the component is not as pronounced as previously suggested.

Railway. Although not the specific subject of an ALSF project, Brown's sphere of activity was captured by a number of funded initiatives, including *The Middle Thames Northern Tributaries Project* (MTNT), and the *Greater Thames Survey of Known Mineral Extraction Sites*. Because of his recording practices, this material is still useful today. Brown marked the artefacts he found carefully with details of date, depth, and the nature of the deposit from which they came (Fig. 5.1). It also seems that he kept a notebook recording further details of these finds; it is likely that this was kept with his artefact collection when it was sold on after his death, but seems subsequently to have been lost. However, using artefact markings alone, it is possible to reconstruct the basic stratigraphy of the deposits he was investigating (Fig. 5.2; Scott 2011, 32–62). This demonstrates that the handaxes and Levallois flakes collected by Brown from a series of pits around Slough actually come from different stratigraphic positions, whilst reanalysis of the artefacts themselves shows them to be in different physical condition. Thus, through relating these observations to more recent geological investigations of the extant deposits in the area, it has been shown that Levallois flaking, as elsewhere in the Thames Valley (Scott *et al.* 2011), was rarely practised at the same time as handaxe manufacture, and that it is likely to date to around 250,000 BP (Ashton *et al.* 2003). So, observations made over 125 years ago can be used to address questions being posed now about the technological strategies early Neanderthals used to survive.

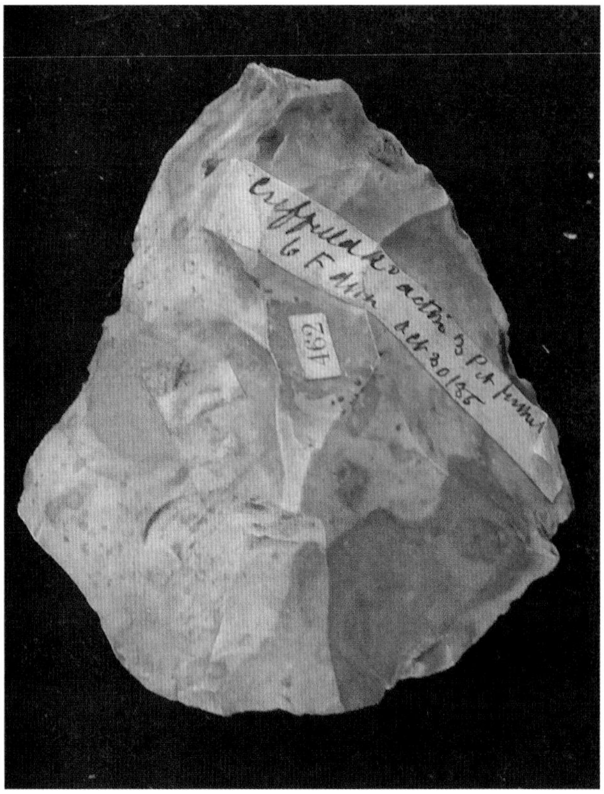

Fig. 5.1 A Levallois core from Creffield Road, Acton, showing the manner in which John Allen Brown marked artefacts. The label reads: 'Creffield Rd Acton 3 pit further W 6F down Oct 30/85'

A large number of ALSF projects included an important archival element that demanded these collectors were investigated (eg TVPP, ProSWeB, Stopes Palaeolithic Project; Welton-le-Wold). For example, the careful observations of Charles Bean formed a significant part of APSC; his skills as a professional surveyor proved invaluable 100 years later when modern scholars returned to his records of the famous chert handaxe site at Broom, Dorset (Hosfield and Green 2013). Similarly, the previously unrecorded collection of Henry Stopes from an area of ongoing intense development around Swanscombe, Kent identified a significant number of previously unknown sites, thus contributing to the management of the modern historic environment (Box 5.5).

Late Victorian collectors were often prevented by their day jobs from spending too much time searching gravel pits. Allen Brown, for instance, took up Palaeolithic archaeology having retired from the family jewellery business. Most opted to pay workmen for retaining finds for them – the more conscientious insisting that careful note be taken of context (O'Connor 2007, 86). Socio-economic status thus had an impact upon what a collector might actually be able to secure; for instance, the remarkable London and Luton archaeologist and illustrator Worthington George Smith made a costly mistake early in his archaeological career when he published the location of the London pits from which he was collecting. Smith was not a wealthy man, and he was quickly priced out of the market by other better-off collectors (O'Connor 2007, 87). These wealthier collectors[1] continue to cause irritation to the modern Palaeolithic archaeologist too; many were concerned only with securing the biggest and best implements, whereas researcher-collectors like Worthington Smith were assiduous in retaining *everything* from a particular site. Thus, depending on the calibre of the local collector, the value of extant museum collections can vary enormously. Derek Roe (1981), in

[1] And modern wealthy collectors can still cause problems today. When the TVPP attempted to purchase the remainder of George Turton's collection from the Hilton-Beeston area at auction (Bridgland *et al.* in press), they were spectacularly outbid by a local collector who had no truck with museums or academics. Turton's son had fortunately allowed the project to record and photograph the collection before the sale, but the current whereabouts of the artefacts is unknown. They may just as well have been discarded. Priceless Upper Palaeolithic material (including flints, bones and charcoal) from Kent's Cavern in Devon – all displayed on museum mounting boards – was similarly lost to science that day, this time without record.

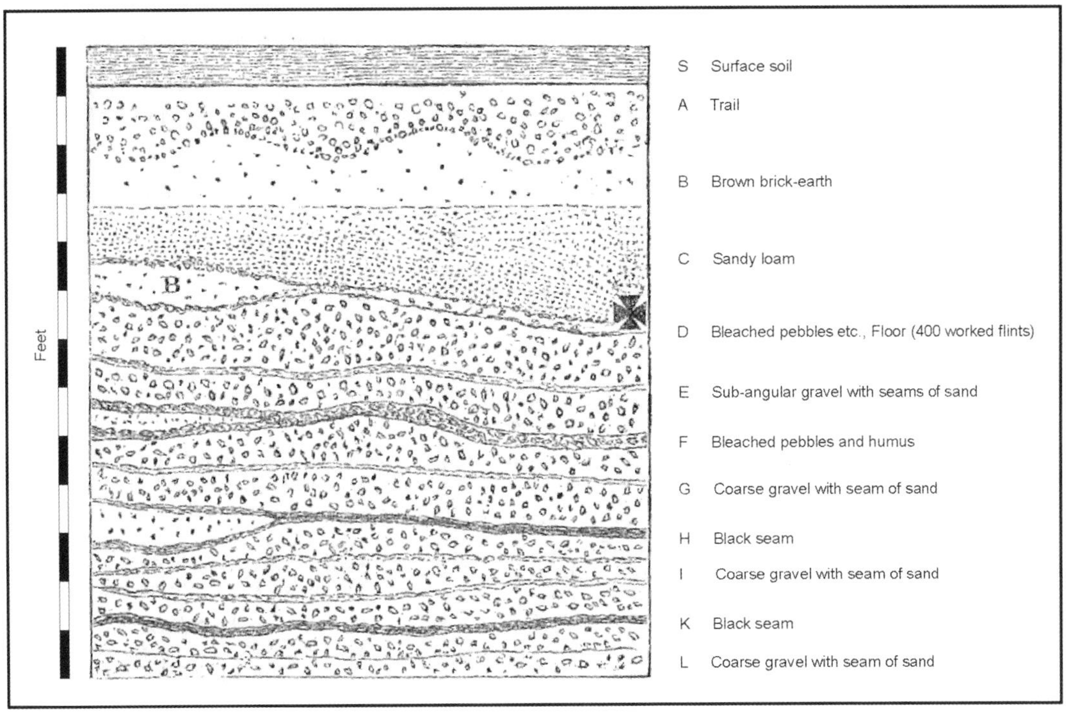

Fig. 5.2 John Allen Brown's section of Pit 2 in the St Barnard's area of Creffield Road, Acton (after Allen Brown 1886). Cross marks position of main artefact level

common with many researchers who have tried to reconstruct the archaeology of the gravel pits between Yiewsley and West Drayton (Middle Thames), has bemoaned the fact that Robert Garraway Rice dedicatedly wrote his name and the fact that he was a Fellow of the Society of Antiquaries on every piece in his collection, rather than details of depth or context!

Old collections can thus be used to address many aspects of current research agendas, and can supply information to modern HER records that may not be available within published sources. They may also provide curators and units with an impression of an area's value and potential at the desktop assessment stage. However, dealing with them requires careful treatment, and a respect for the level of reliable information a particular collection can provide. Before beginning a full reassessment of any museum collection, a nested approach can be taken to assessing its potential value:

- *What is the curation history of a given collection?* This can be defined by consulting all original accession documentation and museum archives (purchase and transfer documents; curatorial notes) to assess how it was obtained, whether it was obtained in its entirety, and what elements may have been lost from (or added to) the collection over time. A visual examination of the collection may be necessary to confirm whether the paper records accurately reflect the composition of the collection: are elements present with different markings (ie handwriting or catalogue numbers)?
- *How reliable is the collector in question?* This requires assessment of published sources; any extant documentation (letters, artefact catalogues, markings on artefacts) may also provide evidence of collection policy – did the collector cherry-pick, or retain everything? Did they visit gravels pits themselves, or purchase second-hand from other collectors on the ground? A visual survey of the collection may also indicate collection policy – does the collection only comprise retouched tools, or is there much small debitage, indicating that everything was retained
- *How much detail concerning position and context can the collection and its associated documentation provide?* An assessment of the paper record, and a visual examination of the artefacts themselves, will indicate what level of detail can be extracted from a given collection

In short, it is critical to maintain rigorous standards of sample hygiene when dealing with old collections.

TYPES, TECHNIQUES AND TOOLKITS: LOWER AND MIDDLE PALAEOLITHIC ARTEFACTS

The handaxe casts a long historical and aesthetic shadow. Easily the most identifiable of all Palaeolithic artefacts, it is predominantly handaxes that have always made it into the hands of quarry workers, collectors, and – eventually – into local HERs. Indeed, the fact that handaxes are so recognisable has led to the impression that they are the only

STOPES PALAEOLITHIC PROJECT

The Stopes Palaeolithic Project (Wenban-Smith 2004, 2009) focused on the work of a single, dedicated collector, Henry Stopes (1852–1902). Stopes amassed an estimated 100,000+ artefacts in the late 19th century. He did not publish widely, and thus is not well known. However, his collection and associated documentation form a critical resource for identifying sites in the Swanscombe area that were not yet recognised and incorporated into either the Southern Rivers Project or the Kent Historic Environment Record. The Swanscombe area (within the Lower Thames corridor) is both a key area for the Palaeolithic and also subject to intense ongoing development. The primary objectives of the project were:

- To identify the locations of Stopes' find-spots, especially locations with surviving Pleistocene sediments not yet recorded by other projects
- To identify the stratigraphic context of Stopes' artefacts, and to relate this to mapped Pleistocene sedimentary units
- To assess the research potential of the artefacts in the Stopes collection
- To determine appropriate evaluation and/or mitigation strategies for surviving deposits at Stopes' sites

The extant Stopes collection comprises at least 20,000 artefacts, around half of which are Palaeolithic, and which predominantly come from the Swanscombe area. Crucially, Stopes maintained a detailed catalogue of his finds, allotting each a number indicating the locality it came from, and other information on its source and provenance. Some detailed catalogue entries provide indications of site location and specific stratigraphic context. He was also one of those collectors who kept everything, so his collection gives a good snapshot of the knapping techniques and range of tool types at certain sites that were the focus of his collecting activity, in particular Dierden's Pit, Knockhall and Barnfield Pit, Swanscombe.

The Stopes Palaeolithic Project successfully used this information to reconstruct where Stopes had collected from, in combination with technological analysis of the collection, now housed in the National of Museum of Wales. Often specific sites had been given slightly different names which needed combining; other sites were not clearly named, but could be relocated by reconstructing changing pit location and building work in the Swanscombe area through map regression. More than 50 individual Palaeolithic find spots were identified, a major enhancement of Kent HER data. Significantly, a previously unknown major site (Bevan's Wash Pit) was identified within a block of land to be impacted upon by development around Ebbsfleet International Station.

Matching-funding for the curatorial side of the Stopes Palaeolithic Project was provided by the National Museum of Wales. A notable portion of the Stopes collection was repacked, reflecting the relative significance of different elements of the collection, and each artefact was documented to item-level to enhance its accessibility to academic researchers. The project additionally involved a number of outreach initiatives, forming a core theme within the National Museum Cardiff exhibition 'Why we Collect'; artefacts from the collection were used in guided handling by visitors, as well as within educational settings from primary schools to universities. An index of all archive material consulted during the project was lodged with Dartford Borough

5.5.1 Lithic artefacts marked by Stopes

Library, English Heritage, National Museum of Wales, Kent County Council (Archaeology Section) and the Centre for Kentish Studies, Maidstone. The Stopes Palaeolithic Project demonstrates the rich resource that museum collections and archives represent in terms of the Palaeolithic heritage. When carefully handled, this museum resource can help address major academic research questions and enhance protection of the surviving Palaeolithic heritage, and, crucially, communicate how this is achieved to a broader public audience.

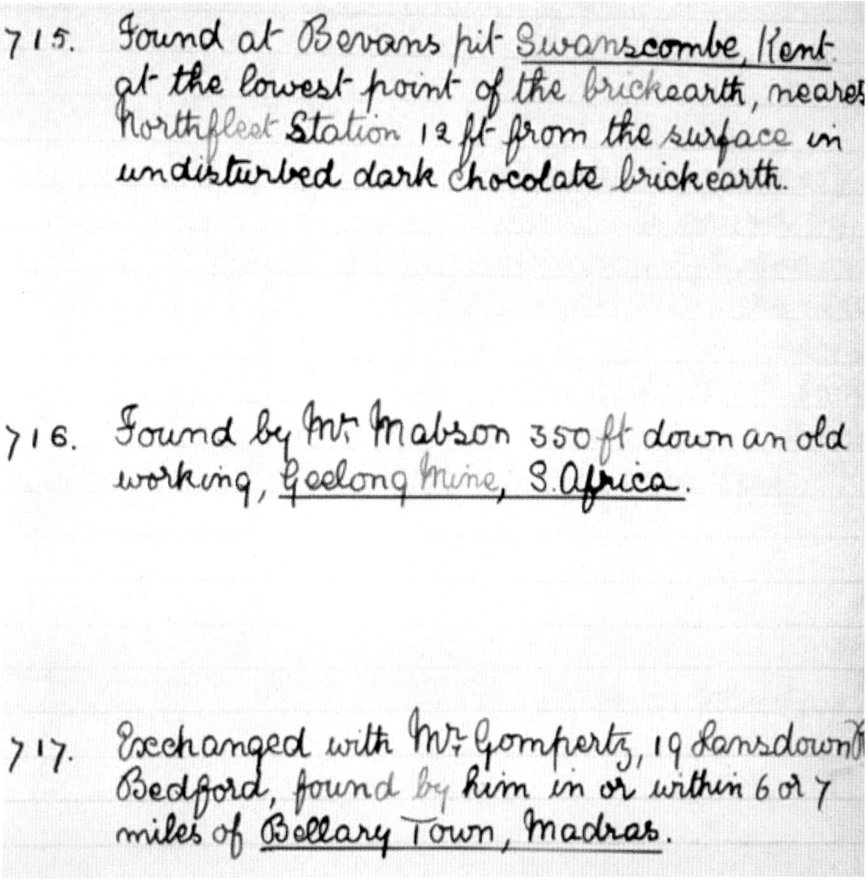

715. Found at Bevans pit Swanscombe, Kent at the lowest point of the brickearth, nearest Northfleet Station 12 ft from the surface in undisturbed dark chocolate brickearth.

716. Found by Mr. Mabson 350 ft down an old working, Geelong Mine, S. Africa.

717. Exchanged with Mr. Gompertz, 19 Lansdowne Rd Bedford, found by him in or within 6 or 7 miles of Bellary Town, Madras.

5.5.2 Typical entries from Stopes' catalogue

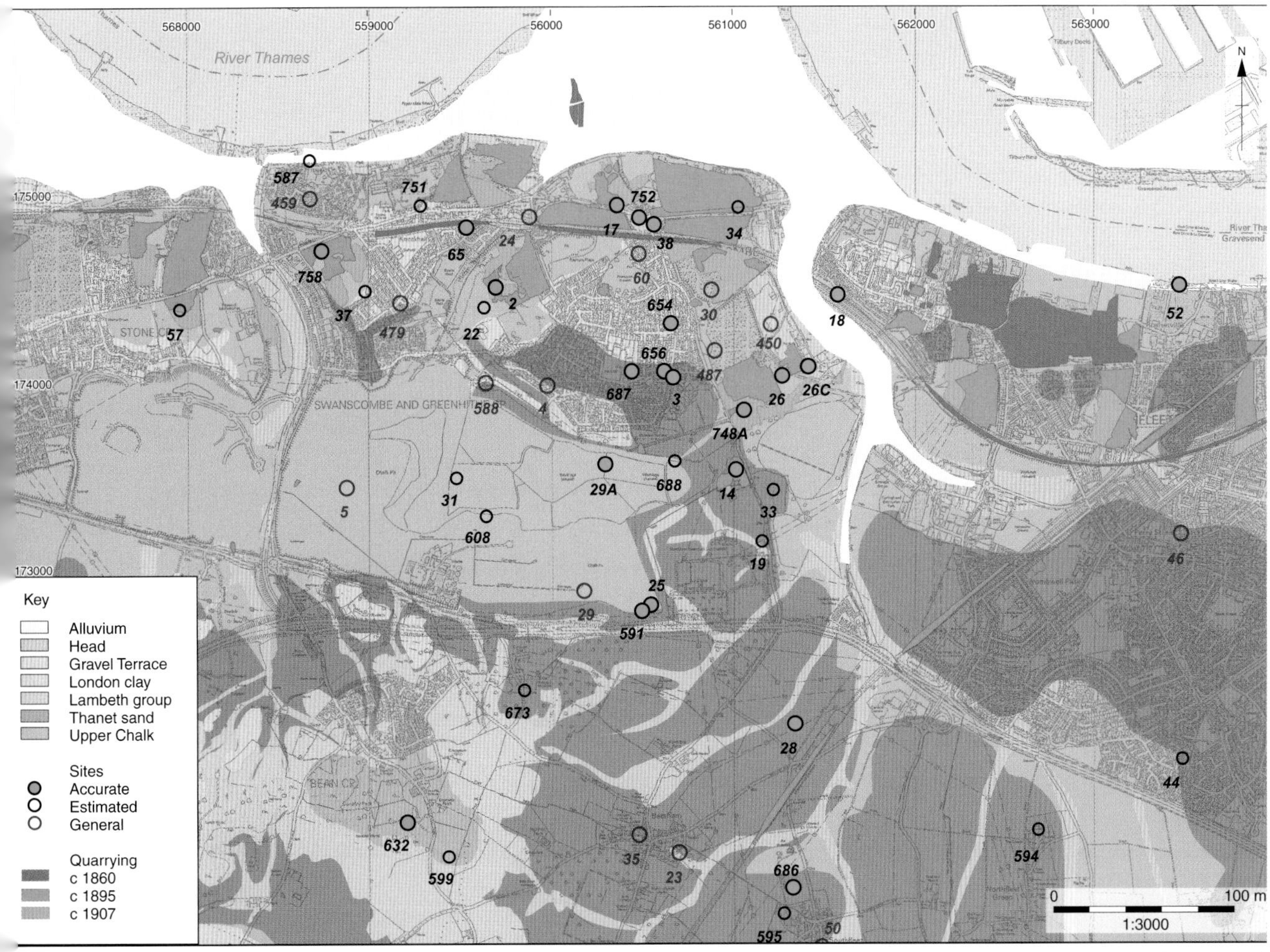

5.5.3 GIS screenshot, Stopes' findspots around Swanscombe, Kent (Stopes Palaeolithic Project Area 2, Wenban-Smith 2004)

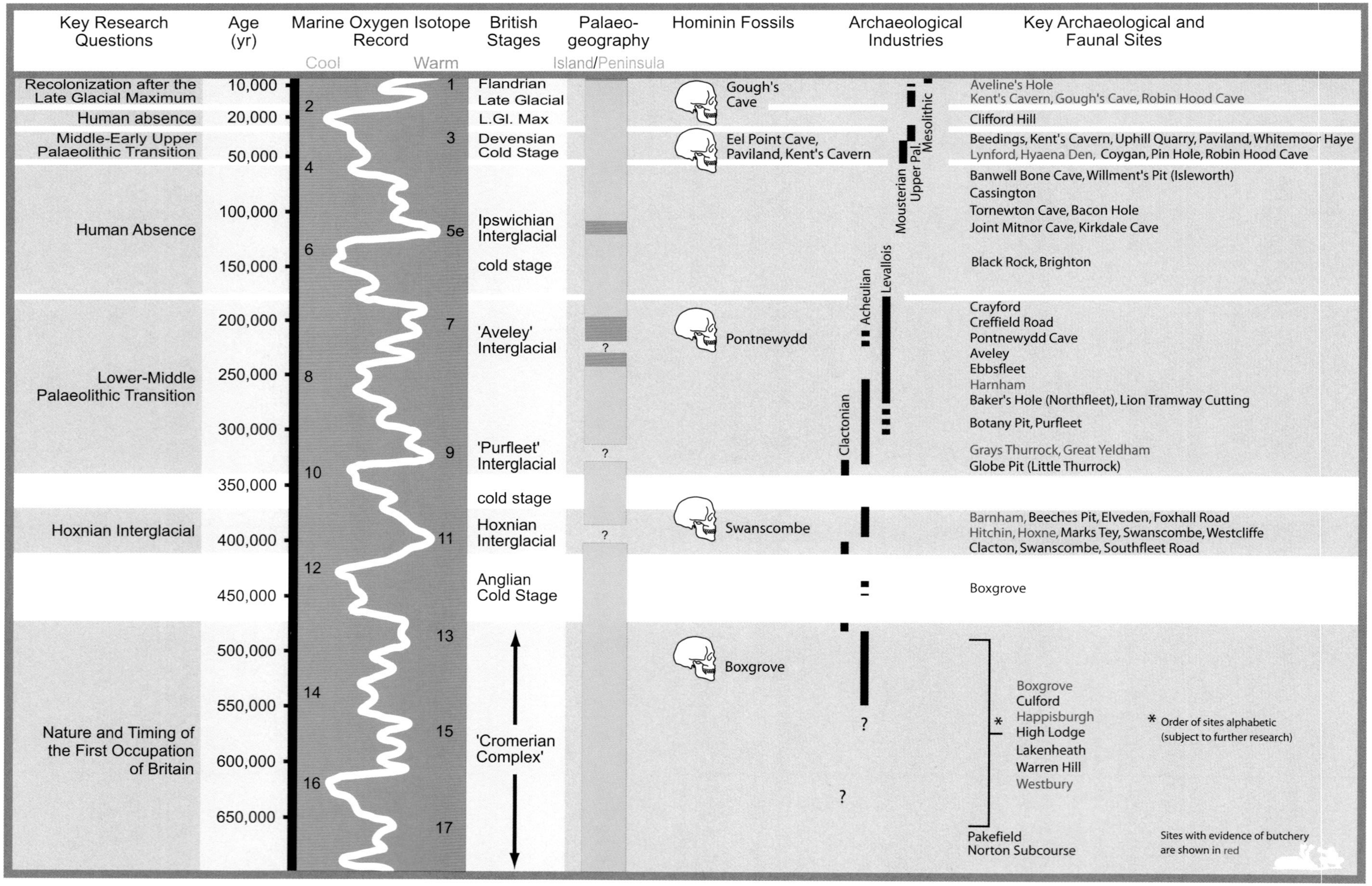

Fig. 5.3 Quaternary chronology of Britain, showing key British sites, archaeological industries, palaeogeography, and major warm periods and ice advances for the past 700,000 years. Image reproduced courtesy of the AHOB project

significant class of artefact that might be recovered from Pleistocene deposits – an impression only reinforced by a tendency amongst some researchers to talk about debitage products as 'waste' flakes. In fact, all classes of lithic artefact have the potential to provide evidence of past technologies and the ways in which early humans engaged with their material world.

The earliest occupation

Thus far, we have no evidence that the first hominins to colonise northern Europe manufactured handaxes; flint tools from Happisburgh (dated to at least 800,000 BP) on the north Norfolk coast comprise cores, flakes, and a number of retouched tools (Box 5.7; Parfitt *et al.* 2005). Certainly, no handaxes have been recovered from the earliest deposits at the site, and neither have any flakes which unequivocally result from their manufacture, and which might indicate that handaxes were made in the area, but were carried away and discarded elsewhere. The technology used to produce the Happisburgh assemblage is simple, and one which persists throughout the Lower Palaeolithic: fine-grained, brittle stone – like flint or chert – is struck in a controlled manner with a stone, bone or antler hammer in order to detach flakes. These flakes may be struck either in order to shape an internal volume (in which case, the resultant flakes may well be 'waste' material), or to produce flakes as an end in themselves.

The products – core and flakes – resulting from the process can vary enormously, depending on a number of factors (Fig. 5.4). Because lithic raw material is not malleable (like for example the clays used in ceramics) working stone is an irreversible process. Importantly, many of the choices made during stone working leave particular sorts of 'landmark' on the worked stone. Lithic specialists can read these landmarks and so build up a picture of the particular actions and gestures used to produce each artefact. This applies just as much to 'waste' material as to deliberately shaped artefacts: each flake retains on its dorsal face the scars of previous removals, which can be used to recreate the flaking sequence through which it was produced. Much of the work done on Palaeolithic artefacts involves recreating the choices made by hominins when working stone, and inferring why such choices were made; this is the process of building up a picture of the 'reduction sequence' or *chaîne opératoire* (see below). Precisely because lithic material is so durable (even when repeatedly reworked by a river) lithic artefacts are our primary source of insight into past hominin action.

Simple core and flake working, as described above, typifies the Lower Palaeolithic; flakes may have been used in their unretouched state, or deliberately modified in order to change (or conserve) the functional properties of their edges. Flakes that have been modified in this way are usually referred to as 'flake tools'. In the Lower Palaeolithic these usually comprise scrapers (a flake on which one or more edges has been repeatedly retouched to become stronger and steeper than it was in its unretouched state) or flaked flakes – flakes from which a further flake ('notch'), or series of flakes ('denticulates'), has been struck. Sometimes it is difficult to tell whether a flake worked in this manner would have been used as a tool, or has simply been used as a core itself (Ashton *et al.* 1991).

Lower Palaeolithic handaxe and non-handaxe assemblages

From about 500,000 BP, Palaeolithic archaeology becomes much more visible in Europe as a whole. From this point onwards over much of western Europe handaxes seem to be the main instrument around which the Lower Palaeolithic toolkit is conceived, although these occur within the background of cores and flakes/flake tools described above. In part, this enhanced visibility of the Palaeolithic record reflects the elevated likelihood of such tools being collected (in comparison to simple cores and flakes), but it also reflects the fact that humans equipped with such tools were much more successful at exploiting northern European environments than the human groups that preceded them. Handaxes were often manufactured using bone or antler hammers which, being slightly elastic, produced flakes markedly different from those produced using a hard hammer – they tend to be thinner and show less exaggerated percussion features such as bulbs of percussion. Such artefacts have a propensity to be under-represented within coarse-grained secondary context situations, being susceptible to breakage and winnowing; handaxes, however, are robust, heavy and highly visible. Although usually fairly symmetrical in planform, handaxes can vary enormously in terms of shape, refinement, degree of working, and techniques of resharpening – and much ink has been spilt discussing the factors that influence such variability (eg Ashton and McNabb 1994; White 1998; McPherron 1999; 2006; Ashton and White 2003). Handaxe assemblages were a key focus for many ALSF projects, including TVPP, MVPP, Stopes Palaeolithic Project, PRoSWeB and NIAN, to name just a few.

Not all Lower Palaeolithic sites contain handaxes, and much research attention has historically focussed upon why this might be so. In Britain, a particular interval of the Lower Palaeolithic – between 426,000 and 394,000 BP (early MIS 11) – is currently viewed as a period within which the regular manufacture of handaxes was not practiced. This peculiarity is referred to as the 'Clactonian', after Clacton-on-Sea, where Samuel Hazzledine Warren first noted this lack (Warren 1912; 1926). The Clactonian has been interpreted – or argued away – in a number of ways. As with the earliest, non-handaxe sites, it is always difficult to know whether one is dealing with simply a site that lacks evidence for handaxe manufacture, or whether the pattern is robust, and holds true on a wider spatial and tem-

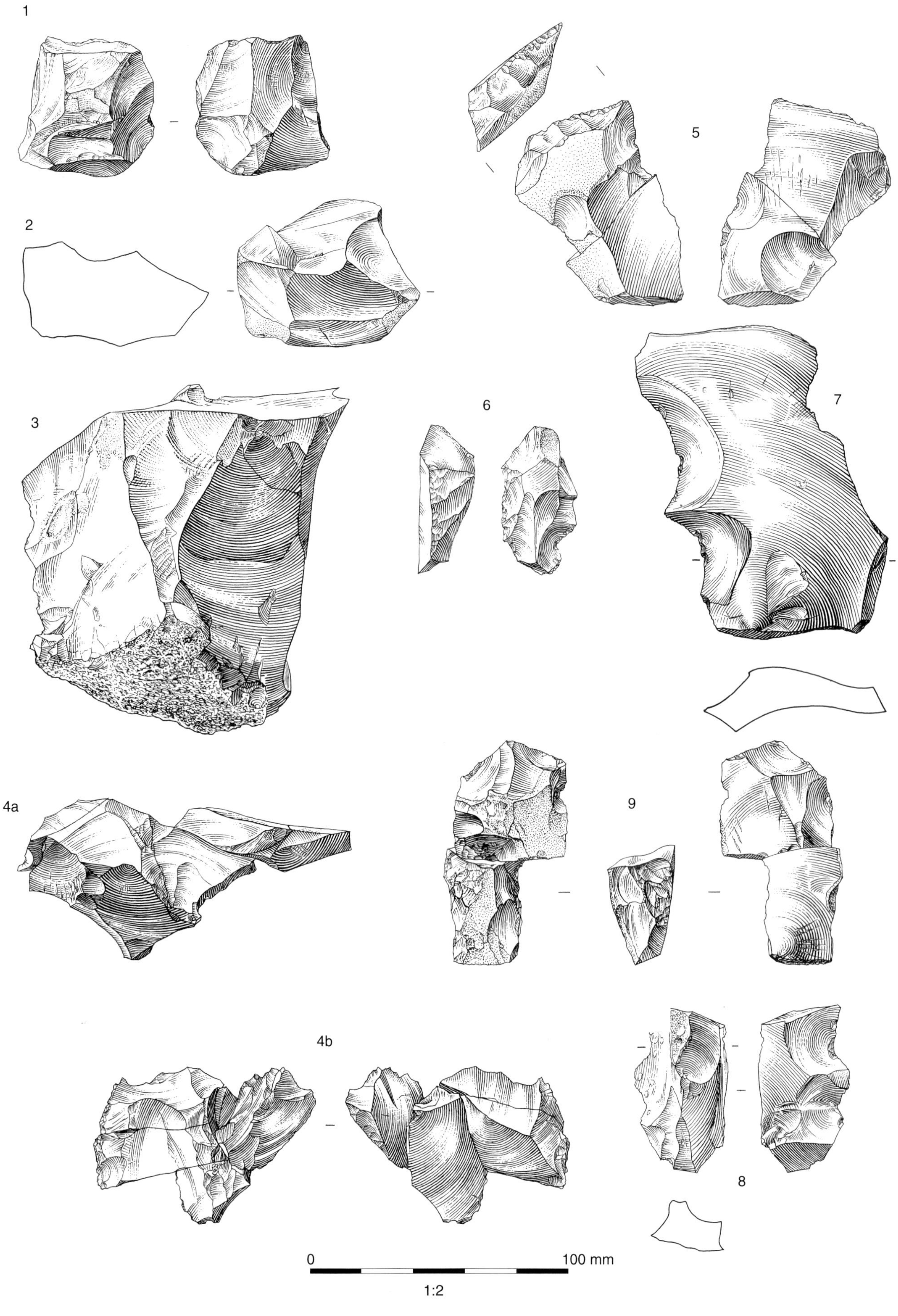
1
2
3
4a
4b
5
6
7
8
9
0
100 mm
1:2

poral scale. Secondary context assemblages actually hold the key to answering such questions. If a large collection of artefacts, derived from an extended spatial catchment and reflecting time-averaged behaviour, lacks handaxes, then the observation that handaxes were not routinely manufactured at that time in that region becomes increasingly robust (White 2000). The fact that there are only three artefacts (amongst many hundreds of thousands) that can be described as handaxes which can be shown to have originated from the Swanscombe Lower Gravels (albeit 'non-classic'; cf. Ashton and McNabb 1994; McNabb 1996a), is strong evidence that the Clactonian is a robust feature of the Palaeolithic record of the Thames Valley. However, it is a pattern that requires continuous testing, rather than a feature that can be regarded as fact.

It is tempting to regard the Lower Palaeolithic as something of a monolithic, and monotonous, entity – certainly in technological terms. However, it is arguable that this perspective results from failing to 'tack' (cf. Gamble 1996) successfully between scales of analysis – the secondary context sites, that illuminate the 'hard framework' of adaptation, and the flagship sites, that spotlight individual moments in time. As the chronological resolution of the Palaeolithic record continues to improve through refinements in AAR and OSL dating, so changes within the Lower Palaeolithic begin to become visible. Hosfield and Chambers' (2004; 2009) work at Broom illustrates this: Broom is one of several sites allotted to late MIS 9 – early MIS 8 that exhibits novel technological features when compared to earlier, handaxe-dominated sites (in this case, elevated asymmetry in handaxe planform).

Levallois and the beginnings of the Middle Palaeolithic

The most striking example of this emerging technological novelty is the site of Purfleet, in the Lower Thames Valley. Here, artefacts have been recovered from throughout gravels of the Mucking Formation of the River Thames, largely as a result of the efforts of Andrew Snelling, who collected material during quarrying at Botany, Greenlands and Bluelands Pits during the 1960s. Artefacts from the Purfleet gravels recorded the presence of humans throughout MIS 9 and as cooling began leading into the MIS 8 glaciation. Notably, there are typo-technological differences between the assemblages collected from different parts of the terrace; handaxes are largely absent from the earliest deposits, but present when the temperate climate sediments that comprise the majority of the sequence accumulated. However, the assemblage from the uppermost units (Botany Member) is particularly interesting. Many of the cores display features that show that they were being worked in a different, and perhaps more thoughtful, fashion. Care was taken to prepare a platform, and then to preferentially flake only one surface of the core, removing one or several large, flattish flakes. This is in contrast to the way that working of Lower Palaeolithic cores usually proceeded – relying on alternate flaking sequences, with platforms being shifted around as they became exhausted – and is analogous to Levallois flaking (see below) in terms of how stone working was organised (White and Ashton 2003). Purfleet is one of a select handful of European sites that illustrate the different ways in which Levallois flaking emerged in different places around MIS 9/8. Recent ALSF-funded studies have shown a similar technology at the contemporaneous site at Dunbridge (Box 5.6).

After the end of the MIS 8 glaciation, the British Palaeolithic record is dominated by one technological strategy – Levallois flaking. Levallois flaking is a technique that involves deliberately shaping a core surface so that if a removal is struck across this prepared surface, a flake of predetermined size and shape is produced. The specific manner in which this surface is prepared means that the knapper can choose to manufacture particular types of product, and adapt what they are doing throughout reduction (Fig. 5.5). Thus particular techniques produce points, others blades, and still others broad flakes

Fig. 5.4 (opposite) A series of typical Lower Palaeolithic flint cores (1-3), a group of refitting flakes (4), scrapers (5-6), flaked flakes (5, 7-8) and a denticulate (9). All from Barnham, Suffolk. Images reproduced courtesy of the British Museum

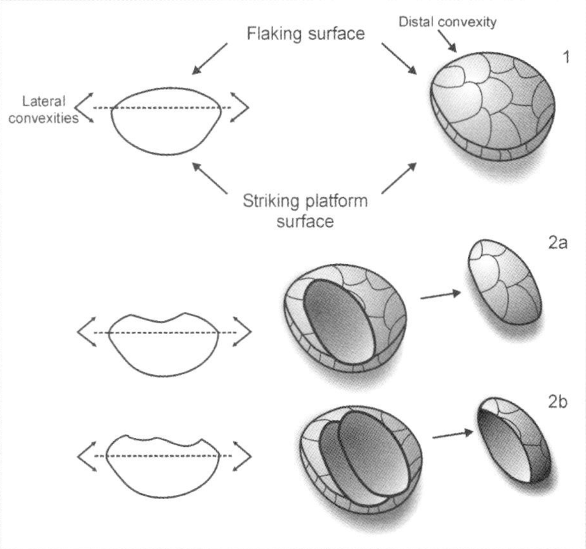

Fig. 5.5 Schematic depiction of the process of Levallois flaking. The Levallois concept is defined by the volumetric construction of the core (distal and lateral convexities). It is asymmetric and divided by a secant plane, one surface functioning solely as a striking platform surface, the other as a flaking surface. Flakes are removed from the upper flaking surface, parallel to the plane of intersection (2a and 2b). The number of predetermined blanks produced is limited by the volume existing between the Levallois preparation surface and the plane of intersection (after Boëda 1988)

EARLY LEVALLOIS FLAKING

The ALSF funded work at Dunbridge, Hampshire was carried out in order to enhance understanding of the context and dating of archaeology recovered from the area. Almost 1000 handaxes have been recovered from Dunbridge – a very substantial concentration for the Solent area – predominantly in the early 20th century by White (1912) and Dale (1912, 1918). Significantly, early Levallois material was also recorded (Roe 1968).

The emergence of Levallois technology is a tipping point in human cultural evolution. Few sites in Britain have as much relevance to this as Purfleet in the Lower Thames Valley (White and Ashton 2003; White *et al.* 2011), where Acheulean and Levalloisian artefacts were recovered from gravels exposed in four separate quarries. These gravels represent the Lynch Hill/Corbets Tey formation of the Thames, banked up against a steep chalk ridge, separating them from the modern river. Towards the top of each sequence, Levallois appears. Andrew Snelling recovered large numbers of artefacts from Botany Pit described as 'proto-Levallois' (Wymer 1968) or 'reduced' Levallois – which appear to show the evolution of the technique from handaxe manufacture (White and Ashton 2003). Notably, such cores are not well represented in the earliest gravels at Purfleet, where the technological strategy was focused around the production of handaxes. The assemblage at Dunbridge is of a similar age, and therefore potentially important to this ongoing research programme

Dunbridge is located on the western side of the River Test, some 500m south of the Dun confluence. Between 1991and 2007 a watching brief was conducted at Kimbridge Farm Quarry.

Artefacts were recovered from both the quarry and the wash plant. Artefacts from the wash plant were provenanced by relating the discovery date to records of changes in the extent or direction of quarrying between visits. Overburden was removed from the entire site before quarrying, except at the very edges of the excavations. 198 artefacts were recovered during monitoring, 60 within the quarry itself, and 190 of which could be related to position. This included 61 handaxes and roughouts (most of which are rolled and stained), 3 developed Levallois cores (sharp or only slightly rolled, with incipient cones on their faces), and 3 simple prepared cores in similar condition to the handaxes. Dunbridge thus represents the best evidence for the appearance of Levallois flaking in the region. The co-occurrence of simple prepared and developed Levallois cores in different states of condition suggests that, as at Purfleet, the sequence may record the local emergence and adoption of the technique.

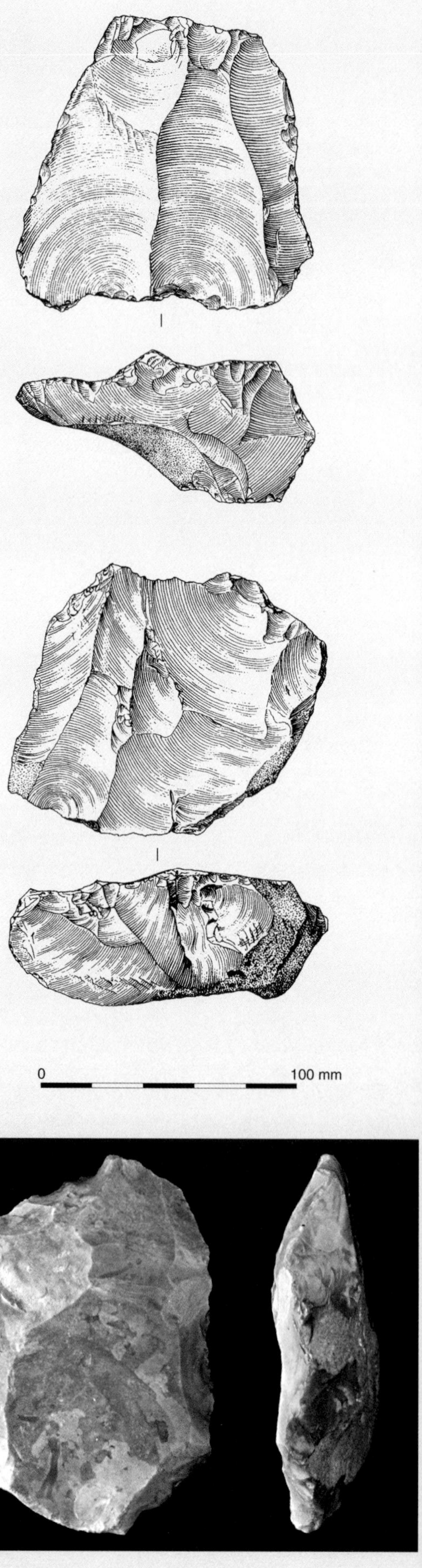

5.6.1 Simple prepared cores from Purfleet, Essex (adapted from Pettitt and White 2012)

BOX 5.6

Two main fluvial units were identified at Dunbridge; the Belbin and Mottisfont Formations. The Belbin Formation is higher (and older) and is a well-bedded fluvial gravel; the Mottisfont gravel is fluvially bedded, frequently within a loamy matrix, which suggests a solifluncted contribution to the river's bedload. Most artefacts came from the Belbin gravel; the simple prepared cores were recovered from the Wash Plant when only these gravels were being worked, indicating that they could not have come from anywhere else in the quarry.

The significance of Dunbridge is twofold. First, maintaining a long-term watching brief was a pioneering attempt to integrate the investigation and protection of the Palaeolithic resource into the process of aggregate extraction. As the significance of this resource has been increasingly accepted by curators, provision has been made to incorporate more targeted sampling strategies, directed towards the quantification of artefacts and the recovery of palaeoenvironmental remains (see Chapter 2). Dunbridge was one of the pioneering projects through which different approaches and protocols were tested in the field. Secondly, Dunbridge represents a location at which simple prepared cores (in this instance with handaxes) were recovered from a situation stratigraphically subjacent to gravel containing fully developed Levallois flaking. The former, secondary context industry is dated to MIS 10/9, and the latter to MIS 8. Thus Dunbridge seems to represent another British location at which the mosaic process of the development and adoption of Levallois flaking is attested – a process which occurs at different times in different ways across Europe and the wider world (White and Ashton 2003, White *et al.* 2011).

5.6.2 Simple prepared cores from Dunbridge, Hampshire

5.6.3 Fully developed Levallois core(s) from Dunbridge, Hampshire

(Boeda 1986; 1995; Van Peer 1992). Levallois flaking is both a very economical and a very flexible technological strategy – a hominin carrying a Levallois core could reconfigure it to meet any number of future requirements, freeing them up from the need to remain close to sources of raw material. Indeed, on the continent, where raw material sourcing studies are possible, Levallois cores and flakes, especially when retouched, tend to be transported much further than other types of artefact (Geneste 1989; Turq 1989; Feblot-Augustins 1999).

Although Levallois flaking dominates the British Palaeolithic record after the MIS 8 through to when Britain was abandoned by humans in advance of the MIS 6 glaciation, this does not mean that all Levallois artefacts, or deposits containing Levallois artefacts, can be dated to this interval – the British early Middle Palaeolithic (cf. White and Jacobi 2002). This is a fact often not appreciated by geologists, who since the earliest years of the 20th century have desperately sought to use artefacts as 'zone fossils' (eg Harding *et al.* 2012). The apparent restriction of particular techniques to particular points in time is again a question that requires testing, especially as there are suggestions that such patterns may be only regionally robust. Whilst Levallois flaking appears to be the favoured problem solving strategy adopted by hominins in the Thames Valley between MIS 8–6, handaxes being rarely manufactured, if at all, the same cannot be said of Wales and south-west England. For instance, the site of Pontnewydd (MIS 7) has produced a substantial lithic assemblage, predominantly manufactured on local volcanic material of variable workability. Handaxes are the most common tool type, though Levallois flaking was also practised (Green 1984; Aldhouse-Green *et al.* 2012). Similarly, the site of Harnham in Wiltshire, which includes refitting material, is dominated by evidence of handaxe manufacture; OSL dating places somewhere within MIS 8 (Whittaker *et al.* 2004). A number of ALSF projects were focussed on this period of major technological and behavioural change, including Stanton Harcourt and Welton-le-Wold.

An interesting feature of the archaeological record from MIS 7 onwards is that human groups seem to have been using their landscapes in new ways – ways which, crucially, impacted upon the likelihood of their tools actually entering the archaeological record at all, let alone being recovered in the context of modern aggregate extraction or construction. Whereas during the Lower Palaeolithic (prior to MIS 8) human groups seem to have preferentially discarded their tools in locations where the necessary materials for survival co-occur – fresh water, prey, and workable stone – from MIS 8 onwards they seem to deliberately target particular places in the landscape for specific purposes. Thus they targeted one place as somewhere to extract raw material, gear up with Levallois cores and flakes, and then moved off to actually use these tools elsewhere in the landscape. So, in Britain there is a pronounced contrast between these two types of site – extraction and production sites, on one hand, and ephemeral, or 'use' sites, on the other (Scott 2011, 187–189). In fact, the potential for the recovery of ephemeral/use sites (Turq 1989) is very limited for a number of reasons:

- Ephemeral sites may only comprise a tiny collection of artefacts with a reduced likelihood of being seen, even during pre-WW1 manual quarrying
- Extraction and production sites are generally located in direct association with raw material sources (for instance, coarse gravel river banks and bars). Such raw material sources have historically become targeted for aggregate extraction, bringing these sites to light
- The material discarded at ephemeral/use sites is often heavily curated, and thus small and worked down. This pattern reflects the fact that Levallois technology freed humans up from the need to constantly access raw material. They were travelling equipped to exploit unpredictable opportunities, and discarding material wherever they needed to use it, rather than it being concentrated at specific points that were repeatedly visited
- Ephemeral/use sites are therefore 'off site' contexts – they are likely to exist in places where we have historically failed to look – for instance, within isolated capture points on the downland away from river valleys, such as solution features and fissures

Because of these factors, our picture of Neanderthal behaviour in Britain from MIS 8 onwards is partial at best. Concentrating only on those sites already known through historical focus on the gravel archives of rivers has blinded us to the potential of other types of capture points, and potentially skewed the British view of the record. For instance, there are very few British archaeological sites that date to the end of MIS 7/beginning of MIS 6 (only Crayford, and this is as yet poorly age-constrained; Scott 2009), whilst such sites are common on the continent. In continental Europe they are usually recovered from fine-grained deposits (such as loess) collected within solution features, dry valleys, or on top of terraces. Although less thick and widespread than on the continent, loess deposits have historically been targeted for brickmaking throughout south-east England, but are under-researched in terms of their archaeological potential. Similarly, such capture points, away from the extraction sites associated with outcropping flint, have the potential to inform us about whole patterns of Neanderthal behaviour – how they moved, used stone tools, and hunted – away from the river valleys. Logistically, however, and particularly from the point of the developer and curator, finding these sites is like looking for the proverbial needle in a haystack, and depends largely on luck.

EVIDENCE OF ABSENCE AND OTHER STORIES

As an island at the northwestern-most edge of the Palaeolithic world, Britain offers some distinct advantages to the Palaeolithic archaeologist. Situated close to a limit of ice advance during cold periods, Britain would have been amongst the first areas of Europe to be directly affected by global cooling. Thus, human groups colonised Britain repeatedly when conditions allowed but also went repeatedly and locally extinct. This resulted in a stochastic pattern of human presence and absence, as reflected by both absolute numbers of artefacts and numbers of sites (cf, Ashton and Lewis 2002; White *et al.* 2006; Scott *et al.* 2011, Pettitt and White 2012). At the edge of their range, hominins are acting at the limits of their biological and cultural adaptations; thus, establishing basic patterns of presence and absence is key to understanding how their adaptive capabilities changed over time as well as how and why particular behavioural packages caught on (Roebroeks *et al.* 2011).

The effects of a group expanding to the limits of its tolerance is compounded by the alternating island-peninsula nature of Britain (see Chapter 3). At different times, it may have been more difficult – or even impossible – to get into Britain, and particular routes may not have been passable. Understanding when early humans and other animals were present and absent in Britain, compared to adjacent areas of the continent, may allow us to understand how accessible Britain was, and when different routes across the submerged landscapes of the North Sea plain and Channel River valley were impassable.

Investigating these questions involves building up an accurate picture of human presence and absence. These questions have been a central focus of the AHOB project (Ashton *et al.* 2011). A key result has been the realisation that humans were able to colonise Britain much earlier than had previously been thought, as shown by the discoveries at Pakefield and Happisburgh. (Parfitt *et al.* 2005; Parfitt *et al.* 2010), and that they were capable of adapting successfully to boreal conditions similar to those found in southern Sweden today. These discoveries together pushed back the earliest occupation of Europe to over 300,000 years earlier than had previously been thought.

It is extremely important, however, to note that the Cromer Forest Bed, the geological deposit within which both sites were discovered, was previously best known for not producing any humanly worked artefacts, despite being a magnet location for collectors since the late Victorian era. The Cromer Forest Bed is not only rich in faunal remains, which initially attracted collectors to the area, but was also one of the key deposits from which 'Pre-Palaeoliths', or 'Eoliths' were collected in the early 20th century (O'Connor 2007). These were flints that are now known not to result from human workmanship but from natural processes, yet early collectors would spend enormous amounts of time searching the exposures of the Cromer Forest Bed around the north Norfolk coast in the hope of finding them. Despite over a century of prospection, these deposits refused to yield evidence for an early human presence (Roebroeks 2005). Thus it becomes even more important not to disregard sediment exposures because they have not previously produced artefacts, or because they date to a period where, presently, we do not think people were there. Any such supposition requires testing.

In a similar vein, a strong body of evidence suggests that Britain was not occupied during MIS 5e (see Chapter 2). A review of all sites confidently dated to this interval in Britain demonstrated that none contained incontrovertible evidence for a human presence (Lewis *et al.* 2011). This is a pattern in marked contrast to the continent, and may therefore tell us something about the accessibility of Britain as an island during this warm phase. However, the fact that humans have not thus far been shown to be present in archaeologically visible numbers in Britain during this period does not mean that all deposits laid down during this interval are of no archaeological significance. Not only do we need to test whether humans were absent, but also to explain why – through rigorously building models of climate and environment in relation to changing human adaptations. In the Palaeolithic, the old archaeological truism that absence of evidence is not evidence of absence has never held more true.

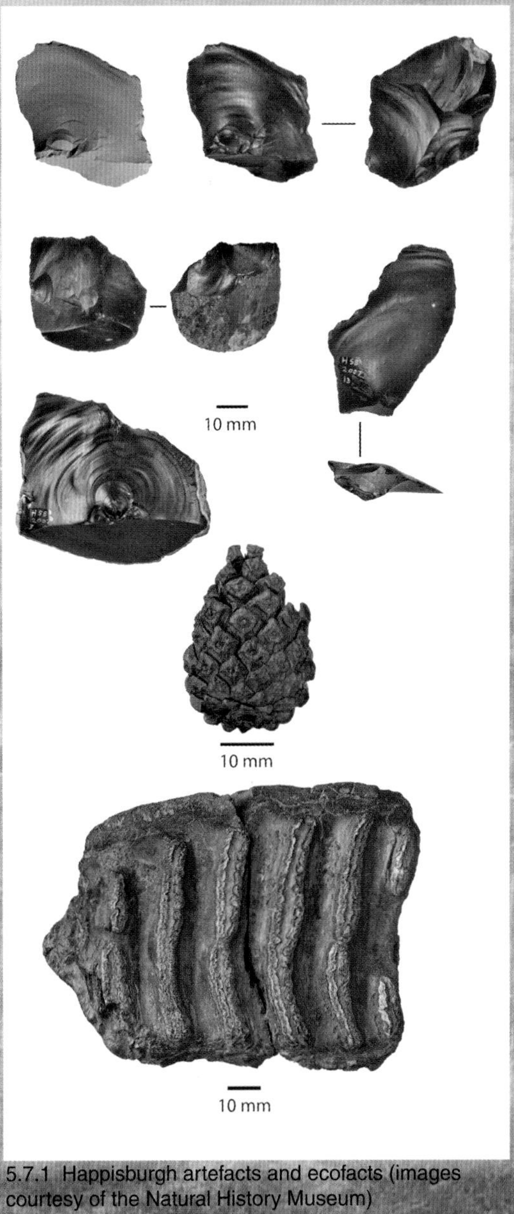

5.7.1 Happisburgh artefacts and ecofacts (images courtesy of the Natural History Museum)

Hiatus

Thus far, very few artefacts have been recovered from deposits laid down between the beginning of MIS 6 and the early MIS 3 (Box 5.7). It therefore appears that Britain was for a long time abandoned by humans, and not successfully reoccupied during the warm conditions of MIS 5e, when sites certainly are known from the near continent (eg Caours: Antoine *et al.* 2006). Of those artefacts that have been found, questions have been raised concerning whether they are true artefacts, whether they are indeed contemporary with the deposits from which they came, and the reliability of the dating methods used (Lewis *et al.* 2011). However, as emphasised in Chapter 2, the suggestion that humans were not present during this period remains a hypothesis that requires testing. It cannot be taken as a given, and all deposits of this date ignored from an archaeological point of view (Box 5.7). Again, though, from the point of view of developer-funded archaeology, deposits from MIS5e-4 may reasonably be given a light touch until properly funded research projects have determined whether this absence is real or not, but they should not be ignored. It is a well-worn axiom that the absence of evidence is not evidence of absence, and only one convincing site is needed to overturn an absence. Moreover, if the hiatus is real, it is only through environmental examination of sites of the right age that we might be able to further unravel the reasons behind it.

The late Middle Palaeolithic

The first significant evidence for human groups reoccupying Britain occurs around 60,000 BP. Although fossils from mainland Britain are sparse, these human groups were classic Neanderthals – in both phenotypic and behavioural terms. Their technology is marked by a return to the regular manufacture of handaxes, whilst Levallois flaking appears no longer to have been practised in Britain.

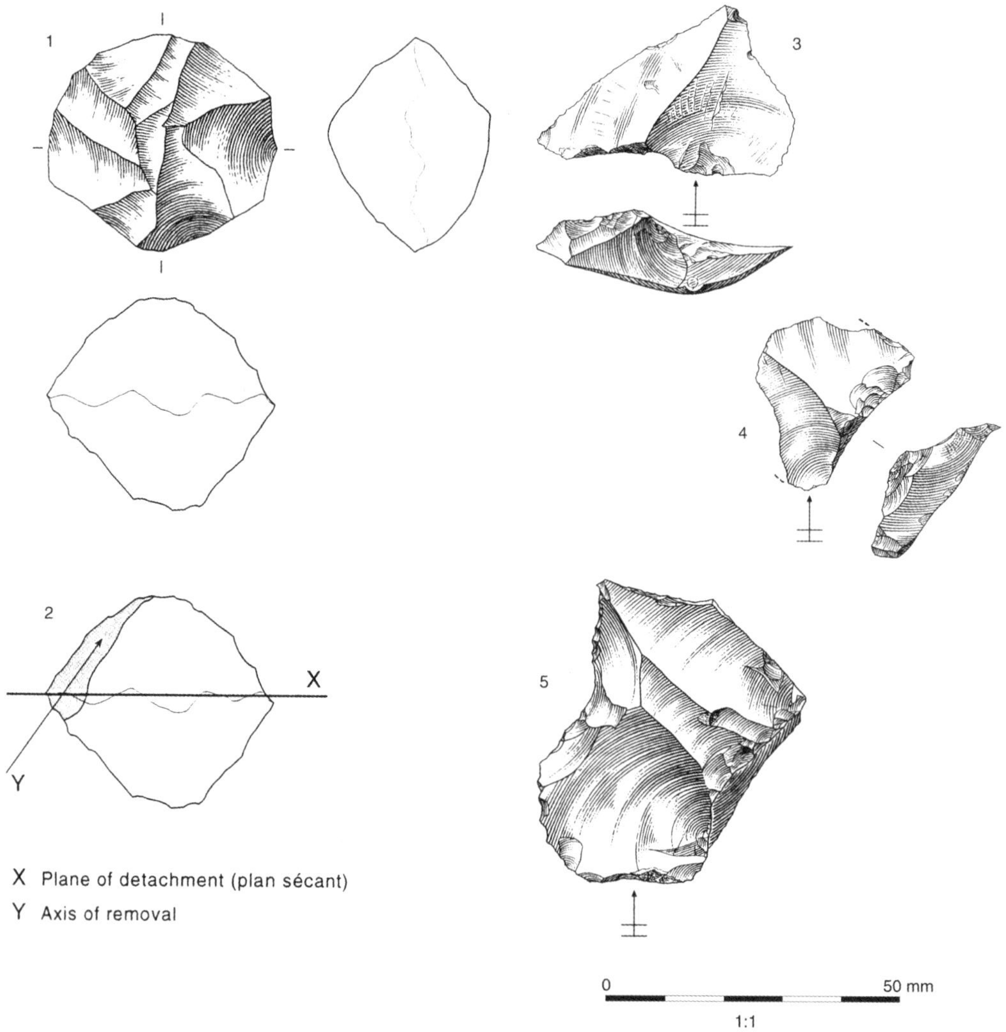

Fig. 5.6 Diagrammatic representation of the technique of discoidal flaking: (1) view in plan and cross-section and (2) schematic representation of the method of flake removal (after Boëda 1993) together with a series of chordal flakes (3-6) from Oldbury, Kent, reproduced courtesy of the Lithic Studies Society

Instead, the working life of cores is prolonged in a different way; they were worked alternately from a continuous platform extending around the core, with each flake removal serving to recreate the correct angle to continue flaking. These cores become flattened when extremely exhausted, and almost disc-shaped – witness the fact that this technique is called 'discoidal flaking' (Fig. 5.6). Discoidal flaking is a very economical way of working stone, and results in a variety of short, squat flakes that are ideal for retouching as scrapers (Cook and Jacobi 1998). In Britain, discoidal cores and flakes seem to be more common away from areas where lithic raw material was freely available; thus it was not frequently used in the south of England, but is well represented where humans occupied limestone caves in the north and west (for example at Creswell Crags).

Even in the south, when Neanderthals travelled over the dissected plateau of the Kent and Sussex Weald, they used this flaking strategy to keep them going over the flint-impoverished Greensand uplands. Although as yet undated, numerous discoidal cores have been collected and excavated from around Oldbury Hatch, near Ightham, in Kent, by the legendary late Victorian polymath and grocer, Benjamin Harrison (Cook and Jacobi 1998). These cores are associated with small handaxes of a very particular type (see below), which have been reworked and remodelled many times. In fact, discoidal cores and handaxes from the area were often transformed from one to the other – handaxes becoming small, reduced discs, used as sources of flakes, and cores becoming flattened, with continuous cutting edges. The date and depositional context of the Oldbury material is as yet poorly understood, but the geographical situation is significant; most of the material probably came from a flattish area below a continuously eroding, soft cliff (Folkestone Beds), and was probably sealed and preserved by the slope deposits derived from these. The area itself commands excellent views over the Darenth Valley, right across to the chalk hills of the Medway. Thus Oldbury probably has the potential to tell us much about late Neanderthal behaviour away from the river valleys, and represents another potential form of geological capture point which is curiously under-researched in Britain.

Although discoidal flaking is important in late Neanderthal Britain, the quintessential tool was once again the handaxe (White and Jacobi 2002). However, these handaxes seem to have been different in conception than those manufactured in the Lower Palaeolithic; often, particular areas around their edge were modified in different ways – to form a scraper, or a notch – or were deliberately blunted, to form a hand-hold opposed to a working edge. In effect, although still a core tool, handaxes were being used as tool supports – blanks that could be retouched and remodelled in the same way as a Levallois flake. They also seem to have been worked and shaped in very separate phases (Boëda 2001 and Cliquet *et al.* 2001). Moreover, particular handaxes show deliberate imposition of form – there seems to be an idea that a particular tool had to look a certain way. These handaxes have 'D-shaped' tips, curiously flat bottoms and noticeably cut off corners, and are usually termed *'bout coupés'*. Where dated, they seem to be restricted to the interval 59,000–41,000 BP, and may well represent a particular, British regional variant of the Mousterian of Acheulian Tradition (MTA) in northern France – where the equivalent regional form is a flat-butted triangular handaxe (White and Jacobi 2002). 'True' *bout coupés* (cf Tyldesley 1987) are often found as single finds (ephemeral/use sites) – and sometimes seem to have been deliberately cached (as at Coygan Cave in south Wales). However, ALSF funding allowed the excavation and publication of a substantial late Middle Palaeolithic assemblage from Lynford Quarry, Norfolk which has dramatically changed our understanding of this period in Britain (Box 5.8).

INTERPRETING PALAEOLITHIC ARTEFACTS

Precisely because stone tools are durable, the vast majority of the Palaeolithic record is made up of this one class of evidence. Organic tools and materials must have comprised a significant component of hominin tool kits. European evidence suggests that hafting using pitch mastic was practised by at least 190,000 BP (Mazza *et al.* 2006), and in exceptional circumstances wooden javelins and composite (hafted) tools have actually been excavated (eg Schöningen: Thieme 1997), whilst in others, the pseudomorphs left by wooden furniture remain within cave sites (eg Abric Romani, Spain: Castro-Curell and Carbonell 1995). The sole British wooden artefact remains the Clacton spear, recovered in 1911 by Samuel Hazzledine Warren from the Temperate Beds at Clacton-on-Sea (Warren 1911); while Boxgrove has yielded percussors of antler and bone. Given this apparent paucity, it is to stone tools that we must turn for most evidence for human activity, although both researchers and units should be aware of the potential for preservation of wood and other organics (they are found for example at High Lodge, Happisburgh, Cudmore Grove, amongst others), some of which may one day prove to be artefactual.

Three main questions can be addressed using lithic evidence: firstly, how the assemblage itself formed (taphonomy); secondly, what actions were undertaken at the site itself; and thirdly, how the actions undertaken at the site itself relate to those undertaken elsewhere in the landscape (technology). Broadly speaking, it is necessary to examine each of these areas in turn to accurately move onto the next.

Taphonomy

Two principles underpin the use of artefacts as a taphonomic tool; firstly, that artefacts, like any other clast subject to movement, will experience damage.

OF MAMMOTHS AND MEN

BOX 5.8

In spring 2002, an archaeological watching brief undertaken by John Lord at Lynford Quarry in Norfolk revealed a spectacular *in situ* association of mammoth bones and a substantial stone tool assemblage within a palaeochannel infilled with rich organic sediments. Excavation was funded by the ALSF, supported by the quarry owners, Ayton Asphalt. The restricted size of the palaeochannel, the quality of the organic remains preserved within it, and the association of near primary context stone tools with well-preserved faunal remains, provided a rare opportunity to investigate late Neanderthal behaviour in Britain on an ethno-historical scale. Schreve (this volume) has already discussed the environmental data and Neanderthal subsistence strategies. Here we discuss the results of the lithic analysis and what it can tell us about Neanderthal technology at the micro and meso-scale.

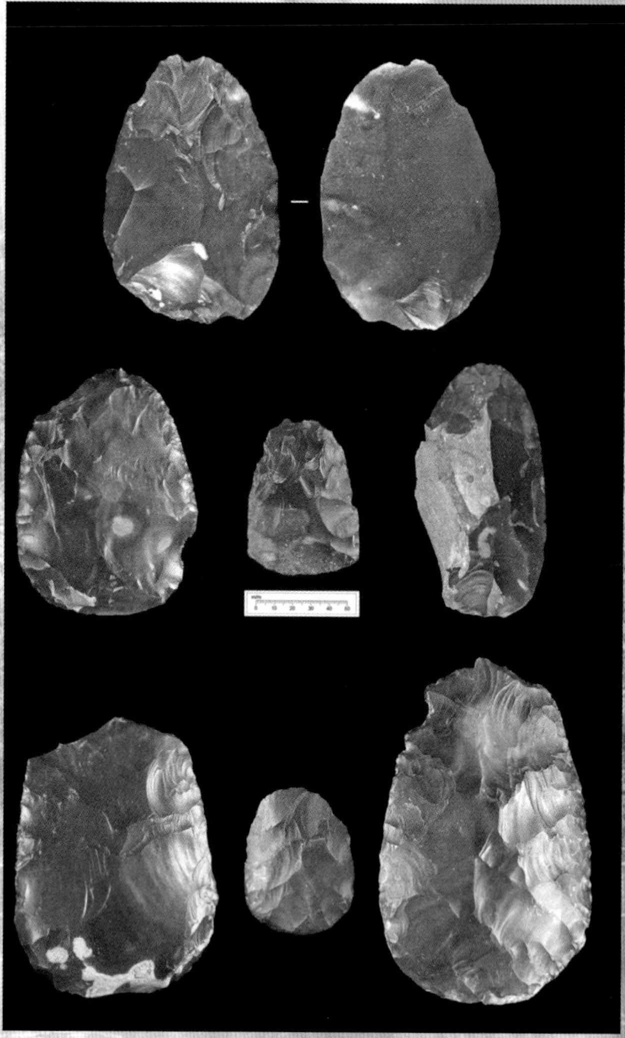

5.8.1 Handaxes from Lynford (from Pettitt and White 2012)

The main depositional unit of organic silts and sands (Association B) produced a lithic assemblage comprising 2,720 artefacts, some of which could be refitted (technological refits, as well as breaks). 41 complete and 6 broken handaxes were recovered; these are predominantly cordiform, ovate and subtriangular in planform, and included the exaggerated, classic bout coupé form. The refitting pieces reflect the use, modification and recycling of tools, especially handaxes — one large example shows a distinctive break to the tip, probably caused by twisting and applying significant force. The flake assemblage primarily reflects the later stages of handaxe production — thinning and finishing; large, cortical flakes such as might result from flint selection and roughing out are not present. The largest and best-made handaxes from the site are the most extensively worked and rejuvenated, suggesting that they were carried in ready-made. Other less intensively worked pieces were also manufactured on local cobbles and flakes; Neanderthals at Lynford were employing both curated and expedient technological solutions in combination (White 2012). The only other British open air site from which a substantial handaxe collection has been recovered is Little Paxton, Cambridgeshire (Paterson and Tebbutt 1947), which shows a similar dichotomy between well-made imported handaxes and less intensively worked examples on local cobbles. The Lynford excavations also produced a sandstone block, which is interpreted as bearing traces resulting from rubbing a softer material against it – perhaps in the context of fire-lighting.

The Lynford excavations exemplify best practice in terms of co-operation between archaeologists and the aggregates industry; Aggregates Levy funding permitted the total excavation of this extraordinary locale, without placing the entire funding burden upon the quarry company unlucky enough to expose such remains. The site itself provides an unparalleled opportunity to investigate late Neanderthal behaviour at the north-western edge of Europe on an ethno-historical scale, and in relation to fine-grained environmental proxies. The Lynford faunal and lithic assemblage allows behaviour at the site to be reconstructed, but also allows inference concerning how British Neanderthals engaged with their wider landscapes.

Late Neanderthal archaeology is poorly represented in Britain; most British sites of this date comprise only a handful of pieces, with Lynford being only the second substantial handaxe-dominated site yet known. In fact, the period reflects the inverse pattern to that apparent for the earlier Middle Palaeolithic, where extraction sites dominate — these are unknown for the middle Devensian. In part, this might reflect the inaccessibility of most fluvial middle Devensian sites, many of which lie below the modern floodplain, but also might reflect the difficulties of surviving in Britain during the 'failed interglacial' conditions of MIS 3. Neanderthals may only have been sporadic summer visitors to Britain (White 2006). Given how little we still know about the late Neanderthal inhabitants of Britain, the contribution Lynford makes to our understanding of the interval cannot be understated — and yet one site remains one site. Until we can access and excavate sedimentary contexts of equivalent date, it provides a rare glimpse of the vistas more familiar to continental workers.

This is usually divided into two categories – edge damage (where chips have been taken out of the delicate, sharp edges of the stone) and abrasion, where the intersections between flake scars have begun to become rounded. In extreme cases, a handaxe can become so heavily edge-damaged and abraded that only the shadows of flake scars survive, with no sharp edges being visible at all. Certain raw materials are more prone to damage than others; generally, the more granular the stone, the more heavily it will abraded. This has the knock-on effect that in flint impoverished regions, where quartzites and volcanic rocks may be used, artefacts have less chance of surviving once they enter an active sedimentary context, such as a river. These factors may have a significant impact upon apparent patterns of occupation investigated during ALSF-funded projects, with the Palaeolithic English Midlands (TVPP) and south-west seeming sparsely populated at best (ProSWeB).

Evaluating the degree of damage, and thus transport and redeposition, that an assemblage has undergone also requires an assessment of context. For instance, heavily rolled and edge-damaged artefacts within a fine-grained, fluvial deposit do not belong there – the damage that they have suffered could not have been inflicted by such a quiescent sedimentary regime. Usually, degree of damage is assessed by dividing material into ordinal categories, splitting up the continuum of variation from mint fresh (as if they had been knapped that day) to heavily abraded (Wymer 1968). This approach has the benefit of being extremely quick and easy, and requiring no specialist equipment. The broad assumption is made that the most heavily rolled and edge-damaged artefacts have travelled further, or within a more energetic sedimentary regime, than those which are not as damaged. This approach is a useful taphonomic tool, allowing the analyst to divide an assemblage into groups that have undergone more or less movement, and adapt the questions they ask of the material accordingly. However, it is worth noting that degree of rolling does not directly reflect how far travelled an artefact might be, as demonstrated by a pair of rolled, but refitting, artefacts from the cobble band at Barnham (Nick Ashton pers. comm.). These two pieces appear to have sat among a cobble band and been battered by passing clasts.

Chambers (2003) has developed a more detailed methodology for analysing changes to artefact state resulting from transport which was applied during several ALSF projects including APSC and Welton-le-Wold. It is based upon the microscopic measurement of the intersection between flake scars, as advocated by Shackley (1974). Taking account of the fact that any artefact, once incorporated within a fluvial system, behaves like a clast (cf. Harding *et al.* 1987), she proposed that microscopic recording of abrasion to different areas of the handaxe can be used to build up a picture of how each artefact has been moved, through comparison with experimental (flume tank) data. On this basis, she proposed that the Broom assemblage (Box 5.4) has in general travelled less than 300m, and that the primary mode of displacement for the handaxes was saltation. However, this methodology has not been widely applied to secondary context sites, relying as it does upon transporting equipment, experience in applying the method and untested assumptions regarding state and distance.

The second principle that underpins the use of artefacts as a taphonomic tool is the fact that, because stone working is a reductive process, particular elements must have been present at some point during working. Thus one can compare what should be there (ie by comparison with experimentally produced assemblages) with what is actually there, and work out what is missing – as well as what processes could have removed it. Probably the best example of this is the fact that most of the volume of material resulting from any knapping episode is actually tiny chips (< 20mm). Such material is small, light, and, in a fluvial context – or even on an exposed land surface – is easily transported away by natural action (Schick 1987). If an assemblage comprises mostly large pieces, then, depending on depositional context, it could be interpreted as a lag, left behind when smaller, lighter pieces have been winnowed away. These coarse taphonomic approaches are suitable for dealing with material from secondary or near primary context; however, dealing with less heavily modified, or near *in situ* assemblages, more precise taphonomic methods are required.

Technology

It is forgivable to think that it is only through the analysis of pristine, refitting assemblages of stone tools that one can begin to build up a picture of the technological choices made by past hominins. Much academic emphasis has been placed upon this as a route for reconstructing technology, and, more esoterically, the mental constructs underlying these technical choices. In Francophone literature, the study of how technical choices are made is termed the study of the *chaîne opératoire* (sequence of operations); in Anglo-American literature the term more normally used is reduction sequence – which means broadly the same thing, though largely stripped of its socio-cognitive implications. Studying reduction choices is, however, possible using assemblages recovered from a variety of preservational gradients; as ever, the key to extracting useful information is to ask questions of appropriate scale. Indeed, when dealing with refitting lithic material, it is sometimes too tempting to become bogged down in the intricate details of any individual refitting group, seduced by the intimacy of recreating each and every gesture – which ultimately, may inform us only about that isolated moment in time. Such individual moments are useful only if animated within their historical and landscape context.

The way in which stone tools were made and used can be reconstructed in very different ways, depending on the taphonomic history of the assemblage in question. Again, the interpretative statements that can be made vary in terms of the scale of question. The irreversible nature of lithic-working means that it is possible to read something of how an individual artefact was produced from the artefact itself. The scars left by striking previous flakes from the same core, or from the surface of a bifacial tool, are retained on the artefact. Specific 'landmarks' allow one to reconstruct technological features, such as the direction flakes were struck from, how many flakes were struck, how hard, and what type of percussor was used. Thus it is possible to build up a picture of the acts and gestures through which even a single artefact was shaped – and why particular choices may have been made. Thus, even artefacts from secondary-context sites that combine material from a wide geographical (basin wide) catchment can shed light upon chosen technological options at particular times.

Just as comparing an archaeological lithic assemblage with an experimentally generated one can be a useful tool for understanding what natural processes have affected it (see taphonomy above), so the same principle can be used to assess what pieces of the expected reduction sequence are missing because of human action. According to the overall technological strategy adopted, characteristic products are associated with different points in the reduction sequence. At the beginning of reduction, large, thick flakes bearing a lot of cortex (the outer rind of the nodule) are produced. So, collections of material resulting from selecting nodules, roughing them out, and preparing cores or handaxes, contain a lot of these flakes. This is the case with the artefacts from near the cliff in the Boxgrove palaeolandscape (Box 5.1; Pope and Roberts 2005). Conversely, the assemblage from Lynford (Box 5.8) lacks these sort of flakes in the proportions one would expect if all stages of handaxe manufacture – from raw material selection to remodelling and discard – had been undertaken at the same place (White 2012). In fact, the Lynford assemblage contains many flakes that are characteristic of the final stages of handaxe working and remodelling: small flakes scars with scar patterns coming in from converging directions, and pieces that refit to broken tips (ibid.).

The lack of these characteristic products within *in situ* or minimally modified sites with refits allows a picture to be made of what general actions have been undertaken at a particular place, and thus helps to reanimate the static residues preserved within them. Where taphonomic factors can be filtered out, the same patterns can be extended to assemblages further along the preservational gradient, where assemblages may have been rearranged, but reflect repeated action within a given place. For instance, many early Middle Palaeolithic sites in the Thames Valley contain signatures reflecting raw material extraction, Levallois core preparation and exploitation, and the export of particular products from them (Scott 2006; 2011). Very few of these contain refitting products, but their technology is still informative on a meso-scale. At Creffield Road, near Acton, for example, it is obvious that parts of the reduction sequence must be missing; the site is dominated by a peculiar combination of, on one hand, very large Levallois points, and on the other, exceedingly small Levallois point cores. The cores are totally exhausted, having been reworked many times, and the final attempt to exploit them appears to have been a failure. If all the technical stages between the production of these big points, and the discard of these small cores had been undertaken at the site, then one very characteristic type of flake (a *débordant*, or core edge flake) should be present. None have been recovered, and it is impossible to account for this lack in terms of taphonomic factors or collection history (Scott 2011, 61–62). Rather, we are dealing with a lithic signature that shows how Neanderthals went to Creffield Road to tool-up before going out into the landscape to carry on the day-to-day routines of hunter-gatherers, then returning to replenish their stocks again once the tools and cores were used up. Thus it is possible to look from an old assemblage, recovered by quarrymen working for a collector in the 1880s, out into the wider taskscapes created by the humans moving through them.

DISCUSSION

Projects funded through the ALSF reflect the full texture of the Palaeolithic artefact record as generally encountered in Britain, and exemplify the approaches adopted and adapted to dealing with sites and the archaeological material recovered from them. The strength of the British Palaeolithic record is undoubtedly its history and the actions of the indefatigable researchers – modern researchers are adept at standing on the shoulders of such giants, and wringing blood from old stones. ALSF projects that reflect this tenacity in mining the existing museum resources to answer new research questions include the *Stopes Palaeolithic Project*, together with work on the artefact collections from Broom and Welton-le-Wold. The Stopes project in particular demonstrates that unpublished archives must be used to extract a full picture of where artefacts have historically been collected, while Broom and Welton-le-Wold show what value can be added to existing collections by a very limited amount of fieldwork. Indeed, Palaeolithic artefacts are essentially ornaments without a well-understood geological, temporal, and environmental context.

ALSF projects encompassed material derived from contexts which accumulated from very different spatial and temporal catchments: from material reworked into secondary context 'dredgers', such as Broom, Dunbridge and Chard Junction to the isolated snapshots apparent within the Boxgrove palaeolandscape. Combining such different preservational catchments involves adopting a nuanced and flexible approach, and asking questions at a scale appropriate to the assemblage being studied. Moreover, small scale (*in situ*) is not necessarily 'better' when dealing with the Palaeolithic record, unless reanimated by being placed within a broader behavioural and landscape context. For example, reconstructions of Neanderthal behaviour at Lynford, as recorded by the faunal and human assemblages, has been extrapolated well beyond the confines of the site itself, to broader engagement with the regional environment.

Dealing with the Palaeolithic record requires a complete change in approach – moving away from simply responding to where material is already known, to a more nuanced approach, which acknowledges the potential of particular types of geological capture point away from the river valleys and evaluates how these help us to build a more complete picture of past hominin lives throughout the entire Lower and Middle Palaeolithic. Such capture points include fissures (frequently impacted upon through quarrying Greensand, as in West Kent and Sussex) and solution features on the chalk (often exposed in road cuttings and similar works), both of which trap loess and other fine grained sediments capable of preserving primary context, if not *in situ* archaeology. If our reconstructions of the lost landscapes of the Palaeolithic are to cease to be dominated by fluvial basins – White's 'normal' locations (Pettitt and White 2012) – then we need to start considering these landscapes in their entirety.

Chapter 6: Lost landscapes of the British Palaeolithic: where do we go from here?

by Mark White

R.I.P. ALSF, 2002-2011

This volume was commissioned to disseminate and celebrate the many successful Palaeolithic and Pleistocene projects funded by the Aggregates Levy Sustainability Fund during the nine years of its short life. In attempting to realise these aspirations, the work has used key case studies to open up to a wide audience the nature, potential and pitfalls of the Pleistocene record, and to engender an understanding of these factors at a variety of scales. I hope that the volume will be seen as successful in its aims and that it will help usher in a new era of understanding and co-operation between the many stakeholders – one that can ultimately only be for the good of the discipline and, if achieved, will ensure that the results of the ALSF long outlast the life of the fund itself.

As noted in Chapter 1, English Heritage had already commissioned a series of three benchmark reviews aimed at assessing the impact of the ALSF (Miller *et al.* 2008; Flatman *et al.* 2008; Richards 2008), with the headline conclusion that the ALSF most certainly had facilitated better understanding. All three reports emphasised the fact that the ALSF had helped develop a more comprehensive baseline of knowledge for particular regions or resources affected by aggregate extraction and had helped to synthesise large datasets that might otherwise have lain dormant. Miller *et al.* (2008) noted that the profile of research had been raised among the aggregates industry, although Richards (2008) observed that the aggregates industry felt that its support was not widely acknowledged. Given the stalemate reached between the National Ice Age Initiative and the Mineral Products Association (MPA) detailed in Chapter 4, this urgently needs addressing at national level. That said, the particular benefits of the ALSF project results to development controllers, curators, HER officers, as well as university academics must equally be acknowledged. There was a feeling amongst the various authors, however, that the ALSF had failed to gain widespread recognition and had not developed a real identity.

With the demise of the scheme, many of the pointers to the future contained in these documents will probably not be taken forward, although they still have much resonance: the need for the various stakeholders to promote mutual understanding, the need for all stakeholders to be able to access a range of data reported in a standard understandable fashion, the potential utility of an ALSF Funding Council and the importance of 'social projects'. The last of these issues may be summarised in one word: IMPACT. Impact has assumed a massive importance in UK academic circles due to the Government's 'Impact Agenda', as measured through the periodical Research Excellence Framework 2014 (REF – formally Research Assessment Exercise, eg RAE2008). This demands that university research must have social, economic or cultural impact or benefit beyond academia. Now, as fists pound and doors slam in ivory towers across the land, even the quickest glance at the ALSF's many mission statements outlined in Chapter 1 will show that English Heritage, Natural England and DEFRA were at least a decade ahead of the game. The aggregates industry has also embraced these philosophies far better than many academics (cf Mineral Products Association 2012). ALSF had impact, in all senses of the word. The tragedy, then, is that the scheme has been withdrawn, the dream is over just as its vision was about to be realised.

In this chapter, I will not provide a summary of earlier ones. Instead I will discuss the issues that I (and hopefully my fellow authors) believe face the British Palaeolithic in the post-ALSF years. Building on the themes that have recurred throughout this volume, I will explore the current frameworks, and suggest ways in which the lessons of the ALSF might encourage us to divert from existing courses onto new paths of strategic resource enhancement. It is unashamedly polemical, but will hopefully ring true with some stakeholders.

'WE HAVEN'T GOT A PLAN SO NOTHING CAN GO WRONG' (SPIKE MILLIGAN)

Modern Palaeolithic archaeologists in Britain benefit from a long tradition of multi-disciplinary study that can be traced right back to the Victorian beginnings of our subject. This long heritage has a major downside, however. The pioneering appetite for discovery and excavation was rapacious, unstructured and often very poorly executed, leaving the modern scholar begging for scraps (or, more literally, gobbets of cave earth stuck high up on a cave wall, denuded spoil heaps and empty pits; cf White and Pettitt 2011; Pettitt and White 2012). The rate of early discoveries is staggering when compared to modern levels, and as Derek Roe famously stated, many British sites were simply discovered too early for their own good (Roe 1981). Year after year as new exciting discoveries are announced across Eurasia and Africa, most scholars in this country find themselves once again sifting through the same dusty materials. Granted, celebrity finds on the Cromer Coast put Britain in the international spotlight. But the truth is that this fame lasts for the notorious 15 minutes, and on their own they are simply not enough. Pakefield and Happisburgh provide only two new data points; yes, they are very old, and yes they challenge ideas about the timing and adaptive constraints of human dispersal into northern latitudes, but we need more. Clive Gamble once said that advances would not come from major new discoveries, but from theoretical developments. I have been a fan of Clive's work all my career, but I am afraid that I simply cannot agree with this statement in relation to Britain. Without a substantial increase in new discoveries, an enhancement of our current database or very significant new analytical techniques or trustworthy dating methods, the British Palaeolithic will decline in significance, and cease to have anything new to say on a European scale. Along this path, the future can only hold decades of fruitless debate over competing hypotheses built on different but equally valid readings of the same tired material – infinite equifinality.

These are the challenges we face in the post-ALSF, economically-squeezed times. We desperately need a new plan to help the British Palaeolithic grow out of this austerity. I believe that the ALSF provides the key.

FRAMEWORKS

There have been two English Heritage commissioned framework documents for the British Palaeolithic: *Research Frameworks for the Palaeolithic and Mesolithic of Britain and Ireland* (1999) and the *Research and Conservation Framework for the British Palaeolithic* (2008). During the years in between these publications, the Mesolithic was seemingly granted a divorce and given custody of Ireland (Blinkhorn and Milner 2014). In editing this book and thinking about future directions that the British Palaeolithic might take, I have perceived two basic problems with both of these documents.

First, the research priorities they outline – however they may be framed – revolve around an evergreen set of questions that have pertained since Prestwich and Evans stepped off the boat back from Amiens (Gamble and Kruszynski 2009). They include: culture and society; environments and ecology; settlement systems and colonisation; dating; continental connections; subsistence and technology; behaviour in different landscape settings (caves vs open air). The absence of statements regarding the need to discover new sites in this pioneering period emphasises that discovery of sites was a defacto given in the context of widespread quarrying (and the concomitant development) activity across much of the country. Today only the specifics and the theoretical paradigms within which they have been investigated have changed. Moreover, as we have seen many times throughout this volume, since the 1940s the rate of discovery has all but collapsed, leaving archaeologists with no option but to re-examine the same aging datasets. The question that must be asked, then, is do we actually need to continuously re-write these research frameworks, re-iterating questions that we have known for generations, or do we need something that aims to enhance the record and give us more to work with in achieving these research objectives?

Following on from this, I think that the present research frameworks are not talking to the right people. They were written by, and talk almost exclusively to, academics. Now, academics are perfectly placed to write such priorities – and most are well aware of each and every one of the issues raised above – but do they really need to? The research would probably have been done anyway and one might be forgiven for thinking that the framework document is a propaganda leaflet aimed at framing personal designs rather than designing strategic frameworks. Conservation and enhancement appear bolted on as an after-thought, without any real commitment.

An examination of the achievements of the 1999 *Framework*, as listed in the 2008 *Framework*, illustrates where these designs lie (Table 6.1). Of the 17 'Research Themes' listed in 1999, 16 were achieved by 2008 (although given the fact that they will continue to be researched, the idea that any one of these priorities can ever really be 'achieved' is dubious in itself). Education, display and information exchange were even more successful deemed to have hit all its targets bar one. Survey and assessment initiatives – those that could potentially enhance the value of our existing materials and add new data – did not fare so well. Only three of the 13 stated action points were even partly achieved:

With these issues in mind, I intend to side-step the principal research themes of the 2008 *Framework* document (not to mention the knotty question of protection and legislation), and move straight to its 'Strategic Research and Conservation Themes'. Leaving the details aside, these themes can all be viewed as capacity building, designed at enhancing and enlarging the database. They are listed below with a summary of what each aims to achieve, cast in the values expressed throughout this volume.

- *Areas* – this basically re-enforces the need to understand Palaeolithic occupation in a landscape context at multiple scales. This may operate at the level of the river valley, region or nation or indeed wider area, and may involve one or more of the terrestrial, transitional or marine landscapes, as discussed in Chapters 2-4
- *Understanding the record* – before we can understand the social and behavioural significance of our data, we need to understand how it formed. This involves an appreciation of geomorphological processes, taphonomy, preservation, collection and curation, as outlined in Chapter 5
- *Dating frameworks* – without accurate dating frameworks, we can have no understanding of patterns and processes. All appropriate dating methods should be explored, and all stakeholders should be aware of the potential (and indeed, limitations) of the different techniques
- *Curation and conservation* – mechanisms need to be in place for the collation, archiving and long term protection of the resource. These should include methods of prospection and recording in a variety of development contexts
- *Dealing with development* – we urgently need to capitalise on the results of the ALSF to create meaningful collaboration between archaeologists and aggregates extractors (as discussed in Chapter 4), and to promote a 'developer-facing' approach. The importance of the work we do, its intrinsic interest and potential minimal impact on commercial operations, needs to be emphasised. Mechanisms need to be developed to ensure that all stakeholders from the curatorial, development and commercial sector are aware of the value of the resource. Professional bodies and academics may take a lead role in dissemination
- *Collections and records enhancement* – ideally this would be an on-line shared resource for museums and other stakeholders to deposit details of finds, archive, location and accessibility
- *Outreach and education* – at the point when the 2008 Framework was being written it was acknowledged that universities did not always value this activity. Although not really falling under the category of impact as expressed in the REF documentation, public engagement and social/cultural benefits are vital to the healthy future of our discipline

ALSF LEGACY: STRATEGIC AGENDAS FOR A RICHER TOMORROW

These research priorities can and should be made to engage all stakeholders. The first six areas outlined above can be further distilled into three basic strategic aims, each of which subsumes outreach and education:

- Extending the Pleistocene record
- Enhancing the Pleistocene Record
- Engaging with the Pleistocene Record

These are not purely academic priorities – they are intended to preserve and enhance the Palaeolithic record in all its forms. Academic research will benefit, but specific research questions are not at the front of the agenda here, and nor should they be. What I, or anybody else, wants to study, and whatever empirical or theoretical stance we wish to take, is utterly irrelevant to the protection and enhancement of our deep past. We need to adopt a nested or scalar approach to our frameworks, beginning with these macro-scale concerns – which I would argue should be the focus of national funding bodies – moving down to the micro-scale of individual academic pursuits. In other words, academics are free to target sites or landscapes to answer specific questions, and free to attract funding from charities and research councils, but national agendas need to be larger, reflect national initiatives and be centrally funded. They also need to have benefits outside academia and speak to the impact agenda by canvassing the widest possible audience.

A number of factors highlighted throughout this volume pertaining to the three principles outlined above – Extending, Enhancing and Engaging – can talk to all stakeholders.

1) Extending the Pleistocene record

In my terms, extending the record describes the need for more sites. Research excavations are unlikely to achieve this on their own, and development is critical. As noted elsewhere, some of the most significant finds of the past decade have been made in advance of construction, for example Southfleet Road (Wenban-Smith *et al.* 2006; Wenban-Smith 2013) and Glaston (Cooper *et al.* 2012). Others have been made during watching briefs in quarries, such as Lynford (Boismier *et al.* 2012).

The most significant unifying principle here is the need for predictive modelling aimed at helping curators and planners make decisions, calming the grieving archaeologists, and assuaging the fears of interference within industry. This will demand the mapping of palaeolandscapes, establishing where humans were most likely to have been active and why, thus enhancing the importance of archaeological landscapes without archaeology (cf Chapter 2). It will also require us to understand the effects of bedrock geology on human mobility and settlement (cf Chapter 3), the distribution of plants and animals (Chapter 4), and changes in human behaviour through time (Chapter 5). Predictive modelling as part of the desk-top survey should occur at the point of conception, alerting the curator and developer to potential contingency measures for excavation or watching brief and comfortably falls within the scope of the National Planning Policy Framework.

2) Enhancing the Pleistocene record

The last comprehensive study of museum collections of early Palaeolithic material was by Derek Roe (1968), which was then used in the 1990s by John Wymer as the basis for TERPS' artefact counts and distribution maps. A lot has happened over the past 48 years, and we urgently need an up-to-date online national database of collections and archives. We also need to increase the scope of previous gazetteers to include all Middle and Upper Palaeolithic material, to include if possible material in private hands and material registered with HERs (much of this is still left over from the 1999 *Framework*).

This is easier said than done. Museums have literally hundreds of thousands of Palaeolithic artefacts. The whereabouts of some historical collections can be difficult to track down, as museums have merged/closed and material has been relocated or even sold. Some material is in private hands (like the Trent handaxes mentioned in Chapter 5), but a simple web-based campaign or initiative similar to the Public Catalogue Foundation's picture gallery should help bring these to light. Archival material also needs databasing, scanning and publishing online, as the information it contains can totally transform the value of old collections and, in effect, render them new sites – as has been done for Baker's Hole and Foxhall Road. Regional and national scale assessments, predictive modelling and curatorial decisions utterly depend on such databases. These suggestions complement the findings and suggestions of the recently published Archaeological Archives and Museums document (Edwards 2013), supported by English Heritage, the Society of Museum Archaeologists, and the Federation of Archaeological Managers and Employers, highlighting the fact that this problem is endemic in archaeology, not just the Palaeolithic.

Likewise, the value of well-known sites can be massively enhanced through the application of new analytical techniques and dating programmes, sometimes with very small-scale sondages to target critical deposits (eg TVPP, MVPP).

3) Engaging with the Palaeolithic Record

The initiatives started by the *National Ice Age Network* need to be revisited. There was nothing wrong with the original philosophy and aspirations of NIAN – to get a better long-term 'deal' for significant Pleistocene remains brought to light during commercial quarrying, and an agreement in principle about recording/recovering remains in quarries. It also had the backing of English Heritage, English Nature, the Quaternary Research Association, the Geologists' Association, the Council for British Archaeology, UKRIGS and the Prehistoric Society. Still, for the reasons outlined in Chapter 4, they were very badly received by the some key players within the quarrying industry, even though as a whole NIAN was seen as being 'pro-industry' within the industry itself. Obviously each stakeholder sees things through different lenses (see below), but we need to resurrect these cross-party talks, with constituent members drawn from the full range of constituencies.

TOWARDS MUTUAL UNDERSTANDING

We have spoken a lot in this volume about mutual understanding among stakeholders (see also Last *et al.* 2013). Hopefully, most of the stakeholders in the heritage sector already do understand each other to a greater or lesser degree, depending on proximity of interests. It is parties with other priorities that we need to reach out to in a genuine way, not as lip service, and begin exploring how we deal with points 1 and 3 above. Many archaeologists are so passionate about the past that they regard anything that affects our heritage with hostility, be it a road through a historical landscape, a housing development on a deserted medieval village, a quarry exploiting 400,000 year old sands and gravels, or metal detecting night-hawks. Archaeologists in general will tell you about the value of the past, how it enhances social and cultural lives, how it links the living with the dead, people to places, and provides a sense of national pride. The number of TV shows and internet sites devoted to the past, genealogy, history etc, shows that this is most certainly the case. Archaeology matters.

The MPA recognises this:

> "Mineral extraction often produces archaeological finds that give us a better understanding of our past. Disturbing ground can create a risk of destroying valuable archaeology, and the industry has long accepted its responsibility not just to cooperate but to fund advance investigation work. In a typical year, operators pay for work covering more than 600 hectares, around half of that before planning permission has been granted. The MPA is a co-signatory of 'Mineral extraction and archaeology: practice guide' published by English Heritage."
>
> (MPA 2012, 6)

I cannot imagine that RCUK-funded projects can make such a claim in respect to the scale of funded excavations, so the first thing we need to be clear on is that the aggregates industry is one of the most important facilitators of archaeological research in the country.

Mineral extraction and archaeology: a practice guide – written by the archaeologist Clive Waddington – also recognises the different needs, which are paraphrased here:

- A steady, adequate and sustainable supply of minerals is essential to the nation's prosperity, infrastructure and quality of life
- Minerals are finite and irreplaceable resources

that can only be worked where they occur (ie geology dictates the positioning of quarries)

- Archaeological remains are a finite and irreplaceable resource that may occur anywhere
- Archaeological resources are not all equal in value
- It is the role of the planning system to reconcile the needs of the historic environment and minerals development in the context of sustainable development (Waddington 2008, 4)

It also recognised that the best way to deal with Palaeolithic archaeology that occurs within an aggregate body is through monitoring sensitive landform units, and that the *in situ* preservation will rarely be practical or justified. This means that all or any of the techniques described in Chapter 2 might be of relevance, depending on context and significance.

This was all part and parcel of the NIAN initiative but outside archaeological circles, Point 1 above is most relevant to the people and government of Great Britain. These quotes should readily explain why.

> "No industry pumps more materials into the arteries of UK life and the economy than mineral products. Over one million tonnes in a typical day, worth £9bn a year and providing jobs for 70,000 people. But what is really significant about our industry is the extent to which it supports others and, in doing so, is essential to the UK economy. We estimate that the knock-on benefit of what we do supports over £400 billion in terms of turnover in industries we supply and over 2.5 million jobs in the economy as a whole."

> "Mineral products enable us to build and improve our housing stock, transport networks, commercial and industrial buildings, utilities, schools and hospitals. While markets have suffered significant decline during recent years, the sheer scale of the £250 billion investment identified by Infrastructure UK and the outstanding need to increase the availability of housing, demonstrate the critical role we will play in delivery."

> "The value of such assets to the UK is huge. For example, the strategic road network of motorways and trunk roads in England [is] built with mineral products and dependent on them for maintenance ...Some products we make possible are not so obvious. Without limestone, there would be no steel. Take away sand, and there would be no glass. Remove lime, and water would not be fit for drinking."
> (MPA 2012, 2-3)

So, if an important new site was discovered, what is the best we could hope for? One thing is for certain – not a cessation of operations. Too much else is at stake. It would involve negotiation between operator and archaeologist. There would be no blanket policy, but personal talks about what area could be left fallow for excavation, for how long, whether the operator would be prepared to contribute, or whether emergency funds should be sought from RCUK (cf. Norton Subcourse which was funded by a combination of a NERC urgency grant, the QRA, the Royal Society and the Leverhulme Trust (via AHOB) or elsewhere (cf Lynford). Predictive modelling will again help curators assess the impact on Pleistocene remains at the planning and mineral permission stage, which can be factored in to long-term extraction plans.

Another important point is what constitutes an important site. I would argue that it would not include a few rolled handaxes and a scrappy mammoth tooth but would require *in situ* finds of the quality of Boxgrove or Lynford. The excavations at the latter, incidentally, involved an area of around 200m^2 at the very edge of a quarry hundreds of times that size. The scale of archaeological excavations (usually restricted by costs) appears to be overestimated by quarry operators who are probably more used to dealing with major later-period excavations on the land above – but that is a wholy different issue that I do not intend to tackle here.

What other measures could be suggested? Funds could be made available to train quarry workers to monitor faces as they extract sand and gravel, rapid responses (local units or universities) could be co-ordinated to rescue and bulk sample materials in a fashion that can be meaningfully analysed in the laboratory without stopping productions (as was successfully done at the Maastricht-Belvedere quarry in the Netherlands), and suitably trained archaeologists with Quarry Safety Passports could be allowed periodically to monitor and record, to develop those personal relationships and negotiate sensitively if anything of real importance is uncovered. The MPA will also need assurances that they will not be horribly surprised by an unexpected bill outside any contingency factored in at the planning stage.

The critical thing is that something is in place to enable the sites to be identified in the first place. But without the ALSF and projects like NIAN, are these just pipe dreams?

CONCLUSIONS

The next decade will be extremely challenging for Palaeolithic archaeology. With continued economic uncertainties everybody is nervous. The academic faces falling student numbers and lack of research funds. Developers are stretched to the limit in a country where the market can hardly be described as buoyant. Development controllers find themselves in the spotlight if they are seen not to favour the developer and in the news if a decision upsets the local community. Quarry operators face continued taxation through the aggregates levy, even though the money is no longer channelled into affected communities, and have expressed frustration over what they perceive as excessive levels of archaeological investigation (cf. Last *et al.* 2013); while the MPA has openly stated it has little faith in NPPF to deliver certainty (newsfeed on 18th March 2013 at http://www.mineralproducts.org). Meanwhile, the woman on the Clapham Omnibus is worried about her job, her mortgage, how Jenny will afford her university fees, and whether archaeology really is such a good choice of subject.

The answer to all – the Lost Landscapes of the Pleistocene do deserve some level of protection, but this needs to be balanced with all these other factors and anchored in economic reality. The opportunity for both archaeologist and industry to positively impact upon science and community is real, but we need to understand each other's needs, hopes and fears as they really are, and not grotesque caricatures. If the door between NIAN and the MPA is not locked, then there is just one question left to ask the multitude of different stakeholders: 'can we please talk?'.

Appendix 1:
ALSF Palaeolithic Project Resources

The following appendix includes a summary of ALSF Palaeolithic projects referred to in this volume whose digital archives have been deposited with the Archaeological Data Service (ADS). The projects are arranged by ALSF project number as they appear on the ADS website. **http://archaeology-dataservice.ac.uk/archives/view/alsf/** In addition the results of several projects have been published in academic monographs and papers and references are included where relevant.

3253/5881: LYNFORD QUARRY
Norfolk Archaeological Unit, Northamptonshire Archaeology, Royal Holloway, UoL
A pdf of the full academic monograph published in 2011 can be downloaded from the English Heritage website:
http://www.english-heritage.org.uk/publications/neanderthals-among-mammoths/
Boismier, W, Gamble, C, and Coward, F, 2011 *Neanderthals Among Mammoths: Excavations at Lynford Quarry, Norfolk*, English Heritage

3263/3913: THAMES THROUGH TIME, VOLUME 1
Oxford Archaeology
An academic monograph was published in 2011:
Morigi, T, Schreve, D, White, M, Hey, G, Garwood, P, Robinson, M, Barclay, A, and Bradley P, 2011 *Thames Through Time: The Archaeology of the Gravel Terraces of the Upper and Middle Thames – Early Prehistory to 1500BC*, Thames Valley Landscapes Monograph, Volume 1

3277/3543: SUBMERGED PALAEO-ARUN AND SOLENT RIVERS: RECONSTRUCTION OF PREHISTORIC LANDSCAPES
Sanjeev Gupta, Jenny Collier, Andy Palmer-Felgate, Julie Dickinson, Kerry Bushe, Stuart Humber
The final integrated project report can be downloaded from the ADS website:
http://archaeologydataservice.ac.uk/archives/view/palaeoarun_eh_2007/
Gupta, S, Collier, J, Palmer-Felgate, A, Dickinson, J, Bushe, K, and Humber, S, 2004 *Submerged Palaeo-Arun River: Reconstruction of Prehistoric Landscapes and Evaluation of Archaeological Resource Potential, Integrated Projects 1 and 2*

3282: THE LEA VALLEY MAPPING PROJECT (LVMP)
Museum of London Archaeology
An academic monograph was published in 2011:
Corcoran, J, Halsey, C, Spurr, G, Burton, E, and Jamieson, D, 2011 *Mapping Past Landscapes in the Lower Lea Valley: A Geoarchaeological Study of the Quaternary Sequence*, Museum of London Archaeology, MOLA Monograph 55

3279: THE PALAEOLITHIC ARCHAEOLOGY OF THE SUSSEX/HAMPSHIRE COASTAL CORRIDOR (PASHCC)
Martin Bates, Francis Wenban-Smith, Rebecca Briant, Richard Bates
The GIS datasets and final report can be downloaded from the ADS website:
http://archaeologydataservice.ac.uk/archives/view/pashcc_eh_2007/overview.cfm
Bates,M R, Wenban-Smith,F, Braint, R, and Bates, C R, 2007 *Curation of the Sussex / Hampshire Coastal Corridor Lower/Middle Palaeolithic Record*

3310: MIDDLE THAMES NORTHERN TRIBUTARIES (MTNT)
Essex County Council, University of Wales Trinity St David, Hertfordshire County Council
The GIS datasets and final report can be downloaded from the ADS website:
http://archaeologydataservice.ac.uk/archives/view/mtnt_eh_2007/
Bates, M, Heppell, E, and Gascoyne, A, 2006 *Assessment Report: Middle Thames Northern Tributaries*. Final Report as submitted to English Heritage.

3322: ARTEFACTS FROM THE SEA
Wessex Archaeology
The following reports can be downloaded from the ADS website:
http://archaeologydataservice.ac.uk/archives/view/artefactssea_eh_2007/
Wessex Archaeology, 2003 *Artefacts from the Sea.* Source Appraisal, ref: 51541.01
Wessex Archaeology, 2003 *Artefacts from the Sea.* Year 1 Report, ref: 51541.02
Wessex Archaeology, 2003 *Artefacts from the Sea.* Year 2 Report, ref: 51541.03

Wessex Archaeology, 2003 *Artefacts from the Sea. Catalogue of the Michael White Collection*, ref: 51541a and b

3338: STOPES PALAEOLITHIC ARCHIVE
Francis Wenban-Smith
The final report and project maps can be downloaded from the ADS website:
http://archaeologydataservice.ac.uk/archives/view/stopes_eh_2007/
Wenban-Smith, F, 2004, *Stopes Palaeolithic Project.* Final Report as submitted to English Heritage

3361: THE ARCHAEOLOGICAL POTENTIAL OF SECONDARY CONTEXTS
Robert Hosfield, Jenni Chambers, Phil Toms
The following reports can be downloaded from the ADS website:
http://archaeologydataservice.ac.uk/archives/view/apscontexts_eh_2007/
Hosfield, R T and Chambers, J C, 2004: *The Archaeological Potential of Secondary Contexts.* English Heritage Project Report (Project No. 3361), English Heritage Archive Report: London
Toms, P S, Hosfield, R T, Chambers, J C, Green, P C, and Marshall, P, 2005 *Optical Dating of the Broom Palaeolithic Sites, Devon and Dorset*, Centre for Archaeology Report 16/2005, English Heritage, London

3362: RE-ASSESSMENT OF THE ARCHAEOLOGICAL POTENTIAL OF CONTINENTAL SHELVES
Justin Dix, Rory Quinn, Kieran Westley
The following report can be downloaded from the ADS website:
http://archaeologydataservice.ac.uk/archives/view/continentshelves_eh_2008/
Westley, K, Dix, J, and Quinn, R, 2004 *Re-assessment of the Archaeological Potential of Continental Shelves.* English Heritage ALSF project no. 3362. School of Ocean and Earth Science, University of Southampton

3388: THE SHOTTON PROJECT: A MIDLANDS PALAEOLITHIC NETWORK (SEE ALSO NIAN)
Lang, A, 2004 The Shotton Project: A Midlands Palaeolithic Network, *PAST* 46
http://www.le.ac.uk/has/ps/past/past46.html

3426: CRESWELL CRAGS LIMESTONE HERITAGE AREA MANAGEMENT ACTION PLAN
Creswell Heritage Trust, Archaeological Research and Consultancy at the University of Sheffield
The Management Plan is available to download from the ADS website:
http://archaeologydataservice.ac.uk/archives/view/creswellcrags_eh_2011/
Davies, G, Badcock, A, Mills, N, and Smith, B, 2004 *Creswell Crags Limestone Heritage Area Management Action Plan*

3447: WELTON-LE-WOLD, LINCOLNSHIRE: AN UNDERSTANDING OF THE ICE AGE HERITAGE LINCOLNSHIRE
The project report is available to download from the ADS website:
http://archaeologydataservice.ac.uk/archives/view/weltonlewold_eh_2011/
Aram, J, Hambly, and Rackham, J, 2004 *Towards and Understanding of the Ice Age at Welton-le-Wold, Lincolnshire*, Heritage Lincolnshire report for English Heritage

3495: TRENT VALLEY PALAEOLITHIC PROJECT (TVPP)
Mark White, Andy J. Howard, David Bridgland
The educational booklet for local outreach is available to download from the ADS website:
http://archaeologydataservice.ac.uk/archives/view/tvpp_eh_2008/
The Trent Valley: Landscape and Archaeology of the Ice Age
Published monographs and papers include:
Bridgland, D R, Howard, A J, White, M J, White, T S, 2014 *Quaternary of the Trent*, Oxbow Books
Howard, A J, Bridgland, D R, Knight, D, McNabb, J, Rose, J, Schreve, D, Westaway, R, White, M J, and White, T S, 2007 The British Pleistocene fluvial archive: East Midlands drainage evolution and human occupation in the context of the British and NW European record, *Quaternary Science Reviews* 26, 2724-2737
White, T S, White, M J, Bridgland, D R, and Howard, A J, 2008 Lower Palaeolithic quartzite artefacts from the River Trent at East Leake, Nottinghamshire: New light on a hidden resource, *Quaternary Newsletter*

3502: CRESWELL CRAGS: MANAGEMENT OF PLEISTOCENE ARCHIVES AND COLLECTIONS
Creswell Heritage Trust
The following report accompanied by a series of tables is available for download at the ADS website:
http://archaeologydataservice.ac.uk/archives/view/creswellcrags_eh_2006/
Wall, I J, and Jacobi, R E M, 2000 *An Assessment of the Pleistocene Collections from the Cave and Rockshelter Sites in the Creswell Area*, Creswell Heritage Trust

3790/3952: NATIONAL ICE AGE NETWORK (NIAN)
Royal Holloway, University of London, University of Leicester, University of Birmingham
The leaflets, recognition sheets and a number of other promotional materials are available for download from the ADS website. The digital archive also contains the Palaeolithic GIS created for the West Midlands by staff at Birmingham Archaeology (University of Birmingham) http://archaeologydataservice.ac.uk/archives/view/nian_eh_2010/

3836: THE MEDWAY VALLEY PALAEOLITHIC PROJECT (MVPP)

Francis Wenban-Smith

The two reports for Essex and Kent can be downloaded from the ADS website:
http://archaeologydataservice.ac.uk/archives/view/medway_eh_2009/

Wenban-Smith, F F, Bates, M R, and Marshall, G, 2007 *Medway Valley Palaeolithic Project Final Report: The Palaeolithic Resource in the Medway Gravels (Essex)*

Wenban-Smith, F F, Bates, M R, and Marshall, G, 2007 *Medway Valley Palaeolithic Project Final Report: The Palaeolithic Resource in the Medway Gravels (Kent)*

Published papers include:

Wenban-Smith, F F, 2004 Handaxe typology and Lower Palaeolithic cultural development: ficrons, cleavers and two giant handaxes from Cuxton, *Lithics* 25, 11-21
http://eprints.soton.ac.uk/41481/

3847: THE PALAEOLITHIC RIVERS OF SOUTHWEST BRITAIN (PRoSWeB)

Tony Brown, Robert Hosfield, Laura Basell, Phil Toms, S. Hounsell, R. Young

The ADS digital archive consists of the project report along with various outreach resources and selected artefact images. Individual images can be cross-referenced to the Artefacts Database:
http://archaeologydataservice.ac.uk/archives/view/proswb_eh_2007/

Hosfield R T, Brown, A G, Basell, L S, Hounsell, S and Young, R, 2007 *The Palaeolithic Rivers of Southwest Britain: Final Report (Phases I & II)*, English Heritage Project Report (Project No. 3847)

Project Booklet: The Palaeolithic Rivers of South-West Britain

Project Flyer: The Palaeolithic Rivers of South-West Britain Project

Project Poster: The Palaeolithic of the South-West

School Teaching Resources: Palaeolithic Stone Tools; Hominin Species; Palaeolithic Chronology; Pleistocene Climate, Flora & Fauna; Pleistocene Landscapes; Palaeolithic Lifestyles & Behaviour

Published monographs and papers include:

Hosfield, R, and Green, CP (eds) *2013 Quaternary History and Palaeolithic Archaeology in the Axe Valley at Broom, South West England*, Oxbow, Oxford

Brown, A G, Basell, L S, and Toms, P, 2015 A stacked Late Quaternary fluvio-periglacial sequence from the Axe valley, southern England with implications for landscape evolution and Palaeolithic archaeology, *Quaternary Science Reviews* 116, 106-121

3854: CHRONOLOGY OF BRITISH AGGREGATES USING AMINO ACID RACEMIZATION AND DEGRADATION

Kirsty Penkman, Matthew Collins, David Keen, Richard Preece

The ADS digital archive currently consists of the project report accompanied by data tables:

Penkman, K, Collins, M, Keen, D, and Preece, R, 2008 *British Aggregates: an Improved Chronology using Amino Acid Racemization and Degradation of Intracrystalline Amino Acids (IcPD)*, English Heritage Research Department Report Series 6-2008, ISSN 1749-8775

Published Papers include:

Ashton, N, Lewis, S, Parfitt, S, Candy, I, Keen, D, Kemp, R, Penkman, K, Thomas, G, and Whittaker, J, 2005 Excavations at the Lower Palaeolithic site at Elveden, Suffolk, UK, *Proceedings of the Prehistoric Society* 71, 1-61

Collins, M J, Cappellini, E, Buckley, M, Penkman, K E H, Griffin, R C, and Koon, H E C, 2005 Analytical methods to detect ancient proteins, in Gunneweg, K, Greenblatt, C, and Adriaens, A, (eds) *Bio- and Material Cultures at Qumran*, 33-40

Langford, H E, Bateman, M D, Penkman, K E H, Boreham, S, Briant, R M, Coope, G R, and Keen, D H, 2007 Age-estimate evidence for Middle-Late Pleistocene aggradation of River Nene 1st Terrace deposits at Whittlesey, eastern England, *Proceedings of the Geologists' Association* 118 (2)

Parfitt, S A, Barendregt, R W, Breda, M, Candy, I, Collins, M J, Coope, G R, Durbidge, P, Field, M H, Lee, J R, Lister, A M, Mutch, R, Penkman, K E H, Preece, R C, Rose, J, Stringer, C B, Symons, R, Whittaker, J E, Wymer, J J, and Stuart, A J, 2005 The earliest humans in Northern Europe: artefacts from the Cromer Forest-bed Formation at Pakefield, Suffolk, UK, *Nature* 438, 1008-1012

Preece, R C, Parfitt, S A, Bridgland, D R, Lewis, S G, Rowe, P J, Atkinson, T C, Candy, I, Debenham, N C, Penkman, K E H, Griffiths, H I, Whittaker, J E, and Gleed-Owen, C, 2007 Terrestrial environments in MIS 11: Evidence from the Palaeolithic site at West Stow, Suffolk, UK, *Quaternary Science Reviews* 26, 1236-1300

Preece, R C, and Penkman, K E H, 2005 New faunal analyses and amino acid dating of the Lower Palaeolithic site at East Farm, Barnham, Suffolk, *Proceedings of the Geologists' Association* 116, 363-377

Schreve, D C, Harding, P, White, M J, Bridgland, D R, Allen, P, Clayton, F, Keen, D H, and Penkman, K E H, 2006 A Levallois knapping site at West Thurrock, Lower Thames, UK: its Quaternary context, environment and age, *Proceedings of the Prehistoric Society* 72, 21-52

3876/4600/5684 SEABED PREHISTORY

Wessex Archaeology

The Seabed Prehistory ADS archive comprises eight reports of which Volume I presents an introduction to the project, Volumes II to VII focus on the individual study areas and Volume VIII presents the results and conclusions of the project overall:
http://archaeologydataservice.ac.uk/archives/view/seaprehist_eh_2009/

Wessex Archaeology, 2008 *Seabed Prehistory: Gauging the Effects of Marine Aggregate Dredging* Volumes I–VIII, ref. no. 57422.31-38
An academic monograph was published in 2015: Tizzard, L, Bickert, A, and De Loecker, D, 2015 *Seabed Prehistory. Investigating the Palaeogeography and Early Middle Palaeolithic Archaeology in the Southern North Sea*, Wessex Archaeology Report 35, Wessex Archaeology Ltd, Salisbury

4620: VALDOE ASSESSMENT SURVEY
Matthew Pope
The ADS digital archive consists of a combined volume of specialist reports:
http://archaeologydataservice.ac.uk/archives/view/valdoe_eh_2010/
Micropalaeontological Report *John Whittaker*
Assessment of vertebrate remains from Valdoe Pit, West Sussex *Simon Parfitt*
Pollen Analysis *Phil Gibbard & Sylvia Peglar*
Molluscan Analysis *Richard Preece*
Amino Acid Racemization *Kirsty Penkman*
Site photographs
Sediment logs
Lithics spreadsheets
Published papers include:
Pope, M, Roberts, M, Maxted, A and Jones, P, 2009 The Valdoe: Archaeology of a locality within the Boxgrove Palaeolandscape, West Sussex, *Proceedings of the Prehistoric Society* 75, 239-263

4996: ARCHAEOLOGICAL POTENTIAL OF CAVE AND FISSURE DEPOSITS IN LIMESTONE
Archaeological Research and Consultancy at the University of Sheffield
The project report can be downloaded from the ADS website:
http://archaeologydataservice.ac.uk/archives/view/caves_eh_2011/
Oliver, J, and Davies, G, 2008 *Caves as Cultural Heritage: Research into the Impact of Limestone Quarries on Archaeological Caves and Fissures and their Protection through Planning*. ARCUS Report No. 1081.b (1)

5088: THE J J WYMER ARCHIVE
Lorraine Mepham
John Wymer's Field Note Books have been digitised in eight volumes and can be viewed on the ADS website:
http://archaeologydataservice.ac.uk/archives/view/wymer_eh_2008/

5266: LOWER AND MIDDLE PALAEOLITHIC OF THE FENLAND RIVERS OF CAMBRIDGESHIRE (FRCPP)
Durham University
The ADS digital archive contains several key outputs available for download, including a gazetteer of Lower and Middle Palaeolithic sites in Cambridgshire; a project bibliography; and a project report/booklet:
http://archaeologydataservice.ac.uk/archives/view/palaeofen_eh_2010/
White, T S, Boreham, S, Bridgland, D R, Gdaniec, K, and White, M J ,2008 *The Lower and Middle Palaeolithic of Cambridgeshire*

5285: SOMERSET AGGREGATES LITHICS ASSESSMENT (SALSA)
Somerset County Council
The following report can be downloaded from the ADS website:
http://archaeologydataservice.ac.uk/archives/view/salsa_eh_2008/
Firth, H, and Faxon, K, 2008 *Somerset Aggregates Lithics Assessment (SALSA), Aggregates Levy Sustainability Fund Project Number 5285*, Somerset County Council Heritage Service

5703: KIMBRIDGE FARM QUARRY, DUNBRIDGE
Wessex Archaeology
The deposit modelling report, artefact database and photographs can be downloaded from the ADS website:
http://archaeologydataservice.ac.uk/archives/view/dunbridge_eh_2012/
Wessex Archaeology, 2011 *Palaeolithic material from Dunbridge, Hampshire: Deposit modelling report*, ref: 69592.01

THE LOST LANDSCAPES ARTEFACT DATABASE (LLAD)
A number of ALSF projects included Palaeolithic artefact databases and gazetteers in various formats. Where sufficient data was available these have been collated into a single database to be hosted on the ADS in due course on a dedicated project page. The Lost Landscapes Artefact Database (LLAD) is primarily an update of The English Rivers Project (TERPS) database. It includes data from the ALSF projects, but also all of the original TERPS datasets.

The TERPS dataset comprises some 3600 records of sites and findspots originally listed by John Wymer on index cards, and subsequently issued as the six unpublished volumes (regionally based) of the Southern Rivers Palaeolithic Project, then the English Rivers Palaeolithic Project, between 1993 and 1997. This dataset essentially summarises information for each Lower and Middle Palaeolithic findspots in England, detailing location, geology, circumstances of discovery, numbers and types of artefacts and their current location, current nature of site, and bibliographic sources (including references to TERPS mapping). This data formed the basis of The Lower Palaeolithic Occupation of Britain, published in 1999.

Some new and updated data were subsequently added by John Wymer, and the database, created in 2008, was also augmented by a few new entries from two ALSF Palaeolithic projects the Medway Valley Palaeolithic Project (MVPP) and the Palaeolithic Archaeology of the Sussex/Hampshire Coastal Corridor (PASHCC)

Following a review of the data as part of the Lost Landscapes project it became apparent that many of the ALSF project datasets included historical and HER data already in the TERPS database, and in these instances records have been identified and updated with ALSF project numbers and additional references. As each site entry in the TERPS database had a unique identifier number it was considered most efficient to update TERPS at the outset rather than create a separate database in order to avoid duplication of records. In some instances ALSF projects identified additional findspots from HER records and other historical sources and these, along with recently investigated sites, form new entries in the database. Additional fields within the site table of the database allows ALSF entries to be filtered by project.

OTHER WEB-BASED PALAEOLITHIC RESOURCES

The English Rivers Project (TERPS)
http://archaeologydataservice.ac.uk/archives/view/terps_eh_2009/

Ancient Human Occupation of Britain (AHOB) project
http://www.ahobproject.org/

The Boxgrove Project
https://boxgroveproject.wordpress.com/

Research and Conservation Framework for the British Palaeolithic (2008)
http://www.english-heritage.org.uk/publications/research-and-conservation-framework-for-british-palaeolithic/palaeolithic-framework.pdf/

National Heritage Protection Plan
http://www.english-heritage.org.uk/professional/protection/national-heritage-protection-plan/all-about-NHPP/

Appendix 2:
National Ice Age Network 'Recognition sheets'

Introduction

Welcome to the Vertebrate Fossil Recognition Sheet, one of a series o factsheets produced by the National Ice Age Network, coverin Pleistocene (Ice Age) sediments, vertebrate fossils, plants, shells an stone tools.

Complete fossil skeletons are rare and only individual bones and teeth, o fragments of them, are usually found. Only in exceptional circumstances such as the permafrost zones of Alaska and Siberia or the arid caves of Chil and Australia, will the soft tissues of animals be preserved – these can giv direct insight into the appearance, diet and health of Ice Age vertebrate (animals with a backbone), as well as preserving ancient DNA. The firs stage in analysis is to identify the part of the body represented, then th species, before establishing age, sex and numbers of individuals present.

The following panels provide a guide to the identification of some of th most common vertebrate forms found in Britain. As well as the physica remains of animals, their past presence may also be indirectly inferre from preserved trackways, carnivore or rodent gnaw marks, fossilised droppings as well as depiction in Palaeolithic (Old Stone Age) art.

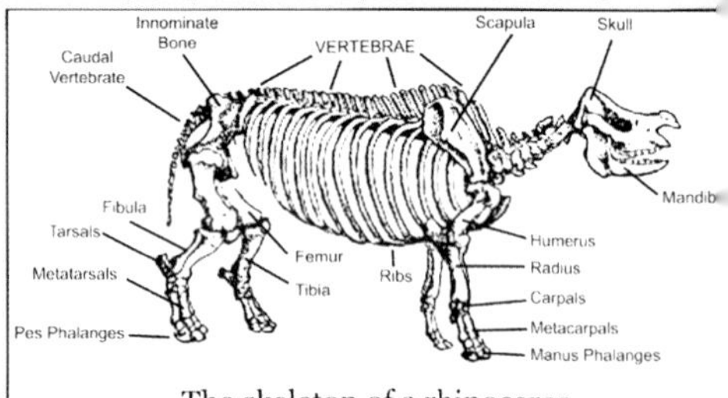

The skeleton of a rhinoceros

Small Vertebrates

Fish remains commonly include vertebrae (the backbone), fin spines, teeth and, occasionally, the fragile scales. Amphibians such as frogs and toads are characterised by their vertebrae and 'fluted', hollow long bones, and reptiles by their vertebrae, although tortoise shell fragments may also be found. Bird remains are rare, particularly on open sites, and are light and hollow; the beak and limb bones being most recognisable.

Most small mammals are readily distinguished to species level by their teeth, particularly the rodents (e.g. mice, voles, lemmings, squirrels and beavers), which possess two pairs of long, curving enamel incisors and 3-4 cheek teeth in each jaw. Vole and lemming molars resemble small radiators from the side and consist of a complex series of interlocking enamel triangles when viewed from the biting surface, whereas mice have low-crowned, rounded molars. Insectivores such as hedgehogs, shrews and moles have a long row of sharply pointed teeth.

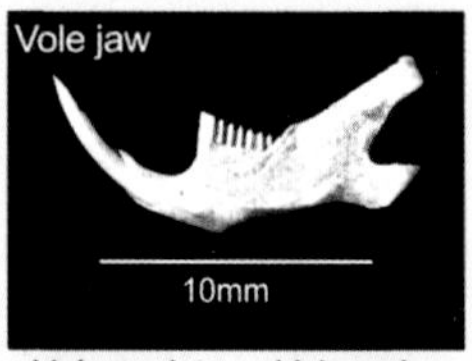

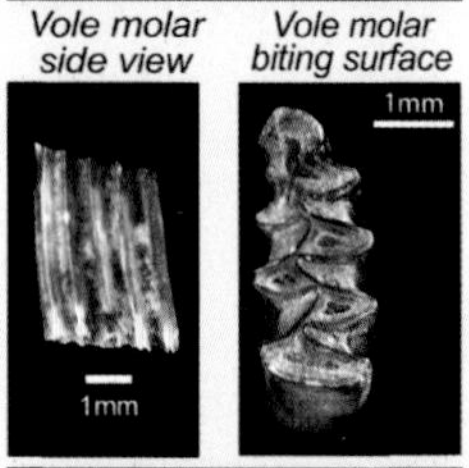

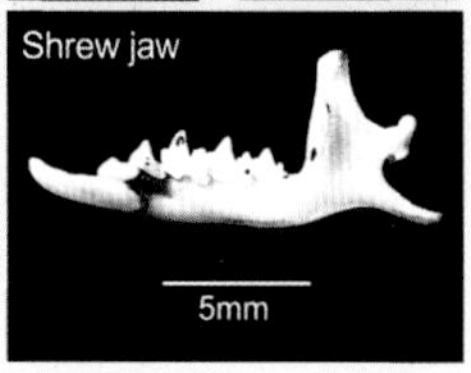

Carnivores

A range of large carnivores occurs in British Ice Age terrestrial deposits, particularly in caves, including cave and brown bears, lions, sabre-toothed cats, leopards, wolves and spotted hyaenas. Smaller predators include foxes, wild cats and mustelids (otters, weasels and their relatives).

The carnivores are readily identified by their prominent canine teeth (in sabre-toothed cats, these evolved into dagger-like points with serrated edges) and by the presence of carnassial teeth (except in bears). The carnassial teeth comprise the first lower molar and the fourth upper premolar and have a blade-like structure for shearing meat. Depending on the dietary adaptation of the carnivore in question, a range of slicing, crushing or grinding teeth will also be present. Bears differ from the general carnivore plan by having only low-crowned cheek teeth, thereby reflecting their omnivorous diet.

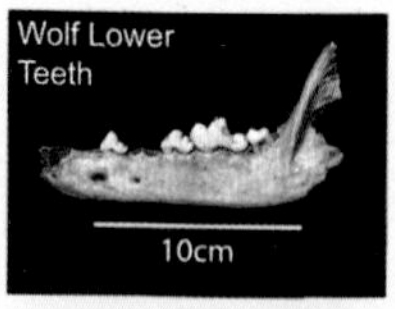

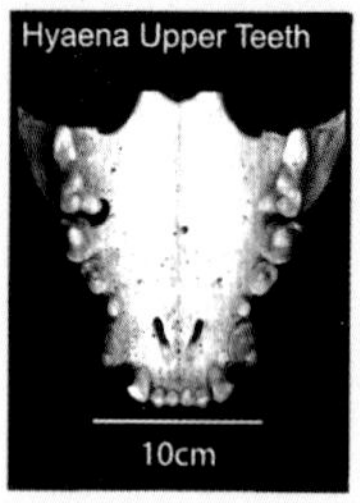

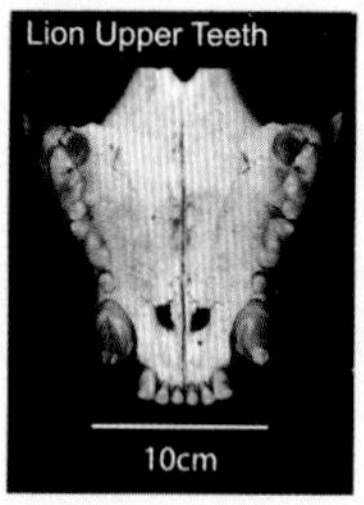

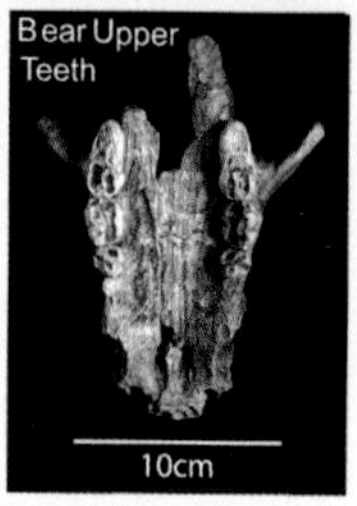

Rhinos and Horses

Rhinos and horses are members of the mammalian Order Perissodactyla, meaning that they have an odd number of toes (3 in rhino and 1 in horse). The limb bones and toes are therefore very diagnostic, in particular the cannon bone (3rd metacarpal or metatarsal - see the skeleton in introduction) of horse and the digits. Several species of rhino are known from Ice Age interglacials, adapted to either woodland or grassland habitats, whereas the woolly rhino is a characteristic component of cold stage faunas. Horses are common to both.

Rhinos have large, robust teeth with a complex pattern of ridges and thick enamel. The upper molars are square-ish, whereas the lower are 'w' shaped. The woolly rhino has an additional isolated enamel ring in the upper molars that distinguishes it from interglacial species. Horses possess tall, column-like teeth with complex enamel folds in both upper and lower sets.

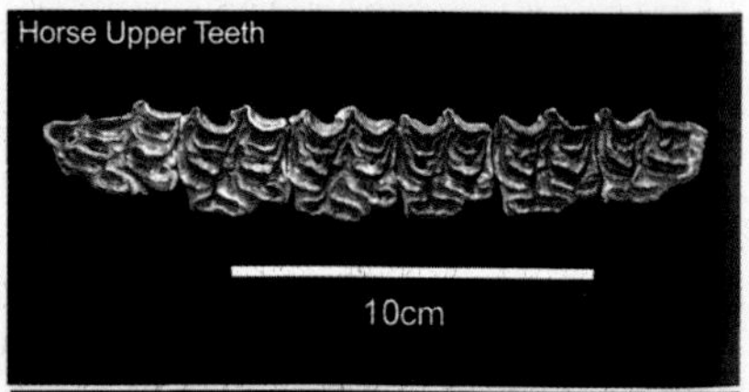

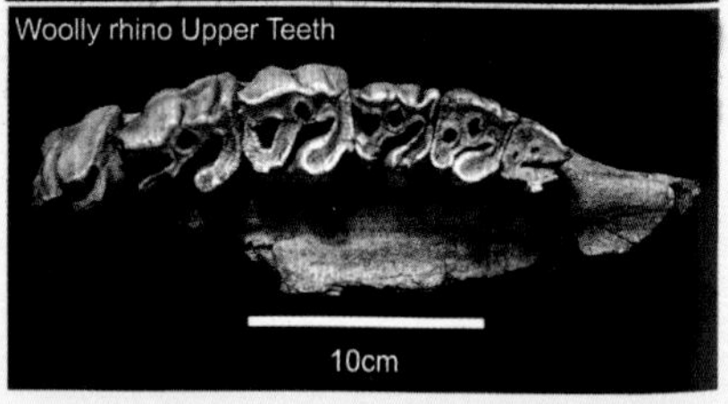

Interpretation

Many Ice Age vertebrates or their close relatives are still alive today. Studying these fossil remains can shed light on past environments (by examining anatomical adaptations and modern habitat preferences), as well as revealing how many species (particularly mammals and birds) changed their size and shape in response to Ice Age climate change. Many mammal lineages show clear patterns of evolution and extinction, in addition to local patterns of presence and absence, that may be used to construct faunal histories. As with all palaeontological studies, an understanding of the taphonomy (i.e. how the bone assemblage formed) is critical.

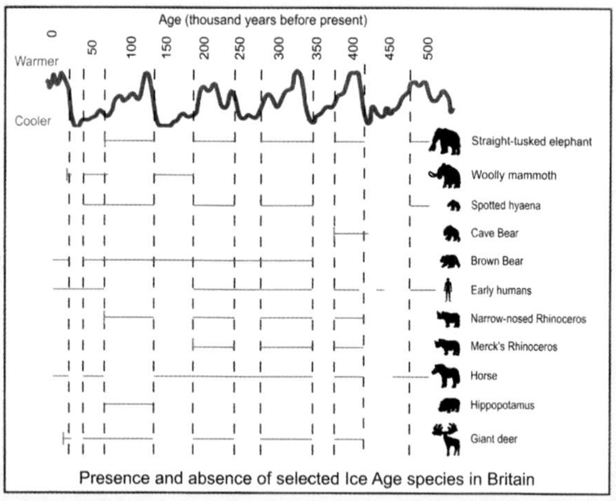

Presence and absence of selected Ice Age species in Britain

Ice Age Mammal Localities

'ossilised vertebrate remains have been found in an enormously wide range ·f environments in Britain, including limestone caves and fissures, former akeshores and beaches, shallow marine sediments, the Fenland peats and ven on the floor of the North Sea!

)ne of the most common places to find vertebrate fossils is in fluvial and stuarine deposits laid down by former rivers. Many such finds have been nade on the north Norfolk coast in the Cromer Forest-bed Formation, as vell as in sand and gravel pits in ancient river deposits in the Thames, Trent, Varwickshire / Vorcestershire Avon and other river alleys. These finds epresent both animals that would ave lived in the vater and other pecies that may ave died on the loodplain and been vashed in, or which nay have become nired at the water's edge, been hunted here or even drowned n the water.

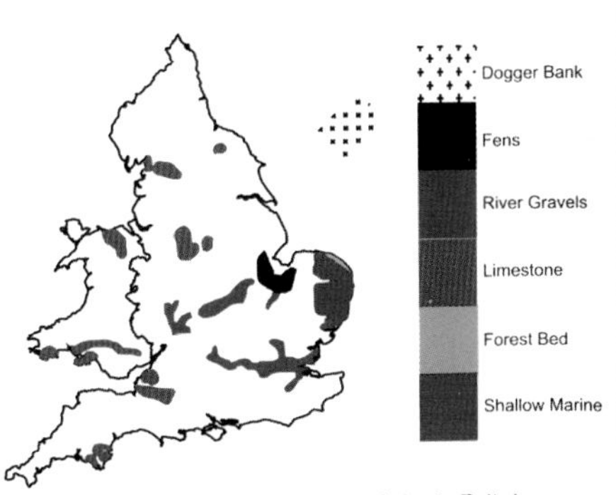

The main Ice Age mammal localities in Britain

Excavation & Sampling

Most fossils in soft sediments can be excavated by hand using a standard pointing trowel, switching to a wooden or plastic implement when near the bone surface so as not to damage it. The specimen should preferably be recorded in three dimensions, tied into a site plan. As a minimum, however, recording should include descriptions of the bed where the specimen was found, a photograph or sketch of its position in the ground or section, and an OS grid reference for the site.

Specimens can be cleaned with warm water and a soft brush prior to being allowed to dry slowly (never in direct sunlight) but more fragile remains may require consolidation *in situ* (e.g. using a plaster jacket) and lifting as a block for later excavation. Full records of conservation measures taken should be kept and specialist advice sought, as required, especially prior to the application of any glues or consolidants as these can affect on later analyses.

Bulk sediment samples (a minimum of 10 litres/10-20kg) should be taken for wet-sieving for microvertebrate remains, which cannot easily be seen in the field with the naked eye. These normally consist of column samples from the base to the top of a section, so that any change through the sequence can be identified. All sediment should be wet-sieved using a 0.5mm mesh. Once the residue is clean and dry, it can then be sorted under a low-power (10x) binocular microscope for specimens. Identification of remains is carried out using keys, drawings and reference material.

Excavating a fossil aurochs

Deer and Bovids

The deer and large bovids (aurochs and ›ison - wild cattle) are some of the most abundant Ice Age fossils. The species encountered range from reindeer and nusk ox, which were restricted to cold limate episodes, to fallow deer and aurochs in interglacials. Bison, red deer, giant deer are common to both, although he latter occupied only open habitats on account of their enormous antler span up to 3m, see cover).

Both deer and bovids have typical erbivore teeth, consisting of linked crescent-shaped molars with enamel nfoldings. In deer, the antlers are most diagnostic, in particular the surface exture, the arrangement of tines projections off the main beam) and the degree of palmation or flattening of the nd. The shape of the horn core in bovids s also characteristic – the single upward ilt in bison, the upward and forward projection in aurochs and the 'helmeted' orm of the musk ox. The limb bones are imilar in both, although those of the deer re relatively longer and more slender.

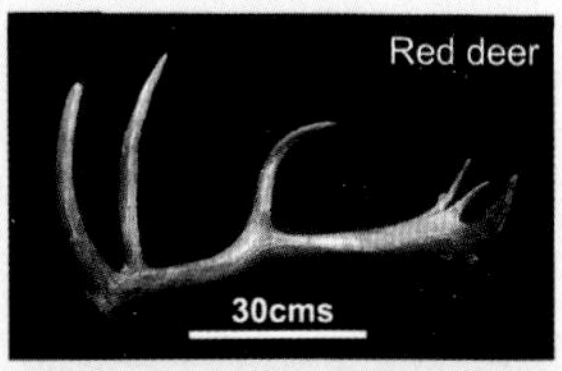

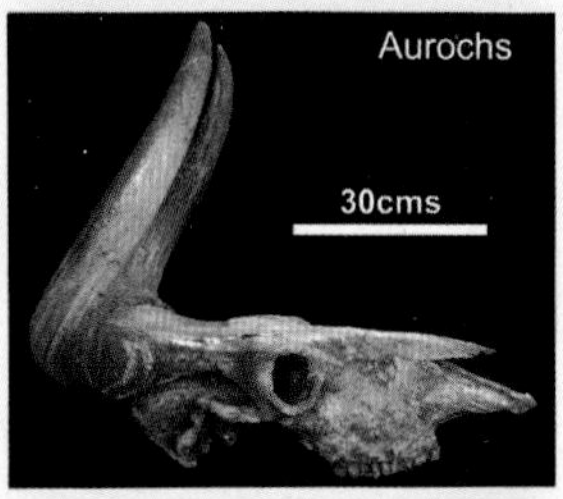

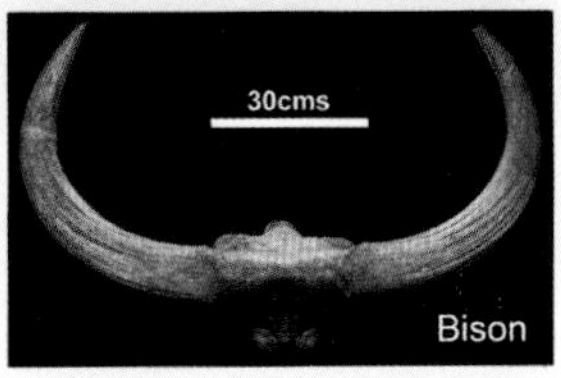

Elephants

Elephants (including mammoths) were the largest of the Ice Age megafauna (all animals weighing more than one ton) in Europe. The straight-tusked elephant (*Palaeoloxodon antiquus*) was found exclusively under temperate (warm) conditions whereas the mammoth (*Mammuthus*) lineage was present in both warm and cold episodes. The ivory tusks of these animals are immediately recognizable – long and straight in *Palaeoloxodon* and downward-spiralling in *Mammuthus*.

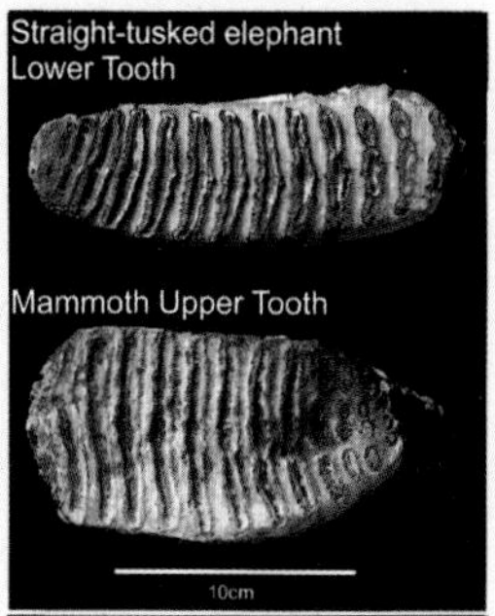

Elephants have only four teeth in their jaws at any one time and go through a succession of six sets in their lifetime. The teeth are comprised of large enamel lamellae or 'plates' stacked one behind the other; where the enamel is worn away at the surface, it creates a characteristic pattern of diamond shapes in *Palaeoloxodon* and parallel strips in *Mammuthus*. Over the last 2.6 million (Ma) years, as mammoths moved from temperate habitats, where they ate soft vegetation, into cold steppes, their molars doubled in height and in the number of enamel plates present, in order to cope with a diet of abrasive grasses.

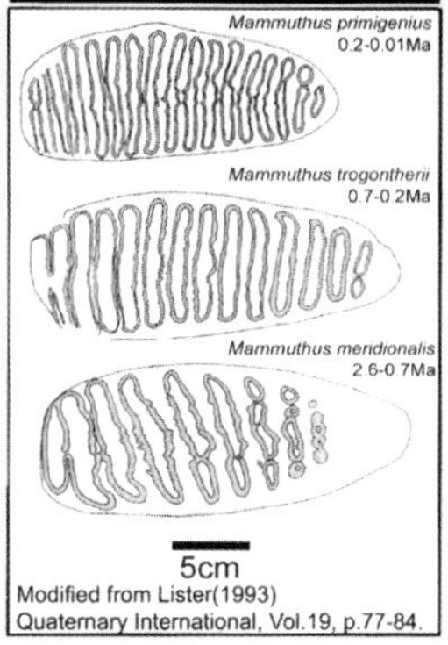

Modified from Lister(1993) Quaternary International, Vol.19, p.77-84.

Vertebrates and Interactions with Stone Age Peoples

Vertebrate remains, particularly mammals, sometimes bear evidence of modification by early humans, such as cutmarks left by stone tools. These can be distinguished from scratches and other natural marks by their position, usually arranged as parallel incisions near joints or major muscle blocks, and by their sharp, v-shaped cross section under the microscope. Other bones may have a characteristic 'spiral fracture' where the fresh bone was broken and twisted apart for marrow extraction. As well as supplying meat, fat and marrow that were important in the diet, animals also provided a source of furs, fuel (burning fat or dung) and raw materials for making tools or art objects.

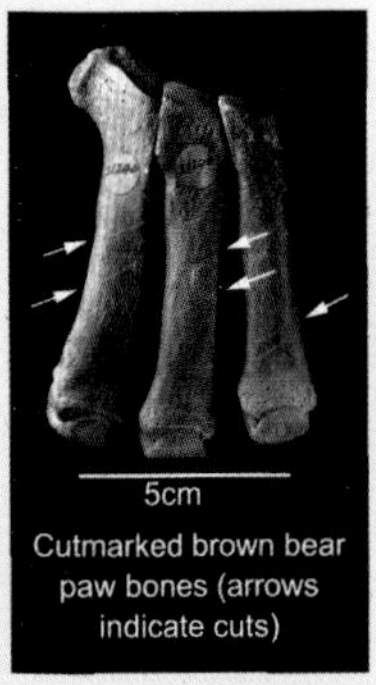

Cutmarked brown bear paw bones (arrows indicate cuts)

Carved Mammoth Figure

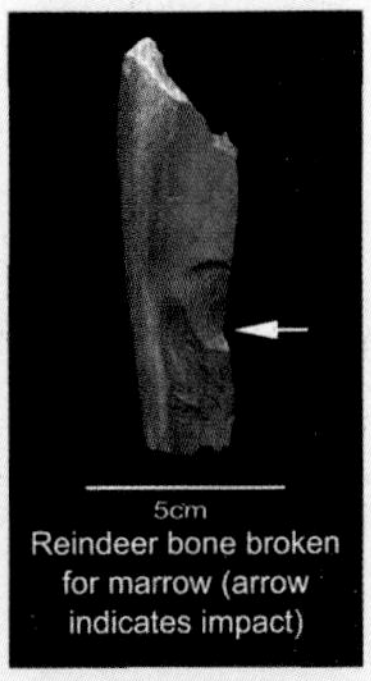

Reindeer bone broken for marrow (arrow indicates impact)

Leaflet Text & Design: Dr B Silva & Dr D Schreve. With thanks to the Natural History Museum Photographic Unit for many of the pictures used in this publication.

Contact your local 'National Ice Age Network' centre by email to info@iceage.org.uk or write to:

North & West Midlands
Birmingham Archaeology,
University of Birmingham,
Edgbaston,
Birmingham,
B15 2TT

SUPPORTED BY
ENGLISH HERITAGE

East Midlands
School of Archaeology & Ancient History,
University of Leicester
University Road,
Leicester,
LE1 7RH

NATIONAL ICE AGE NETWORK

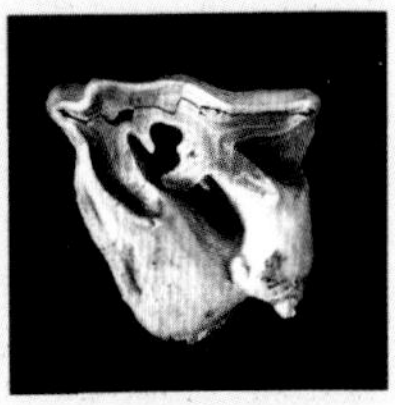

www.iceage.org.uk

South West
Centre for the Archaeology of Human Origins,
Avenue Campus,
University of Southampton,
Southampton,
SO17 1BF

SUPPORTED BY
ENGLISH NATURE

South East
Department of Geography,
Royal Holloway,
University of London,
Egham, Surrey,
TW20 0EX

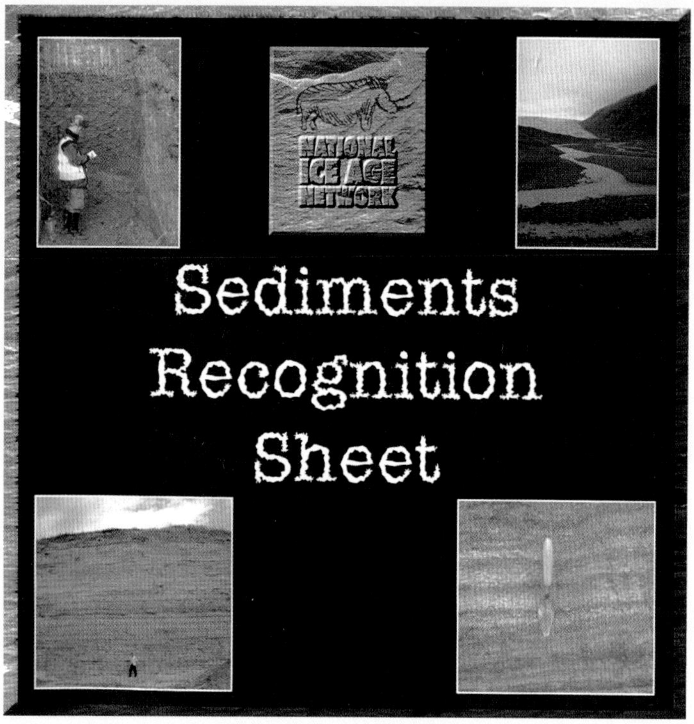

Introduction

Welcome to the Sediments Recognition Sheet, one of a series of factshee produced by the National Ice Age Network, covering Pleistocene (Ice Ag stone tools and vertebrate, molluscan, insect and plant fossils.

Sediments are fragments of rocks or minerals that are transported ar deposited by water, wind or ice. Soils are a horizon of organic and inorgan weathered materials that accumulate and develop on stable surfaces. Tl identification of certain types of sediments and soils can thus provic important information on the depositional environment and help build picture of the past landscapes in Britain that our ancestors may have facec

The deposition of sediments in layer-cake sequences (i.e. younger sediments overlying older sediments) is very useful for understanding past environmental and climatic changes. However, layer-cake sequences are rarely preserved in Britain due to erosion by successive glaciations, thus we must piece the information together from different locations.

The following panels provide a guide to the description, identification, and formation of the main sediment types to be found in Britain.

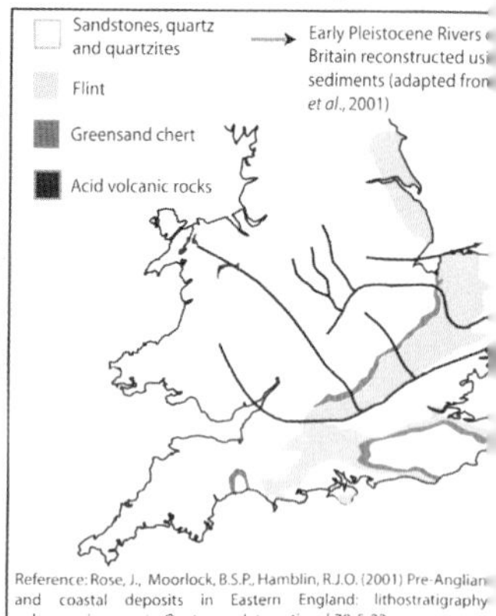

Reference: Rose, J., Moorlock, B.S.P., Hamblin, R.J.O. (2001) Pre-Anglian and coastal deposits in Eastern England: lithostratigraphy palaeoenvironments. *Quaternary International*, 79, 5-22.

How are sediments described?

Sedimentary investigations are best carried out on open section faces so that vertical and horizontal variations can be carefully recorded. Before commencing fieldwork, the section should be cleaned of slumped material, and a 'fresh' face revealed by cutting back into the exposure.

Sediments are typically described in terms of their grain sizes, sorting (to what degree are the grains of a similar size: well-sorted = grains are all of a similar size; poorly sorted = grains are of widely different sizes), roundedness of pebbles, colour (using comparative colour charts e.g. Munsell), texture (e.g. gritty or smooth?), and the nature of the contacts between different sediment types (e.g. sharp contacts indicate erosion of the underlying layer).

a)

b)

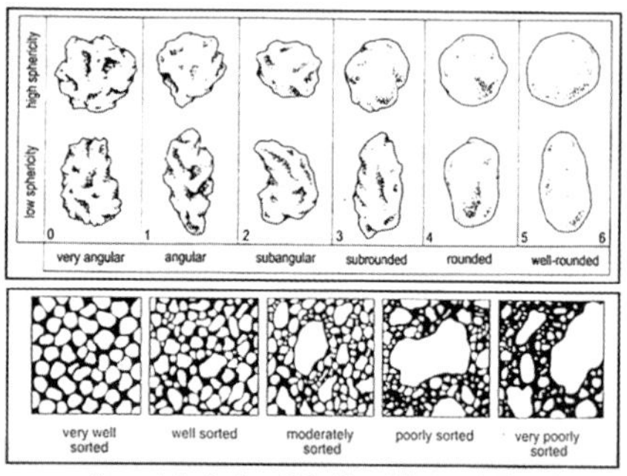

Categories of:
a) roundedness,
and b) sorting.

Roundedness and sorting images source: Jones, A.P., Tucker, M.E., Hart, J.K. (1999) The Description and Analysis of Quaternary Stratigraphic Field Sections. QRA technical guide 7, QRA, London.

Glacial Till

'Till' or 'boulder clay' is typically a deposit of clay that is full of boulders (poorly sorted), which is formed in and beneath ice sheets and glaciers. As the till is the result of the abrasion of the older rocks over which the ice has travelled, it takes its colour from them, e.g. where the ice has passed over chalk the clay may be quite pale and chalky. Boulders may be angular, sub-angular, or well-rounded, and frequently bear grooves and scratches caused by contact with other rocks while held firmly in the moving ice. Like the clay in which they are borne, the boulders belong to districts over which the ice has travelled. By the nature of the contained boulders it is often possible to trace the path along which a vanished ice-sheet moved; thus in the till of the east coast of England many rocks from north Britain can be recognized.

A modern glacier ploughing through the landscape and mixing up sediments in its path.

Typical poorly sorted glacial till with pebbles in a clay matrix.

Buried Soils

Soils form on stable ground surfaces by the action of chemical, biological and physical weathering processes over time. Relict buried soils may thus be good indicators of past warm interglacial conditions and their features may be compared to modern soils for information on past climatic conditions. Weak soils also form, however, in cold climates and are dominated by the physical action of freeze-thaw cycles.

The most important property for identifying a soil is that it has vertically differentiated layers (or 'horizons') due to the movement of weathering products up and down the soil profile. Typically, however, in buried soils the topmost 'A' horizon has been eroded and only the underlying 'B' horizon is preserved. Important diagnostic features of the 'B' horizon include colour, texture (e.g. high clay content), and enrichment (e.g. soils of semi-arid climates) or depletion (acid soils) of the carbonate content (a white mineral).

Left: Brown-red palaeosol of a former warm (interglacial) climate in England.

Right: Ice wedge cast of a soil formed under Arctic conditions and permafrost.

Cave and Lake Deposits

Caves and lakes form natural sediment traps where sediments can accumulate and provide detailed information on past climatic and environmental changes. Sediments have accumulated in caves in Britain through stream deposition, wind action and deposition associated with prehistoric man (e.g. ash/charcoal from hearths, bones, teeth and shells) and animals (e.g. bones in hyena dens). Sediments also form within the caves themselves through the deposition of roof fall and the formation of stalactites and stalagmites (or 'speleothems').

Lakes that have formed in front of glaciers ('proglacial lakes') may produce annually rhythmic layers of fine sand/silt and clay (termed 'varves'). The coarser sand and silt are deposited first leaving the clay in suspension. During winter the lake freezes over and the suspended clay particles gradually settle forming a layer of clay.

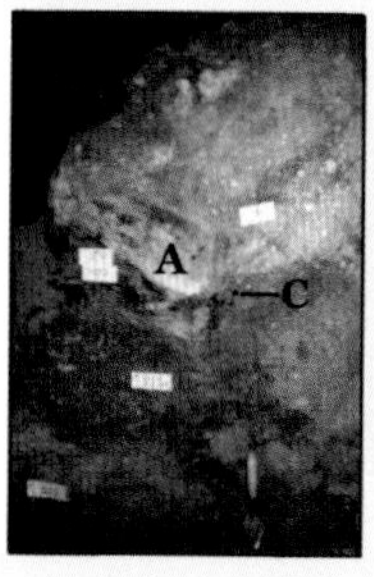

Left: Grey ash (A) and black charcoal (C) in cave sediments.

Right: Ice Age lake clays from England.

Identifying different sediment types

Sediments can be classified in terms of their size, ranging from fine sediments such as clay (0.001-0.004 mm) and silt (0.004-0.063 mm) to boulders (>256 mm) which as a rough rule of thumb is 'bigger than your head'!. The size of sediments indicates the energy and power of their depositional environment. For example, layers of clay are deposited in quiet water lakes; silt is blown by wind; silt, sand, gravels (or 'pebbles') and cobbles are transported by rivers; large boulders are transported by glaciers.

In soils, clays often become concentrated down-profile due to weathering and being washed downwards in Britain's moist climate.

How are different pebble types identified?

As sediments are fragments of rock or minerals, it is possible to identify the parent rock or mineral type. From geological mapping we know where certain rock types and minerals occur in Europe and so we can therefore determine from where and in what direction the sediment originally came from. This has been particularly important for working out the flow paths of major ancient rivers and where the ice sheets in Britain came from (e.g. North Britain or Scandinavia?).

Some of the main rock/mineral types found in British river gravels, and their origin (scale: one grid square width = 1 cm):

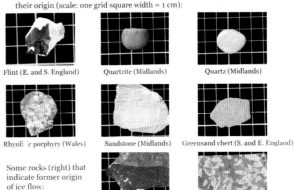

Flint (E. and S. England)

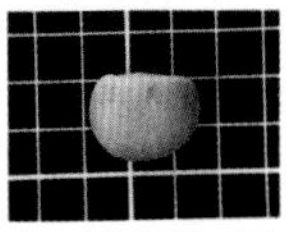

Quartzite (Midlands)

Quartz (Midlands)

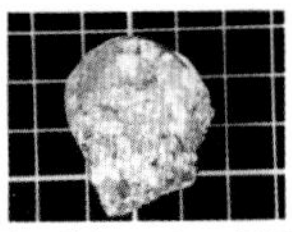

Rhyoli`c porphyry (Wales)

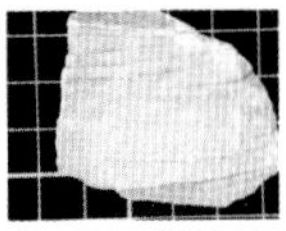

Sandstone (Midlands)

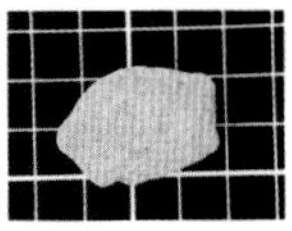

Greensand chert (S. and E. England)

Some rocks (right) that indicate former origin of ice flow:

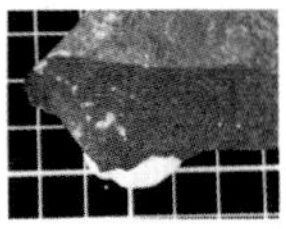

Dolerite (N. England/Scotland)

Rhomb porphyry (Norway)

Marine Sediments

The sea level in Britain has varied dramatically in response to climate change. The growth of ice sheets in northern Europe locked up much of the ocean water and so sea levels fell and Britain became a peninsula of Europe. As the ice sheets melted, sea levels rose again. Marine deposits in Britain are typically found in coastal areas and may be testament to higher sea levels in the past. Beach deposits can be recognised by very well-sorted and well-rounded pebbles. Beach pebbles are typically covered in "chatter-marks" due to agitation caused by tidal action. Marine fossil shells preserved in sands are also good indicators of past marine conditions.

Raised beach sediments at Brighton, south England.

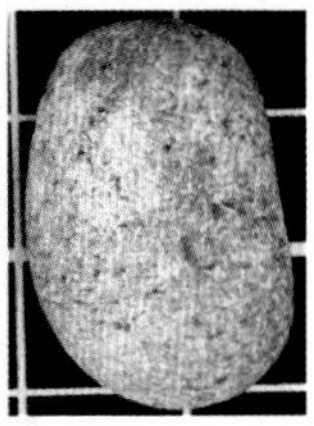

A "chatter-marked" pebble.

River Sediments

Britain is currently enjoying a warm interglacial period, and our rivers are mainly meandering, cutting sinuous valleys with single channels. During cold glacial periods, however, Britain was dominated by large braided rivers that carried vast quantities of sediment fed by the meltwaters from giant ice sheets. Braided rivers were large with numerous shifting channels and bars of sand and gravel. River deposits are typically well to moderately sorted and have rounded to sub-rounded gravels.

Evidence for past warm interglacial rivers and streams may come from dark, organic-rich silts and sands. These are very important for preserving shells, microfossils (e.g. pollen), vertebrate fossil remains and even evidence for early humans (e.g. stone tools and bones).

Top left: Modern braided river in Iceland with shifting bars of sand and gravel.

Top right: Ice Age braided river sediments in England.

Bottom left: Modern meandering river in England.

Bottom right: Past interglacial organic river channel in England.

Wind-Blown Sediments

Silt is mainly produced by the grinding action of glaciers. The silt is transported in large volumes by glacial rivers and may be subsequently picked up by the wind and deposited elsewhere. Particles of silt are preferentially picked up and blown by wind and large deposits (termed 'loess') accumulated during cold periods in Europe. Loess is typically a pale yellow colour and small patches can be found in Britain. Analysis of wind-blown deposits at sites from Kent to south Devon has revealed a westward decrease in particle size – indicating that the loess had been transported by easterly winds from river plains in the North Sea basin that were exposed as much of the sea water was tied up in ice sheets (Catt, 1977).

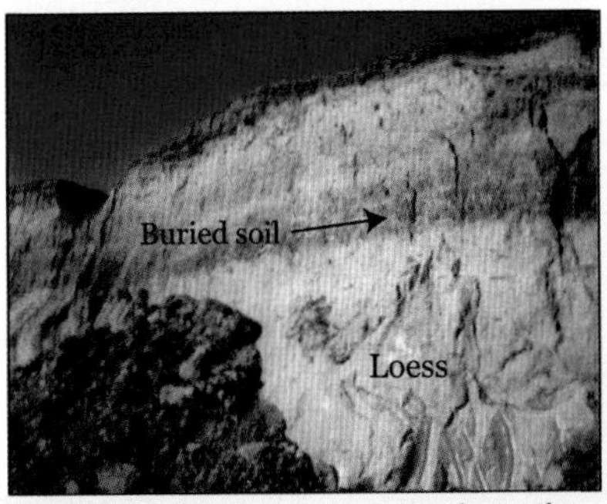

A 5 m-thick cliff section of loess with interbedded buried soils.

eference: Catt, J.A. (1977) Loess and coversands. In: Shotton, F.M. (ed.) British Quaternary tudies - Recent Advances. Oxford University Press, Oxford, 22-229.

Cave and Lake Deposits

Caves and lakes form natural sediment traps where sediments can accumulate and provide detailed information on past climatic and environmental changes. Sediments have accumulated in caves in Britain through stream deposition, wind action and deposition associated with prehistoric man (e.g. ash/charcoal from hearths, bones, teeth and shells) and animals (e.g. bones in hyena dens). Sediments also form within the caves themselves through the deposition of roof fall and the formation of stalactites and stalagmites (or 'speleothems').

Lakes that have formed in front of glaciers ('proglacial lakes') may produce annually rhythmic layers of fine sand/silt and clay (termed 'varves'). The coarser sand and silt are deposited first leaving the clay in suspension. During winter the lake freezes over and the suspended clay particles gradually settle forming a layer of clay.

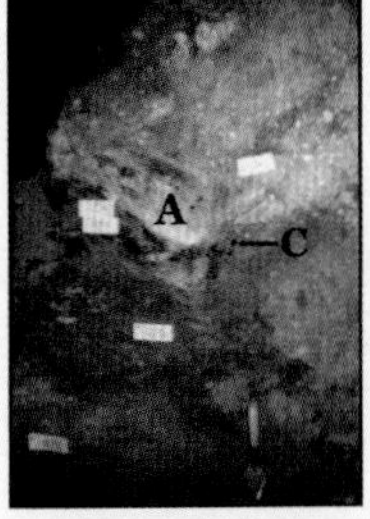

Left: Grey ash (A) and black charcoal (C) in cave sediments.

Right: Ice Age lake clays from England.

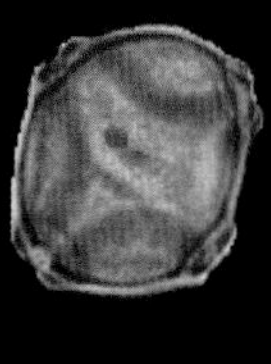

Mollusc, Insect & Plant Fossils Recognition Sheet

Introduction

Welcome to the Mollusc, Insect and Plant Fossils Recognition Sheet, one c series of factsheets produced by the National Ice Age Network, cover Pleistocene (Ice Age) sediments, vertebrate fossils and stone tools. This sh provides information on fossil molluscs (snails), insects and plants, and h these are used to reconstruct Ice Age environments.

Land and freshwater molluscs (a term that includes snails, mussels and slugs) are probably the most common fossils in Ice Age deposits. The mollusc fauna of Britain today consists of about 220 species, although not all of these have been found as fossils. Most Ice Age snails have no English name and are identified by their Linnean (Latin) names only.

Modern distributions of two sn species which lived in Ice Age Brita

Molluscs are known from all Ice Age sediments dating back 2.5 million years. During this time few new species have evolved and very few have become extinct. Thus, Ice Age species can be used to reconstruct past environments as they still have living descendants whose habitats are well known.

The chemical composition of shells can also be analysed to estimate ancient water temperatures (from isotopes of oxygen in the shells) and furthermore, the shells can be dated by measuring their fossil protein (amino acid) or radiocarbon content.

Finding Ice Age Molluscs

Molluscs are usually found in sand or mud rather than in gravel or clays. Silted-up river channels exposed by gravel quarrying are often the most productive, containing an abundance of freshwater shells, but also land shells washed into the river by floods. Occasional sandy deposits in large rivers like the Thames may also be very rich in shells, including the largest bivalves. Shells are often noticed because they have been bleached white over time although the original shell colours may also sometimes be preserved.

Warm interglacial period deposits usually contain a wide variety of species (70 or 80), whereas those from cold conditions have fewer species (10 or so), but with many individuals. Because many shells are small (usually under 5 mm) only the largest species are visible in deposits, although sediment faces wetted by rain may show shells that have been washed clean. Shells can also be found in more unusual settings, including hollows in fossil animal bones and skulls that they have colonised after the death and decomposition of the host animal.

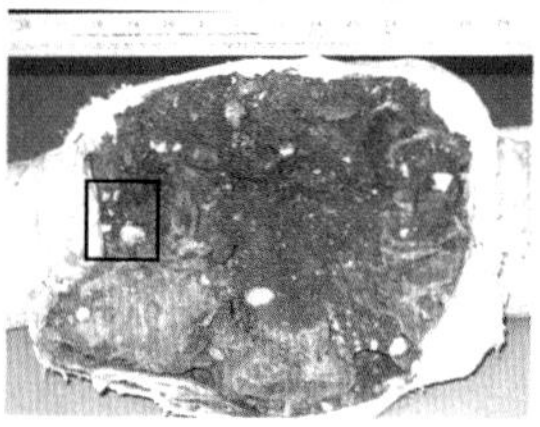

Corbicula shells within an aurochs' (wild cattle) skull

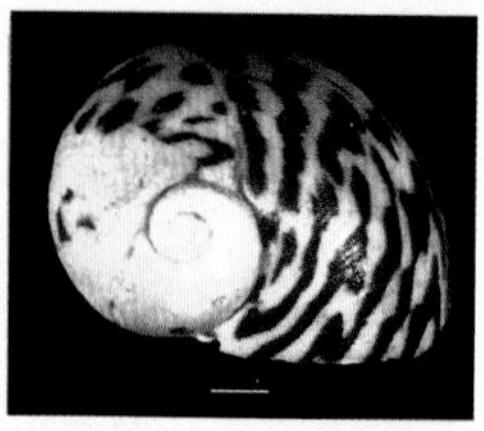

A 500,000 year old *Theodoxus danubialis* shell excavated from Swanscombe in Kent

Molluscs Types

Bivalves

Bivalves (mussels and clams) consist of two 'valves' (shell halves) joined by a hinge that is held together by an elastic ligament. The animal can open the two valves of the shell to feed, breathe and reproduce but can also hold the shell closed as a defence against predators or fast moving water.

Bivalves live only in water where they either burrow into the bottom sediments or attach themselves to stones or other hard parts of river beds. Some species, however, are only found in freshwater (e.g. *Potamida littoralis* and *Unio crassus*, both freshwater mussels), whilst others are more tolerant of saline conditions (e.g. *Corbicula fluminalis*, which can live in estuarine environments). The presence or absence of species in the fossil assemblage can also have a climatic significance, with both *Corbicula fluminalis* and *Pisidium clessini* being associated exclusively with warm, interglacial conditions.

Unio crassus

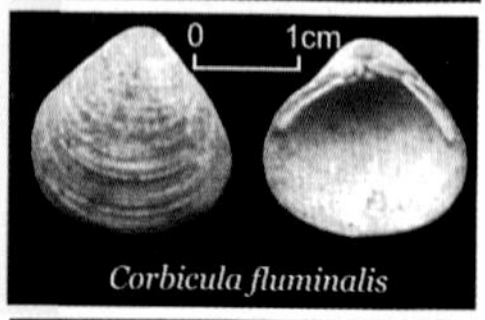

Corbicula fluminalis

Pisidium clessini

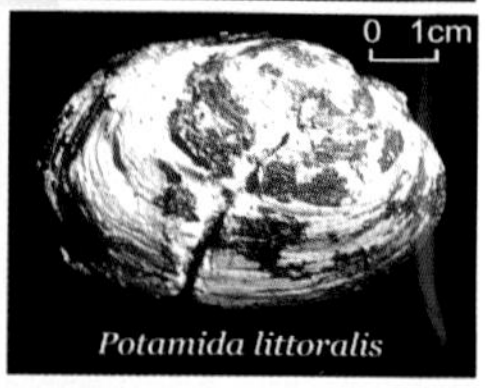

Potamida littoralis

Plant Macrofossils

Plant macrofossils are defined as fragments of plant material which are visible to the naked eye. The fragments can represent any part of a plant, most often seeds, leaves, stems and roots, but sometimes larger fragments such as tree trunks, are found. These tend to be best preserved in organic deposits such as peat horizons or silt and fine sand river channel infills.

The particular advantage of plant macrofossils over pollen (see next panel) is that they are frequently recognisable to species level so precise information can be obtained about past environments. Also, as they are relatively large and tend to only travel short distances, the presence of plant macrofossils generally provides good evidence that a specific plant once grew at, or close to, the fossil deposit. They are therefore reliable indicators of how local environmental conditions have changed over time.

Plant fossils are also sometimes found in association with animal remains giving us important insights into their diets. For example, plant remains embedded in woolly rhino teeth from the Whitemoor Haye Quarry, Staffordshire, indicate a diet of grasses and herbs.

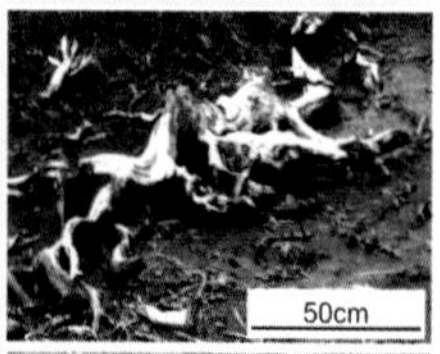

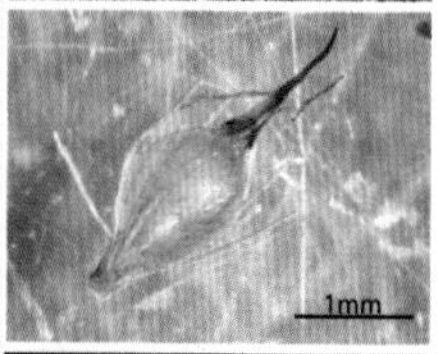

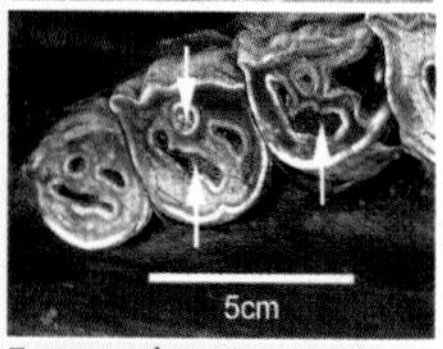

From top to bottom:
Fossil Pine tree stumps buried in peat in Scotland; A sedge seed magnified 40x; Plant fragments embedded in the teeth of the Whitemoor Haye woolly rhino.

Microscopic Fossil Remains

Pollen Grains

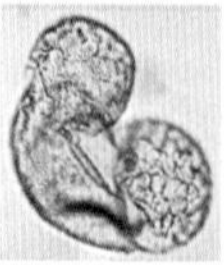

Pine pollen grain x1000

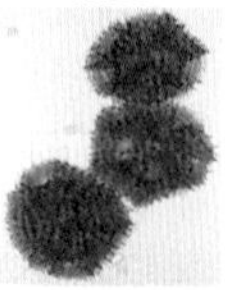

Dandelion pollen grains x1000

Despite not being visible to the naked eye, many Ice Age sediments preserve pollen grains, millions of which are produced and dispersed by the flowers of trees and plants. All pollen grains are microscopic, with few exceeding 1/10th of a millimeter in size, and are identified and counted under high-powered microscopes. Unlike plant macrofossils, they can usually only be identified to family level (e.g. *Betula* = birch family). However, due to their high preservation in many sediments and wide dispersal rates, pollen grains can provide valuable insights into regional vegetation cover and, indirectly, into climatic conditions.

Chironomids

Chironomideae are a family of midges (flies); the adults look similar to mosquitoes but do not suck blood. Chironomids are extremely sensitive to changes in environmental conditions, particularly temperature. Juvenile chironomids hatch from eggs into aquatic larvae before becoming winged adults. The larval outer 'casing' preserve well in sediments and are easily identifiable. Statistical techniques can then be used, comparing fossil and modern communities, to produce estimates of past temperatures. This procedure has been most successful in reconstructing conditions from the last glacial period onwards.

Chironomid head capsule x 1000

Mollusc Habitats

Different species of molluscs occupy a range of habitats including water bodies (from the largest rivers to small ponds), grasslands, scrub and woodlands. Calcium carbonate-rich limestone bedrock and a relatively humid climate provide favourable conditions for land species, whilst flowing, well-oxygenated water with a good lime content is best for freshwater species.

Molluscs are also adapted to more specific niches. Thus the arctic/alpine species *Columella columella* only lives in unshaded places in tundra or mountains whilst *Clausilia pumila* is solely found in mature woodlands in central Europe. Although neither of these species lives in Britain today, both have been found here as Ice Age fossils. These 'specialisations' allow researchers to use fossil 'assemblages' (groups of individual fossils) to produce detailed reconstructions of Ice Age environments in the past.

At Marsworth in Buckinghamshire, analysis of the fossil mollusc assemblages based on modern ecologies illustrates the drying out of the site, from freshwater pond to dry land 200,000 years ago.

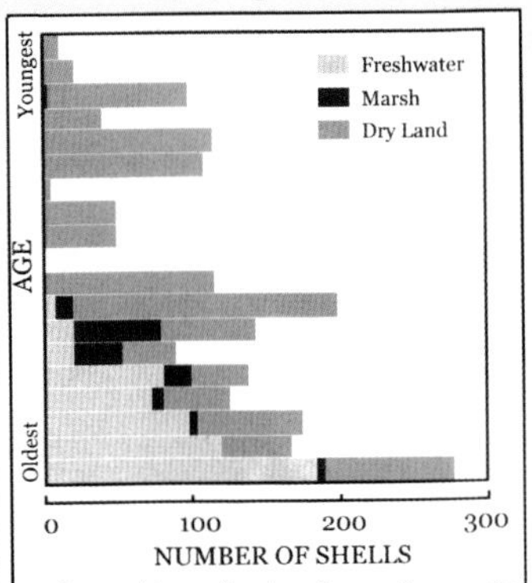

Mollusc evidence for changing environments 200,000 years ago in Buckinghamshire

Sampling for Molluscs

As not all mollusc shells are obvious to the naked eye, bulk samples (a minimum of 10 litres/10-20kg) should be taken from the sediments of interest. These are normally taken as column samples from the base to the top of a section, in order to identify any changes through the sequence.

Due to the generally small size of the shells, their separation from the sediment is a job for experts, involving washing sediment samples through fine sieves down to a mesh size of 0.5 mm, drying the residues and then extracting the shells.

This method may sometimes produce thousands of shells from only a few grams of sediment, although such occurrences are usually restricted to lake marls (calcium carbonate-rich clays) of limestone areas, where preservation is exceptionally good.

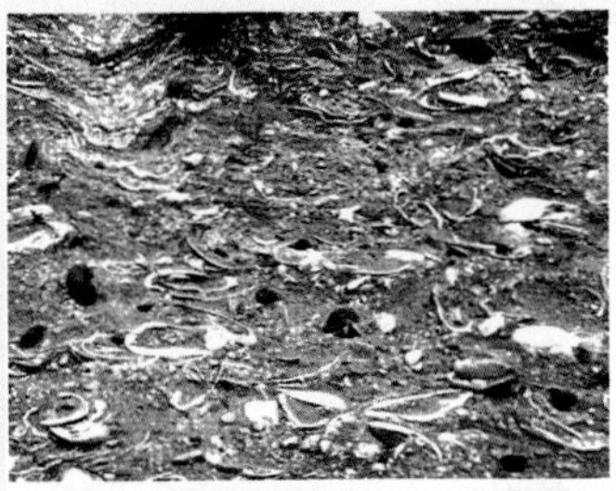

Top: Shells exposed in the sands of the Thames
Bottom: The shells after sieving

Mollusc Types
Gastropods

Gastropods (snails) have coiled or cone-shaped shells and include both terrestrial and aquatic species. They move by contractions along a muscular "foot" on the underside of the animal and can retract their soft parts into the shell to avoid danger or drought.

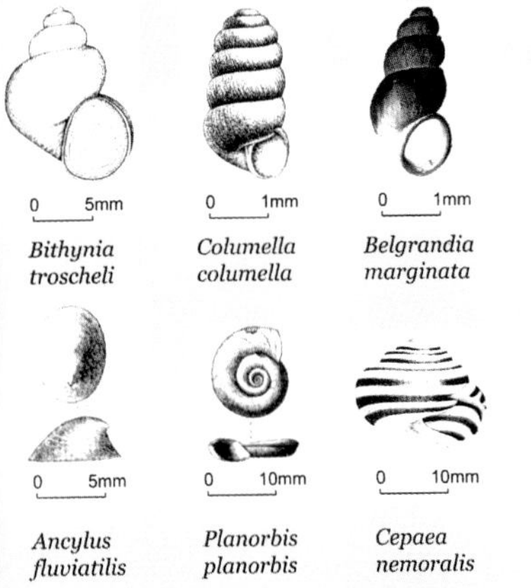

Some examples of common gastropod species (adapted from: Kerney, M.P. and Cameron, R.A.D, 1979, 'A field guide to the land snails of Britain and North-West Europe' Collins.)

The figure on the left shows a few examples of common land and freshwater gastropods found in Britain.

Bithynia troscheli (here pictured on the far left) was one of the fossil molluscs found at Pakefield in Suffolk. Dating the shells by measuring the fossil protein (amino acid) content helped to establish the age of the Pakefield archaeological site as being 700,000 years old, thereby pushing back the date of the earliest human colonisation of Britain by 200,000 years.

Plant and Insect Fossils

Plant and insect fossil remains can provide valuable insights into former vegetation cover (whether a landscape was covered by forest or grassland for example) and past climates (understanding the modern preferences of the species found can be used to reconstruct past landscapes as well as local and regional climatic conditions).

Plant fossil remains are also sometimes found in association with animal remains and can provide interesting insights into animal diet. Fossil insects, interpreted with reference to modern ecologies, can also indirectly indicate the presence of other animals or vegetation, e.g. some beetle species are solely dependent on particular plants or trees. Plant and insect fossils found in archaeological sites can provide information about which plants ancient peoples would have utilised in the past, not only as food but also as a fuel source (e.g. charcoal), and to make tools (e.g. twine or hunting implements).

To analyse sediments for plant and insect fossils, bulk samples (a minimum of 10 litres/10-20kg) should be taken normally as column samples from the base to the top of a section, to identify any changes through the sequence. To isolate the plant and insect macro fossils (those visible with the naked eye), the sediment should be wet-sieved using a fine (200μm) mesh. Once the residue is clean and dry, it can then be sorted under a low-power (10x) binocular microscope for specimens. To analyse microscopic fossils (e.g. pollen and chironomids), small sub samples are taken from the column (1cm³), and the fossils concentrated using various chemical treatments. Both plant and insect fossils are then identified using keys, drawings and reference material.

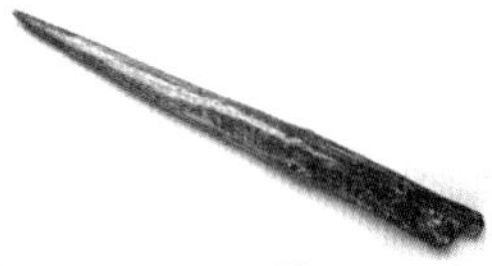

A 400,000 year old spear point made from Yew

Beetles

Twenty five per cent of all known animal species are beetles. Different beetle species occupy almost all habitats from freshwater bodies to scrubland and woods. Many beetle species are specialists adapted to particular environments and/or narrow temperature ranges. For example, *Stephanocleonus eruditus* is a weevil that is only found near snowfields in the alpine tundra of Siberia. Other beetle species have specific dietary needs, for example dung beetles require the presence of large herbivores locally to provide their food source.

The beetle fauna of Britain today consists of more than 3800 species. They are best preserved in fine grained sediments such as silts and sands and organic deposits within gravel bodies. However, beetles do not tend to survive intact and generally what remains will be the wing cases and thorax (the 'shell' between neck and abdomen). As beetles have not evolved or 'changed' over the last 2 million years, the distinctive species features are the same for fossil beetles as for modern beetles living today. This means that fossils can be directly interpreted with reference to the diet and habitat of modern beetle specimens. Fossil beetle assemblages, once subjected to statistical analysis, are invaluable in providing very detailed climatic reconstructions of the Ice Age.

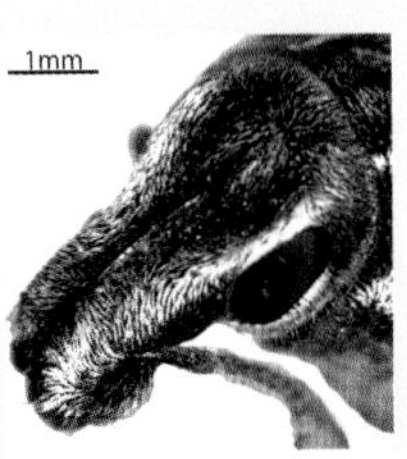

Stephanocleonus eruditus head capsule

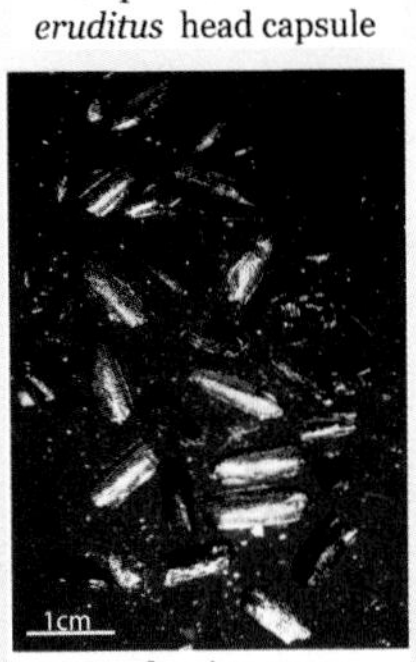

Beetle wing cases

Finding Ice Age Molluscs

Molluscs are usually found in sand or mud rather than in gravel or clays. Silted-up river channels exposed by gravel quarrying are often the most productive, containing an abundance of freshwater shells, but also land shells washed into the river by floods. Occasional sandy deposits in large rivers like the Thames may also be very rich in shells, including the largest bivalves. Shells are often noticed because they have been bleached white over time although the original shell colours may also sometimes be preserved.

Warm interglacial period deposits usually contain a wide variety of species (70 or 80), whereas those from cold conditions have fewer species (10 or so), but with many individuals. Because many shells are small (usually under 5 mm) only the largest species are visible in deposits, although sediment faces wetted by rain may show shells that have been washed clean. Shells can also be found in more unusual settings, including hollows in fossil animal bones and skulls that they have colonised after the death and decomposition of the host animal.

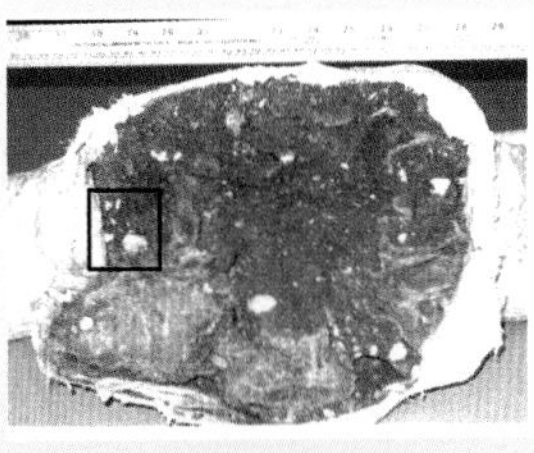

Corbicula shells within an aurochs' (wild cattle) skull

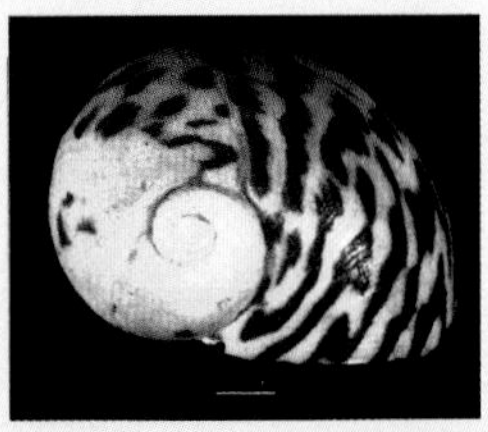

A 500,000 year old *Theodoxus danubialis* shell excavated from Swanscombe in Kent

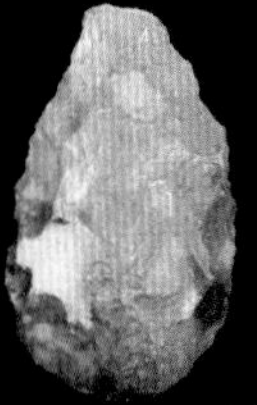

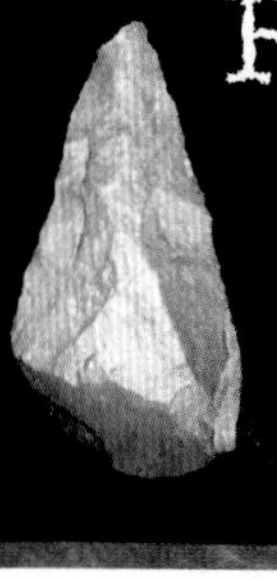

Palaeolithic Artefact Recognition Sheet

INTRODUCTION

Welcome to the Palaeolithic Artefact Recognition Sheet, one of a series of introductory facts produced by the National Ice Age Network, which will include Pleistocene (Ice Age) sedim fossil animals, plants and shells and lithic artefacts (stone tools).

Palaeolithic literally means 'Old Stone Age', and in Britain the oldest manufactured artefac over half a million years old. Due to this great age only very durable types of artefact - such as tools - have survived for study by the archaeologists of today. This makes stone tools a uniqu of evidence for reconstructing the technologies, habits and behaviours of the earliest h inhabitants of our country. The timeline shows when different species of human (*hominins*) ar in Britain and an overview of their technologies.

This sheet will introduce you to the main types of Lower and Middle Palaeolithic artefact, from simple *flakes* and the *cores* they come from to *handaxes* and *Levallois* techniques.

All the artefacts described in this sheet were produced by *knapping* - *knapping* is the process of removing *flakes* from blocks of stone and the shaping of suitable materials into a desired end product.

The *knapping* techniques focused on here are *direct percussion* (hitting) techniques. *Direct percussion* may be done using a *hard hammer* made of stone, or a *soft hammer* usually made of antler. Both *hammer* types can be used to detach and shape *flakes* and *cores* and to *retouch flakes* into other tools.

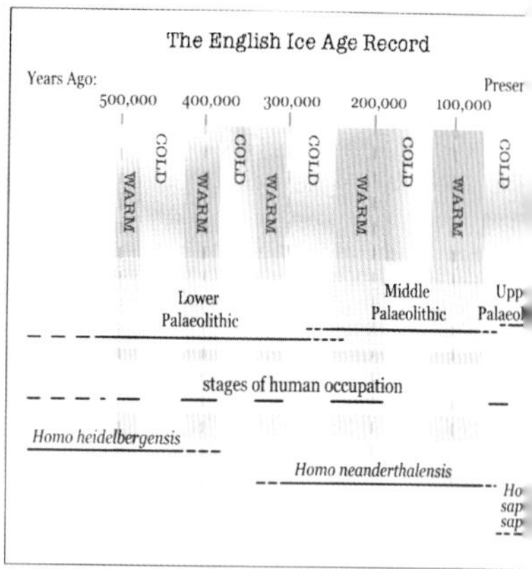

SIMPLE CORES

Cores are the pieces of lithic raw material from which *flakes* are detached. Just like *flakes*, *cores* have a series of diagnostic features known as *negative flake scars* that help us distinguish humanly-made artefacts from naturally fractured stones.

Negative Flake Scar(s): when *flakes* are detached from the *core* they leave a hollowed out depression of their shape in the *core*. This *negative flake scar* shows a marked hollow corresponding to the 'positive' *bulb of percussion* present on the detached *flake*, and *ripples* indicating the direction from which the *flake* was detached from the *core*.

Each *flake* removed creates a *negative flake scar* on the *core* and as *knapping* of the *core* continues these *negative scars* may overlap and overprint one another - the most complete *negative flake scars* belong to the *flakes* that were removed last.

Sample Core

Flake 1 was removed first. The *core* was then rotated 90° and the *scar* of the first *flake* used as a *platform* for *flake* removals 2 and 3. The *core* was then re-rotated 90° and *flakes* 4 and 5 removed from the *core*. Further *flake* removals from the same location as 4 and 5 would have been possible.

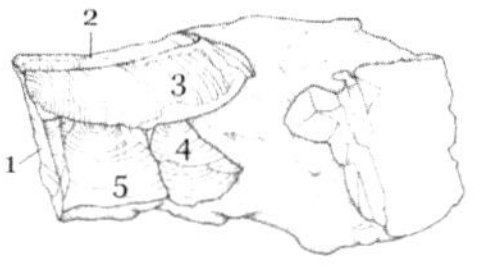

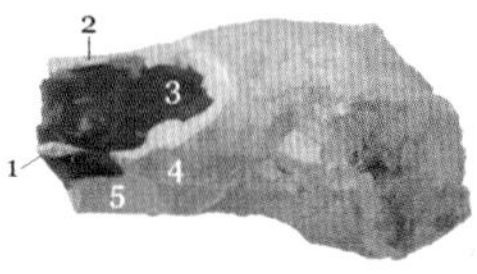

Negative Flake Scars can also tell us about the way in which the *core* was *knapped*.

Single Removal

A single *flake* is detached from the *core* - perhaps to test the quality of the raw material

Parallel Flaking

2 or more *flakes* are detached from the *striking platform*

Simple Alternate Flaking

1 or more *parallel flakes* are removed, then the *core* is rotated through 90° and the *scars* of these removals used are as the *striking platform* for further *flakes*

Classic Alternate Flaking

A single *flake* is removed, then the *core* is rotated 90°, and the *scar* used as the *striking platform* for detaching the second *flake*. More flakes may be removed, rotating the core 90° before each removal

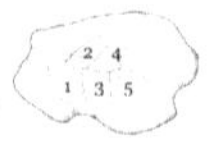

after Ashton *et al.* 1998

LEVALLOIS

Levallois technique is the name of a specific type of *prepared core technology*, usually asso with the Middle Palaeolithic and the Neanderthals. As the name implies, the *core* is first pre so that a *flake* of predetermined size and shape can be removed.

Levallois schematic

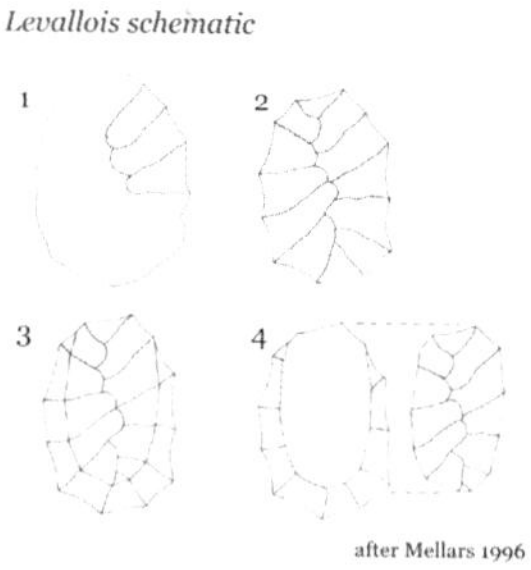

after Mellars 1996

Levallois techniques create a conical *core* with a convex upper surface, which controls the shape of the final removal, the *Levallois flake*. The shape of this *'tortoise core'* allows several *Levallois flakes* to be removed with little further modification of the *core*.

Levallois flakes have a distinctive *dorsal scar pattern*, testifying to the earlier *core* preparation.

Preparation of a Le 'tortoise core'.

Flint Levallois core.

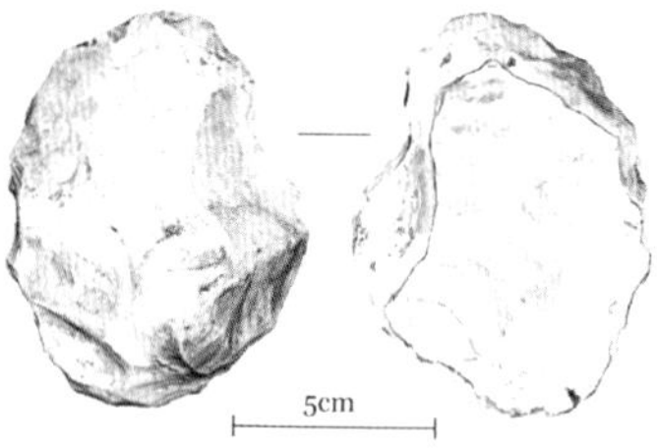

Location of *Levallois flake* removal marked in red.

Levallois flakes.

Levallois photographs © Birmingham Museums & Art Gallery

WHAT IS A HANDAXE?

The most commonly recognised type of Palaeolithic tool recovered in this country is the *handaxe*. The *handaxe* is the diagnostic tool type of the Lower Palaeolithic Acheulean technology. The oldest *handaxes* known from this country are over half a million years old.

HOW WERE THEY MADE?

Handaxes are also known as *bifaces*, and this alternative name alludes to how they were made - the *handaxe/biface* is a tool that has been extensively shaped and flaked on both faces. These tools dominate the Palaeolithic record because they are large (larger than most *flakes*), durable and easily recognisable as humanly-made artefacts.

Handaxes can be made in 2 different ways. Firstly a nodule may be reduced by *hard hammer flaking* to create a *roughout* - an approximation of the shape of the finished *handaxe* - then finally shaped using a *soft hammer*. Alternatively if you have access to large *nodules* of raw material then very *large flakes* known as *blanks* can be produced; these are then flaked further to produce the handaxe.

Core reduction method of handaxe production:

after Gamble 1999

WHAT WERE THEY MADE FROM?

Handaxes have been recovered in this country in a range of raw materials including *andesitic tuff, quartz, quartzite, chert* and *flint*. The Raw Material Map should give you an idea of the most dominant raw material in your local area. Remember though that 'exotic' raw materials may also have been present and could have been used to make stone tools.

WHAT WERE THEY USED FOR?

Handaxes are considered to be multipurpose tools - sometimes referred to as the Palaeolithic 'Swiss Army Knife'. Many experiments have shown *handaxes* to be highly efficient butchery tools. They are also easily resharpened which both extends the useful life of the *handaxe* and can also provide a source of sharp *flakes* if required.

HANDAXE SHAPES & SIZES

There is no standard size for a *handaxe*. Occasionally very large examples (over 30cm long) smaller specimens (approx. 5cm long) are found, though these artefacts are more typically siz fit comfortably in the hand (as the name implies).

Handaxes are found in a wide range of shapes and with varying degrees of 'refinement'. It was thought that *handaxe* forms evolved through time and that crude stone-struck examples were than more finely flaked forms. Sites such as Boxgrove in West Sussex with 'finely' made *handa* an early date, finally disproved this theory. It is now recognised that 'refinement' is not a r indicator of the age of a *handaxe*. Similarly, whilst *handaxe* shapes were once considere represent different 'cultural' groups, variations are now thought to relate to more 'practical' rea such as raw material size or tool function. Some of the common *handaxe* shapes are shown b (after Wymer 1968).

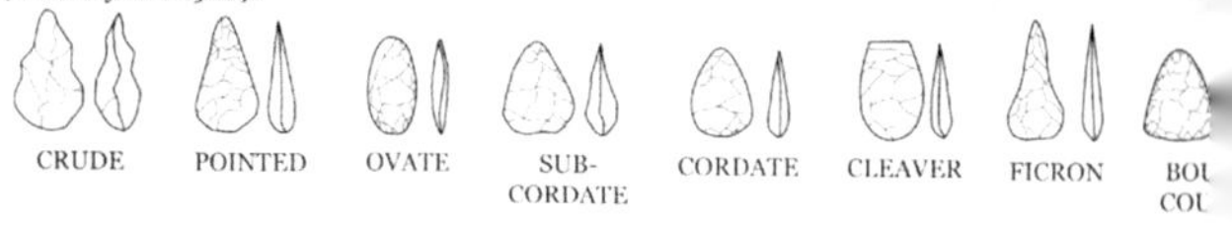

A lightly stained Flint Handaxe

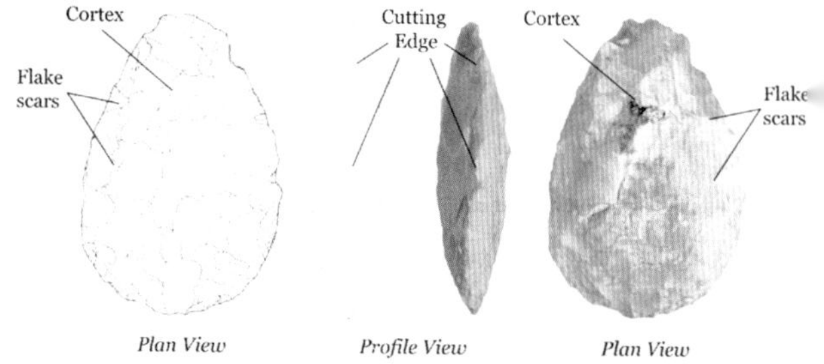

RAW MATERIALS

In Europe, *flint* was the most widely used lithic raw material in Palaeolithic times. *Flint* is a fine-grained, very homogenous stone, similar to glass in its mechanical properties. This means that not only does it create very sharp edges as it fractures, it does so in a predictable and consistent manner. *Flint* fractures conchoidally (literally 'shell-like') so as it is *knapped* a series of recognisable *percussion features* are produced.

Flint forms in Chalk, and both large and small nodules can be found where Chalk outcrops. *Flint* collected from eroding Chalk outcrops would have provided early humans (*hominins*) with high quality raw materials for tools. *Flint* would also have been available in secondary sources such as river gravels – though the size and quality of these flint pebbles and cobbles would have been very variable.

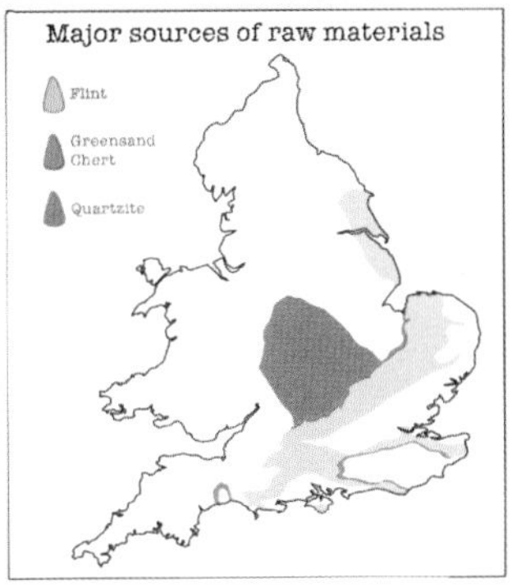

Most, but by no means all, of the Palaeolithic artefacts from England are made of *flint*. However, flint was not always available and then Palaeolithic people used other suitable rocks such as *quartzite* and *Greensand chert* and less common materials such as *andesitic tuff* (a very ancient volcanic deposit) to make tools.

The raw material map should give you an idea of what materials Palaeolithic artefacts in your area are likely to be made from – though remember that non-local 'exotic' materials may also have been utilised!

Many of the examples in this sheet are *flint* artefacts, because not only are they the most commonly found material, but *flint* is also the easiest stone in which to "read" the distinctive *percussion features;* however we have also included other raw materials. We hope that you can use this recognition sheet to help identify more Lower and Middle Palaeolithic stone tools, in different locations across England, and in a variety of raw materials. If you would like further advice about stone tool identification please contact the National Ice Age Network or your local museum.

IDENTIFYING ARTEFACTS

Bulb of Percussion: this occurs just below the place where the core was struck to remove a flake - on flakes this bulb is a pronounced swelling and on cores a corresponding hollow.

Flake Scars: the evidence on an artefact for earlier *flake* removals. They are made up of *ripples* and a 'hollowed out' *negative bulb of percussion*. Multiple *negative flake scars*, help us to identify *deliberate knapping* as natural processes do not usually create a series of complete *negative flake scars.*

Retouched Flakes: the removal of small flakes that alter the shape and/or the angle of the edge can be a good indicator of artefact status. However, when dealing with Ice Age river gravels it is always worth remembering that such small flakes may have been removed by natural processes, damaging the edges of the artefact.

Handaxes: handaxes or *bifaces* are among the easiest types of artefact to identify, due to the intensive degree of shaping and flaking evidence they preserve. Use the pictures on this sheet as a guide to identifying any potential artefacts you find.

Artefact Size & Shape: Palaeolithic artefacts come in a wide range of sizes and shapes. As a very rough guide, *handaxes* are generally approximately hand-sized, and *flakes* somewhat smaller. *Cores* can be any size. Due to the ferocity of Ice Age rivers it can be difficult to prove that very small pieces are genuine artefacts as the features they display may well result from impacts with cobbles in fast flowing water.

Artefact Colour & Physical Condition: many Palaeolithic artefacts will show iron staining of an orangey colour. Artefacts may also have been damaged by processes such as river transportation; most typically this shows as abrasion to the ridges between the negative flake scars and/or chipping to the edges of the piece.

References:

Ashton, N., Lewis, S.G. & Parfitt, S. 1998. *Excavations at the Lower Palaeolithic site at East Farm, Barnham, Suffolk 1989-94.* British Museum Occasional Paper 125, British Museum Press, London.
Gamble, C. 1999. *The Palaeolithic Societies of Europe.* Cambridge University Press, Cambridge.
Mellars, P. 1996. *The Neanderthal Legacy.* Princeton University Press, Princeton.
Wymer, J. 1968. *Lower Palaeolithic Archaeology in Britain as represented by the Thames Valley.* John Baker, London.

Credits:

Text and design by Dr. Jenni Chambers & Bryony Ryder

FLAKES

Flakes are the simplest type of lithic artefact; quick to produce, very sharp and easily *retouched* into other tool types. *Knapping* creates a series of recognisable attributes on both the *flake* and the *core* it is detached from. It is these *percussion features* that allow us to recognise Palaeolithic artefacts.

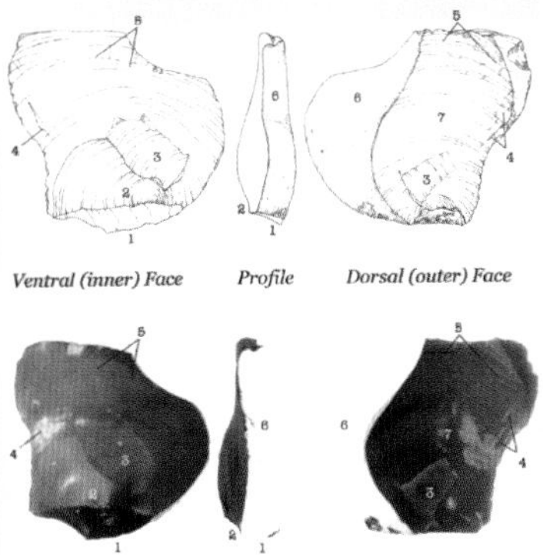

1 = Striking Platform: this is the flat area where the *hammer* strikes the *core* to remove the *flake*
2 = Bulb of Percussion: adjacent to where the *hammer* strikes, the force of the impact produces a conical swelling
3 = Eraillure Scar: a small secondary *flake* that may be removed as the *bulb of percussion* forms
4 = Radial Fissures: small cracks known as *'Hackles'* may be present and point towards the *bulb of percussion*
5 = Ripples: *ripples* radiate from the *bulb of percussion*, travelling the length of the *flake*. *Ripples* indicate the direction of the blow that removed the *flake* from the *core*
6 = Cortex: the 'outer skin' of a *nodule*
7 = Dorsal Flake Scar(s): evidence of previous flaking may be present on the *dorsal* (outer) surface of the *flake* as *ripples*, or complete *negative scars* which have a hollow where the *bulb of percussion* of the previous *flake* formed

The example above is a modern replica of an ancient *flake*. Archaeological examples you might find are more likely to be stained, patinated or coated in minerals from their long exposure to chemicals in the soil. Orange, brown, yellow and cream are the most common stains for *flint* to develop. On other raw materials such as *chert* and *quartzite* this staining is harder to see due to the natural colouration of these materials.

A *flint flake* stained orangey brown

A *chert flake*, naturally dark brown, showing some orange staining

RETOUCHED FLAKES

Freshly *knapped flakes* are extremely sharp, and would have been used for a variety of cutting tasks. However, this very sharp, thin edge quickly becomes worn down and blunted with use. *Retouching* the edge of a flake makes it much more durable and suitable for tasks such as wood working and hide processing which would quickly blunt a *non-retouched flake.*

Retouch is the removal of a series of small *flakes* to modify the shape or edge of an artefact, when done to one face of an edge this is called *unifacial retouch* and when both faces of an edge are *retouched* this is called bifacial retouch. Retouch removals may be made with a small *hard hammer* (stone) or a *soft hammer* (antler) - both *direct percussion* methods.

Illustrated are some common *unifacial retouched* tool types:

Scraper:
Small *retouch flakes* are removed from one side of the *flake*, creating a durable working edge that could be used for hide or wood working.

Notch:
Larger *retouch removals* concentrated in one location produce this distinctive *notch*. It has been suggested *notches* were used for wood working.

Denticulate:
Small *retouch removals* create a 'saw' like edge, that could have been used for meat or wood processing tasks.

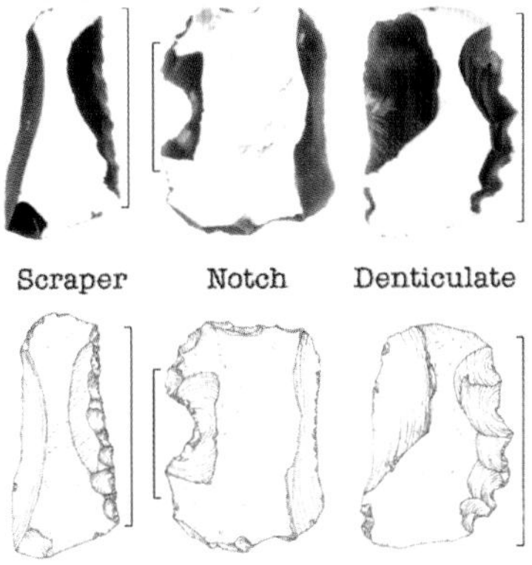

EXAMPLES OF HANDAXES FOUND IN GRAVEL DEPOSITS AROUND ENGLAND

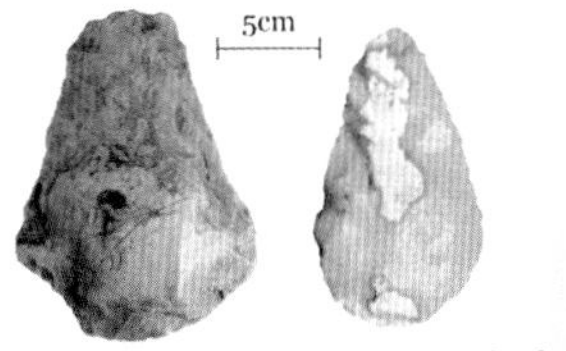

Flint handaxes occur in many parts of England, and have been found in a wide range of shapes and sizes. Commonly they are iron-stained, as shown above. *Handaxes* from gravels may also show abrasion and/or damage similar to the *handaxe* on the left.

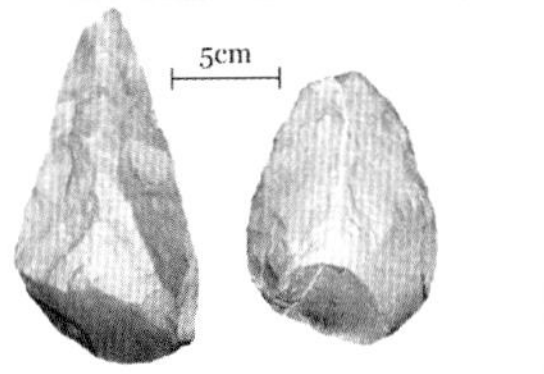

Quartzite cobbles suitable for *handaxe* manufacture are scattered throughout central England. *Handaxes* are commonly made on split *quartzite* cobbles like those above.

Greensand Chert is mechanically similar to *flint*, though it often looks much coarser. The largest numbers of *Greensand Chert* artefacts occur in the Southwest of England.

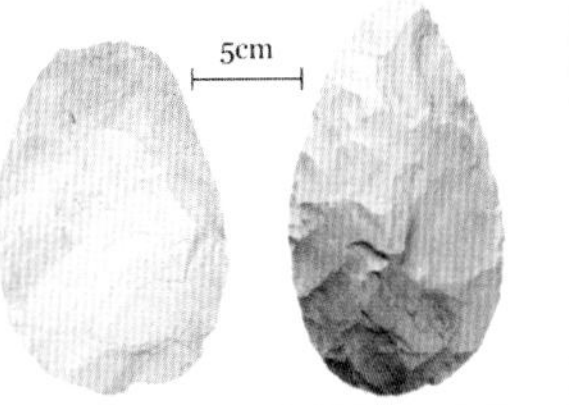

Andesitic tuff is an ancient volcanic deposit, suitable for stone tool manufacture. Palaeolithic *handaxes* of *andesitic tuff* have been found mainly in the Midlands.

Contact your local 'National Ice Age Network' centre by email at info@iceage.org.uk or write to:

North & West Midlands
Birmingham Archaeology,
University of Birmingham,
Edgbaston,
Birmingham,
B15 2TT

SUPPORTED BY
ENGLISH HERITAGE

East Midlands
School of Archaeology & Ancient History,
University of Leicester
University Road,
Leicester,
LE1 7RH

NATIONAL ICE AGE NETWORK

www.iceage.org.uk

South West
Centre for the Archaeology of Human Origins,
Avenue Campus,
University of Southampton,
Southampton,
SO17 1BF

SUPPORTED BY
ENGLISH NATURE

South East
Dept of Geography,
Royal Holloway,
University of London,
Egham,
Surrey,
TW20 0EX

Bibliography

Aitken, M J, 1998 *Introduction to Optical Dating*, Oxford

Alabaster, C, and Straw, A, 1976 The Pleistocene context of faunal remains and artefacts discovered at Welton-le-Wold, Lincolnshire, *Proceedings of the Yorkshire Geological Society* 41, 75-94

Aldhouse-Green, H S, Peterson, R, and Walker E A, 2012 *Neanderthals in Wales: Pontnewydd and the Elwy Valley Caves*, Oxford

Allen, J R L, 2001 Late Quaternary stratigraphy in the Gwent Levels (southeast Wales): the sub-surface evidence, *Proceedings of the Geologists' Association* 112, 289-315

Allen, L G, and Gibbard, P L, 1993 Pleistocene evolution of the Solent river of southern England, *Quaternary Science Reviews* 12, 503-528

ALSF Annual Report 2002-3, English Heritage, http://www.english-heritage.org.uk/publications/extract-02-03/

ALSF Annual Report 2003-4, English Heritage, http://www.english-heritage.org.uk/publications/extract-03-04/

ALSF Annual Report 2004-5, English Heritage, http://www.english-heritage.org.uk/publications/extract-04-05/

ALSF Annual Report 2005-6, English Heritage, http://www.english-heritage.org.uk/publications/extract-05-06/

ALSF Annual Report 2006-7, English Heritage, http://www.english-heritage.org.uk/publications/extract-06-07/

ALSF Annual Report 2007-8, English Heritage, http://www.english-heritage.org.uk/publications/extract-07-08/

Antoine, P, Limondin-Lozouet, N, Auguste, P, Locht, J-L, Galheb, B, Reyss, J-L, Escude, É, Carbonel, P, Mercier, N, Bahain, J-J, C, F, and Voinchet, P, 2006 Le tuf de Caours (Somme, France): mise en évidence d'une séquence eemienne et d'un site paléolithique associé, *Quaternaire* 17, 281–320

Aram, J, Hambly, J, and Rackham, J, 2004 Towards an understanding of the ice age at Welton-le-Wold, Lincolnshire, unpubl rep., Heritage Lincolnshire, Heckington

Ashton, N M, and McNabb, J, 1994 Bifaces in perspective, N Ashton and A David (eds), *Stories in Stone*, Lithic Studies Occasional Paper 4, London, 182–191

Ashton, N M, and Lewis, S G, 2002 Deserted Britain: declining populations in the British late Middle Pleistocene, *Antiquity* 76, 388-396

Ashton, N M, and White, M, 2003 Bifaces and raw materials: flexible flaking in the British Early Palaeolithic, in M Soressi and H L Dibble (eds), *Multiple Approaches to the Study of Bifacial Technologies*, University of Pennsylvania, Philadelphia, 109-123

Ashton, N M, Dean, P, and McNabb, J, 1991 Flaked flakes: what, when and why? *Lithics: The Journal of the Lithics Studies Society* 12, 1-12

Ashton, N M, Cook, J, Lewis, S G, and Rose, J, 1992 *High Lodge: excavations by G de G Sieveking 1962–68 and J Cook 1988*, London

Ashton, N M, Lewis, S G, and Parfitt, S A, 1998 *Excavations at Barnham, 1989-1994*, British Museum Occasional Paper 125, London

Ashton, N M, Jacobi, R, and White, M, 2003 The dating of Levallois sites in West London, *Quaternary Newsletter* 99, 25-32

Ashton, N M, Lewis, S, Parfitt, S, Candy, I, Keen, D, Kemp, R, Penkman, K, Thomas, G, Whittaker, J, and White, M J, 2005 Excavations at the Lower Palaeolithic site at Elveden, Suffolk, UK, *Proceedings of the Prehistoric Society* 71, 1-61

Ashton, N, Lewis, S, Parfitt, S, and White, M, 2006 Riparian landscapes and human habitat preferences during the Hoxnian (MIS 11) Interglacial, *Journal of Quaternary Science* 21, 497–506

Ashton, N M, Lewis, S G, Parfitt, S, Penkman, K E H, and Coope, G R, 2008 New evidence for complex climate change in MIS 11 from Hoxne, UK, *Quaternary Science Reviews* 27, 652-668

Ashton, N, Lewis, S G, and Hosfield, R, 2011 Mapping the human record: population change in Britain during the early Palaeolithic, in N M Ashton, S G Lewis and C B Stringer (eds), *The Ancient Human Occupation of Britain*, Amsterdam, 39–52

Austin, L, 1994 Life and death of a Boxgrove biface, in N M Ashton and A David (eds), *Stories in Stone*, London, 119-27

Banham, P H, Gibbard, P L, Lunkka, J P, Parfitt, S P, Preece, R C, and Turner, C, 2001 A critical assessment of 'A new glacial stratigraphy for eastern England', *Quaternary Newsletter* 93, 5–14

Barham, A J, and Bates, M R, 1994 *Strategies for the use of boreholes in archaeological evaluations: a review of methodologies and techniques*, Institute of Archaeology, University College, London, Geoarchaeological Service Facility, Technical Report 94/01, London

Basell, L S, Brown, A G, and Toms, P S, 2011 Chard Junction Quarry and the Axe Valley gravels, in L S Basell, A G Brown, and P S Toms (eds), *The Quaternary of the Exe Valley and Adjoining Areas,* Quaternary Research Association Field Guide, London, 93-102

Bassinot, F C, Labeyrie, L D, Vincent, E, Quidelleur, X, Shackleton, N, Lancelot, Y, 1994 The astronomical theory of climate and the age of the Brunhes-Matuyama magnetic reversal, *Earth and Planetary Science Letters* 126, 91-108

Bates, M R, 1993 Quaternary aminostratigraphy in north-western France, *Quaternary Science Reviews* 12, 793-809

Bates, M, 2001 The meeting of the waters: raised beaches and river gravels of the Sussex coastal plain/Hampshire basin, *Lithic Studies Society Occasional Papers* 7, 27-45

Bates, M R, and Heppell, E, 2007 Assessment report: Middle Thames northern tributaries, unpubl. rep., University of Wales Lampeter and Essex County Council

Bates, M R, and Wenban-Smith, F F, 2011 Palaeolithic geoarchaeology: palaeolandscape modeling and scales of investigation, *Landscapes* 2012 (1), 69-96

Bates, M R, and Stafford, E, 2013, *Thames Holocene: A Geoarchaeological Approach to the Investigation of the River Floodplain for High Speed 1,* Oxford Wessex Archaeology Monograph, Salisbury

Bates, M R, Roberts, M B, and Parfitt, S A, 1997 The chronology, palaeogeography and archaeological significance of the marine Quaternary record of the West Sussex coastal plain, southern England, UK, *Quaternary Science Reviews* 16, 1227 – 1252

Bates, M R, Lambrick, G, Welsh, K, and White, M J, 1999 Evaluation of Palaeolithic deposits at Purfleet, Essex, *Lithics* 19, 72-87

Bates, M R, Barham, A J, Pine, C A, and Williamson, V D, 2000 The use of borehole stratigraphic logs in archaeological evaluation strategies for deeply stratified alluvial areas, in Roskams, S (ed.), *Interpreting Stratigraphy: Site Evaluation, Recording Procedures and Stratigraphic Analysis,* BAR Int. Ser. 910, Oxford, 49–69

Bates, M R, Keen, D H, Whittaker, J E, Merry, J S, and Wenban-Smith, F F, 2002 Middle Pleistocene molluscan and ostracod faunas from Allhallows, Kent, UK, *Proceedings of the Geologists' Association* 113, 223–236

Bates, M R, Keen, D H, and Lautridou, J-P, 2003 Pleistocene marine and periglacial deposits of the English Channel, *Journal of Quaternary Science* 18, 319–337

Bates, M R, Wenban-Smith, F F, Briant, R M, Marshall, G, 2004 Palaeolithic archaeology of the Sussex/Hampshire coastal corridor, Project Number 3279, unpubl. rep. for English Heritage, London

Bates, M R, Briant, R M, Wenban-Smith, F F, Bates, C R, 2007a Curation of the Sussex/Hampshire coastal corridor Lower/Middle Palaeolithic record, Project Number 3279, unpubl. rep. for English Heritage, London

Bates, M R, Bates, C R, and Whittaker, J E. 2007b Mixed method approaches to the investigation and mapping of buried Quaternary deposits: examples from southern England, *Archaeological Prospection* 14, 104-129

Bates, M R, Bates, C R, and Briant, R M, 2007c Bridging the gap: a terrestrial view of shallow marine sequences and the importance of the transition zone, *Journal of Archaeological Science* 34, 1537-1551

Bates, C R, Bates, M R, and Dix, J, 2009 Contiguous Palaeo-Landscape Reconstruction (Transition Zone Mapping for marine-terrestrial archaeological continuity), ALSF rep., University of St Andrews

Bates, M R, Bates, C R, Gibbard, P L, Keen, D H, Parfitt, S A, Peglar, S M, Schwenninger, J-L, Wenban-Smith, F F, and Whittaker, J E, 2009 West Street, Selsey, in: R M Briant, M R Bates, R T Hosfield, and F F Wenban-Smith (eds), *The Quaternary of the Solent Basin and West Sussex Raised Beaches,* Quaternary Research Association Field Guide, London

Bates, M R, Briant, R M, Rhodes, E J, Schwenninger, J L. and Whittaker, J E, 2010 A new chronological framework for Middle and Upper Pleistocene landscape evolution in the Sussex/Hampshire coastal corridor, *Proceedings of the Geologists' Association* 121, 369–392

Bates, M R, Nayling, N, Bates, C R, Dawson, S, Huws, D, And Wickham-Jones, C, 2012 A multidisciplinary approach to the archaeological investigation of a bedrock-dominated shallow-marine landscape: an example from the Bay of Firth, Orkney, UK, *International Journal of Nautical Archaeology* 42, 24-43

Bates, M R, Wenban-Smith, F F, Bello, S M, Bridgland, D R, Buck, L T, Collins, M J, Keen, D H, Leary, J, Parfitt, S A, Penkman, K, Rhodes, E, Ryssaert, C, and Whittaker, J E, 2014 Late persistence of the Acheulian in southern Britain in an MIS 8 interstadial: evidence from Harnham, Wiltshire, *Quaternary Science Reviews* 101, 159-186

Behre, K-E, 2007, A new Holocene sea-level curve for the southern North Sea, *Boreas* 36, 82-102

Bell, M, 2007, *Prehistoric Coastal Communities: the Mesolithic in Western Britain,* CBA Res. Rep. 149, York

Bell, M, and Walker, M J C, 2005 *Late Quaternary Environmental Change* (2nd edn), Harlow

Bell, M, Chisham, C, Dark, P and Allen, S, 2006 Mesolithic sites in coastal and riverine contexts in southern Britain: current research and the management of the archaeological resource, in E Rensink and H Peeters (eds), *Preserving the Early Past: Investigation, Selection and Preservation of Palaeolithic and Mesolithic Sites and Landscapes,* Nederlandse Archeologische Rapporten 31, Amersfoort, 25-39

Berendsen, H J A, and Stouthamer, E, 2001 *Palaeogeographic Development of the Rhine-Meuse*

Delta, the Netherlands, Assen
Blinkhorn, E, and Milner, N, 2014 *Mesolithic Research and Conservation Framework 2013*, York
Boëda, E, 1986. Approche technologique du concept Levallois et évaluation de champ d'application, unpubl. PhD thesis, Univ. Paris
Boëda, E, 1988 Le concept Levallois et évaluation de son champ d'application, in M Otte M (ed.), *L'Homme de Néandertal* 4: *la Technique*, Etudes et Recherches Archéologiques de l'Université de Liège 31, Liège, 13-26
Boeda, E, 1993 Le débitage discoïde et le débitage levallois récurrent centripète, *Bulletin de la Société Préhistorique Française* 90, 392-404
Boëda, E, 1995 Levallois: a volumetric reconstruction, methods, a technique, in H L Dibble and O Bar–Yosef (eds), *The Definition and Interpretation of Levallois Technology*, Madison, 41–68
Boëda, E, 2001 Détermination des unités techno-fonctionnelles de pièces bifaciales provenant de la couche acheuléenne C'3 base du site de Barbas, in D Cliquet (ed.), *Les Industries á Outils Bifaciaux du Paléolithique Moyen d'Europe Occidentale*, Études et Recherches Archéologiques de l'Université de Liège 98, Liège, 51–75
Boismier, W A, 2003 A Middle Palaeolithic site at Lynford Quarry, Mundford, Norfolk: interim statement, *Proceedings of the Prehistoric Society* 69, 315-324
Boismier, W A, Gamble, C, and Coward, F, 2012 *Neanderthals Amongst Mammoths: Excavations at Lynford Quarry, Norfolk*, London
Bos, J A A, and Janssen, C R, 1996 Local impact of Palaeolithic Man on the environment during the end of the Last Glacial in the Netherlands, *Journal of Archaeological Science* 23, 731-739
Bos, J A A, van Geel, B, Groenewoudt, B J, and Lauwerier, R C G M, 2005 Early Holocene environmental change: the presence and disappearance of early Mesolithic habitation near Zutphen (The Netherlands), *Vegetation History and Archaeobotany* 15, 27-43
Bowen, D Q, Hughes, S, Sykes, G A, and Miller, G H, 1989 Land-sea correlations in the Pleistocene based on isoleucine epimerization in non-marine molluscs, *Nature* 340, 49–51
Briant, R M, Bates, M R, Schwenninger, J-L, and Wenban-Smith, F, 2006 An optically stimulated luminescence dated Middle to Late Pleistocene fluvial sequence from the western Solent Basin, southern England, *Journal of Quaternary Science* 21, 507 – 523
Briant, R M, Bates, M R, Marshall, G D, Schwenninger, J-L, and Wenban-Smith, F F, 2012 Terrace reconstruction and long profile projection: a case study from the Solent river system near Southampton, England, *Proceedings of the Geologists' Association* 123, 438–449
Bridgland, D R, 1988 The Pleistocene fluvial stratigraphy and palaeogeography of Essex, *Proceedings of the Geologists' Association* 99, 291–314
Bridgland, D R, 1994 *Quaternary of the Thames*, London
Bridgland, D R, 1996 Quaternary river terrace deposits as a framework for the Lower Palaeolithic record, in C Gamble and A Lawson (eds), *The English Palaeolithic Reviewed*, Salisbury, 23–39
Bridgland, D R, 1999 Wealden rivers' north of the Thames: a provenance study based on gravel clast analysis, *Proceedings of the Geologists' Association* 110, 133–148
Bridgland, D R, 2000 River terrace systems in north–west Europe: an archive of environmental change, uplift and early human occupation, *Quaternary Science Reviews* 19, 1293–1303
Bridgland, D R, 2003 The evolution of the river Medway, SE England, in the context of Quaternary palaeoclimate and the Palaeolithic occupation of NW Europe, *Proceedings of the Geologists' Association* 114, 23–48
Bridgland, D R, 2006 The Middle and Upper Pleistocene sequence in the Lower Thames; a record of Milankovitch climatic fluctuation and early human occupation of southern Britain. Henry Stopes Memorial Lecture, *Proceedings of the Geologists' Association* 117, 281–305
Bridgland, D R, 2010 The record from British Quaternary river systems within the context of global fluvial archives, *Journal of Quaternary Science* 25, 433–446
Bridgland, D R, 2014 Lower Thames terrace stratigraphy: latest views, in D R Bridgland, P Allen and T S White (eds), *The Quaternary of the Lower Thames and Eastern Essex*, Quaternary Research Association Field Guide, London, 5–17
Bridgland, D R, and Sutcliffe, A J, 1995 East Mersea Hippopotamus Site, in D R Bridgland, P Allen and B A Haggart (eds), *The Quaternary of the Lower Reaches of the Thames*, Quaternary Research Association Field Guide, London, 275-276
Bridgland, D R, and Allen, P, 1996 A revised model for terrace formation and its significance for the lower Middle Pleistocene Thames terrace aggradations of north east Essex, U.K. in C Turner (ed.), *The Early Middle Pleistocene in Europe*, Rotterdam, 121–134
Bridgland, D R, and Gibbard, P L, 1997 Quaternary river diversions in the London Basin and the eastern English Channel, *Géographie Physique et Quaternaire* 51, 337–346
Bridgland, D R, and Maddy, D, 2002 Global correlation of the long Quaternary fluvial sequences: a review of baseline knowledge and possible methods and criteria for establishing a database, *Netherlands Journal of Geosciences* 81, 265–281
Bridgland, D R, and Westaway, R, 2007 Climatically controlled river terrace staircases: a worldwide Quaternary phenomenon, *Geomorphology* 98, 285–315
Bridgland, D R, Currant, A P, and Preece, R C, 1995 East Mersea Restaurant site, in D R Bridgland, P Allen, and B A Haggart (eds), *The Quaternary of the Lower Reaches of the Thames*,

Quaternary Research Association Field Guide, London, 271–274

Bridgland, D R, Field, M H, Holmes, J A, McNabb, J, Preece, R C, Selby, I, Wymer, J J, Boreham, S, Irving, B G, Parfitt and S A, and Stuart, A J, 1999 Middle Pleistocene interglacial Thames/ Medway deposits at Clacton-on-Sea, England: reconsideration of the biostratigraphical and environmental context of the type Clactonian Palaeolithic industry, *Quaternary Science Reviews* 18, 109–146

Bridgland, D R, Crowe, K, Preece, R C, Roe, H M, Tipping, R M, Coope, G R, Field, M H, Robinson, J E, and Schreve, D C, 2001 Middle Pleistocene interglacial deposits at Barling, Essex, England: evidence for a longer chronology for the Thames terrace sequence, *Journal of Quaternary Science* 16, 813-840

Bridgland, D R, Schreve, D C, Keen, D H, Meyrick, R, and Westaway, R, 2004 Biostratigraphical correlation between the late Quaternary sequence of the Thames and key fluvial localities in central Germany, *Proceedings of the Geologists' Association* 115, 125–140

Bridgland, D R, Antoine, P, Limondin-Lozouet, N, Santisteban, J I, Westaway, R, and White, M J, 2006 The Palaeolithic occupation of Europe as revealed by evidence from the rivers: data from IGCP 449, *Journal of Quaternary Science* 21, 437–455

Bridgland, D R, Westaway, R, Howard, A J, Innes, J B, Long, A J, Mitchell, W A, White, M J, and White, T S, 2010 The role of glacio-isostasy in the formation of post-glacial river terraces in relation to the MIS 2 ice limit: evidence from northern England, *Proceedings of the Geologists' Association* 121, 113–127

Bridgland, D R, Harding, P, Allen, P, Candy, I, Cherry, C, Horne, D J, Keen, D H, Penkman, K E H, Preece, R C, Rhodes, E J, Scaife, R, Schreve, D C, Schwenninger, J, Slipper, I, Ward, G R, White, M J, White, T S, and Whittaker, J E, 2012 An enhanced record of MIS 9 environments, geochronology and geoarchaeology: data from construction of the High Speed 1 (London–Channel Tunnel) rail-link and other recent investigations at Purfleet, Essex, UK, *Proceedings of the Geologists' Association* 124/3, 417–76

Bridgland, D R, Howard, A J, White, M J, and White, T S, 2014 *Quaternary of the Trent*, Oxford

Bridgland, D R, Howard, A J, White, M J, White, T S, and Westaway, R, 2015 New insight into the Quaternary evolution of the River Trent, UK, *Proceedings of the Geologist's Association*, http://dx.doi.org/10.1016/j.pgeola.2015.06.004

Brown, J, 1840 Notice of a fluvio-marine deposit containing mammalian-remains occurring in the parish of Little Clacton on the Essex coast, *Magazine of Natural History* Ser. 2/4, 197–201

Brown, T, 2012 Monitoring and modeling of the Palaeolithic archaeological resource at Chard Junction Quarry, Hodge Ditch, Phases II and III. Assessment Stage (5695). Project report Stage II, unpubl rep., University of Southampton

Brown, T, and Basell, L, 2008 New lower Palaeolithic finds from the Axe Valley Dorset, *Past* 60, 1–3

Brown, A G, Basell, L S, and Toms, P, 2015 A stacked Late Quaternary fluvio-periglacial sequence from the Axe valley, southern England with implications for landscape evolution and Palaeolithic archaeology, *Quaternary Science Reviews* 116, 106-121

Brown, T, Hosfield, R, Basell, L, Toms, P, Hounsell, S, and Young, R, 2008 The Palaeolithic Rivers of South-West Britain, York: Archaeology Data Service (doi:10.5284/1000027)

Bull, W B, 1991 *Geomorphic Responses to Climatic Change*, Oxford

Buteux, S, Brooks, S, Candy, I, Coates, G, Coope, R, Currant, A, Field, M, Greenwood, M, Greig, J, Howard, A, Limbrey, S, Paddock, E, Schreve, D, Smith, D, and Toms, P, 2003 The Whitemoor Haye Woolly Rhino Site, Whitemoor Haye Quarry, Staffordshire (SK 173127): assessment report on scientific investigations funded by the ALSF through a grant administered by English Nature, unpubl. rep., University of Birmingham Field Archaeology Unit

Buteux, S, Chambers, J, and Silva, B, 2009 *Digging up the Ice Age. Recognising, Recording and Understanding Fossil and Archaeological Remains Found in British Quarries: a Guide and Practical Handbook*, Oxford

Butzer, K W, 1982 *Archaeology as Human Ecology*, Cambridge

Castro-Curel, Z, and Carbonell, E, 1995 Wood pseudomorphs from level I at Abric Romani, Barcelona, Spain, *Journal of Field Archaeology* 22, 376-384

Chambers, J C, 2003 Like a rolling stone? The identification of fluvial transportation damage signatures on secondary context bifaces, *Lithics* 24, 66–77

Chen, W, Xuanqing, Z, Naihua, H, and Yongyhong, M, 1996 Compiling the map of shallow-buried palaeochannels on the North China Plain, *Geomorphology* 18, 47–52

Chew, K J, 1995 Data modelling: a general-purpose petroleum geological database, in: J R A Giles (ed.), *Geological Data Management*, Geological Society Special Publication 97, London, 13–23

Clayton, C R I, Matthews, M C, and Simons, N E, 1995 *Site Investigation*, Oxford

Cliquet, D, Ladjadj, J, Lautridou, J-P, Leportier, J, Lorren, P, Michel, D, Pruvost, P, Rivard, J-J, and Vilgrain, G, 2001 Le Paléolithique moyen à outils bifaciaux en Normandie: état des connaissances, in D Cliquet (ed.), *Les Industries á Outils Bifaciaux du Paléolithique Moyen d'Europe Occidentale*, Études et Recherches Archéologiques de l'Université de Liège 98, Liège, 115–27

Cohen, K M, 2005 3D geostatistical interpolation and geological interpretation of palaeo-groundwater rise in the Holocene coastal prism in the Netherlands, in L Giosan and J P Bhattacharya, *River Deltas: Concepts, Models and Examples*, SEPM Special Publication 83, Tulsa, 341–64

Cohen, K M, MacDonald, K, Joordens, J C A, Roebroeks, W, and Gibbard, P L, 2012 The earliest occupation of north-west Europe: a coastal perspective, *Quaternary International* 271, 70-83

Cohen, K M, Gibbard, P L, and Weerts, H J T, 2014 North Sea palaeogeographical reconstructions for the last 1 Ma, *Geologie en Mijnbouw/Netherlands Journal of Geosciences* 93, 7-29

Coles, B, 1998 Doggerland: a speculative survey, *Proceedings of the Prehistoric Society* 64, 45-81

Conneller, C, 2007 Inhabiting new landscapes: settlement and mobility in Britain after the last glacial maximum, *Oxford Journal of Archaeology* 26, 215-37

Conway, B W, McNabb, J, and Ashton, N, 1996 *Excavations at Barnfield Pit, Swanscombe, 1968-72*, British Museum Occasional Paper 94, London

Cook, J, and Jacobi, R, 1998 Discoidal core technology in the Palaeolithic at Oldbury, Kent, in N Ashton, F Healy and P Pettitt (eds), *Stone Age Archaeology: Essays in Honour of John Wymer*, Oxford, 124–136

Coope, G R and Tallon, P W J, 1983 A full glacial insect fauna from the Lea Valley, Enfield, North London, *Quaternary Newsletter* 40, 7–12

Cooper, L, Thomas, J S, Beamish, M G, Gouldwell, A, Collcutt, S N, Williams, J, Jacobi, R M, Currant, A, and Higham, T, 2012 An early Upper Palaeolithic open-air station and mid-Devensian hyaena den at Grange Farm, Glaston, Rutland, UK, *Proceedings of the Prehistoric Society* 78, 73–93

Corcoran, J, Halsey, C, Spurr, G, Burton, E, and Jamieson, D, 2011 *Mapping Past Landscapes in the Lower Lea Valley: a Geoarchaeological Study of the Quaternary Sequence*, Museum of London Archaeology Monograph 55, London

Culshaw, M G, 2005 From concept towards reality: developing the attributed 3D geological model of the shallow subsurface, *Quarterly Journal of Engineering Geology and Hydrogeology* 38, 231–284

Currant, A P, and Jacobi, R M, 2001 A formal mammalian biostratigraphy for the Late Pleistocene of Britain, *Quaternary Science Reviews* 20, 1707–1716

Dale, W, 1912 The implement-bearing gravel beds of the lower valley of the Test, *Proceedings of the Society of Antiquaries* 24, 108–116

Dale, W, 1918 Report as local secretary for Hampshire, *Proceedings of the Society of Antiquaries* 30, 20–23

Department for Communities and Local Government, 2012, National Planning Policy Framework (NPPF), https//www.gov.uk/government/uploads/attachment_data/file/6077/2116950.pdf

Dewey, H, 1926 The river gravels of the south of England. Their relationship to Palaeolithic man and to the glacial period, *XIII Congnis Geologique International* (1922), 1429-1446

Duller, G A T, 2008 *Luminescence Dating: Guidelines on using luminescence dating in archaeology*, English Heritage, London

Edwards, R, 2013 *Archaeological Archives and Museums, 2012*, Society of Museum Archaeologists, http://www.socmusarch.org.uk/docs/Archaeological-archives-and-museums-2012.pdf

English Heritage and The Prehistoric Society, 1999 *Research Frameworks for the Palaeolithic and Mesolithic of Britain and Ireland*, Salisbury

Essex County Council and Kent County Council, 2004 Archaeological Survey of Mineral Extraction Sites in the Greater Thames Estuary, Aggregates Levy Sustainability Fund 1, unpubl. rep.

Essex County Council and Kent County Council, 2011 Archaeological Survey of Mineral Extraction Sites around the Thames Estuary [data set], York: Archaeology Data Service (doi:10.5284/1000016)

Evans, J, 1860 On the occurrence of flint implements in undisturbed beds of gravel, sand, and clay, *Archaeologia* 13, 280-307

Féblot-Augustins, J, 1999 Raw material transport patterns and settlement systems in the European Lower and Middle Palaeolithic: continuity, change and variability, in C Gamble and W Roebroeks (eds), *The Middle Palaeolithic Occupation of Europe*, Leiden, 193-214

Fischer, A, 2004 Submerged Stone Age: Danish examples and North Sea potential, in N C Flemming (ed.), *Submarine Prehistoric Archaeology of the North Sea: Research Priorities and Collaboration with Industry*, CBA Res. Rep. 141, York, 21-36

Fitch, S, Thomson, K and Gaffney, V L, 2005 Late Pleistocene and Holocene depositional systems and palaeogeography of the Dogger Bank, North Sea, *Quaternary Research* 64, 185-96

Flatman, J, Short, J, Doeser, J, and Lee, E (eds) 2008 *Sustainable Heritage: Aggregates Extraction and the Historic Environment*, ALSF Dissemination Project, 2002-07, benchmark report, London

Flemming, N C, 2002 *The Scope of Strategic Environmental Assessment of North Sea Areas SEA3 and SEA2 in Regard to Prehistoric Archaeological Remains*, SEA3_TR014, Department of Trade and Industry, London

Flemming, N C, (ed.) 2004 *Submarine Prehistoric Archaeology of the North Sea: Research Priorities and Collaboration with Industry*, CBA Res. Rep. 141, York

Foley, R A, 1981 *Off-site Archaeology and Human Adaptation in Eastern Africa*, Cambridge Monographs in African Archaeology 3, BAR Int. Ser. 97, Oxford

Gaffney, V L, Thomson, K, and Fitch S, (eds) 2007 *Mapping Doggerland: the Mesolithic landscapes of the southern North Sea*, Oxford

Gaffney, V L, Fitch, S, and Smith, D, 2009 *Europe's Lost World: the Rediscovery of Doggerland*, CBA Res. Rep. 160, York

Gamble, C, 1992 Southern rivers Palaeolithic project, *Quaternary Newsletter* 66, 38-40

Gamble, C, 1996 Hominid behaviour in the Middle Pleistocene: an English perspective, in C S Gamble and A J Lawson (eds), *The English Palaeolithic Reviewed*, Salisbury

Gamble, C, and Kruszynski, R, 2009 John Evans, Joseph Prestwich and the stone that shattered the time barrier, *Antiquity* 83, 461-475

Geneste, J-M, 1989 Economie des resources lithiques dans le mousterien du sud-ouest France, in L Freeman and M Patou (eds), *L' Homme de Néandertal 6: la Subsistance*, Etudes et Recherches Archéologiques de l'Université de Liège 33, Liège, 75-97

Gibbard, P L, 1977 Pleistocene history of the Vale of St Albans, *Philosophical Transactions of the Royal Society of London* B280, 445–483

Gibbard, P L, 1979 Middle Pleistocene drainage in the Thames Valley, *Geological Magazine* 116, 35–44

Gibbard, P L, 1985 *Pleistocene History of the Middle Thames Valley*, Cambridge

Gibbard, P L, 1994 *Pleistocene History of the Lower Thames Valley*, Cambridge

Gibbard, P L, 1995 Formation of the Strait of Dover, in R C Preece (ed.), *Island Britain: A Quaternary Perspective,* Geological Society Special Publication 96, London, 15-26

Gibbard, P L, 2007 Europe cut adrift, *Nature* 448, 259-260

Gibbard, P L, and Cohen, K M, 2008 Global chronostratigraphical correlation table for the last 2.7 million years, *Episodes* 31, 243-7

Gibbard, P L, and Lewin, J, 2003 The history of the major rivers of southern Britain during the Tertiary, *Journal of the Geological Society*, London, 160, 829–845

Gibbard, P L, and Lewin, J, 2008 River incision and terrace formation in the Late Cenozoic of Europe, *Tectonophysics* 474, 41–55

Gijssel, K van, 2006 A continent-wide framework for local and regional stratigraphies: application of genetic sequence and event stratigraphy to the Middle Pleistocene terrestrial succession of north-west and central Europe, unpubl. PhD thesis, Univ. Leiden

Gowlett, J A J, Chambers, J C, Hallos, J, and Pumphrey, T R J, 1998 Beeches Pit: first views of the archaeology of a Middle Pleistocene site in Suffolk, UK, in European context, *Anthropologie* 36, 91-97

Gowlett, J A J, Hallos, J, Hounsell, S, Brant, V, and Brant, N C D, 2005 Beeches Pit: archaeology, assemblage dynamics and early fire history of a Middle Pleistocene site in East Anglia, UK, *Journal of Eurasian Prehistory* 3, 3–40

Graf, A, 2002 Lower and Middle Palaeolithic Leicestershire and Rutland: progress and potential, *Transactions of the Leicester Archaeological and Historical Society* 76, 1–46

Green, C P, and McGregor, D F M, 1980 Quaternary evolution of the river Thames, in D K C Jones (ed.), *The Shaping of Southern England*, London, 177–202

Green, C P, Branch, N P, Coope, G R, Field, M H, Keen, D H, Wells, J M, Schwenninger, J-L, Preece, R C, Schreve, D C, Canti, M G, and Gleed-Owen, C P, 2006 Marine Isotope Stage 9 environments of fluvial deposits at Hackney, North London, UK, *Quaternary Science Reviews* 25, 89–113

Green, C P, 1984 *Pontnewydd Cave; a Lower Palaeolithic Hominid Site in Wales*, Cardiff

Gupta, S, Collier, J, Palmer-Felgate, A, Dickinson, J, Bushe, K, and Humber, S, 2004 Submerged Palaeo-Arun River: reconstruction of prehistoric landscapes and evaluation of Archaeological Resource Potential Integrated Projects 1 and 2, unpubl. rep., English Heritage, London

Gupta, S, Collier, J S, Palmer-Felgate, A, and Potter, G, 2007 Catastrophic flooding origin of shelf valley systems in the English Channel, *Nature* 448, 342–345

Harding, P, and Gibbard, P L, 1983 Excavations at Northwold Road, Stoke Newington, north-east London, 1981, *Transactions of the London and Middlesex Archaeological Society* 34, 1–18

Harding, P, Gibbard, P L, Lewin J, Macklin, M G, and Moss, E H, 1987 The transport and abrasion of flint handaxes in a gravel-bed river, in G. de G. Sieveking and M H Newcomer (eds), *The Human Uses of Flint and Chert*, Proceedings of the Fourth International Flint Symposium Held at Brighton Polytechnic, Oct-15 April 1983, 115–126, Cambridge University Press, Cambridge

Harding, P. Bridgland, D R, Allen, P, Bradley, P, Grant, M J, Peat, D, Schwenninger, J-L, Scott, R, Westaway, R, and White, T S, 2012 Chronology of the Lower and Middle Palaeolithic in north-west Europe: developer-funded investigations at Dunbridge, Hampshire, southern England, *Proceedings of the Geologists' Association* 123, 584–607

Hazell, Z J, 2008 Off shore and intertidal peat deposits, England: a resource assessment and development of a database, *Environmental Archaeology* 13, 101–10

Hijma, M P, Cohne, K M, Roebroeks, W, Westerhoff, W E, and Busschers, F S, 2012 Pleistocene Rhine-Thames landscapes: geological background for hominin occupation of the southern North Sea region, *Journal of Quaternary Science* 27, 17-39

Hosfield, R T, 1999 *The Palaeolithic of the Hampshire Basin: a regional model of hominid behaviour during the Middle Pleistocene*, BAR Brit. Ser. 286, Oxford

Hosfield, R T, and Chambers, J C, 2004 The

Archaeological Potential of Secondary Contexts, English Heritage Project Report (Project No. 3361), London

Hosfield, R T and Chambers, J C, 2009 Genuine diversity? The Broom biface assemblage, *Proceedings of the Prehistoric Society* 75, 65-100

Hosfield, R, and Green, C P (eds), 2013 *Quaternary History and Palaeolithic Archaeology in the Axe Valley at Broom, South-west England*, Oxford

Hosfield R T, Brown, A G, Basell, L S, Hounsell, S, and Young, R, 2007 The Palaeolithic Rivers of Southwest Britain: Final Report (Phases I and II), English Heritage Project Report (Project No. 3847), London

Hosfield, R, Green, C, Toms, P, Scourse, J, Scaife, R, and Chambers, J, 2011 The Middle Pleistocene deposits and archaeology at Broom, in L S Basell, A G Brown, and P S Toms (eds), *The Quaternary of the Exe Valley and Adjoining Areas*, Quaternary Research Association Field Guide, London, 103-127

Howard, A J, Bridgland, D R, Knight, D, McNabb, J, Rose, J, Schreve, D, Westaway, R, White, M J, and White, T S, 2007 The British Pleistocene fluvial archive: east Midlands drainage evolution and human occupation in the context of the British and NW European record, *Quaternary Science Reviews* 26, 2724-2737

Howard, A J, Carney, J N, Greenwood, M T, Keen, D H, Mighall, T, O'Brien, C, and Tetlow, E, 2011 The Holme Pierrepont sand and gravel and the timing of middle and late Devensian floodplain aggradation in the English Midlands, *Proceedings of the Geologists' Association* 122, 419–431

Huntley, D J, Godfrey-Smith, D I, and Thewalt, M L W, 1985 Optical dating of sediments, *Nature* 313, 105-7

Hublin, J-J, Weston, D, Gunz, P, Richards, M, Roebroeks, W, Glimmerveen J, and Anthonis, L, 2009 Out of the North Sea: the Zeeland Ridges Neandertal, *Journal of Human Evolution* 57, 777–85

Isaac, G L, 1989 Towards the interpretation of occupation debris: some experiments and observations, in B Isaac (ed.), *The Archaeology of Human Origins: Papers by Glynn Isaac*, Cambridge, 191-205

Jelgersma, S, 1979 Sea-level changes in the North Sea Basin, in E Oele, R T E Schuttenheim and A J Wiggers (eds), *The Quaternary History of the North Sea*, Uppsala, 233–48

Jones, T A, 1992 Extensions to three-dimensional: introduction to the sections of 3D geologic block modelling, in D E Hamilton and T A Jones (eds), *Computer Modelling of Geologic Surfaces and Volumes*, AAPG Computer Applications in Geology 1, Tulsa, 175–182

Kavanagh, K E, and Bates, M R, in press 'Semantics of the Sea' in N. Campion and J. Bezant (eds), *Celtic Myth: Land, Sea and Sky*, University of Wales Press, Cardiff

Keen, D H, 2001 Towards a late Middle Pleistocene non-marine molluscan biostratigraphy for the British Isles, *Quaternary Science Reviews* 20, 1657–1665

Keen, D H, Hardaker, T, and Lang, A T O, 2006 A Lower Palaeolithic industry from the Cromerian (MIS 13) Baginton Formation of Waverley Wood and Wood Farm Pits, Bubbenhall, Warwickshire, UK, *Journal of Quaternary Science* 21, 457–470

Kennard, A S, 1942 Faunas of the High Terrace at Swanscombe, *Proceedings of the Geologists' Association* 53, 105

Kerney, M P, 1971 Interglacial deposits in Barnfield Pit, Swanscombe, and their molluscan fauna, *Journal of the Geological Society of London* 127, 69–93

Kiden, P, and Törnqvist, T E, 1998 Can river terrace flights be used to quantify Quaternary tectonic uplift rates? *Journal of Quaternary Science* 13, 573–575

Kiden, P, Denys, L, and Johnston, P, 2002 Late Quaternary sea-level change and isostatic and tectonic land movements along the Belgian-Dutch North Sea coast: geological data and model results, *Journal of Quaternary Science* 17, 535–46

Laban, C, 1995 The Pleistocene glaciations in the Dutch sector of the North Sea: a synthesis of sedimentary and seismic data, unpubl. dissertation, Univ. Amsterdam

Laban, C, Cameron, T D J, and Schiittenhelm, R T E, 1984 Geologie van het Kwartair in de zuidelijke bocht van de Noordzee, *Mededelingen van de Werkgroep Tertiaire en Kwartaire Geologi*e 21, 139–154

Lake, R D, Ellison, R A, Hollyer, S E, and Simmons, M, 1977 *Buried Channel Deposits in the South-East Essex Area: Their Bearing on Pleistocene Palaeogeography*, Institute of Geological Sciences Report 77/21, London

Lake, R D, Ellison, R A, Henson, M R, and Conway, B W, 1986 *Geology of the Country Around Southend and Foulness*, Memoirs of the British Geological Survey, 1: 25 000 sheets 258 and 259, New Series, London

Lang, A T O, and Keen, D H, 2005a 'At the edge of the world...'. Hominid colonisation and the Lower and Middle Palaeolithic of the West Midlands, *Proceedings of the Prehistoric Society* 71, 63–83

Lang, A T O, and Keen, D H, 2005b A further andesite handaxe from Waverley Wood Quarry, Warwickshire, *Lithics* 24, 32–36

Last, J, Brown, E J, Bridgland D R, Harding P, 2013 Quaternary geoconservation and Palaeolithic heritage protection in the 21st century: developing a collaborative approach, *Proceedings of the Geologists' Association* 124, 625–637

Lee, J R, Rose, J, Hamblin, R J O, and Moorlock, B S P, 2004 Dating the earliest lowland glaciation

of eastern England: a pre-MIS 12 early Middle Pleistocene Happisburgh glaciation, *Quaternary Science Reviews* 23, 1551–1566
Lewin, J and Gibbard, P L, 2010 Quaternary river terraces in England: forms, sediments and processes, *Geomorphology* 120, 293–311
Lewis, S G, Parfitt, S A, Preece, R C, Sinclair, J, Coope, G R, Field, M H, Maher, B A, Scaife, R G, and Whittaker J E, 2004 Age and palaeoenvironmental setting of the Pleistocene vertebrate fauna at Norton Subcourse, Norfolk, in D C Shreve (ed.), *The Quaternary Mammals of Southern and Eastern England*, Quaternary Research Association Field Guide, London, 5–17
Lewis, S G, Ashton, N, and Jacobi, R, 2011 Testing human presence during the Last Interglacial (MIS 5e): a review of the British evidence, in N M Ashton, S G Lewis, and C B Stringer (eds), *The Ancient Human Occupation of Britain*, Amsterdam
Lisiecki, L E, and Raymo, M E, 2005 A Pliocene-Pleistocene stack of 57 globally distributed benthic $\delta^{18}O$ records, *Palaeoceanography* 20, PA10003, doi:10.1029/2004PA001071
Locht, J L, Sellier, N, Coutard, S, Antoine, P, and Feray, P, 2010 La détection de sites du Paléolithique ancien et moyen dans le nord de la France : une approche particulière, in P. Depaepe and F. Séara (eds) *Le Diagnostic des Sites Paléolithiques et Mésolithiques*, Les Cahiers de l'Inrap, 3
Lovell, J H, and Nancarrow, P H A, 1983 The sand and gravel resources of the country around Chichester and north of Bognor Regis, Sussex, *British Geological Survey Mineral Assessment Report* 138, London
Lowe, J J, and Walker, M J C, 1997 *Reconstructing Quaternary Environments*, Harlow
Lowe, J, and Walker, M, 2015 *Reconstructing Quaternary Environments* (3rd edn) Routledge, Abingdon

Maddy, D, 1997 Uplift-driven valley incision and river terrace formation in southern England, *Journal of Quaternary Science* 12, 539–545
Maddy, D, and Bridgland, D R, 2000 Accelerated uplift resulting from Anglian glaciostatic rebound in the Middle Thames Valley, UK? Evidence from the river terrace record, *Quaternary Science Reviews* 19, 1581–1588
Maddy, D, Coope, G R, Gibbard, P L, Green, C P, and Lewis, S G, 1994 Reappraisal of Middle Pleistocene fluvial deposits near Brandon, Warwickshire and their significance for the Wolston glacial sequence, *Journal of the Geological Society of London* 151, 221–233
Martinson, D G, Pisias, N G, Hays, J D, Imbrie, J, Moore, T C, and Shackleton, N J, 1987 Age dating and the orbital theory of the ice ages: development of a high resolution 0-300,000 year chronostratigraphy, *Quaternary Research* 27, 1–29
Mazza, A P P, Martini, F, Sala, B, Magi, M, Perla, M, Colombini, G G, Landucci, F, Lemorini, C, Modugno, F, and Ribechini, E, 2006 A new Palaeolithic discovery: tar-hafted stone tools in a European mid-Pleistocene bone-bearing bed, *Journal of Archaeological Science* 33, 1310–1318
McCarroll, D, 2002 Amino-acid geochronology and the British Pleistocene: secure stratigraphical framework or a case of circular reasoning? *Journal of Quaternary Science* 17, 647–51
McNabb, J, 1996a More from the cutting edge: further discoveries of Clactonian bifaces, *Antiquity* 70, 428–436
McNabb, J. 1996b Through a glass darkly: An historical perspective on archaeological research at Barnfield Pit, Swanscombe, *c* 1900–1964, in B Conway, N M Ashton and J McNabb (eds), *Excavations at Barnfield Pit, Swanscombe, 1968–72*, British Museum Occasional Paper 94, London
McNabb, J, 2001 An Archaeological Resource Assessment and Research Agenda for the Palaeolithic of the East Midlands (part of Western Doggerland), East Midlands Archaeological Research Framework, unpublished report
McNabb, J, 2006 The Palaeolithic, in N J Cooper (ed.), The Archaeology of the East Midlands, *An Archaeological Resource Assessment and Research Agenda,* Leicester Archaeology Monographs 13, 11–51
McNabb, J, 2007 *The British Lower Palaeolithic: Stones in Contention*, London and New York
McNabb, J, 2012 *Dissent with Modification: Human Origins, Palaeolithic Archaeology and Evolutionary Anthropology in Britain, 1859–1901*, Oxford
McPherron, S P, 1999 Ovate and pointed handaxe assemblages: two points make a line, *Préhistoire Européenne* 14, 9-32
McPherron, S P, 2006 What typology can tell us about Acheulian handaxe production, in N Goren-Inbar and G Sharon, *Axe Age: Acheulian Toolmaking from Quarry to Discard*, London, 267–286
Miller, J, Poulter, A, Hewson, M, and Penrose, S, 2008 Rich deposits: aggregates extraction and the knowledge pool, ALSF Dissemination Project, 2002-07, Benchmark Report, Atkins Heritage, London
Mineral Products Association, 2012 The mineral products industry's contribution to the UK, London, (http://www.mineralproducts.org/documents/MPA_MTL_Document.pdf)
Mitchell, G F, Penny, L F, Shotton, F W, and West, R G, 1973 *A Correlation of Quaternary Deposits in the British Isles,* Geological Society of London Special Report 4, London
Morigi, A, Schreve, D, and White, M, 2011 *The Thames Through Time: The Archaeology of the Gravel Terraces of the Upper and Middle Thames, Early Prehistory to 1500 BC, Part 1 – the Ice Ages,* Thames Valley Landscapes 32, Oxford
Murray, A S, and Wintle, A G, 2000 Luminescence dating of quartz using an improved single-aliquot regenerative-dose protocol, *Radiation Measurements* 32, 57–73
Murton, D K, and Murton, J B, 2012 Middle and Late Pleistocene glacial lakes of lowland Britain

and the southern North Sea Basin, *Quaternary International* 260, 115-142

National Planning Policy Framework, 2012, see Department for Communities and Local Government, 2012

O'Connor, A, 2007 *Finding Time for the Old Stone Age: a History of Palaeolithic Archaeology and Quaternary Geology in Britain, 1860–1960*, Oxford

Parfitt, S A, Barendregt, R W, Breda, M, Candy, I, Collins, M J, Coope, R G, Durbridge, P, Field, M H, Lee, J R, Lister, A M, Mutch, R, Penkman, K, Preece, R C, Rose, J, Stringer, C B, Symmons, R, Whittaker, J E, Wymer, J J, and Stuart, A J, 2005 The earliest record of human activity in Northern Europe, *Nature* 438, 1008–1012

Parfitt, S A, Ashton, N M, Lewis, S G, Abel, R L, Coope, G R, Field, M H, Hoare, P G, Larkin, N R, Leis, M D, Karloukovski, V, Maher, B A, Peglar, S M, Preece, R C, Whittaker, J E, and Stringer, C B, 2010 Early Pleistocene human occupation at the edge of the boreal zone in northwest Europe, *Nature* 466, 229–233

Paterson, T T, and Tebbutt, C F, 1947 Studies in the Palaeolithic succession in England no. III: palaeoliths from St. Neots, Huntingdonshire, *Proceedings of the Prehistoric Society* 13, 37–46

Peeters, H, Murphy, P, and Flemming, N, 2009 *North Sea Prehistory Research and Management Framework (NSPRMF)*, Amersfoort

Penkman, K E H, Collins, M, Keen, D, And Preece, R C P, 2008 An improved chronology using amino acid racemization and degradation of intercrystalline amino acids (IcPD), English Heritage Research Department Report Series no. 6-2008, London

Penkman, K E H, Preece, R C, Bridgland, D R, Keen, D H, Meijer, T, Parfitt, S A, White, T S, and Collins, M J, 2011 A chronological framework for the British Quaternary based on Bithynia opercula, *Nature* 476, 446–449

Pettitt, P, Gamble, C, and Last, J (eds), 2008 *Research and Conservation Framework for the British Palaeolithic*, London

Pettitt, P, and White, M, 2012 *The British Palaeolithic: Human Societies at the Edge of the Pleistocene World*, London

Pope, M I, 2002 The significance of biface-rich assemblages: an examination of the behavioural controls on lithic assemblage formation in the Lower Palaeolithic, unpubl. Ph.D. thesis, Univ. Southampton

Pope, M, 2004 Placing Boxgrove in its Prehistoric Landscape: The Raised Beach Mapping Project. *Archaeology International*, 2003/4 (7), 13–16

Pope, M I, and Roberts, M B, 2005 Observations on the relationship between Palaeolithic individuals and artefact scatters at the Middle Pleistocene site of Boxgrove, UK, in C Gamble and M Porr (eds), *The Hominid Individual in Context: archaeological investigations of Lower and Middle Palaeolithic landscapes, locales and artefacts*, London, 81–97

Pope, M, Roberts, M B, Maxted, A, and Jones, P, 2009 The Valdoe: archaeology of a location within the Boxgrove landscape, *Proceedings of the Prehistoric Society* 75, 239–263

Posnansky, M, 1963 The Lower and Middle Palaeolithic industries of the English east Midlands, *Proceedings of the Prehistoric Society* 29, 357–394

Preece, R C, Gowlett, J A J, Parfitt, S A, Bridgland, D R, and Lewis, S G, 2006 Humans in the Hoxnian: habitat, context and fire use at Beeches Pit, West Stow, Suffolk, UK, *Journal of Quaternary Science* 21, 485–496

Preece, R C, and Parfitt, S A, 2012 The Early and early Middle Pleistocene context of human occupation and lowland glaciation in Britain and northern Europe, *Quaternary International* 271, 6–28

Prestwich, J, 1855 On a fossiliferous deposit in the gravel at West Hackney, *Quarterly Journal of the Geological Society* 11, 107–110

Prestwich, J, 1860 On the occurrence of flint-implements, associated with the remains of animals of extinct species in beds of a late geological period, in France at Amiens and Abbeville, and in England at Hoxne, *Philosophical Transactions of the Royal Society of London* 150, 277–317

Reid, C, 1904 On the probable occurrence of an Eocene outlier off the Cornish Coast, *Quarterly Journal of the Geological Society* 60, 1–4

Reid, C, 1913 *Submerged Forests*, Oxford

Reumer, J, Rook, L, van der Borg, K, Post, K, Mol, D, and de Vos, J, 2003 Late Pleistocene survival of the sabre-toothed cat *Homotherium* in North-western Europe, *Journal of Vertabrate Palaeontology* 23, 260-263

Richards, J, 2008 The sands of time: aggregates extraction, heritage and the public. ALSF Dissemination Project 2002-2007 benchmark report, English Heritage, London

Rhodes, E J, 1988 Methodological considerations in the optical dating of quartz, *Quaternary Science Reviews* 7, 395–400

Roberts, M B, 1986 Excavation of the Lower Palaeolithic site at Amey's Eartham Pit, Boxgrove, West Sussex: a preliminary report, *Proceedings of the Prehistoric Society* 52, 215–245

Roberts, M B, and Parfitt, S A, 1999 *Boxgrove: a Middle Pleistocene Hominid Site at Eartham Quarry, Boxgrove, West Sussex*, English Heritage Archaeological Report 17, London

Roberts, M B, and Pope, M I, 2009 The archaeological and sedimentary records from Boxgrove and Slindon, in R M Briant, R T Hosfield and F Wenban-Smith (eds), *The Quaternary of the Solent Basin and the Sussex Raised Beaches*, Quaternary Research Association Field Guide, London, 96–122

Roe, D A, 1968 *A Gazetteer of British Lower and Middle Palaeolithic Sites*, CBA Res. Rep. 8, London

Roe, D A, 1981 *The Lower and Middle Palaeolithic Periods in Britain*, London
Roe, H M, 1999 Late Middle Pleistocene sea-level change in the southern North Sea: the record from eastern Essex, UK, *Quaternary International* 55, 115–128
Roe, H M, 2001 The late Middle Pleistocene biostratigraphy of the Thames Valley, England: new data from eastern Essex, *Quaternary Science Reviews* 20, 1603–1619
Roe, H M, and Preece, R C, 1995 A new discovery of the Middle Pleistocene Rhenish fauna in Essex, *Journal of Conchology* 35, 272–273
Roe, H M, Coope, G R, Devoy, R J N, Harrison, C J O, Penkman, K E H, Preece, R C, Schreve, D C, 2009 Differentiation of MIS 9 and MIS 11 in the continental record: vegetational, faunal, aminostratigraphic and sea-level evidence from coastal sites in eastern Essex, UK, *Quaternary Science Reviews* 28, 2342–2373
Roe, H M, Penkman, K E H, Preece, R C, Briant, R M, and Wenban-Smith, F F, 2011 Evolution of the Thames Estuary during MIS 9: insights from the Shoeburyness area, Essex, *Proceedings of the Geologists' Association* 122, 397–418
Roebroeks, W, 2005 Archaeology: life on the Costa del Cromer, *Nature* 438, 921–922
Roebroeks, W, Hublin, J-J, and MacDonald, K, 2011 Continuities and discontinuities in Neanderthal presence: a closer look at north-western Europe, in N M Ashton, S G Lewis, and C B Stringer (eds), *The Ancient Human Occupation of Britain*, Amsterdam
Roep, T B, Holst, H, Vissers, R L M, Pagnier, H, and Postma, D, 1975 Deposits of southward-flowing Pleistocene rivers in the Channel region, near Wissant, NW France, *Palaeogeography, Palaeoclimatology, Palaeoecology* 17, 289–308
Rose, J, 1994 Major river systems of central and southern Britain during the Early and Middle Pleistocene, *Terra Nova* 6, 435–443
Rose, J, 2009 Early and Middle Pleistocene landscapes of eastern England, *Proceedings of the Geologists Association* 120, 3–33
Rose, J, and Allen, P, 1977 Middle Pleistocene stratigraphy in south east Suffolk, *Journal of the Geological Society of London* 133, 83–102
Rose, J, Lee, J A, Candy, I, and Lewis, S G, 1999 Early and Middle Pleistocene river systems in eastern England: evidence from Leet Hill, southern Norfolk, *Journal of Quaternary Science* 14, 347–360

Schreve, D C, 2001 Differentiation of the British late Middle Pleistocene interglacials: the evidence from mammalian biostratigraphy, *Quaternary Science Reviews* 20, 1693–1705
Schreve, D C, 2006 The taphonomy of a Middle Devensian (MIS 3) vertebrate assemblage from Lynford, Norfolk, UK, and its implications for Middle Palaeolithic subsistence strategies, *Journal of Quaternary Science* 21, 543–556
Schreve, D C, 2012 The vertebrate assemblage, in W A Boismier, C Gamble, and F Coward (eds), *Neanderthals Among Mammoths: Excavations at Lynford Quarry, Norfolk*, Swindon
Schreve, D C, unpubl rep. for the Kent RIGS group on mammalian fossils from Aylesford, Kent, viewed at Maidstone Museum, 2004, unpubl rep. for English Nature, London
Schreve, D, Howard, A J, Currant, A, Brooks, S, Buteux, S, Coope, R, Crocker, B, Field, M, Greenwood, M, Greig, J, and Toms, P, 2013 A Middle Devensian woolly rhinoceros (*Coelodonta antiquitatis*) from Whitemoor Haye Quarry, Staffordshire (UK): palaeoenvironmental context and significance, *Journal of Quaternary Science* 28, 118–130
Scott, B, 2006 The early middle Palaeolithic of southern Britain: origins technology and landscape, unpubl. PhD thesis, Univ. Durham (Rebecca Scott)
Scott, B, 2009 The Crayford brickearths project, *Quaternary Newsletter* 117, 44–48
Scott, B, 2011 *Becoming Neanderthals*, Oxford
Scott, B, Ashton, N, Lewis, S G, Parfitt, S, and White, M, 2011 Technology and landscape use in the early Middle Palaeolithic of the Thames Valley, in N M Ashton, S G Lewis, and C B Stringer (eds), *The Ancient Human Occupation of Britain*, Amsterdam
Shackleton, N J, 1987 Oxygen Isotopes, ice volume and sea-level, *Quaternary Science Reviews* 6, 183–190
Shackleton, N J, and Opdyke, N D, 1973 Oxygen isotope and paleomagnetic stratigraphy of equatorial Pacific core V28-238: oxygen isotope temperatures and ice volumes on a 10^5 year and 10^6 year scale, *Quaternary Research* 3, 39–55
Shackleton, N J, Berger, A, and Peltier, W R, 1990 An alternative astronomical calibration of the lower Pleistocene timescale based on ODP Site 677, *Transactions of the Royal Society of Edinburgh: Earth Sciences* 81, 251–261
Shackley, M L, 1974 Stream abrasion of flint implements, *Nature* 248, 501–502
Schick, K, 1987 Modelling the formation of early stone age artefact concentrations, *Journal of Human Evolution* 16, 789-807
Shotton, F W, Keen, D H, Coope, G R, Currant, A P, Gibbard, P L, Aalto, M, Peglar, S M, and Robinson, J E, 1993 The Middle Pleistocene deposits of Waverley Wood Pit, Warwickshire, England, *Journal of Quaternary Science* 8, 293–325
Singer, R, Gladfelter, B G, and Wymer, J J, 1993 *The Lower Palaeolithic Site at Hoxne, England*, Chicago
Smith, B W, Aitken, M J, Rhodes, E J, Robinson, P D, and Geldard, D M, 1986 Optical dating: methodological aspects, *Radiation Protection Dosimetry* 17, 229–33
Smith, W G, 1883 Palaeolithic implements of north-east London, *Nature* 27, 270–274
Smith, W G, 1884 On a Palaeolithic floor at north-

east London, *Journal of the Anthropological Institute* 13, 357–384
Smith, W G, 1894 *Man, the Primeval Savage: His Haunts and Relics from the Hill-tops of Bedfordshire to Blackwall*, London
Steffensen, J P, Andersen, K K, Bigler, M, Clausen, H B, Dahl-Jensen, D, Fischer, H, Goto-Azuma, K, Hansson, M, Johnsen, S J, Jouzel, J, Masson-Delmotte, V, Popp, T, Rasmussen, S O, Rothlisberger, R, Ruth, U, Stauffer, B, Siggard-Andersen, M-L, Sveinbjornsdottir, A E, White, J W C, 2008 High-resolution Greenland ice core data show abrupt climate change happens in few years, *Science* 321, 680–684
Stephens, M, Challis, K, Graf, A, Howard, A J, Rose, J, and Schreve, D, 2008 New exposures of Bytham river deposits at Brooksby, Leicestershire, UK: context and importance, *Quaternary Newsletter* 115, 14–27
Straw, A, 2005 *Glacial and Pre-Glacial Deposits at Welton-le-Wold, Lincolnshire*, Exeter

Tester, P J, 1965. An Acheulian site at Cuxton, *Archaeologia Cantiana* 80, 30–60
Thieme, H, 1997 Lower Palaeolithic hunting spears from Germany, *Nature* 385, 807–810
Tizzard, L, Bickert, A, and De Loecker, D, 2015 *Seabed Prehistory. Investigating the Palaeogeography and Early Middle Palaeolithic Archaeology in the Southern North Sea*, Wessex Archaeology Report 35, Salisbury
Trigger, B G, 1989 *A History of Archaeological Thought*, Cambridge
Turq, A, 1989 Exploitation des matières prémières lithiques et occupation du sol: l'exemple du Moustérien entre Dordogne et Lot, in H Laville (ed.), *Variation des Paleomilieux et Peuplement Préhistorique*, Paris, 179–204
Tyldesley, J A, 1987 *The Bout Coupé Handaxe: A Typological Problem*, BAR Brit. Ser. 170, Oxford

Vandenberghe, J, 2003 Climate forcing of fluvial system development; an evolution of ideas, *Quaternary Science Reviews* 22, 2053–2060
Vandenberghe, J, 2007 The fluvial cycle at cold–warm–cold transitions in lowland regions: a refinement of theory, *Geomorphology* 98, 275–284
Van Peer, P, 1992 *The Levallois Reduction Strategy*, Monographs in World Archaeology 13, Madison
Vos, Pm, 2015 Origin of the Dutch Coastal Landscape, Barkhuis, Groningen

Waddington, C, 2008 *Mineral Extraction and Archaeology: A Practice Guide*, London
Walker, M, 2005 *Quaternary Dating Methods*, Chichester and New York
Warren, S H, 1911 On a Palaeolithic (?) wooden spear, *Quarterly Journal of the Geological Society* 67, xcix
Warren, S H, 1912 A Late Glacial stage in the valley of the river Lea, subsequent to the epoch of River-Drift Man, with reports on the organic remains and on the mineral composition of the Arctic Bed, by various authors, *Quarterly Journal of the Geological Society of London* 68, 213–251
Warren, S H, 1915 Further observations on the Late Glacial, or Ponder's End, stage of the Lea Valley, *Quarterly Journal of the Geological Society of London* 71, 164–178
Warren, S H, 1926 The classification of the Lower Palaeolithic with especial reference to Essex, *South East Naturalist* 31, 38–50
Weerts, H J T, Westerhoff, W E, Cleveringa, P, Bierkens, M F P, Veldkamp, J G, and Rijskijk, K F, 2005 Quaternary geological mapping of the lowlands of the Netherlands: a 21st-century perspective, *Quaternary International* 133–134, 159–78
Wenban-Smith, F F, 1994 Managing the Palaeolithic heritage: looking backwards, looking forwards, in N Ashton and A David (eds), *Stories in Stone*, Lithic Studies Society Occasional Paper 4, London, 104–11
Wenban-Smith, F F, 1995a Square pegs in round holes: problems of managing the Palaeolithic heritage, in M Cooper, A Firth, J Carman and D Wheatley (eds), *Managing Archaeology*, London, 146–62
Wenban-Smith, F F, 1995b Managing the Palaeolithic heritage IV: the end of the beginning, in J Schofield (ed.), *Lithics in Context: Suggestions for the Future Direction of Lithic Studies*, Lithic Studies Society Occasional Paper 5, London, 115–24
Wenban-Smith, F F, 2004 Stopes Palaeolithic Project: final report, unpubl rep., English Heritage, London
Wenban-Smith, F F, 2009 Henry Stopes (1852–1902): engineer, brewer and anthropologist, *Lithics: the Journal of the Lithic Studies Society* 30, 65–84
Wenban-Smith, F F (ed), 2013 *The Ebbsfleet Elephant: Excavations at Southfleet Road. Swanscombe in Advance of High Speed 1, 2003-2004*, Oxford Archaeology Monograph 20, Oxford, 17–56
Wenban-Smith, F, and Bates, M, 2011 Palaeolithic and Pleistocene investigations, in A Simmonds, F Wenban-Smith, M Bates, K Powell, D Sykes, R Devaney, D Stansbie and D Score, *Excavations in North-West Kent 2005-2007*, Oxford Archaeology Monograph 11, Oxford
Wenban-Smith, F F, Allen, P, Bates, M R, Parfitt, S A, Preece, R C, Stewart, J R, Turner, C, and Whittaker, J E, 2006 The Clactonian elephant butchery site at Southfleet Road, Ebbsfleet, UK, *Journal of Quaternary Science* 21, 471–483
Wenban-Smith, F F, Bates, M R, and Marshall, G, 2007a Medway Valley Palaeolithic Project Final Report: the Palaeolithic resource in the Medway Gravels (Kent), unpubl. report for English Heritage, http://archaeologydataservice.ac.uk/archives/view/medway_eh_2009/
Wenban-Smith, F F, Briant, R M, and Marshall, G, 2007b Medway Valley Palaeolithic Project Final Report: the Palaeolithic Resource in the Medway

Gravels (Essex), unpubl. report for English Heritage http://archaeologydataservice.ac.uk/archives/view/medway_eh_2009/

Wenban-Smith, F F, Bates, M R, Schwenninger J-L, 2010 Early Devensian (MIS 5d–5b) occupation at Dartford, southeast England, *Journal of Quaternary Science* 25, 1193–1199

Wessex Archaeology, 2008 Seabed prehistory: gauging the effects of marine aggregate dredging, Round 2, final report, vol. VII: Happisburgh and Pakefield exposures, unpubl. rep. 57422.37 for English Heritage

West, R G, and Sparks, B W, 1960 Coastal interglacial deposits of the English Channel, *Philosophical Transactions of the Royal Society of London. Series B, Biological Sciences* 243(701), 95–133

Westaway, R C, 2011 A re-evaluation of the timing of the earliest reported human occupation of Britain: the age of the sediments at Happisburgh, eastern England, *Proceedings of the Geological Society* 122, 383–396

Westaway, R, and Bridgland, D R, 2010 Causes, consequences and chronology of large-magnitude palaeoflows in Middle and Late Pleistocene river systems of northwest Europe, *Earth Surface Processes and Landforms* 35, 1071–1094

Westaway, R C, Bridgland, D R, and White, M J, 2006 The Quaternary uplift history of central southern England : evidence from the terraces of the Solent River system and nearby raised beaches, *Quaternary Science Reviews* 25, 2212–2250

White, H J O, 1912 *The Geology of the Country around Winchester and Stockbridge*, Memoir of the Geological Survey, London

White M J, 1998 On the significance of Acheulian biface variability in southern Britain, *Proceedings of the Prehistoric Society* 64, 15–44

White, M J, 2000 The Clactonian question: on the interpretation of core-and-flake assemblages in the British Lower Palaeolithic, *Journal of World Prehistory* 14, 1–63

White, M J, 2006 Things to do in Doggerland when you're dead: surviving OIS3 at the northwestern-most fringe of Middle Palaeolithic Europe, *World Archaeology* 38, 547–575

White, M J, 2012 The lithic assemblage, in W A Boismier, C Gamble, and F Coward, (eds.), *Neanderthals Among Mammoths: Excavations at Lynford Quarry, Norfolk*, Swindon

White, M J, and Pettitt, P, 1995 Technology of early Palaeolithic western Europe: innovation, variability and a unified framework. *Lithics: the Journal of the Lithic Studies Society* 16, 27–40

White, M J, and Schreve, D C, 2000 Island Britain-peninsula Britain: palaeogeography, colonisation and the Lower Palaeolithic settlement of the British Isles, *Proceedings of the Prehistoric Society* 66, 1–28

White, M J, and Jacobi, R M, 2002 Two sides to every story: *Bout Coupé* handaxes revisited, *Oxford Journal of Archaeology* 21, 109–133

White, M J, and Ashton, N, 2003 Lower Palaeolithic core technology and the origins of the Levallois method in North-Western Europe, *Current Anthropology* 44, 598-609

White, M, and Pettitt, P, 2011 The British late Middle Palaeolithic: an interpretative synthesis of Neanderthal occupation at the northwestern edge of the Pleistocene World, *Journal of World Prehistory* 24, 25–97

White, M J, Scott, B, and Ashton, N M, 2006 The early Middle Palaeolithic in Britain: archaeology, settlement history and human behaviour, *Journal of Quaternary Science* 21, 525–41

White, T S, Bridgland, D R, Howard, A J, and White, M J, 2007a *The Quaternary of the Trent Valley and Adjoining Regions*, Quaternary Research Association Field Guide, London

White, T S, Bridgland, D R, Howard, A J, O'Brien, C E, Penkman, K E H, Preece, R C, and Schreve, D C, 2007b Norton Bottoms Quarry (SK 863588), in T S White, D R Bridgland, A J Howard, and M J White (eds), *The Quaternary of the Trent Valley and Adjoining Areas*, Quaternary Research Association Field Guide, London, 105–109

White, T S, Boreham, S, Bridgland, D R, Gdaniec, K, and White, M J, 2008a The Lower and Middle Palaeolithic of Cambridgeshire. An introduction to the work of the fenland rivers of Cambridgeshire Palaeolithic project, available as digital archive in Durham University (2010) Lower and Middle Palaeolithic of the Fenland Rivers of Cambridgeshire, Archaeology Data Service, York (doi:10.5284/1000113)

White, T S, White, M J, Bridgland, D R, and Howard, A J, 2008b Lower Palaeolithic quartzite artefacts from the River Trent at East Leake, Nottinghamshire: new light on a hidden resource, *Quaternary Newsletter* 114, 10–19

White, T S, White, M J, Bridgland, D R, and Howard, A J, 2009 Palaeolithic and Quaternary research in the Trent Valley (UK): contributions by early collectors, *Proceedings of the Geologists' Association* 120, 223–232

White, T S, Bridgland, D R, Westaway, R, Howard, A J, and White, M J, 2010 Evidence from the Trent terrace archive, Lincolnshire, UK, for lowland glaciation of Britain during the Middle and Late Pleistocene, *Proceedings of the Geologists' Association* 121, 141–153

Whittaker, K, Beasley, M, Bates, M, and Wenban-Smith, F, 2004 The lost valley, *British Archaeology* 74, 22–27

Wymer, J J, 1968 *Lower Palaeolithic Archaeology in Britain as Represented by the Thames Valley*, London

Wymer, J J, 1985 *Palaeolithic Sites of East Anglia*, Norwich

Wymer, J J, 1988 Palaeolithic archaeology and the British Quaternary sequence, *Quaternary Science Reviews* 7, 79–98

Wymer, J J, 1992 *Region 3 (The Upper Thames Valley, the Kennet Valley) and Region 5 (The Solent*

Drainage System), Southern Rivers Palaeolithic Project Report 1, Salisbury
Wymer, J J, 1993 *Region 4 (South of the Thames) and Region 1 (South-west England)*, Southern Rivers Palaeolithic Project Report 2, Salisbury
Wymer, J J, 1994 *Region 6 (Sussex Raised Beaches) and Region 2 (Severn River)*, Southern Rivers Palaeolithic Project Report 1, Salisbury
Wymer, J J, 1996a. *Regions 7 (Thames) and 10 (Warwickshire Avon)*, English Rivers Palaeolithic Project Report 1, Salisbury
Wymer, J J, 1996b *Regions 9 (Great Ouse Drainage) and 12 (Yorkshire and Lincolnshire Wolds)*, English Rivers Palaeolithic Project Report 2, Salisbury
Wymer, J J, 1997 *Regions 8 (East Anglian Rivers) and 11 (Trent Drainage)*, English Rivers Palaeolithic Project Report 3, Salisbury
Wymer, J J, 1999 *The Lower Palaeolithic Occupation of Britain*, Salisbury
Wymer, J J, 2001 Palaeoliths in a lost pre-Anglian landscape, in S Miliken and J Cook, (eds), *A Very Remote Period Indeed*, Oxford, 174–179
Wymer, J J, and Straw, A, 1977 Hand-axes from beneath glacial till at Welton-le-Wold, Lincolnshire, and the distribution of palaeoliths in Britain, *Proceedings of the Prehistoric Society* 43, 355–360

Zeuner, F E, 1945 *The Pleistocene Period: Its Climate, Chronology and Faunal Succession*, 1st edn, Ray Society Publication 130, London
Zeuner, F E, 1959 *The Pleistocene Period: Its Climate, Chronology and Faunal Succession*, 2nd edn, London

Index